HIDDEN ®

Boston
& Cape Cod

"A good source of information on the region."
—*Los Angeles Times*

"If you're planning to explore the coast of Massachusetts, take along
Hidden Boston & Cape Cod."
—*Better Homes & Gardens*

"This book covers Boston in more depth than you'll find in
most guidebooks."
—*San Diego Tribune*

"The definitive guide to Martha's Vineyard, Nantucket and the
Massachusetts Coast along with Boston and Cape Cod."
—*Touring America*

"*Hidden Boston & Cape Cod* will tell you about standard attractions
of the Massachusetts Coast as well as some of those lesser-known places
that make a trip special."
—*Buffalo News*

"Can any places be truly hidden in such a heavily developed area? You
bet and this book finds them."
—*Ashbury Park Press*

HIDDEN®
Boston
& Cape Cod

*Including Cambridge,
Lexington, Concord, Provincetown,
Martha's Vineyard and Nantucket*

SIXTH EDITION

Ulysses Press®
BERKELEY, CALIFORNIA

Copyright © 1991, 1995, 1997, 1999, 2001, 2003 Ulysses Press.
All rights reserved, including the right to reproduce this book or
portions thereof in any form whatsoever, except for use by a
reviewer in connection with a review.

Published by: ULYSSES PRESS
P.O. Box 3440
Berkeley, CA 94703
www.ulyssespress.com

ISSN 1524-1262
ISBN 1-56975-328-8

Printed in Canada by Transcontinental Printing

20 19 18 17 16 15 14 13 12 11 10 9

MANAGING EDITOR: Claire Chun
PROJECT DIRECTOR: Summer Block
COPY EDITOR: Lily Chou
EDITORIAL ASSOCIATES: Marin Van Young, Kate Allen
TYPESETTER: Lisa Kester
CARTOGRAPHY: Pease Press
COVER DESIGN: Leslie Henriques, Sarah Levin
INDEXER: Sayre Van Young
COVER PHOTOGRAPHY: Robert Holmes (Nobska Light,
   Woods Hole)
ILLUSTRATOR: Norman Nicholson

Distributed in the United States by Publishers
Group West and in Canada by Raincoast Books

HIDDEN is a federally registered trademark
of BookPack, Inc.

Ulysses Press 🐢 is a federally registered trademark
of BookPack, Inc.

The author and publisher have made every effort to ensure the
accuracy of information contained in *Hidden Boston & Cape Cod*,
but can accept no liability for any loss, injury or inconvenience
sustained by any traveler as a result of information or advice
contained in this guide.

Write to us!

If in your travels you discover a spot that captures the spirit of Boston, Cape Cod and the Massachusetts Coast, or if you live in the region and have a favorite place to share, or if you just feel like expressing your views, write to us and we'll pass your note along to the author.

We can't guarantee that the author will add your personal find to the next edition, but if the writer does use the suggestion, we'll acknowledge you in the credits and send you a free copy of the new edition.

ULYSSES PRESS
3286 Adeline Street, Suite 1
Berkeley, CA 94703
E-mail: readermail@ulyssespress.com

❋

Ulysses Press would like to thank the following readers who took the time to write in with suggestions that were incorporated into this new edition of *Hidden Boston & Cape Cod*:

Cathy Chun of Denver, CO; Julie Colombero of Aliso Viejo, CA; Gary B. Gaines via e-mail; Jayne and Paul Sorrell of Reading, England; and John Worden of Boston, MA.

What's Hidden?

At different points throughout this book, you'll find special listings marked with a hidden symbol:

◄ HIDDEN

This means that you have come upon a place off the beaten tourist track, a spot that will carry you a step closer to the local people and natural environment of Boston, Cape Cod and the Massachusetts Coast.

The goal of this guide is to lead you beyond the realm of everyday tourist facilities. While we include traditional sightseeing listings and popular attractions, we also offer alternative sights and adventure activities. Instead of filling this guide with reviews of standard hotels and chain restaurants, we concentrate on one-of-a-kind places and locally owned establishments.

Our authors seek out locales that are popular with residents but usually overlooked by visitors. Some are more hidden than others (and are marked accordingly), but all the listings in this book are intended to help you discover the true nature of Boston, Cape Cod and the Massachusetts Coast and put you on the path of adventure.

Contents

Maps

OUTDOOR ADVENTURE SYMBOLS

The following symbols accompany national, state and regional park listings, as well as beach descriptions throughout the text.

⛺	Camping	🏄	Surfing
🥾	Hiking	🎿	Waterskiing
🚲	Biking	🏄	Windsurfing
🐴	Horseback Riding	🛶	Canoeing or Kayaking
⛷	Downhill Skiing	🚤	Boating
🎿	Cross-country Skiing	🛥	Boat Ramps
🏊	Swimming	🐟	Fishing
🤿	Snorkeling or Scuba Diving		

ONE

Boston, Cape Cod & the Massachusetts Coast

Boston has been dubbed both the "hub of the universe" and the Athens of America by its own residents—Bostonians certainly don't need lessons in self-esteem. Of course, travelers will forgive them that bit of pride, considering the riches the Boston area has to offer.

Boston and its history-packed surroundings are a mecca for American history buffs. It would be almost impossible to discover another place so densely packed with historical treasures: from the spot where the *Mayflower* landed to the back rooms where the American Revolution was plotted to the fields where the fighting began. You can barely take a step without stumbling over a Colonial battlefield, a historic site or monument, or an 18th-century house. There's a certain magic, too, in visiting spots where Paul Revere rode, Thoreau and Emerson philosophized, Hawthorne, Melville and Dickinson wrote, and John Kennedy grew up.

This is a territory of firsts: first college in the New World (Harvard), first public school, oldest lighthouse. Before your very eyes will come to life all that you learned in school about the birth of the United States. And every few years, another nearby town celebrates its 350th anniversary.

But history is not all you'll find. Modern Boston, and Cambridge across the Charles River, beat to the pulse of the new millennium. Downtown, the classic 1795 Massachusetts State House looks out over a city that also has postmodern financial buildings, new and refurbished shopping arcades and sparkling highrise hotels. The high-tech boom of the '60s and '70s added a reputation for business acumen and technological know-how to an area already respected as the site of five major universities and dozens of smaller centers of learning.

Visitors will also discover, within a day's drive of the city, 168 miles of splendor along the Massachusetts coastline, which stretches above and below Boston and curves a great arm out into the Atlantic to form Cape Cod. Here are miles and miles of white-sand beaches fringed with dunes and marsh grasses and seaside villages where elegant yachts as well as working fishing vessels bob in the harbor. Standing fast before time, old wooden saltbox houses have weathered into the colors of the very ground that made them. Directly to the south of the Cape, the wealthy island retreats of Martha's Vineyard and Nantucket float in pristine loveliness.

Whether you're in the northernmost villages of Rockport and Newburyport or in Provincetown on the tip of Cape Cod, the ocean is never far from anyone's mind. Fishing blessed all who settled here, from the American Indians and the Pilgrims to the 19th-century whalers and today's fishermen of Gloucester, New Bedford and Plymouth. Residents of Cape Cod and the rest of the Massachusetts coast have always been premier shipbuilders and sailors, and today visitors can still take great pleasure aboard an excursion boat, a tiny sailboat or a vintage whaler.

The ocean also tempers the weather, making summers cooler and winters less fierce, although Boston itself can be notoriously humid in summer, and the winds along the Charles are sometimes bone-chilling from November through May.

Bostonians and Cape Cod natives revere their Revolutionary War–era, Federal and Greek revival homes and landmark buildings, and their chowder made with milk, not tomato juice, thank you. To a real Massachusetts Yankee, there's nothing quite like the first clambake on the beach. To give them credit, many dour old Bostonians have expanded their tastes to include the flowers, glass arcades and gourmet restaurants of Faneuil Hall Marketplace and whimsical things like balloon festivals. Still, in spite of the downtown highrises, there is little of glitz about this region. It's not an invented attraction but a real place, one that stands on the legitimacy and integrity of its origins.

This book was designed to help you explore Boston, Cape Cod and the Massachusetts coast. Besides leading you to countless popular spots, it will also take you to many off-the-beaten-path locales, places usually known only by locals. The book will tell the story of the region's history, its flora and fauna. Each chapter will suggest places to eat, to stay, to sightsee, to shop and to enjoy the outdoors and nightlife, covering a range of tastes and budgets.

Beginning in Boston proper, this book takes visitors from its Revolutionary War sites to Beacon Hill, Back Bay, the Fenway and all the other corners of this city of neighborhoods and ethnic charm. In Chapter Three, we cross the Charles River to visit Cambridge, site of Harvard University and dozens of bookstores and museums, then go on to Lexington and Concord, now idyllic spots where the Revolutionary War's first shots were fired. Chapter Four joins the hordes of visitors traveling to Cape Cod, where moors, salt marshes and breathtaking dunes lead out to the artsy enclave of Provincetown, and to the jewels of Martha's Vineyard—where a visitor might run into a member of the Kennedy clan, Spike Lee, Carly Simon or Walter Cronkite—and the smaller island of Nantucket. In Chapter Five, we travel the Massachusetts coast: first we head north of Boston toward infamous Salem and the quietly beautiful old fishing and resort villages that hug the shoreline, then south to the Plymouth area, where Pilgrim memorials abound, and finally to New Bedford, made famous by Melville in *Moby Dick* and still a crusty old sea town.

Generations of travelers have come to the Boston area, searching for pieces of America's past that echo off brick pavements, seeking out its centers of learning, or just looking for a quiet spot in a cottage by the sea. Many have found there's too much here to contain in a single visit, and they return again and again.

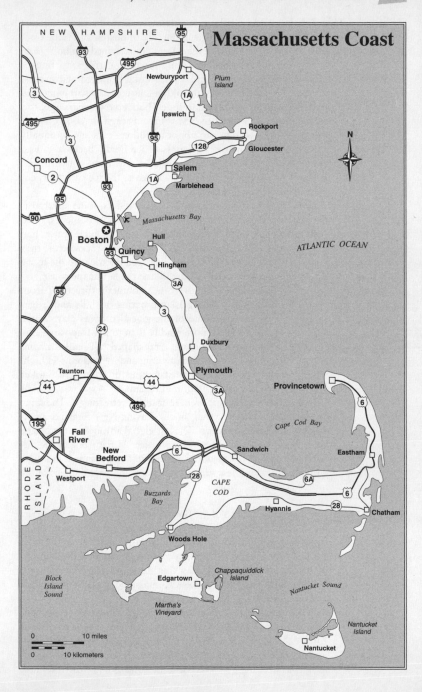

Massachusetts Coast

The Story of Boston & Cape Cod

GEOLOGY

Geology is destiny, you might say. Certainly this is true in the case of Boston and Cape Cod. Some of the region's most famed symbols, from stone walls, mill towns and rivers, to Bunker Hill, Walden Pond and Cape Cod, sprang from geologic events.

New England is one of the oldest continuously surviving land masses on earth. In Cambrian times, half a billion years ago, this entire area was covered by a vast inland sea. The Ice Age seized the region in a frozen grip about a million years ago, gradually spreading and growing. The mass of ice finally became so vast and heavy that its own weight pushed it down and outward, and it began to move. For thousands of years, the ice cap grew, engulfing all of New England.

As it moved, the ice cap picked up boulders, some as large as houses, and carried them along with it. Fields of boulders, filled with rocks of all sizes, are common in New England. Farmers had to clear their fields of countless rocks before they could plant, and they used the rocks to make the stone walls that still line the landscape today.

Melting glacial ice formed kettle-hole lakes, deep bodies of water with a rounded shape—Walden Pond is a good example. Kettle lakes make for fine ice-skating and ice-fishing.

The ice moved in a southerly direction, from Canada to Long Island, paring off hills and ledges as it went. Some of the glacial till was clay, which sticks to itself more readily than to ice. Deposited clay formed into low-lying, oval-shaped hills called *drumlins*, many a mile or more long and a hundred feet high. Some of the region's most famous drumlins are Bunker Hill and World's End located in Hingham.

The glaciers came and went four times, retreating and advancing for over a million years, finally leaving New England about 10,000 to 12,000 years ago. The last glacial advance formed Cape Cod, Martha's Vineyard and Nantucket. At the front of the advancing ice sheet, released rock debris built up a terminal moraine, a ridge of rubble. These islands and coasts are what remains of the morainal ridges.

PREHISTORY The American Indians of the Boston and Cape Cod area were part of the greater Algonquin nation of tribes, which covered territory from the Carolinas to Canada and from the Atlantic to the Mississippi. Along the Massachusetts coastline and islands lived dozens of Algonquin tribes, including the Massachusett, Narragansett, Wampanoag, Nauset, Mattakese, Cummaquid, Pamet, Monomoyk and Pawtucket.

Radiocarbon tests performed on artifacts discovered near Ipswich in 1949 suggest that humans lived here at least as early as 7500 B.C. They were nomadic hunters, drawn here by large animals, mostly caribou, that fed on the tundra left behind by retreating glaciers. As their prey died off, the nomads had to adapt, move or die. Adapt they did; they learned to eat oysters, scallops, crabs and quahogs. They also learned to spear and catch fish in nets.

Reliable food sources enabled the early American Indians to form larger, more stable living groups, or tribes. Agriculture began between 1000 and 2000 years before the Plymouth Colony. One staple, corn, which was originally developed from a grass in Central America about 7000 years ago, passed from tribe to tribe until it reached coastal New England approximately 800 years ago. The Massachusett tribe arranged their fields in a pragmatic way: they planted the corn on small hills, then planted squash, beans and pumpkins among the stalks and between the hills. The cornstalks served as beanpoles and the thick, wide leaves of the squash vines smothered weeds.

Archaeologists know from inspecting their skeletons that the pre-1620 natives of coastal Massachusetts were, for the most part, tall, strong people with good teeth—even the elderly often had full sets—and thick, healthy hair. We know of no malnutrition among these people. Until the Europeans began making frequent trips to the New World and spreading infectious diseases through their waste, the native people had never suffered from the outbreaks and plagues that regularly wiped out crowded areas of Europe.

Before the first permanent European settlement was founded in Plymouth, an epidemic of smallpox carried by European fishermen killed approximately 85 percent of the people who lived in coastal Massachusetts. Initial relations between the few natives who were left to greet the English settlers were not necessarily acrimonious; the Narragansett provided food that helped the Plymouth Colony survive the first difficult winters. As more Europeans arrived and settled, however, relations quickly deteriorated.

Unlike the Puritan settlers, the natives believed that nature was an organic whole; every human, animal and plant had a distinct role that was to be followed and respected. Waste of any kind was abhorrent to the natives and absent from their cultures. This explains why there are few remnants of their society to analyze.

HISTORY

Boston and its environs make up America's scrapbook, telling a tale of a nation conceived on hardship and perseverance, faith and dreams. It is a riveting story of high adventure and the struggle for freedom, of ingenuity and despotism, of victory over adverse conditions.

The opening pages find navigator John Cabot, on assignment from England's King Henry VII, seeking a Northwest Passage to the East. Cabot explored the coast of Massachusetts in 1497. He found no such pass but claimed a considerable chunk of the New World—everything north of Florida and east of the Rockies—for the British crown.

Italian explorer Giovanni da Verrazano staked out the same coast some 27 years later, claiming the territory for his employer nation, France. Just prior to his visit, navigator Miguel Corte Real had been checking out the terrain for Portugal.

In 1614, English captain John Smith mapped the Massachusetts coast and was taken by its beauty. A soldier of fortune, Smith wrote a glowing report of the intriguing land, describing its "sandy cliffes and cliffes of rock" planted with cornfields and gardens.

Though captivated by the new region, none of these adventurers did what seemed the most logical thing: settle the place. Of course, this white man's frontier had been inhabited at least five centuries by Algonquin tribes. A peaceful people who dwelled in wigwams, they were expert growers of corn, tobacco, pumpkins and other crops. They hunted forests plentiful with moose, deer, turkey and goose, and fished the streams and ocean for bass, salmon, lobster and clams, throwing the area's earliest clambakes.

Religious asylum, not adventure or fortune, is what those first real settlers were seeking in the New World. The Puritans, cut off from Anglican England because of their strict Protestant beliefs, read with interest John Smith's glowing report on the New World. Could it be their Utopia? They were anxious to find out.

In the spring of 1620, the Puritans struck a deal with the Plymouth Company to finance a settlement in the New World. By summer's end, 102 Puritans boarded the *Mayflower* for a rigorous, two-month journey to America. They first sighted land at Cape Cod, then cruised the coast for a month and landed at Plymouth Rock. On December 21, the Plymouth Colony was born.

That first winter proved brutal for the colonists as they fought scurvy, pneumonia and other diseases that killed nearly half their group. But springtime brought relief and the opportunity to plant crops, thanks to help from the Indians who were hospitable to their new neighbors. To celebrate the first anniversary of their friendship, the Pilgrims and Indians feasted together for three days that fall.

As word of the successful colony trickled back to England, more Puritans set out for the New World. In 1630, about 1000 Puritans on 11 ships landed at Salem during the "Great Migration." Drawn by a vast harbor filled with sea life, settlers moved southward and declared Boston their main colony.

By 1636, another 12,000 immigrants had arrived. Puritan ministers, sensing the need to train future leaders, founded Harvard College and set up a general court to govern the colonies. Local matters were dealt with by town leaders at regular meetings, the forerunners of today's town council sessions.

Ironically, those same Puritans who sought the New World for religious freedom would not tolerate other beliefs. In 1651, a visitor from the Rhode Island colony was publicly whipped for being a Baptist. Victims of English persecution, Quakers fleeing the Old World were arrested on ships in Boston Harbor before they ever set foot on the new land. And in 1659, two men and a woman were hanged in Massachusetts for espousing Quaker beliefs. Religious dissidents fled to Rhode Island, which Puritans dubbed "the sewer of New England" and "Rogue's Island."

It was Puritan fanaticism that caused the untimely end of several other unfortunate New England souls. Witches, the Puritans said, were lurking about, possessed by demons and casting spells on innocent minds.

The accusations led to witch trials in Charlestown in 1648 and in Boston in 1655, but the most hideous ordeal occurred in Salem in 1692. After hundreds of people were imprisoned in a "Witch House," 19 were executed, including 80-year-old Giles Corey, who was pressed to death when he pled no-contest.

The Puritans were also a nightmare for the indigenous population. Determined to "save" them from their pagan ways, missionaries translated the Bible into Algonquin and set about converting new Christians. By the 1670s, nearly one-fourth of the Indian population had officially accepted the imposed faith. But it was not enough. The Puritans wanted not just mental converts but a race that would abandon its centuries-old customs and its very mode of existence.

In 1700, Boston was the third busiest port in the British realm, after London and Bristol.

As colonies expanded, the native population got in the way. Several skirmishes ensued, but it was King Philip's War, from 1675 to 1676, that spelled the beginning of the end for the New England Indians. Pressured by colonists to abandon his land, chief Metacomet (King Philip) led a series of battles against his encroachers. He lost a decisive engagement, the "Great Swamp Fight," near Kingston, Rhode Island, when Massachusetts and Connecticut colonists burned wigwams, killing hundreds of women and children and disorganizing Indian forces.

Betrayed by a fellow Indian, King Philip was captured soon thereafter, his body beheaded and quartered. His head was displayed on a gibbet in Plymouth for 20 years as a reminder of white victory. Just four decades after the Indians had welcomed the first Puritans into their home, the Puritans had decimated them.

Although the Indians paid dearly for the colonists arrival in America, the settlers themselves thrived. The colonists found Boston waters teeming with cod and, by the 1640s, were shipping dried cod to the West Indies and the Mediterranean. In exchange, they received sugar, gold and molasses. By the 1670s, Boston dominated the West Indian shipping business.

But Britain resented this young upstart colony and began to impose trade and tax restrictions. In 1764, Britain imposed the

Revenue Act, which levied duties on silk, sugar and some wines. Colonists rebelled and promptly boycotted the tariffs.

England didn't flinch. One year later, it slapped colonies with the Stamp Act, taxing commercial and legal papers such as newspapers and licenses. Outraged, colonists denounced the tax and refused to buy European goods. "No taxation without representation," they cried. Every Colonial stamp agent resigned, and before the law could take effect November 1, Parliament repealed the act.

But Colonial anger was growing, and it soon erupted into riots. The British responded by sending troops to occupy Boston in 1768. Anti-crown tensions climaxed in the Boston Massacre in 1770, a clash between British soldiers and colonists. When the day was over, five Colonials lay dead on King Street, present-day State Street.

England repealed most of the Townshend taxes, leaving duties on imported tea—then the most popular drink in America. New Englanders retaliated by buying smuggled tea. In 1773, when England's Tea Act flooded the market with cheap tea, agents would not accept any deliveries—except for Governor Thomas Hutchinson in Boston.

When three tea-filled ships sailed into Boston Harbor, the Committees of Correspondence and Sons of Liberty—pre-revolutionary activists—blocked the piers. Governor Hutchinson refused to let the ships return to England, so protesters invited him to a little tea party.

Disguised as Indians, 60 Sons of Liberty boarded the ships on the night of December 16, 1773, and dumped 342 chests of tea into the harbor. It was a defiant move and an ominous portent of what was to come: revolution was in the air.

On April 19, 1775, a single musket discharge set off America's first full-scale war. "The shot heard 'round the world" was fired at the Battle of Lexington and Concord, an effort by the Redcoats to crush revolutionary uprisings around Boston.

Forewarned by Paul Revere that "the British are coming," 77 Minutemen crouched in early morning darkness, waiting for the Redcoats to attack. The British advanced, killing eight rebels and wounding ten more on the present-day Lexington Green before continuing to Concord. There they destroyed a cache of arms and were finally driven out.

On June 17, 1775, the colonists fought the Revolutionary War's first major engagement—known as the Battle of Bunker Hill although it was really fought on nearby Breed's Hill—on the Charlestown peninsula near Boston. After enduring two British attacks, the Americans ran short of ammunition and retreated.

Though a technical victory for England, Bunker Hill cost the crown more than 1000 troops—over twice the Colonial losses.

More important, it proved that the Minutemen volunteers were a match for the better-trained British Army. The British fled the city on March 17, 1776, and fighting never again touched Boston.

On July 4, 1776, the Declaration of Independence was adopted by the Continental Congress. Six years of war later, the colonies were free.

After the Americans won their independence, thoughts turned to commerce. But lost British markets pushed Boston into a depression, and the city began looking toward the Far East for trade, bringing in silks, spices and porcelain. Salem grew into a major port known for its China trade.

Fortunes were made by Boston's more prosperous merchants, a group of influential families who came to be known as the "codfish aristocracy." They dubbed themselves Boston Brahmins, smugly adopting the title of India's priestly caste. This small group counted among them the names of Cabot, Lowell and Hancock. They ruled the city with an unapproachable elitism, letting it be known that "the Lowells speak only to the Cabots, and the Cabots speak only to God."

Great minds thrived across the region. Artists, thinkers and literary geniuses would set the dynamic tone in the Boston and Massachusetts coastal areas for centuries to come. Nathaniel Hawthorne lived in Salem, while Rudyard Kipling and Winslow Homer also made their homes on the North Shore, and Henry David Thoreau settled in Cape Cod.

The sea was bountiful for Massachusetts in the 18th century. The coast thrived on its burgeoning whaling industry, with major ports at Nantucket and New Bedford, while the North Shore grew fat with fishing villages. In the 1850s Boston become the premier builder of clipper ships, sending these graceful craft around the world. To accommodate the growing trade, the city built many wharves along its waterfront. But the clipper era was cut short by the rise of steam-powered ships, which conservative Bostonians did not trust and would not build. Merchants shifted their capital to manufacturing, and the harbor went into a long decline.

The mid-19th century also saw the founding of some of Boston's most famed cultural institutions, among them the Boston

BRAINY HILL

The Brahmins built brick monuments to their prosperity on Beacon Hill, an elite residential district that defined the social character of Boston throughout the mid-19th century. Beacon Hill was home to such intellectuals as Francis Parkman, William James, Henry Wadsworth Longfellow, James Russell Lowell, Bronson Alcott, Julia Ward Howe and Horace Mann.

Public Library, the Boston Symphony Orchestra, the Massachusetts Institute of Technology and Boston University, the first to admit women on an equal basis. But political turmoil had not ended with the Revolution—abolitionism grew in the Boston area in the 19th century. William Lloyd Garrison published his *Liberator* newspaper for 34 years, despite being constantly threatened and dragged through the streets by angry mobs.

Into this tumultuous urban area swarmed thousands of immigrants, led in the 1840s by the Irish, who had been forced from their homeland by the potato famine. The influx of Irish changed the character of this Yankee city forever. First blatantly discriminated against by old-line Bostonians ("No Irish need apply"), they grew in numbers great enough to win political power. The first Irish mayor was elected in 1885, and the political influence continues today with such notable Irish as Senator Ted Kennedy and former House Speaker Tip O'Neill.

Boston's cultural richness in the mid-19th century produced a new nickname for the city: "The Athens of America."

By 1860, 61 percent of Boston residents had been born abroad. Boston bloomed into an ethnic rainbow in the 1880s, when waves of Italians, Poles and Russians arrived, multiplying the population 30-fold.

At the same time, the city's area was itself multiplying. In the mid-19th century, Boston had begun filling in the bay between Beacon Hill and Brookline, a neighborhood now known as Back Bay. Other swampy land to the south was also filled and became the South End. By the turn of the century, Boston had tripled its size with landfill.

But soon after, Boston's economy suffered a tremendous decline that would last until the 1960s. The city lost its major port status to New York and Baltimore, and its textile, shoe and glass mills moved south in search of cheaper labor and operating costs. Population shrank in the 1940s and '50s, with Boston the only large city to decline in numbers during the postwar baby boom years. The city languished in the throes of this decline for decades.

Cape Cod, meanwhile, was beginning to bloom as a tourist mecca, while Martha's Vineyard lured writers including Lillian Hellman and Dashiell Hammett to build summer homes along its exotic shoreline. In 1930, the respected Woods Hole Oceanographic Institute opened on the Cape's southeastern tip.

Good times eventually returned to Boston, too. In the 1960s, the Protestant elite and Irish Catholics finally cooperated in managing city affairs. Urban renewal projects created the new Government Center and the landmark Prudential and Hancock towers. The technology revolution of the '70s and '80s enriched the area's economy.

With prosperity came urban problems. In the early 1970s, court-ordered busing among racially imbalanced schools sparked rioting and protests, particularly in South Boston and Charlestown. The crisis lasted several years. In the 1980s, blacks began to gain more power in local and state government and in private business, but racial tension continues in this city.

Today, higher education remains a leading "industry" of Boston, the site of 47 colleges and universities at last count. And tourism is a major source of income in the city and along the coast and Cape Cod.

But beyond the high-tech centers and tourist attractions resounds the inescapable presence of Boston's colorful past: Revolutionary War monuments, 18th-century statehouses, steepled churches that held this country's first congregations. One need only explore Paul Revere's House or the Bunker Hill Monument to recognize the sites of this country's genesis. For Boston's past is America's past. And the region remains a vital part of the nation's present and future.

FAUNA & FLORA

Massachusetts coastal waters hold a bounty of sea life, thanks in large measure to the magnificent salt marshes skirting its shoreline. Among the most productive acres on earth, these marshes are home to plants and minute animals that eventually wash into the ocean and feed fish and shellfish.

A delicately balanced ecosystem that takes about 5000 years to evolve, the marsh at high tide is full of fiddler crabs, fish and water fowl. At low tide, marsh mud flats are alive with shellfish and shorebirds. Not surprisingly, conservationists and developers are at odds over the salt marshes. With the advent of dredging, developers were able to transform swampy marshes into profitable waterfront real estate, and from that point on there has been a battle to protect the salt marshes.

Massachusetts' bays and inlets thrive with marsh-nourished crabs, oysters, quahogs, clams, mussels, scallops, periwinkles and whelks. Farther out to sea swim the species that have made this area one of the richest fishery resources in the world. Long famous for record-size striped bass and giant bluefin tuna, the coastal waters also have a variety of other highly prized fish, including flounder, cod, bluefish, swordfish, squid and shark.

The coast is also home to many endangered and rare species of birds such as the merlin, a small hawk, and sedge wrens. Blue herons, tree swallows, marsh hawks, catbirds, mourning doves, red-starts, orioles, red-winged blackbirds and owls are a mere sampling of coastal birdlife. Canada geese and cormorants have increased their range and numbers, as have ospreys, after being given special nesting platforms on Martha's Vineyard.

Text continued on page 14.

The Land of Lighthouses

Massachusetts' prominence as a shipping and fishing center made lighthouses essential early in its history. The first lighthouse in America was built in Boston Harbor on Little Brewster Island in 1716. During the years to follow, 60 more were built all along the coast.

The majority of lighthouses have been well preserved, and many are still in use, although the lighthouse keeper has gone the way of time. Today, lighthouses are automated and unmanned. Lighted buoys, radio communications, radar and high-tech navigational equipment, electronic fog signals and the Coast Guard offer additional protection to seafaring vessels. Shipwrecks are practically unheard of these days.

A few beacons are privately owned, but most are maintained by the Coast Guard or local historic organizations. What follows is a guide to some of the most beautiful and historically significant lighthouses.

Built in 1797, **Highland Museum and Lighthouse Station** in Truro, Cape Cod, is better known as Cape Cod Light. It stands on clay bluffs overlooking an area once known as "the graveyard of ships" because hundreds of vessels went aground here before the lighthouse was built. Visible 20 miles out to sea, this classic white-and-black lighthouse is surrounded by scenic Cape Cod National Seashore and commands a magnificent view. ~ Phone/fax 508-487-1121.

Located within the Cape Cod National Seashore, **Race Point Lighthouse**, built in 1816, guards the entrance to Provincetown Harbor. Surrounded by wild, windswept dunes, it is accessible only by four-wheel-drive vehicle or by foot. Even after the lighthouse was built, from 1816 to 1946 more than 100 shipwrecks occurred in this treacherous area. ~ 508-487-9930.

Plymouth Lighthouse, established in 1768, is located on a beautiful bluff at the end of a peninsula that stretches from Duxbury to Plymouth Harbor. During the Revolutionary War, a British ship fired a cannonball at the lighthouse, but it barely made a dent. Destroyed by fire in 1801, it was rebuilt in 1843 and is one of Massachusetts' most scenic lighthouses.

On the road to Nauset Beach is **Nauset Light**, a classic red-and-white lighthouse, one of Cape Cod's most photographed sights. ~ Off Route 6, at the end of Cable Road and along Nauset Light Beach Road, Eastham; 508-349-3785.

Scituate Lighthouse, built in 1811 on Cedar Point at the entrance to Scituate Harbor, is maintained by the Scituate Historical Society. It's no longer in use, but an event that took place here during the War of 1812 gave this lighthouse historic distinction. In September 1814, Rebecca and Abigail Bates, the lighthouse keeper's young daughters, were alone in the lighthouse, when they spotted British war ships heading for the harbor. Frantic to do something, they started playing military songs on a drum and fife. The music made the British think the American Army was amassing, and they hightailed it back to the high seas. The girls became local heroes. Closed Sunday. ~ 781-545-1083, fax 781-545-8287.

Minot's Lighthouse, which dates to 1850, is built on a ledge one mile offshore from Cohasset. The ledge can only be seen at low tide. Most of the time the lighthouse looks as if it's floating in water. Since it was built in a highly dangerous area, men working on the lighthouse were washed out to sea by strong waves and currents. In 1851, a ferocious storm destroyed the lighthouses and two keepers died. Because of these tragedies the lighthouse was thought to be haunted by the ghosts of those who perished at sea. A museum in Cohasset contains many artifacts and historical information on the lighthouse.

Annisquam Harbor Lighthouse is on Wigwam Point at the mouth of Annisquam River on the North Shore. Built in 1801, this lighthouse doesn't have historic significance, but it is one of the most scenic in all of Massachusetts. It's off the beaten path: to get there, take Route 127 to Annisquam and turn right at the village church, then right into Norwood Heights and follow the road to the water.

Farther out to sea, Nantucket has three lighthouses. Near the town of Nantucket, **Brant Point Light** was the second lighthouse built in America (1746); since then it has been rebuilt eight times. **Sankaty Head Lighthouse**, one mile north of Siasconset, dates back to 1850 but is now endangered because erosion is undercutting the cliff on which it stands. In 1987 this lighthouse was fitted with a modern airport beacon, and its original lens can now be seen in the Nantucket Whaling Museum. The **Great Point Light**, only 15 years old, is a reproduction of an earlier lighthouse built in 1817. Its battery-powered light is recharged by solar cells. ~ The end of Wauwinet Road, off Polis Road, at the northeast end of the island.

An imposing sight, the great blue heron frequents both fresh-water and saltwater areas and can be seen all over Cape Cod during spring, summer and fall. The largest of American herons, it's usually seen at a distance standing in shallow water, waiting for prey to swim into view. It thrives on fish, reptiles, mice, insects and other small mammals.

Snowy egrets, once common chiefly along the shoreline south of Boston, now can be found throughout Massachusetts coastal marshes, especially in the summer. With its pure white body, yellow feet and black pointed bill, the snowy egret is fairly easy to spot. Around the turn of the 20th century, hunters, coveting the bird's feathers for ladies hats, nearly wiped out the species. Hunting these birds is now illegal.

Belted kingfishers aren't the most cordial of the shore's feathered creatures. They stake out a territory in fresh- or saltwater marsh and try to drive other birds away. Fairly easy to recognize, the birds have a crested head, blue-gray upper coloration and a lighter belt under the throat. The more colorful female has a red band around the stomach.

The Massachusetts state bird is the black-capped chickadee, the state flower is the mayflower, and the state tree is the American elm.

Another common shorebird, the herring gull, nests on islands and in remote coastal areas. You can spot them by their white heads and bodies, light gray backs and black wing tips. The tiny semipalmated sandpipers are often seen in groups, scurrying along sand and mud flats. Sometimes called peeps, little peeps or ox eyes, they have grayish-brown backs, white speckled breasts and black legs. Other shore and ocean birds include shearwaters, petrels, fulmars, gannets, jaegers, skuas, phalaropes, arctic terns and more.

The noble whale is without question the most observed and admired sea mammal in Massachusetts. In the warmer months, hundreds of whale-watching excursions depart daily from ports everywhere along the coast, so visitors can watch 70-foot fin whales, acrobatic humpbacks, 20-foot minke whales and rare right whales, as well as dolphins and porpoises at play in the waters. Hunted extensively in the 19th century, many species of whales are now endangered.

Although birds and fish populate the coast in great numbers, animal wildlife is somewhat limited. Along or near the shoreline you're apt to see muskrats, painted turtles, ribbon snakes, raccoons, quail, pheasant and ruffed grouse. The fallow deer, a native of Asia Minor, was released on Nantucket and Martha's Vineyard. The deer became so numerous that they overran the islands and had to be thinned.

Flora along the eastern edge of Massachusetts varies greatly from spot to spot. Common salt marsh flora includes fragrant sea lavender, a long, slender, stalklike plant that produces tiny flowers in summer; glasswort, a low, edible plant that looks like a skinny pickle; orach, a sharply pointed, arrow-shaped, light-green plant found in the high marsh; stately seaside goldenrod, a tall, colorful high-marsh plant with small vibrant flowers that closely resemble upland goldenrods; and spike-grass, short, wavy grass with large flower heads.

Pitch pines and scrub oaks dominate Cape Cod's landscape, along with sassafras, and oak and pine forests cover Martha's Vineyard. Cranberry bogs lying in deep woods east of Plymouth lead to a crimson spectacle during fall harvesting, and patches of cranberries also grow on Cape Cod and Nantucket. Visitors will also discover lush swamps and forests of beech, cedar and holly. Growing close to the shore are wild roses, beach plums, heather and acres of wavy beach grass.

Nantucket is the only place in America with maritime heathland similar to that found in Scotland, a unique display of lush heather, bayberry and other flora. The island's rolling moors change colors with the seasons—from green and pink in the summer to the dazzling reds and golds that come in autumn.

When to Go

SEASONS

A constant battle rages here in the Boston and Cape Cod area between bristling battalions of cold, dry Canadian arctic air and warm, humid air from the tropics. When these two mix it up, which is frequently, you have New England's legendary changeable weather. The morning may dawn fine and sunny, afternoon turn cold and foggy and nightfall bring a raging northeaster.

In Boston proper, the weather varies from warm, humid summers, when temperatures range from the 60s to the low 90s, to dry, crisp falls hovering in the high 40s (and the low 70s during Indian summer), to very cold winters, when temperatures dip to the 20s and 30s, occasionally falling below zero.

Along the coast and Cape Cod, the weather is milder than in the rest of New England, although winters are still long and cold. Summer temperatures range from the 60s to the 80s. Humidity can be a problem, especially along the North Shore, although ocean breezes keep things from getting too unbearable. In the fall temperatures range from around 45° to 65°.

Tourists flock to Boston for fall-foliage season (mid-September through October), when it can be very difficult to get reservations. During the low seasons of April, May and late October to late December, you'll have a much less crowded vacation and a much easier time getting reservations.

Traditionally the Cape, the Islands and coastal areas have been summer destinations, but more people are beginning to visit in the fall, when prices decline along with the crowds. A bike ride through Nantucket in October when the moors are in bloom is an unforgettable experience. In the rural outskirts of Boston, and in farm country near Plymouth and New Bedford, autumn may be the most wonderful season of all to visit. Fall colors are at their peak, and all the harvests of apples, cranberries and pumpkins are in. Sunny days often warm up to "Indian summer" comfort, energized by cool, crisp nights.

Both autumn and winter are substantially drier than in other locales. Still, rain is unpredictable and can happen at any time of year. In this area it manages to rain, snow or sleet about one day out of three, making for an annual precipitation of 42 inches. Although the 1938 hurricane looms large in natives' memories, when entire coastal communities were swallowed by the sea, hurricanes hardly ever happen. There are about five to ten hurricanes per century, fortunately most much less devastating than the 1938 storm. The most recent destructive summer storm, Hurricane Bob of August 1991, uprooted thousands of trees and tore roofs, shingles and shutters from hundreds of homes on Cape Cod and the South Shore. Some homeowners were still rebuilding several years later.

CALENDAR OF EVENTS

Each year, the Boston and Cape Cod area celebrates its Colonial past by re-enacting historic events. Other annual observances celebrate the area's riches and native skills: shipbuilding, agriculture, arts and crafts, and clam digging.

JANUARY   Boston   The **Chinese New Year** is celebrated in January or February, with three weeks of festivities.

FEBRUARY   Boston   The **New England Boat Show**, one of the largest on the East Coast, brings out the latest and fanciest in power and sail. Four of the city's biggest ice hockey–playing colleges (Harvard, Northeastern, Boston University and Boston College) face off in the **Beanpot Tournament**.

MARCH   Boston   The **New England Spring Flower Show** has been running since 1871, giving a lift to winter-weary Bostonians. The **St. Patrick's Day Parade** thrown by the Irish of South Boston is one of the largest and most festive in America.

APRIL   Boston   The nation's premier running event, the **Boston Marathon**, is only one of several signal events on **Patriot's Day**. Other activities commemorating Revolutionary War events include a parade plus re-enactments of Paul Revere's famous ride and the Battle of Lexington and Concord.
Cape Cod and the Islands   During Nantucket's **Daffodil Festival**, hundreds of these sprightly blooms decorate shop windows.

It ends with an antique car parade. A pancake-eating contest, parade, kayak races, golf and tennis tournaments, and local art show are featured at the **Brewster in Bloom** festival, held the last weekend in April.

Boston **Lilac Sunday** at the Arnold Arboretum finds over 500 lilacs in bloom (over 200 varieties), and the Franklin Park Zoo hosts a colorful **Annual Kite Festival.**

MAY

Cape Cod and the Islands The three-day **Herb Festival** offers a plant sale, lectures, demonstrations, a garden walk and an herb-accented luncheon at the Green Briar Nature Center in Sandwich. **The Arts & Crafts Street Fair** includes over 200 professional artists and craftspeople, live music and jugglers.

Massachusetts Coast The **Salem Seaport Festival** includes food, arts, crafts, antiques, live music and children's activities.

Boston The **Bunker Hill Day Parade** features contemporary patriots dressed in Revolutionary uniforms fighting the famous battle again. The annual **Dragonboat Festival** features traditional Chinese teak boat races, ethnic foods, and live cultural performances and demonstrations.

JUNE

Outside Boston The multicultural diversity of Cambridge comes alive in the **Cambridge River Festival,** with live performances, arts and crafts, and food.

Cape Cod and the Islands At Hyannis' **Annual Chowder Festival,** you can vote for the best chowder and enjoy the live entertainment.

Massachusetts Coast Anything made with fresh strawberries can be served at the **Annual Strawberry Festival** in Ipswich. **St. Peter's Fiesta** in Gloucester is a colorful event with religious activities, fireworks, music, food and a parade.

Boston Every weekend in July and August, **Italian street festivals** in the North End honor patron saints with colorful parades and festivities. The **Boston Harborfest** offers more than 200 activities celebrating the harbor at 30 sites, highlighted by a chowderfest. Local restaurants serve up heaping samples of clam chowder as they battle for the tastiest bowl of "chowdah" as determined by popular vote at the **Chowderfest** on City Hall Plaza. The **Boston Pops Fourth of July Concert** on the Esplanade's Hatch Shell promises an evening of free music and glorious fireworks.

JULY

Cape Cod and the Islands The **Barnstable County Fair,** held in Falmouth, features local and national music acts, a midway, livestock shows, gardening and cooking and crafts exhibits making this fair a popular tradition for Massachusetts families. In early July, the **Annual Indian Pow Wow** is held on 55 acres in Mashpee. The pow-wow attracts American Indians from all over the U.S., as well as from Canada, Mexico and some Central and South

American countries. In Vineyard Haven, the **Tisbury Street Fair** includes quality clothing, jewelry, crafts, food and games. The **Edgartown Yacht Club Regatta** is one of New England's best and most serious yacht races.

Massachusetts Coast In Gloucester, the **Robin Hood Faire at Hammond Castle** has magic shows, music and general renaissance merriment. **Race Week** in Marblehead includes sailboat races, parades and concerts. The **Whaling City Festival** presents lots of crafts, live music and a variety of ethnic foods.

AUGUST

Outside Boston The **Cambridge Carnival International** celebrates food, music, dance and crafts in Central Square.

Cape Cod and the Islands The **Falmouth Road Races** is the event of the year on the lower Cape, where the seven-mile race is run along the beach of the Vineyard Sound. **Peter Rabbit's Animal Fair** in Sandwich is great for kids, with pet rabbit shows, games, music and storytelling. **Dennis Festival Days** are fun-filled with crafts, a parade, kite flying on the beach, antique cars and a lobster roll supper. On Nantucket, the **Annual Antiques Show** offers quality antiques. Imaginations go wild at the **Sandcastle & Sculpture Contest** at Jetties Beach. Also on Nantucket is the **Annual Billfish Tournament**, a big event where anglers compete for the biggest catch of each species. In Oak Bluffs, **Illumination Night** is pure magic, with hundreds of paper lanterns strung between the Gothic homes. The **West Tisbury Agricultural Fair** includes fiddler's contests, the Massachusetts Woodsman Championship, horses and livestock shows, and even ox pulls. **Sails Around Cape Cod** are regattas that circumnavigate the 30 miles of the cape.

Massachusetts Coast New Bedford's **Annual Feast of the Blessed Sacrament**, the largest Portuguese feast in America, offers terrific ethnic food at budget prices. Tall ships, regattas, sailboat races, concerts, parades and fireworks are offered for five days at the **Fall River Celebrates America Festival** in Heritage State Park.

SEPTEMBER

Boston The **Boston Film Festival** includes feature-length movies by major studios as well as more unusual films from independent producers, students and foreign filmmakers.

Cape Cod and the Islands Tasty crustaceans star at the **Annual Bourne Scallop Festival**. The **Harwich Cranberry Festival** includes a week of parades, contests, fireworks and exhibits. **Tivoli Day Festival** is held in the middle of the month in Oak Bluffs, where there's a colorful street fair.

Massachusetts Coast At the **Gloucester Schooner Festival**, you can watch races, a boat parade and other maritime activities.

OCTOBER

Boston More than 5000 rowers from around the world compete in the **Head of the Charles Regatta**, now a two-day rowing spectacular. **Lowell Celebrates Kerouac** stages poetry readings and organizes "beat" tours in honor of '50s literary giant Jack Kerouac, who lived and worked in Lowell.

Outside Boston   Celebrate autumn in Cambridge at the annual **Oktoberfest,** where more than 200 merchants and food vendors join street entertainers and musicians in Harvard square.

Massachusetts Coast   If ever a place looked haunted, it would be **Hammond Castle** in Gloucester during Halloween, where ghosts and ghouls spook and delight you as you tour this romantic castle. **Haunted Happenings,** Salem's citywide Halloween festival, is loaded with haunted-house tours, costume parades, parties, magic shows, psychics and candlelight tours with, of course, witches. Mysterious legends of Essex County are recounted by costumed storytellers in historic houses at Salem's Peabody Museum **Essex Eerie Events**.

Cape Cod and the Islands   The **Green Briar Nature Center Thanksgiving Celebration** in Sandwich offers traditional holiday fare, special exhibits and craft demonstrations. **Felix Neck Sanctuary Fall Festival** on Martha's Vineyard includes nature walks and baked goods.   **NOVEMBER**

Massachusetts Coast   Have a traditional turkey dinner with all the trimmings in America's hometown, Plymouth, during its annual **Thanksgiving Dinner**.

Boston   Staged by the National Center of Afro-American Artists, Langston Hughes' **Black Nativity** is a holiday spiritual tradition. Hundreds of events mark **First Night,** an alcohol-free New Year's Eve celebration held throughout the city. There's a huge pageant, plus choral groups, ice sculptures, storytellers, acrobats, puppeteers and art and drama presentations. The **Boston Tea Party Reenactment** finds patriots dressed as Indians throwing chests of tea into Boston Harbor one more time.   **DECEMBER**

Outside Boston   The **Cambridge Christmas Revels** in Sanders Theatre celebrate the winter solstice with period song and dance; audience participation is traditional.

Cape Cod and the Islands   Main Street looks like something out of Dickens when Nantucket's **Annual Christmas Stroll** takes place, with a weekend of jolly carolers and other Yuletide festivities.

Massachusetts Coast   Salem Holiday Happenings includes crafts, fairs, house tours, auctions, concerts and more.

Like large cities, many small towns have chambers of commerce or visitor information centers; a number of them are listed in this book under the appropriate region.

▼▼▼▼▼▼▼▼
Before You Go

For information on areas throughout the state, contact the **Massachusetts Office of Travel & Tourism**. ~ State Transporta-

VISITORS CENTERS

tion Building, 10 Park Plaza, Suite 4510, Boston, MA 02116; 617-973-8500, 800-227-6277, fax 617-973-8525; www.massvaca tion.com. More detailed information on Boston can be had from the **Greater Boston Convention and Visitors Bureau.** ~ 2 Copley Place, Suite 105, Boston, MA 02116; 617-536-4100, 888-733-2678, fax 617-424-7664; www.bostonusa.com.

PACKING   Packing for a visit to this area is a little trickier than for other destinations. What you must take is dictated by the fickle Yankee weather, which might change at any minute. A warm, sunny day can turn cool and foggy without so much as a by-your-leave. Your best bet is to bring layers of clothing that can be added or subtracted as needed. Even in the summer, bring some long-sleeved shirts, long pants and lightweight sweaters and jackets, along with your T-shirts, jeans and bathing suit.

Fall and spring call for a full round of warm clothing, from long pants and sweaters to jackets, hats and gloves. While fall days are often sunny and warm, fall nights can turn quite crisp and cool. Bring your heaviest, warmest clothes in winter: thick sweaters, knitted hats, down jackets and ski clothes.

Boston can be conservatively dressed at times. Some down-town Boston restaurants have dress codes, requiring men to wear jackets and ties and women to be "appropriately attired." Boston Brahmins notwithstanding, most of this area is a pretty casual place, especially in summer, when everyone has sand in his shoes. No one will look askance if you wear your deck shoes and L. L. Bean pants to dinner at most restaurants, particularly in coastal resort areas. Massachusetts is less casual, however, than a warm-weather resort, and you can't get into most restaurants or bars without a shirt or shoes, or if you're wearing a bathing suit.

Residents are used to rolling up their car windows every night in summer, knowing it may rain any night. Rain, though not usually heavy, is a big part of every season, so be sure to bring an umbrella and a raincoat, even in the summer.

Some of Boston's streets are almost as old as the city itself. On these rough, cobblestone ways you need sturdy, comfortable shoes that can take this kind of beating and be kind to your feet. Women should never attempt to navigate cobblestone streets in high heels. Likewise, some shores can be rocky. A pair of rubber shoes or old sneakers for swimming is sometimes advisable.

Though Cape Cod and the Coast are not the Caribbean, you can get just as impressive a sunburn here. Bring a good sunscreen, especially to the beach, where sand and water reflect the sun's rays more intensely. Bring insect repellent in the summertime as insurance against the greenhead flies at the shore and blackflies in the mountains.

You may want to toss in an antique guide along with your other reading; the country's oldest antiques are for sale here. Last but not least, don't forget your camera for capturing quintessential New England vistas of lighthouses and white-steepled villages.

LODGING

Visiting Massachusetts is your opportunity to stay in some of the most historic lodgings in America. A number of them date back to the 18th century, such as Longfellow's Wayside Inn in Sudbury.

Boston hotels range from grande dames of the past century to glitzy contemporary skyscrapers. They are usually first-rate but tend to be priced for travelers on an expense account, especially in the downtown area.

The coastal regions are thick with historic farmhouses and sea captains' mansions turned into bed and breakfasts. These are often rambling, cozy affairs complete with fireplace, bookshelves and resident cat. But bed-and-breakfast booking agencies, especially in Boston, also list host homes with a spare room, which isn't quite the same thing. Be sure to ask whether a bed and breakfast is an inn or not.

Cape Cod has some of the most beautiful inns in the country, along with hundreds of other accommodations in every price range, location and style imaginable. If you plan to stay for at least a week, think about renting a house, apartment or condo; it's usually less expensive than a hotel. Call or write the **Cape Cod Chamber of Commerce** for names of realtors handling rentals in a particular area. ~ 307 Main Street, Suite 2, Hyannis, MA 02601; 508-862-0700, 888-332-2732, fax 508-862-0727; www.capecodchamber.org, e-mail info@capecodchamber.org.

In addition, accommodations include mom-and-pop motels, chain hotels and rustic seaside cottages where you'll awaken to the sounds of surf and crying gulls. Cities have the most deluxe highrise hotels, but outside urban areas, lodgings are generally casual and lowrise.

Whatever your preference and budget, you can probably find something to suit your taste with the help of the individual chap-

NAVIGATIONAL TOOLS

When you come to Boston, Cape Cod and the Massachusetts coast, you'll need nothing but the best street and road maps. Many roads are winding, poorly marked or not marked at all, following an age-old philosophy that if you live here, you know where you're going, and if you don't, you have no business being here anyway.

ters in this book. Remember, rooms are scarce and prices rise in the high season, which is summer, fall-foliage time and Christmas. Many hotels on Cape Cod and the Islands close in the winter, and reservations are mandatory in the summer.

There are lots of special weekend and holiday packages at the larger hotels, and off-season rates drop significantly, making a week- or month-long stay a real bargain.

Accommodations in this book are organized by region and classified according to price. These refer to high-season rates for a double room, so if you're looking for low-season bargains, be sure to inquire about them.

Budget lodgings generally cost less than $60 a night for two people and are satisfactory and clean but modest. *Moderate*-priced lodgings run from $60 to $120; what they offer in terms of luxury will depend on their location, but in general they provide larger rooms and more attractive surroundings. At *deluxe*-priced accommodations, you can expect to spend between $120 and $175 for a homey bed and breakfast or a double in a hotel or resort. In hotels of this price you'll typically find spacious rooms, a fashionable lobby, a restaurant or two and often some shops. *Ultra-deluxe* facilities, priced above $175, are a region's finest, offering all the amenities of a deluxe hotel plus plenty of luxurious extras, such as jacuzzis and exercise rooms, 24-hour room service and gourmet dining.

> Some restaurants, particularly those that depend on the summer trade in coastal areas, close for the winter.

If you've got your heart set on a room with a water view, be sure to pin that down. Be forewarned that "oceanside" doesn't always mean right on the beach. If you want to save money, try lodgings a block or so away from the water. They almost always offer lower rates than rooms within sight of the surf, and the savings are often worth the short stroll to the beach.

DINING

Succulent native seafood stars at legions of Boston and Cape Cod restaurants, from lobster in the rough and tender bay scallops to codfish, mussels, steamers and milky clam chowder.

Besides seafood and traditional Yankee foods, Boston and Cape Cod restaurants serve up ethnic cuisines of every stripe, plus gourmet foods and fast food. No matter what your taste or budget, there's a restaurant for you.

Within each chapter, restaurants are organized geographically. Each entry describes the cuisine and ambience and categorizes the restaurant in one of four price ranges. Dinner entrées at *budget* restaurants usually cost $9 or less. The ambience is informal, service speedy, the crowd often a local one. *Moderate*-priced eateries charge between $9 and $18 for dinner; surroundings are casual but pleasant, the menu offers more variety and the pace is usually slower. *Deluxe* restaurants tab their entrées above $18; cuisines may be simple or sophisticated, but the decor is plusher and the service more personalized establishments, where entrées begin at $25, are often the gourmet gathering places; here cooking is (hopefully) a fine art, and the service should be impeccable.

Breakfast and lunch menus vary less in price from one restaurant to another. Even deluxe establishments usually offer light breakfasts and luncheons, priced within a few dollars of their budget-minded competitors. These smaller meals can be a good time to test expensive restaurants. All restaurants serve lunch and dinner unless noted otherwise.

Massachusetts is a wonderful place to bring children. Besides many child-oriented museums, the region also has hundreds of beaches and parks, and many nature sanctuaries sponsor children's activities year-round.

TRAVELING WITH CHILDREN

Quite a few bed and breakfasts in this area don't accept children, so be sure of the policy when you make reservations. If you need a crib or cot, arrange for it ahead of time.

Travel agents can help with arrangements; they can reserve airline bulkhead seats where there is plenty of room (but where you can't watch a movie) and determine which flights are the least crowded. If you are traveling by car, be sure to take along such necessities as water and juices, snacks and toys. Always allow extra time for getting places, especially on rural roads.

A first-aid kit is a must for any trip you embark on. Along with adhesive bandages, antiseptic cream and something to stop itching, include any medicines your pediatrician might recommend to treat allergies, colds, diarrhea or any chronic problems your child may have.

At the beach, take extra care with your children's skin the first few days. Children's tender young skin can suffer severe sunburn before you know it. Hats for the kids are a good idea, along with liberal applications of a good sunscreen. Never take your eyes off your children at the shore. If you are traveling in winter, never leave a child alone near a frozen lake.

All-night stores are scarce in rural areas, and stores in small towns often close early. You may go a long distance between stores that can supply you with essentials, so be sure to be well stocked with diapers, baby food and other needs when you are on the go. But all-night stores such as Store 24, Christie's, White Hen Pantry, Cumberland Farms and 7-11 are plentiful in urban areas.

To find specific activities for children, consult local newspapers. The *Boston Globe Calendar* has especially comprehensive listings that cover a good part of the state. ~ www.boston.com/globe/calendar.

Travelers Aid of Boston is a resource for any traveler in need and maintains booths at major transportation terminals. Volunteers can arrange to meet young children traveling alone. ~ 17 East Street, Boston, MA 02111; 617-542-7286, fax 617-542-9545; www.taboston.org.

WOMEN TRAVELING ALONE

Traveling solo grants an independence and freedom different from that of traveling with a partner, but single travelers are more vulnerable to crime and must take additional precautions.

It's unwise to hitchhike and probably best to avoid inexpensive accommodations on the outskirts of town; the money saved does not outweigh the risk. Bed and breakfasts, youth hostels and YWCAs are generally your safest bet for lodging, and they also foster an environment ideal for bonding with fellow travelers.

Keep all valuables well-hidden and clutch cameras and purses tightly. Avoid late-night treks or strolls through undesirable parts of town, but if you find yourself in this situation, continue walking with a confident air until you reach a safe haven. A fierce scowl never hurts.

These hints should by no means deter you from seeking out adventure. Wherever you go, stay alert, use your common sense and trust your instincts. For more hints, get a copy of *Safety and Security for Women Who Travel* (Travelers Tales, 1998).

If you are hassled or threatened in some way, never be afraid to yell for assistance. It's a good idea to carry change for a phone call and to know the number to call in case of emergency. Most areas have 24-hour hotlines for victims of rape and violent crime. In the Boston area, call the **Boston Area Rape Crisis Center**. ~ 617-492-7273. The **Independence House** serves the Cape Cod area. ~ 508-790-1344, 800-439-6507.

GAY & LESBIAN TRAVELERS

While New England is generally not known for its progressive attitudes, the people who live here tend to be very independent minded and not apt to stick their noses in other people's business. This allows gay or lesbian travelers to feel comfortable while visiting here. Whether you're interested in exploring the scenic rural backroads or sightseeing in the region's cities, New England has much to offer. The region also boasts several gay and lesbian hotspots to which this guidebook dedicates special "gay-specific" sections.

The first of these sections covers Boston's gay neighborhood in the city's South End. Both Boston and nearby Cambridge are home to large gay communities, with the South End area of Boston offering the greatest concentration of gay-friendly bars, nightclubs and restaurants (see "Boston Gay Scene" in Chapter Two).

Located at the tip of Cape Cod and attracting gay and lesbian travelers from all over the world is the well-known resort mecca of Provincetown (see "Provincetown" in Chapter Four).

Also check "Gay and lesbian travelers" in the index for more gay and lesbian listings.

These areas offer a number of resource centers and publications of use to the gay, lesbian, transgender and bisexual community. In Boston, the **Gay, Lesbian, Bisexual & Transgendered Helpline** can direct you to your traveling heart's desire, from health services to social possibilities and everything in between. ~ 617-267-9001. If you're in town, stop by the **Cambridge Women's Center** and flip through notebooks filled with helpful information about places to go and places to stay. Check the bulletin boards to see what events are happening in the area. Closed Sunday. ~ 46 Pleasant Street, Cambridge; 617-354-8807, fax 617-354-3109; www.cambridgewomenscenter.org, e-mail wmnscntr@attbi.org.

The Fig Newton cookie was named after the town of Newton, Massachusetts.

Gay and lesbian publications providing entertainment listings and happenings are available. *The Metroline*, a free bi-monthly that you can find in cafés and bookstores, covers Connecticut, Rhode Island, Massachusetts and Maine. ~ 860-233-8334, fax 860-233-8338; www.metroline-online.com, e-mail editor@metro-online.com. For monthly news and art features of a local, national and international scope, pick up *Sojourner: The Women's Forum* at any of the area's independent bookstores. ~ 617-524-0415, fax 617-524-9397; www.sojourner.org, e-mail info@sojourner.org.

In Boston, you can get the weekly *Bay Windows* for entertainment listings. ~ 617-266-6670, fax 617-266-5973; www.baywindows.net, e-mail calendar@baywindows.com. There's also the free *In Newsweekly*, available at cafés and bookstores. ~ 617-426-8246, fax 617-426-8264; e-mail innews@aol.com.

In Provincetown, the **Provincetown Business Guild** publishes a handy directory detailing the area's gay services. ~ 508-487-2313, 800-637-8696; www.ptown.org, e-mail pbguild@capecod.net. Find out about Provincetown/Brewster happenings in the *Provincetown Banner*, an all-inclusive community newspaper that comes out weekly. ~ 508-487-7400, fax 508-487-7144; www.province townbanner.com.

SENIOR TRAVELERS

The Boston area is a hospitable place for senior citizens to visit; countless museums, historic sights and even restaurants and hotels offer senior discounts that cut a substantial chunk off vacation costs. And many golden-agers from hotter climes flock to New England for its cool summers.

The **American Association of Retired Persons** (AARP) offers membership to anyone over the age of 50. AARP's benefits include travel discounts. ~ 601 E Street Northwest, Washington,

DC 20049; 800-424-3410, fax 202-434-6483; www.aarp.org, e-mail member@aarp.org.

Elderhostel offers many, many educational courses in a variety of New England locations that are all-inclusive packages at colleges and universities. ~ 11 Avenue de Lafayette, Boston, MA 02111; 877-426-8056, fax 617-426-0701; www.elderhostel.org, e-mail ireg@elderhostel.org.

Remember that the weather along the Massachusetts coast changes frequently. It's a good idea to carry a lightweight windbreaker at all times; summer or winter, the extra layer will ward off sudden chilly winds. Another precaution for traveling in coastal New England: Much of the charm of the oldest cities and villages comes from their cobblestoned streets and brick sidewalks, which are lovely to look at but are treacherously slippery when wet or icy. No matter what the weather, take your time when you are walking along these pretty streets. You'll save your ankles and knees from undue wear and tear while you get a better view of the old buildings and trees.

> The nation's first human flying stunt occurred in 1757, when John Childs, using a half glider/half umbrella, leaped from the steeple of Boston's Old North Church.

Be sure to bring along needed medications. Consider carrying a medical record with you, including your history and current medical status as well as your doctor's name, phone number and address. Make sure that your insurance covers you while you are away from home.

Travelers Aid of Boston can provide shelter and transportation, help find low-cost accommodations, give directions and information, and assist with train, plane and bus connections. Volunteers can arrange to meet travelers with special needs. ~ 17 East Street, Boston, MA 02111; 617-542-7286, fax 617-542-9545; www.taboston.org.

DISABLED TRAVELERS Massachusetts has made real strides toward making its many attractions and services handicapped-accessible. Parking spaces for the disabled are provided at most services and attractions, although few buses are accessible to people with disabilities.

Special escorted group tours are offered by **The Guided Tour**. ~ 7900 Old York Road, Suite 114-B, Elkins Park, PA 19027; 215-782-1370, 800-783-5841, fax 215-635-2637; www.guidedtour.com, e-mail gtour400@aol.com.

There are many organizations offering general information. Among these are:

The **Society for Accessible Travel & Hospitality** (SATH). ~ 347 5th Avenue, Suite 610, New York, NY 10016; 212-447-7284, fax 212-725-8253; www.sath.org, e-mail sathtravel@aol.com.

The **MossRehab Resource Net.** ~ MossRehab Hospital, 1200 West Tabor Road, Philadelphia, PA 19141; 215-456-9600; www. mossresourcenet.org, e-mail netstaff@mossresourcenet.org.

Flying Wheels Travel. ~ 143 West Bridge Street, Owatonna, MN 55060; 507-451-5005, fax 507-451-1685; www.flyingwheels travel.com, e-mail thq@ll.net.

Also providing information for travelers with disabilities is **Travelin' Talk**, a networking organization. ~ P.O. Box 1796, Wheat Ridge, CO 80034; 303-232-2979, fax 303-239-8486; www.travel intalk.net, e-mail info@travelintalk.net. They also run **Access-Able Travel Service**, with worldwide information online. ~ 303-232-2979; www.access-able.com.

Travelers Aid of Boston can arrange for volunteers to meet disabled travelers. ~ 17 East Street, Boston, MA 02111; 617-542-7286, fax 617-542-9545; www.taboston.org.

Passports and Visas Most foreign visitors are required to obtain a passport and tourist visa to enter the United States. Contact your nearest United States Embassy or Consulate well in advance to obtain a visa and to check on any other entry requirements.

FOREIGN TRAVELERS

Customs Requirements Foreign travelers are allowed to carry in the following items: 200 cigarettes (one carton), 100 cigars or two kilograms (4.4 pounds) of smoking tobacco; one liter of alcohol for personal use (you must be 21 years of age to bring in alcohol); and US$100 worth of duty-free gifts that can include an additional quantity of 100 cigars. You may bring in any amount of currency, but must fill out a form if you bring in more than US$10,000. Carry any prescription drugs in clearly marked containers. (You may have to produce a written prescription or doctor's statement for the customs officer.) Meat or meat products, seeds, plants, fruits and narcotics are not allowed to be brought into the United States. Contact the **United States Customs Service** for further information. ~ 1300 Pennsylvania Avenue Northwest, Washington, DC 20229; 202-927-0230; www.customs.treas.gov.

Driving If you plan to rent a car, an international driver's license should be obtained prior to arrival. United States driver's licenses are valid in Canada and vice versa. Some rental car companies require both a foreign license and an international driver's license along with a major credit card and require that the lessee be at least 25 years of age. Seat belts are mandatory for the driver and all passengers. Children under the age of 5 or 40 pounds should be in the back seat in approved child safety restraints.

Currency American money is based on the dollar. Bills in the United States come in seven denominations: $1, $2, $5, $10, $20, $50 and $100. Every dollar is divided into 100 cents. Coins are the penny (1 cent), nickel (5 cents), dime (10 cents), quarter (25 cents), half-dollar (50 cents) and dollar. You may not use foreign currency to purchase goods and services in the United States. Consider buying traveler's checks in dollar amounts. You may also use credit cards affiliated with an American company such as Interbank, Barclay Card, VISA and American Express.

Electricity and Electronics   Electric outlets use currents of 110 volts, 60 cycles. To operate appliances made for other electrical systems, you need a transformer or other adapter. Travelers who use laptop computers for telecommunication should be aware that modem configurations for U.S. telephone systems may be different from their European counterparts. Similarly, the U.S. format for videotapes is different from that in Europe; National Park Service visitors centers and other stores that sell souvenir videos often have them available in European format on request.

Weights and Measurements   The United States uses the English system of weights and measures. American units and their metric equivalents are as follows: 1 inch = 2.5 centimeters; 1 foot = 0.3 meter; 1 yard = 0.9 meter; 1 mile = 1.6 kilometers; 1 ounce = 28 grams; 1 pound = 0.45 kilogram; 1 quart (liquid) = 0.9 liter.

Outdoor Adventures

CAMPING

Camping is somewhat limited in this area, but you'll find a few campgrounds at parks on Cape Cod and in the New Bedford area. For information on camping at Massachusetts state forest sites, contact the **State Division of Forests and Parks**. ~ State Transportation Building, 251 Causeway Street, Room 600, Boston, MA 02116; 617-727-3180, fax 617-973-8799. A free guide, the *Massachusetts Campground Directory*, is published by the **Massachusetts Association of Campground Owners**. ~ P.O. Box 548, Scituate, MA 02066, 781-544-3475, fax 781-544-3159; www.campmass.com. This guide is also available from the **Massachusetts Office of Travel and Tourism**. ~ 10 Park Place, Suite 4510, Boston, MA 02116; 617-727-3201, 800-227-6277, fax 617-973-8525; www.massvacation.com. Camping is also permitted on several of the Boston Harbor Islands (see the "Beaches & Parks" section of Chapter Three). For more information, contact **Boston Harbor Islands and Web Memorial State Park**. ~ 349 Lincoln Street, Building 45, Hingham; 781-740-1605, fax 781-740-1372. *Note:* Massachusetts does not allow camping outside of designated camping areas in state forests.

BOATING

Boating is one of the most popular activities along the Massachusetts harbor-studded coastline. Sailboats, canoes, windjammers, power boats, cruise boats and ferries all ply the coastline. You can bring your own boat and get your feet wet doing some Massachusetts cruising, or rent or charter a craft here. Each chapter in this book offers suggestions on how to go about finding the vessel of your choice. Charts for boaters and divers are widely sold at marine shops and bookstores throughout the area.

Massachusetts boating information can be obtained from the **Division of Law Enforcement.** ~ 251 Causeway, Boston, MA 02114; 617-727-3905, fax 617-727-8897; www.state.ma.us.

Ever since the Puritans discovered salt cod, New Englanders have been fishing these waters. In the 19th century, men went down to the sea in ships after bigger fish—whales.

FISHING

Today many people fish just for fun, casting a line into the surf off a rock jetty for flounder, striped bass or bluefish, or perhaps going out to sea for such deep-water game fish as bluefin tuna or shark.

Freshwater fishing in streams, lakes and ponds nets rainbow, brook and brown trout, as well as largemouth bass, northern pike, bullhead, perch, sunfish, catfish and pickerel.

The most common saltwater fish are winter flounder and bluefish. Other saltwater species include striped bass, cod, tautog, mackerel, haddock, pollock, weakfish and smelt.

Massachusetts requires a license for freshwater fishing but not for most saltwater fishing, with a few restrictions.

For information on fishing in Massachusetts, contact the **State Division of Fisheries and Wildlife** and ask the Freshwater Hunting and Fishing division for the *Abstracts of the Fish and Wildlife Laws*. ~ 251 Causeway Street, Boston, MA 02202; 617-727-3151, fax 617-626-1517; www.masswildlife.com. The Marine Fisheries division publishes the *Massachusetts Saltwater Fishing Guide*, which includes town-by-town lists of bait shops, boat rentals, jetties and piers, party boats and boat-launching sites.

TWO

Boston

A stately dominion of brick and brownstone, parks and trees, river and harbor, Boston has stood as the preeminent New England city for more than three and a half centuries. Holding fast to the tip of a tiny peninsula jutting into the Atlantic, the city grew and spread south and west through the centuries, but it's still compact and eminently walkable. Despite its tiny size, Boston has played a mighty role in history, a history etched in the minds of all Americans. For this is the birthplace of our nation, where Paul Revere made his dashing midnight ride, where "the shot heard 'round the world" was fired.

A city of fanatical Puritan roots, Boston has been mocked and scorned by more worldly others as dull, pious and provincial, no match for New York or Los Angeles in sophistication. Rich in artistic and intellectual life, Boston has still been notched down on the big-city scoresheet for its lackluster shopping, dining and hotel accommodations.

But Boston is changing its face. While still revering its history and roots, the city is searching for a new identity as a modern, stylish metropolis. In the 1980s, world-renowned chefs set up shop here, winning over Bostonians and food critics alike. The palatial shopping emporium Copley Place opened, anchored by flashy Dallas retailer Neiman Marcus, which would never have dared show its face here in the 1950s. A building boom pushed up skyscraping: First-class hotels like the Westin, the Boston Harbor Hotel and the Four Seasons, as well as gleaming Financial District office towers, add to the city's skyline. At the same time, old treasures like South Station and the Ritz-Carlton Hotel received much-needed facelifts. Change continued in the 1990s. In 1995, the Boston Public Library completed a $50 million restoration project. In September 1995, the FleetCenter, a $160 million contemporary sports arena, opened to replace the antiquated Boston Garden.

The push for class continues with a grand project called the "Big Dig" begun in the late 1980s, which involves carving a giant tunnel to allow for the ugly, elevated Central Artery expressway underground. The project's completion will bring light and spaciousness to the downtown area. And the city's main eyesore—the burlesque district known as the Combat Zone—has all but disappeared. Trendy restaurants, cafés and shops have sprung up in Boston's efforts to demolish the Combat Zone (known to some as the "Ladder District") and expand the nearby theater district. The area has surprisingly become a spot for hip jazz clubs and excellent people watching. Boston's ambitious facelift includes the redevelopment of the Seaport District, a convention center, hotel, shopping and restaurant zone that will replace existing warehouses and will feature a harborfront walkway.

The city's Puritan past took root in 1630, when a small band of English Puritans led by Governor John Winthrop arrived and settled on the peninsula. As the colony thrived along with others that would become the United States, economic tensions mounted that led to the Revolutionary War. Signal events on the road to independence took place in the Boston area: the 1770 clash called the Boston Massacre, in which five colonists were killed; the Boston Tea Party, where Bostonians disguised as Indians let the crown know what they thought of the tea tax—shiploads of tea were dumped into the harbor in a gesture that's still re-enacted today.

The Revolution began in earnest in and around Boston. The first shots were fired at nearby Lexington and Concord in 1775. In the Battle of Bunker Hill, the British drove off the heavily outnumbered Americans, but only after sustaining severe losses. When George Washington fortified Dorchester Heights in a single night, the British were ousted forever.

Two centuries after the Revolution, Boston still has a reputation for liberalism, spearheaded by the reigning scion of the Kennedy clan, Senator Ted Kennedy. Breaking the Irish tradition, today's top city official—Thomas Menino—is the city's first Italian mayor.

Boston the city is home to a scant 589,141 souls. Many are under 30; thousands of students flood the city each September, injecting it with vitality and youthfulness.

The nucleus of Boston proper is a pear-shaped peninsula. At its northernmost tip stands the North End, a small Italian enclave clustered with shops, cafés and restaurants. The downtown area takes up most of the peninsula, winding between the waterfront and Boston Common from north to south and encompassing a Chinatown that is tiny yet rich in tradition.

High above Boston Common in regal splendor sits Beacon Hill, crowned by the State House and graced with bowfront brick homes, window boxes and hidden gardens. To the west of Beacon Hill lies its cousin, stately Back Bay, a place of wide boulevards and imposing brownstones. Back Bay also encompasses the architectural jewels of Copley Square: the Public Library, Trinity Church and the John Hancock Tower. Farther west is the Fenway, sprawling around its marshy gardens and home to baseball's famous Fenway Park.

A bit farther south lies the city's largest neighborhood, the South End, another 19th-century brick residential area in the process of gentrification. Cut off from eastern downtown by the Fort Point Channel, South Boston (not to be confused with the South End) is a primarily commercial area, home to the city's fish piers.

The residential neighborhoods, harking back to English architecture, have led to Boston's being characterized "America's most European city." But since Boston has added new space-age layers to the urban quiltwork of centuries, the city wears a more American and international face. Though the city took its time, it has come a long way from its Puritan roots and the days when books by male and female authors were separated on different shelves.

Somehow we know the Puritan roots will never die; the Sunday blue laws were rescinded fairly recently, in 1994. And Boston will never be mistaken for wilder cities like New York or Los Angeles. It will always remain small, and never a province of punk hairdos. But nowadays, Boston has a lot less to apologize for on the big-city scoresheet and is becoming a first-class city in a class by itself.

The North End

The North End is Boston's oldest, most colorful neighborhood. Today it's a tightly knit, homogeneous Italian community, established after a gradual takeover from pockets of Irish, Portuguese and Jewish residents starting in the late 19th century. The North End's mostly one-lane streets are crowded cheek-by-jowl with Italian restaurants and food stores. Many residents still greet each other in the language of the Old Country and hang their wash out between the alleys. All summer long, Italians celebrate their patron saints with picturesque weekend parades and street festivals.

On the roundish peninsula that is Boston, the North End juts north into Boston Harbor and is cut off from downtown by the elevated Southeast Expressway, which helps keep it a place unto itself. It's a spot where Boston history still lives.

SIGHTS
Probably no name evokes more romance in American history than Paul Revere. His famous ride warning of the British attack in 1775 has been chronicled the world over. The quiet little expanse of North Square, lined with cobblestones and black anchor chain, is where you come upon the **Paul Revere House**. This simple little two-story house with gray clapboards and leaded-glass, diamond-paned windows looks almost out of place in Boston today, and well it might. Built in 1680, it's the only example left in downtown Boston of 17th-century architecture. Revere lived here from 1770 until 1800, although not with all of his 16 children at the same time. Inside are period furnishings, some original Revere family items and works of silver. Closed Monday from January through March. Admission. ~ 19 North Square; 617-523-2338, fax 617-523-1775; www.paulreverehouse.org, e-mail staff@paul reverehouse.org.

Next door to Paul Revere's house and entered through the same courtyard is the **Pierce-Hichborn House**. Built around 1711 for glazier Moses Pierce, it's one of the earliest remaining Georgian structures in Boston. It later belonged to Paul Revere's cousin, boatbuilder Nathaniel Hichborn. Guided tours only; call ahead for schedule. Closed Monday from January through March.

Text continued on page 36.

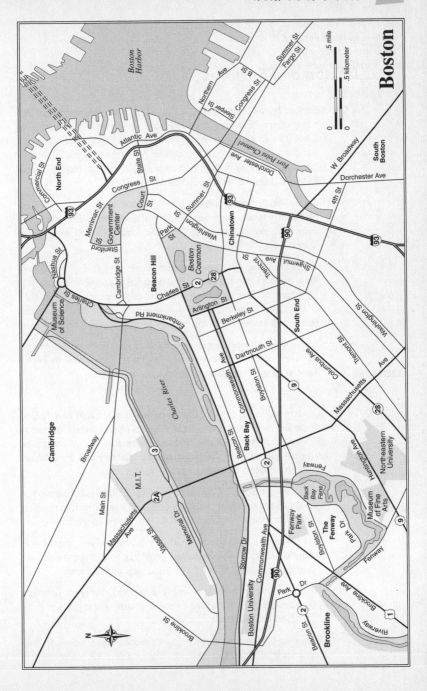

Three-day Weekend

Boston and Environs

DAY 1
- Explore historic Boston on the **Freedom Trail** (pages 44–45). This string of pre-Revolutionary buildings echoing with the footsteps of Samuel Adams and young Ben Franklin provides a good excuse to wander the streets of the city center. Along the way, you're sure to be sidetracked by other attractions such as the huge **Quincy Market** (page 46) at Faneuil Hall Marketplace.

- Take a lunch break midway through your walking tour at **The Marshall House** (page 56), a hidden alternative to the usual Freedom Trail tourist haunts such as the Union Oyster House and Durgin Park.

- Continue under the freeway to the North End to see where Paul Revere rode. Today the North End is an Italian neighborhood boasting some of Boston's best restaurants. Why not try the *pollo all'Arrabbiata* ("angry chicken") at **Lucia's** (page 39), where the ceilings are covered with frescoes by local latter-day Michelangelos.

- Take in a play this evening at one of the city's fine theaters, then top off your history-packed day with a nightcap at the **Bell in Hand Tavern** (page 61), Boston's oldest bar.

DAY 2
- Learn more about some of the ethnic subcultures that have helped shape Boston's unique character. A good place to start is Beacon Hill, once the heart of the city's early-day free black community. Visit the **Museum of Afro-American History** and the **African Meeting House** (page 65).

- Next explore Boston's compact, bustling Chinatown, a very Asian enclave in the center of a Yankee city. Stop in for lunch at the best seafood restaurant in Chinatown, **Chau Chow** (page 58).

- This afternoon, head south to Columbia Point to visit the **John F. Kennedy Library and Museum** (page 95), celebrating the accomplishments of the 20th-century's most famous Bostonian.

- Before returning to the city, enjoy a seafood dinner at **Jimmy's Harborside** (page 96), a long-established eatery that was a favorite of JFK and brother Bobby.

- Take your choice among the many nightclubs that have made Boston a music mecca.

DAY 3
- Cross the river to Cambridge and explore the hallowed halls of **Harvard** (pages 104, 106–107), America's premier university.

- It's an amazing experience just to sit in Harvard Yard, read a book and watch students strolling by. To make a full day of it, visit some of the university's world-class museums. We recommend the **Peabody Museum of Archaeology** (page 106), the **Arthur M. Sackler Museum** (page 106) and the **Fogg Art Museum** (page 106).

- Complete your visit with a special dining experience **Upstairs at the Pudding** (page 111), steeped in Harvard tradition and one of greater Boston's finest restaurants.

Admission. ~ 29 North Square; 617-523-2338, fax 617-523-1775; www.paulreverehouse.org, e-mail staff@paulreverehouse.org.

Also in North Square are the **Seamen's Bethel** (12 North Square) and the **Mariner's House** (11 North Square). An anchor over the door announces the Mariner's House, a place where, since 1838, a seaman has always been able to get a cheap meal and a bed for the night. Said the sailor-preacher of the Seamen's Bethel, "I set my bethel in North Square because I learned to set my net where the fish ran." Once a place where sailors worshipped, it's now a rectory office.

On a street noted for "gardens and governors" lived John F. "Honey Fitz" Fitzgerald, one of Boston's Irish "governors," a ward boss, congressman and mayor. His daughter Rose Kennedy was born in this plain brick building at **4 Garden Court Street**.

The **Old North Church** is the one from which the sexton hung two lanterns the night of Paul Revere's midnight ride ("one if by land, two if by sea"). This beautiful church has Palladian windows and a white pulpit inspired by London designs. The four trumpeting cherubim atop the choir loft pilasters were taken from a French pirate ship. Replicas of the steeple's lanterns may be viewed in the adjacent museum. ~ 193 Salem Street; 617-523-6676, fax 617-725-0559; www.oldnorth.com, e-mail church@oldnorth.com.

Directly behind Old North Church in the **Paul Revere Mall** stands a life-sized statue of Revere astride his horse—one of the city's most photographed scenes.

On the other side of the mall you'll come to **St. Stephen's Church**, a brick Federal-style church designed by the man who established that style, Charles Bulfinch, America's first native-born architect. The only Bulfinch-designed church still standing in Boston, St. Stephen's has a bell and copper dome cast by Paul Revere. Inside are wedding cake–white fluted pillars, balconies and Palladian windows, a pewter chandelier and an 1830s pipe organ. ~ Hanover and Clark streets.

Copp's Hill Burying Ground served as the cemetery for Old North Church in the 17th century. Set high on a little green knoll, it overlooks Boston Harbor and Charlestown, which was bombarded by British guns placed here during the Battle of Bunker Hill. Its simple gray headstones bear pockmarks from British target practice. Buried here are Increase and Cotton Mather, Puritan ministers who wielded considerable political clout. ~ Hull and Snowhill streets.

The widest street in all the North End is **Hanover Street**, a major center for shops and restaurants. Walking south on Hanover Street leads you straight to the **Haymarket–North End Underpass**, which leads under the Southeast Expressway to downtown. The underpass is lined with bright, primitive mosaics done by North End children, a kind of urban folk art. The walls of the

HIDDEN ▶

underpass also sport the work of Sidewalk Sam, a well-known local sidewalk artist who paints brightly colored reproductions of works by the Italian masters.

Boston by Foot gives regular walking tours of the North End, as well as other neighborhoods. Hour-and-a-half tours take place from May through October, rain or shine. Fee. ~ 77 North Washington Street; 617-367-2345, 617-367-3766, fax 617-720-7873; www.bostonbyfoot.com, e-mail bbfoot@bostonbyfoot.com.

DINING

In the Italian North End, you can feast on pasta and regional dishes from one end to the other, stopping at neighborhood "red-sauce" cafés, plush formal dining rooms or late-night espresso bars. Some of the best deals in Boston dining are here, with many restaurants offering moderate prices.

Mamma Maria's Ristorante is the queen of North End gourmet. Highly regarded, it's set in a ritzy townhouse bedecked with brass chandeliers, mirrors and peach-and-gray walls. An upstairs atrium overlooks Paul Revere's little house. Mamma Maria's menu is refreshingly free of red sauce, featuring the lighter, reduced-sauce dishes of Tuscany and Piedmont, which might include grilled swordfish on a bed of pesto garnished with shrimp and baby vegetables. Dinner only. Closed the first week of January. ~ 3 North

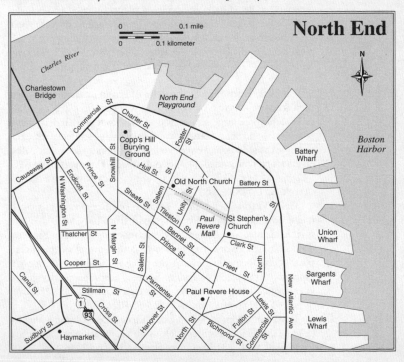

North End

Square; 617-523-0077; www.mammamaria.com, e-mail mamma maria@bicnet.net. DELUXE.

Dark wood wainscotting, terra-cotta walls, ceiling fans, and country-style chairs and tables create a warm and inviting atmosphere at **Antico Forno**. Much of the menu of this Neapolitan-style trattoria originates from a large brick oven tucked in the corner: roasted veal stuffed with spinach, mushrooms and fontina; grilled lamb chops with garlic mashed potatoes; baked fusilli with eggplant, zucchini and goat cheese; and a selection of wood-fired pizzas. You won't walk away hungry from this rustic feast. ~ 93 Salem Street; 617-723-6733; www.terramiaristorante.com. MODERATE TO DELUXE.

> Book a tour with North End resident Michele Topor, who offers an insider's look of her neighborhood's culinary nooks and crannies. ~ 617-523-6032; www.cucinare.com.

In business for only a few years, **Bricco** has already won scores of coveted awards and praise. The restaurant's two floors include a sleek main dining room and an upstairs area for private functions. The menu is classic Italian, but the dishes are presented with a modern flair for simplicity and elegant presentation. The clientele is super-fashionable, especially at the full bar. Dinner only. ~ 241 Hanover Street; 617-248-6800, fax 617-367-0666; www.bricco.com. MODERATE TO ULTRA-DELUXE.

Café Paradiso is a favored haunt of local Italians. There's an espresso bar decorated with hanging plants, mirrors and colorful Italian cake boxes. The gelato and *granite* are freshly churned. The café serves desserts and light Italian fare including pizza, calzone and salad. They also feature a full bar. ~ 255 Hanover Street; 617-742-1768, fax 617-742-7317; e-mail paradiso@aol.com. BUDGET.

Upstairs, **Trattoria a Scalinatella** offers an intimate dining experience with exposed brick walls, a working fireplace, candlelit tables and three large bay windows. The authentic Italian menu is seasonal and may feature squid-ink ravioli stuffed with calamari, Texas wild boar, veal medallions or handmade pastas. Reservations recommended. Dinner only. ~ 253 Hanover Street; 617-742-8240, fax 617-523-8865; e-mail scalinatella@aol.com. DELUXE TO ULTRA-DELUXE.

Caffe Vittoria is the most colorful of the espresso bistros. It might have been shipped here straight from Italy, so Old World is it. A massive and ancient espresso machine stands in the window, and latticework, marble floors and a mural of the Italian coast add to the feeling. Here's the place to indulge in a late-night espresso, cappuccino or Italian liqueur, accompanied by gelato or cannoli. There's also a downstairs cigar lounge. ~ 296 Hanover Street; 617-227-7606, fax 617-523-5340. MODERATE.

Restaurant Pomodoro may be short on decor, but it's long on generous, delicious entrées such as chicken carbonara and olive risotto with veal. ~ 319 Hanover Street; 617-367-4348. MODERATE.

If you can't visit the Sistine Chapel, you can still see its transcendent frescoes covering the ceiling at **Lucia's**. Art critics come to rave and art students to stare in awe. More magnificent ceiling frescoes show Marco Polo's visit to China, the 12 Apostles and the Last Supper. Lucia's chef hails from Abruzzo and prepares specialties from all over Italy, robust to light dishes, something for everyone. Try the *pollo all'Arrabbiata* or *maccheroni all'Arrabbiata* (angry chicken or angry macaroni). No lunch Monday through Thursday. ~ 415 Hanover Street; 617-367-2353, fax 617-367-8952; www.luciaristorante.com. MODERATE.

Pizza is all that's been served at **Pizzeria Regina** since 1926, and that's fine with the loyal clientele who jam the doorway at lunch and dinner waiting for one of the few tables inside. When you get in, you'll sit on high-backed benches at long, heavy wooden tables, where you'll eat slice after slice of pizza served with pitchers of beer, soda or house wine. The service is fast, if sometimes curt, but that's the North End style. Cash only. ~ 11½ Thatcher Street; 617-227-0765, fax 617-227-2662. BUDGET TO MODERATE.

Ristorante Marsala is a glowingly pink place with an intimate and elegant café-style dining room. It serves light dishes from northern Italy, and veal is a house specialty. Closed Monday. ~ 54 Salem Street; 617-742-6999, fax 617-742-6940. MODERATE TO DELUXE.

At **La Famiglia Giorgio's**, the portions are so big and the prices so reasonable, you can't believe it. Locals do believe, and they pack the uproarious place nightly to feast on gargantuan helpings of spaghetti and meatballs, lasagna, linguine with clam sauce and a sautéed seafood platter. As the name suggests, the small, bright low-decor eatery is family-owned. Reservations are required for parties of six or more. ~ 112 Salem Street; 617-367-6711, fax 617-367-6174. MODERATE TO ULTRA-DELUXE.

The North End is a food lover's shopping dream, chock full of wine and cheese shops and bakeries.

SHOPPING

Since **Bova's Bakery**, at the corner of Salem and Prince streets, is open 'round the clock, it's a great place to satisfy late-night hunger pangs. It's also an ideal spot to hear local gossip. The well-connected Bova family owns shops and apartments all over the North End, and the bakery serves as an apartment-hunters' clearinghouse for folks who are in the know. ~ 134 Salem Street; 617-523-5601.

For a pungent whiff of Old World ambience, head for **Polcari's Coffee Store**, a tiny shop brimming with open bags of cornmeal and flour, wooden bins of nuts and jars of coffee beans. Closed Sunday. ~ 105 Salem Street; 617-227-0786.

Trio's Ravioli is full of good smells from their Italian cheeses and delicious homemade pasta and sauces. Closed Sunday. ~ 222 Hanover Street; 617-523-9636.

Overwhelming, tantalizing smells hit the nose in the **Modern Pastry Shop,** which dates to 1931. It's hard to choose among the *pizzaiole, zuppa inglese,* amaretto biscotti and macaroons. ~ 257 Hanover Street; 617-523-3783.

Mike's Pastry is a popular spot for North End–residing yuppies to pick up a boxful of pastries for breakfast meetings downtown. A warning: The volume of goods available here far outweighs their consistent quality, so take your time to peruse the offerings. ~ 300 Hanover Street; 617-742-3050, fax 617-523-2384.

Downtown

The downtown area comprises several distinct neighborhoods that sprawl around the peninsula and loop around Beacon Hill and the Boston Common. Although Boston's compactness makes it very easy to sightsee on foot, there is no convenient way to see these neighborhoods, and you'll find yourself doubling back more than once.

SIGHTS

For visitors who would rather combine all their historic sightseeing into one trip, the **Freedom Trail** (see "Walking Tour," page 44) is Boston made simple. But if you only follow the red line, you'll have missed many of Boston's riches. For visitors with more time and energy, the following tour provides an in-depth look at Boston, old and new. It loops northward from the North End to the old West End, back down through Government Center and Quincy Market, and out to the Waterfront. Then it goes up State Street, down through the Financial District to Chinatown and the Theater District, and finally back up Washington Street to Boston Common. Since all these neighborhoods are so small, there's no need to treat them as separate geographic areas. But when a sight lies within the boundaries of a particular downtown neighborhood, we'll be sure to let you know.

When you come out the North End Underpass, you'll be crossing Blackstone Street, home to **Haymarket** (covering several blocks of Blackstone Street), the country's oldest market, in operation more than 200 years.

HIDDEN ► You'll find the **Boston Stone** easily enough by looking behind the Boston Stone Gift Shop. A round brown stone embedded in the rear corner of the house and dated 1737, it was brought from England and used as a millstone to grind pigment. A tavern keeper named it after the famous London Stone and used it as an advertisement. ~ Marshall and Hanover streets.

Behind Marshall Street is the **Blackstone Block,** tiny alleyways that are the last remnants of Boston's 17th-century byways, the oldest commercial district. Their names, Marsh Lane, Creek Square and Salt Lane, represent the early topography of Boston's landscape.

The **Union Oyster House,** built in the 18th century, became a restaurant in 1826, making it the oldest continuously working

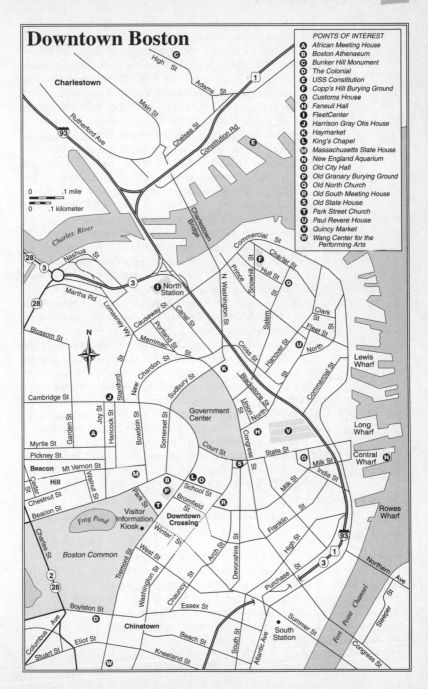

Downtown Boston

Charlestown

POINTS OF INTEREST

- **A** African Meeting House
- **B** Boston Athenaeum
- **C** Bunker Hill Monument
- **D** The Colonial
- **E** USS Constitution
- **F** Copp's Hill Burying Ground
- **G** Customs House
- **H** Faneuil Hall
- **I** FleetCenter
- **J** Harrison Gray Otis House
- **K** Haymarket
- **L** King's Chapel
- **M** Massachusetts State House
- **N** New England Aquarium
- **O** Old City Hall
- **P** Old Granary Burying Ground
- **Q** Old North Church
- **R** Old South Meeting House
- **S** Old State House
- **T** Park Street Church
- **U** Paul Revere House
- **V** Quincy Market
- **W** Wang Center for the Performing Arts

High St

Adams St

Main St

Rutherford Ave

93

Chelsea St

Constitution Rd

0   .1 mile

0   .1 kilometer

Charles River

28

3

Nashua St

28

Martha Rd

Lomasney Wy

Blossom St

Cambridge St

Myrtle St

Pickney St

Beacon

Hill

Cedar St

Chestnut St

Beacon St

Charles St

2

28

Boston Common

Boylston St

Columbus Ave

Stuart St

Eliot St

Chinatown

Garden St

Joy St

Hancock St

Mt Vernon St

Walnut St

Park St

Tremont St

West St

Washington St

Chauncy St

Essex St

Beach St

Kneeland St

N

Staniford St

New Chardon St

Bowdoin St

Somerset St

Sudbury St

Government Center

Court St

School St

Bromfield

Winter St

Visitor Information Kiosk

Downtown Crossing

Frog Pond

Arch St

Devonshire St

South St

Atlantic Ave

Causeway St

Portland St

Canal St

Merrimac St

N Washington St

Cross St

Blackstone St

Union St

Congress St

State St

Milk St

Franklin St

High St

Purchase St

Summer St

South Station

North Station

Commercial St

Charter St

Prince St

Snowhill St

Hull St

Salem St

Hanover St

Clark St

Fleet St

North St

Commercial St

Milk St

India St

Northern Ave

Fort Point Channel

Congress St

Sleeper St

Lewis Wharf

Long Wharf

Central Wharf

Rowes Wharf

93

1

3

restaurant in America. Here Daniel Webster drank a tall tumbler of brandy and water with each half-dozen oysters, and he rarely had fewer than six plates. Before it was a restaurant, exiled French King Louis Philippe taught French here to wealthy ladies. Upstairs in 1771, Isaiah Thomas published *The Massachusetts Spy*, one of the first newspapers in the United States. Closed Sunday. ~ 41 Union Street; 617-227-2750, fax 617-227-2306; www.unionoyster house.com, e-mail uoh@shore.net.

At the western edge of Boston's peninsula, stretching from the Southeast Expressway to Storrow Drive, is an area that used to be known as the West End. Once rich in many-quilted ethnic groups, it's now a mostly commercialized neighborhood. The area around North Station and the Boston Garden has begun to sprout new restaurants, while a few of the old-time sports bars have become trendy hangouts for a younger crowd.

Located next to the site of the hallowed Boston Garden is the state-of-the-art **FleetCenter**. Featuring 19,600 seats, luxury suites, restaurants, spacious concourses and air conditioning, the Center is a far cry from Boston's beloved but outdated Garden. Home to the Boston Celtics and Bruins, the shiny FleetCenter still sports the famous parquet floor and banners. ~ 1 FleetCenter Place, Boston; 617-624-1050, 617-624-1000 (event line), fax 617-624-1127; www.fleetcenter.com.

Not on the peninsula at all but out in the middle of the Charles River is the **Museum of Science**, reached via the Charles River Dam. The star of the museum is the Omni Theater, whose 76-foot domed screen and surrounding sound systems make you feel as though you're actually whizzing down Olympic slopes on skis, moving underwater through the Great Barrier Reef or breaking through the Antarctic's icy underwater depths. The museum also houses live animal exhibits, the Charles Hayden Planetarium and changing displays on foreign cultures. Closed Sunday. Admission. ~ Science Park, O'Brien Highway; 617-723-2500, fax 617-589-0187; www.mos.org, e-mail information@mos.org.

AUTHOR FAVORITE

sights   Whether it's in Mexico or Marrakesh, I am always drawn to the excitement of an open-air market—and that goes for Boston's centuries-old **Haymarket**, where, on Friday and Saturday, open-air vendors hawk fruits and vegetables, meats, fresh fish and crabs, crowding over several blocks. Ancient hanging metal scales are used to weigh purchases. Prices are good here, but don't try to touch anything without permission—the vendor will scream.

The **Harrison Gray Otis House** was the first of three Boston houses Charles Bulfinch designed for his friend Otis, a prominent lawyer and member of Congress. Built in 1796, the three-story brick house is classically symmetrical, with rows of evenly spaced windows and a Palladian window. Inside is one of the most gorgeous interiors in Boston, rich with imported wallpapers, opulent swag curtains and carpeting, gilt-framed mirrors, Adams mantels and neoclassical motifs framing every doorway and window. Surviving abuse as a bathhouse, Chinese laundry and rooming house, the building became the headquarters of the Society for the Preservation of New England Antiquities in 1916. Closed Monday and Tuesday. Admission. ~ 141 Cambridge Street; 617-227-3956, fax 617-227-9204; www.spnea.org.

Right next door is the **Old West Church**, a handsome Federal-style brick building with a cupola and pillars on three stories. The British tore down its original steeple to prevent signaling across the river during the siege of 1776. Rebuilt in 1806, it houses a Charles Fisk organ; there are free organ concerts on Tuesday evenings from June through August. ~ 131 Cambridge Street; 617-227-5088, fax 617-227-7548, e-mail oldwestch@aol.com.

A short walk up Cambridge Street brings you to **Government Center**, a sprawling brick plaza with multilevel stairs and fountains designed by I. M. Pei, an architect who was to change the face of the city in the 1960s, leaving his imprint on many key buildings. The plaza contains two of Boston's most important government structures, the **John F. Kennedy Federal Building** and **City Hall**, a modernistic-looking inverted pyramid. An abstract sculpture entitled *Thermopylae*, inspired by Kennedy's book *Profiles in Courage*, stands facing the JFK Building. A mass of twisting forms, it takes its name from a Greek battle in which the Spartans fought the Persians to the last man.

Some say the **Steaming Teakettle**, a huge copper kettle hung outside the doorway at 65 Court Street at the edge of Government Center, is America's oldest advertising sign. It once announced the operations of the Oriental Tea Company, Boston's largest tea company. Made by city coppersmiths, it holds 227 gallons, two quarts, one pint and three gills. It gives you a warm feeling to see the teakettle steaming away, especially on a cold day. Ironically, it's now advertising a coffee shop.

For a figure so flamboyant as **James Michael Curley**, one statue is not enough. The colorful but corrupt Curley dominated Boston politics for years, from 1914 to the late 1940s, serving as mayor, congressman and governor and figuring prominently in Edwin O'Connor's novel *The Last Hurrah*. This four-term mayor was loved by the poor and fond of calling Boston bankers the "State Street Wrecking Crew." Behind City Hall, two very lifelike bronze statues immortalize Curley, one sitting on a park bench,

The Freedom Trail

This two-and-a-half-mile, one-way route, marked by a red brick or painted line on the sidewalk, links 16 major historical places from downtown to Beacon Hill, the North End and Charlestown. It takes two to three hours to walk, though you can easily spend all day. Guided tours are also available, leaving every half hour from the National Park Service visitors center at 15 State Street opposite the Old State House.

BOSTON COMMON   Start your walk at Boston Common, one of the oldest public parks in the U.S., which has served during its 250-year history as a British Army encampment, a cow pasture and the site of public hangings. Freedom Trail maps are sold at the **Visitor Information Kiosk** on the southeast side of the park, near the Park Street Station. ~ 147 Tremont Street; 617-426-3115. At the corner of the park, **Park Street Church** is often called the "church of firsts"; here, the first Sunday school in the U.S. was held, William Lloyd Garrison gave his first public anti-slavery speech and "My Country 'tis of Thee" was sung for the first time. ~ Park and Tremont streets; 617-523-3383. Behind the church, governors, mayors and three signers of the Declaration of Independence lie in the **Old Granary Burying Ground**.

SCHOOL STREET   Walk northeast on Tremont, past the Granary Burying Ground, to School Street and turn east (right). **King's Chapel**, at the corner, was the first Anglican church in New England and the first church in Boston to have an organ (the Puritans didn't believe in music in church). ~ 58 Tremont Street; 617-523-1749. One block up the street, at the corner of Province Street, is the site of the **Boston Latin School**, the first public school in America, where Benjamin Franklin attended classes. The **Ben Franklin Statue** stands behind the school in Old City Hall Plaza. Another block up School Street, at the corner of Washington, the **Boston Globe Store** not only sold books but published them—including *The Scarlet Letter, Walden* and the *Atlantic Monthly*

the other standing right on the brick pavement with no pedestal. Tourists have been seen patting the stomach of the standing Curley, so temptingly portly is it. ~ Union and Congress streets.

If you walk down the stairs at the rear of Government Center and across Congress Street, you'll be entering Faneuil Hall Marketplace, one of Boston's most popular destinations.

Faneuil Hall was the city's central market in the mid-18th century. The second floor of Faneuil Hall became known as the magazine; it still operates as a bookstore under the ownership of the *Boston Globe* newspaper. Closed Sunday during the winter. ~ 1 School Street; 617-367-4004.

OLD HOUSES   Turn south (right) on Washington and walk one short block to the **Old South Meeting House**, where Samuel Adams and his co-conspirators plotted the Boston Tea Party. Admission. ~ 310 Washington Street; 617-482-6439. Across Milk Street is the house where Benjamin Franklin was born. ~ 17 Milk Street. Next, do an about-face and walk two blocks north to the **Old State House** (c. 1713), the oldest surviving public building in Boston, which is now a museum. Admission. ~ 206 Washington Street; 617-720-3290. Right next door, **Boston National Park Visitor Information** has maps, tour books and brochures. ~ 15 State Street; 617-242-5642.

FANEUIL HALL   Turn east (right) on State Street and walk one block to the corner of Congress Street. Here, a circle of cobblestones marks the **Boston Massacre Site**, where British soldiers killed five colonists, triggering the Revolutionary War. Turn north (left) on Congress. Across the street from the present City Hall, Faneuil Hall Marketplace has been a public market and meeting hall since 1742—and still is. Patriots gave speeches that inspired the American Revolution at Faneuil Hall.

THE NORTH END   Follow the red tour route line carefully as it takes you about one mile north along Union, Marshall and Salem streets to loop around the North End. At the intersection of Salem and Hull streets stands the **Old North Church** (c. 1723); its 191-foot steeple was the tallest structure in Boston when Robert Newman signaled the approach of British troops with his lanterns, launching Paul Revere's midnight ride. ~ 193 Salem Street; 617-523-6676. To find the **Paul Revere House**, follow Tileston Street east past the Paul Revere Mall, take a little jog south at Hanover and Fleet streets, and go south (right) for one and a half blocks. The simple house is the only remaining residence in Boston dating back to the 17th century. Closed Monday from January through March. ~ 19 North Square; 617-523-2338. To complete your tour, return to Salem Street via Richmond Street or catch any bus with a "Downtown" sign back to Boston Common.

"Cradle of Liberty," as it resounded with the patriotic rhetoric of James Otis and Samuel Adams in the years leading to the Revolution. On the fourth floor is a museum and armory of the **Ancient and Honorable Artillery Company**, the nation's oldest military group, founded in 1638. Look up to see the four-foot-long gilded copper grasshopper weathervane, a familiar Boston landmark and symbol. Closed weekends. ~ Off Congress Street; 617-523-1300, fax 617-523-1779; www.faneuilhallmarketplace.com.

Quincy Market is another historic marketplace, built in 1826 by Mayor Josiah Quincy to expand Faneuil Hall. In a move that has been imitated by almost every major city, Faneuil Hall Marketplace, which includes Quincy Market along with its twin flanking arcades, the North and South Markets, was renovated in the 1970s into shops and restaurants that have become a major tourist draw for the city. The cobblestoned mall is a street festival by day, a lively nightspot in the later hours. It's wonderfully decorated during the holidays. ~ Off Congress Street.

A booklet of tickets to six of the most popular sights in Boston, CityPass may save you money and waits in line. ~ 888-330-5008; www.city pass.net, e-mail info@ citypass.net.

If you walk out the rear of the marketplace and under the Southeast Expressway across busy Atlantic Avenue, you'll arrive at the waterfront.

When Atlantic Avenue was built in the 1860s, it sliced right through the center of many of the great old wharves, including **Long Wharf**, the oldest existing one in Boston. Built in 1710, Long Wharf was named for its length—formerly 1800 feet. The British marched up Long Wharf when they occupied the city in 1768, only to retreat back down it when they were evacuated in 1776. Long Wharf also saw the departure of the first missionaries to Hawaii in 1819 and played a role in the 1850s California gold rush, when thousands of New Englanders departed for San Francisco.

Buildings imitating Renaissance palazzos and Greek temples were built in the 19th century along Rowes, India, Central, Long, Commercial, Lewis, Sargent's and Union wharves. **Lewis Wharf**, formerly Clarke's Wharf, was once owned by a Mr. John Hancock. Nathaniel Hawthorne served for a time as a customs inspector at Long Wharf. By the mid-19th century, the wharves were a center of clipper trade with China, Europe, Australia and Hawaii.

Some of the old wharf buildings, which once housed ships' chandlers and sail riggers, have been renovated into shops, offices and restaurants, including the **Pilot House, Mercantile Wharf** and **Chart House**, the only surviving late-18th-century building on the waterfront. ~ Off Atlantic Avenue.

Central Wharf is home to the **New England Aquarium**, just a short walk from Faneuil Hall Marketplace. Bostonians like to congregate to watch the harbor seals in the outdoor pool. Inside, the Giant Ocean Tank is home to 95 species of exotic reef fish, sea turtles, sharks and moray eels. In the Aquarium Medical Center, you can observe medical check-ups of the sea life from behind a glass window. Sea lions perform next door aboard the Discovery, a floating theater. Admission. ~ Central Wharf, off Atlantic Avenue; 617-973-5200, fax 617-367-6615; www.neaq.org.

Waterfront Park is a neatly landscaped pocket park with brick walkways and benches that offers a lovely harbor view along with respite. Dedicated to the late matriarch of the Kennedy clan, the

Rose Fitzgerald Kennedy Garden is a lovely spot at any time of year, but especially when it is in full bloom early in the summer. It's not far from Mrs. Kennedy's birthplace in the North End. ~ North of Long Wharf on Atlantic Avenue.

From the wharves, you can take cruises of Boston Harbor, a great way to while away an afternoon or evening and see the city skyline. One boat line there is **Boston Harbor Cruises**. ~ 63 Long Wharf; 617-227-4321, 877-733-9425; www.bostonharborcruises. com. Another servicing the harbor is **Massachusetts Bay Lines**. ~ 60 Rowes Wharf; 617-542-8000, fax 617-951-0700; www.mass baylines.com.

If you're into intrigue and humor, book passage with the **Boston Harbor Mystery Cruise**. These three-hour dinner cruises depart from Long Wharf and feature a comic murder mystery. Closed November through April. ~ 63 Long Wharf; 617-227-4320, 877-733-9425, fax 617-723-2011; www.bostonharbor cruises.com.

From Long Wharf, walk up State Street. In a couple of blocks, you'll come to the granite Greek Revival **Customs House**, built between 1837 and 1847, where inspectors once examined all cargoes arriving at the wharves. Incongruously, this building also became Boston's first skyscraper in 1915, when the great clock tower was added. The clock, broken for many years, was restored in the late 1980s and its bright blue and gold face now glows handsomely at night, visible from great distances. ~ McKinley Square at State and India streets.

The **Cunard Building** was built in 1902 for the Cunard Steamship Line, owners of the ocean liner *Queen Elizabeth II*. Twin brass anchors flank its doors, festooned with dolphins and seashells. ~ 126 State Street.

The **Old State House** is a pretty little brick building dwarfed by the surrounding skyscrapers. The bronze lion and unicorn atop its gables stand as symbols of the English crown. Until the American Revolution, this was the seat of British government. A ring of cobblestones outside marks the site of the Boston Massacre, the signal event launching the Revolution. A museum since 1882, the Old State House features winding galleries of exhibits on the building's history and architecture, early Boston and maritime history, including memorabilia, a model ship, paintings and prints. Admission. ~ 206 Washington Street, corner of State Street; 617-720-3290, fax 617-720-3289; www.bostonhistory.org, e-mail bos toniansociety@bostonhistory.org.

An outdoor flower market fronting the brick, Colonial-style **Old South Meeting House** adds to its charms. Built in 1729, Old South has high-arching Palladian windows, a white pulpit and candlelight chandeliers. Many crucial meetings leading to the American Revolution took place here, including the debate that launched the Boston Tea Party. Countless notables spoke here, including Samuel Adams, John Hancock and, later, Oliver Wendell Holmes. Though Old South was repeatedly ravaged—the British turned it into a riding school complete with jumping bar, and it was forced to serve as a temporary post office after a devastating fire in 1872—it has been restored to its 18th-century look. Taped presentations re-create the famous Tea Party debate and others. This building offers historical and architectural programs and hands-on exhibits, and still serves as a public forum for community events. Admission. ~ 310 Washington Street, corner of Milk Street; 617-482-6439, fax 617-482-9621; www.oldsouthmeeting house.org.

Milk Street leads into the heart of the Financial District, a warren of streets stretching south from State Street to High Street and east to Washington Street. Dominated by towering banks and office buildings, the Financial District was considerably built up in the 1980s with bold new buildings, provoking controversy over their design in tradition-minded Boston. One of these—the **BankBoston**—is laughingly called Pregnant Alice because of its billowing shape. ~ 100 Federal Street.

In its marching devastation, the **Great Fire of 1872** leveled 60 acres of downtown Boston. The spot where the fire was arrested on its northeastward path is noted on a **bronze plaque** on the front of the U.S. Post Office at Post Office Square. ~ Corner of Milk and Devonshire streets.

HIDDEN ►   Two bonanzas await in the lobby of the **New England Telephone building**. One, a massive mural called *Telephone Men and Women at Work*, encircles the rotunda and depicts decades of telephone workers, from 1880s switchboard operators to later engineers, cable layers and information operators. The other reward is Alexander Graham Bell's Garret, a dark little corner filled with memorabilia surrounding the birth of the telephone in Boston in 1875. The garret looks much as it did when Bell worked in it at its original location at 109 Court Street. (A **bronze plaque** at Government Center in front of the John F. Kennedy Federal Building marks that spot, where sound was first transmitted over wires in the fifth-floor garret.) ~ 185 Franklin Street.

On Summer Street stands a mobile that looks like a giant yellow lollipop tree, an ebullient surprise in a city where there is not much outdoor public art. Bostonians call it "the lollipops," but its real name is **Helion**, one of a group of pieces called "windflowers" by sculptor Robert Amory. ~ 100 Summer Street.

HIDDEN ►

Walk south down Summer Street until you come to **South Station**. South Station was a grand old station house in its day, in fact the largest in the world at the turn of the 20th century. After a thorough restoration completed in 1989, this pink granite beauty

A Taste of China

Compared to Chinatowns in other major cities, Boston's is geographically quite small, just a few blocks long. But this Chinatown was much larger decades earlier, before the Southeast Expressway was built, cutting a wide swath through the district. The Tufts New England Medical Center, too, took a great chunk of Chinatown land when it was built. Now hemmed in by the Expressway and the Combat Zone, Chinatown has little room to grow. But don't be fooled by its physical size: Boston's densely populated Chinatown makes it the third largest Chinese neighborhood in the country.

The Chinese were first brought to Boston to break a shoe industry strike in the 1870s, coming by train from the West Coast. They settled close to South Station because of the convenience of the railroad. First living in tents, the Chinese eventually built houses or moved into places previously inhabited by Syrians, Irish and Italians.

Despite its small size and recent influx of Thai and Vietnamese immigrants, Chinatown is intensely and authentically Chinese. Signs are in Chinese characters, and the area is densely packed with Chinese stores and restaurants. Even the phone booths are covered with Chinese pagodas.

The **Chinatown gates**, a bicentennial gift from Taiwan, stand at the intersection of Beach Street and Surface Road, marking the entrance to Chinatown. White stone with a massive green pagoda on top, they are guarded fore and aft by stone Chinese Foo dogs and sport gold Chinese characters on green marble. The classic characters are not readily translatable in modern Chinese, but they embody such moral principles as propriety, righteousness, modesty and honor.

The large **Unity/Community Chinatown Mural**, painted in 1986, depicts the history of the Chinese in Boston. Among its pigtailed Chinese figures are construction workers, a launderer and women at sewing machines. Other scenes show the Chinese learning to read, protesting to save their housing and gaining access to professional careers. ~ Corner of Harrison Avenue and Oak Street.

Although you may not want to take one home, you can see live chickens squawking in stacks of wire crates at **Eastern Live Poultry**, where locals line up to buy them "live or dressed." ~ 48 Beach Street; 617-426-5960.

stands tall and proud. Ionic columns, a balustrade and a clock with eagle decorate the curved beaux-arts facade stretching for two blocks. South Station today serves as a transportation hub for subway, rail and bus connections. The interior, designed to resemble a European market square, sparkles with polished marble floors and brass railings and is filled with restaurants, shops and pushcart vendors. ~ Summer Street and Atlantic Avenue.

Across the street, you'll see the **Federal Reserve Bank**, which processes millions of dollars worth of currency every day. The Fed's unusual design—it looks like a giant white washboard, and there's a gap where the fifth floor should be—is intended to withstand down drafts and wind pressures. The Fed, which boasts a lobby full of sculpture and murals, also hosts jazz and classical concerts and changing art and crafts exhibits. For a performance schedule, call 617-973-3453. The Fed is not currently open to the public except for pre-scheduled tours. Tours are available to groups of at least ten, and must be booked at least a month in advance. ~ 600 Atlantic Avenue, corner of Summer Street; 617-973-3464, fax 617-973-3511; www.bos.frb.org, e-mail public comm.affairs-bos@bos.frb.org.

HIDDEN ► **Winthrop Lane**, a tiny brick-lined channel between Arch and Devonshire streets, contains one of the most interesting pieces of public art in Boston, entitled *Boston Bricks: A Celebration of Boston's Past and Present.* In 1985 artists Kate Burke and Gregg Lefevre created bronze reliefs of various Boston personages, scenes and stories and placed them along this red-brick shortcut that's used by folks who work in the Financial District. Take the time to peruse the bricks here; you'll recognize some things—the Red Sox, the swan boats in the Public Garden lagoon—and wonder about others.

South Station is just a hop, skip and a jump from **Chinatown**, bounded by Essex and Washington streets and the Southeast Expressway. See "A Taste of China" for more information.

Few people know that **Edgar Allan Poe** had a long history in Boston, so in 1989 a memorial bronze plaque was erected in his memory at the corner of Boylston Street and Edgar Allan Poe Way. Born here, Poe was the son of actors at the Boston Theatre. He published his first book, lectured and enlisted in the Army in Boston.

HIDDEN ► The **Grand Lodge of Masons** is decorated with blue and gold mosaics of masonic symbols, and its grand lobby houses a small exhibit of masonic memorabilia. Closed weekends. ~ 186 Tremont Street, corner of Boylston Street; 617-426-6040, fax 617-426-6115; www.glmasons-mass.org, e-mail grandsec@glmasons-mass.org.

Head south on Tremont Street. In short order you'll be in the Theater District, centered on Tremont Street, Warrenton Avenue and Charles Street South. Boston has a lively and prestigious theater scene, with many tryouts moving on to Broadway. Among the half dozen or so nationally known theaters is the **Colonial**, the oldest continuously operated theater in America, built in 1900. At that time the sumptuously decorated Colonial was considered one of the most elegant theaters in the country, ◆◆◆◆◆◆◆◆◆◆◆◆◆◆◆◆◆◆◆◆◆◆◆◆ with its 70-foot Italian-marble vestibule and foyer rich with ceiling paintings, cupids, plate mirrors, bronze staircases and carved wood. George M. Cohan, Noel Coward, Fred Astaire, Katharine Hepburn and the Marx Brothers have trod its boards. ~ 106 Boylston Street; 617-426-9366, 617-880-2400, fax 617-880-2449; www.broadwayinboston.com, e-mail info@broadwayinboston.com.

At the Colonial Theatre, the original writing table that Rodgers & Hammerstein used when they wrote *Oklahoma!* is located outside the ladies' lounge.

Formerly the Metropolitan Theatre, the splendid **Wang Center for the Performing Arts** was built in 1925 as a palace for first-run movies in the Roaring Twenties. Restored to its original grandeur, it is opulently decorated with gold leaf, crystal, mirrors and Italian marble, and was designed to be reminiscent of the Paris Opera and Versailles. This 3610-seat theater is one of the largest in the world, and has hosted a variety of artists including Yo-Yo Ma, Luciano Pavarotti, Robin Williams, Lauryn Hill and the Alvin Ailey American Dance Theater. The Center is listed on the National Register of Historic Places. ~ 270 Tremont Street; 617-482-9393, fax 617-451-1436; www.wangcenter.org, e-mail info@wangcenter.com.

The **International Society**, opened in 1980, houses a gallery where rotating exhibits of Chinese paintings, sculpture, ceramics and folk art are shown. The institute also produces concerts, community plays, dance recitals and lectures on its stage. Closed Sunday and Monday. ~ 276 Tremont Street; 617-542-4599, fax 617-451-0569; www.internationalsociety.org, e-mail internationalsociety@yahoo.com.

◄ HIDDEN

Eliot Norton Park, with bright lights and green lawns, stands where Chinatown and the Theater District meet Bay Village. The park is appropriately dedicated to the dean of American drama critics. ~ Corner of Tremont Street and Charles Street South.

Boston's famed **Combat Zone** on lower Washington Street should be added to the endangered species list. As the pace of development quickened in the late 1970s, its former horde of topless lounges, sleazy bars and adult bookstores and movies shrank to a pathetic few blocks that would be the scorn of any true big-city habitué.

Downtown Crossing is the heart of downtown shopping. Lunchtime shoppers crowd the brick pedestrian mall fronting on Macy's and Filene's, one of Boston's oldest department stores. Downtown Crossing is street entertainment at its most diverse. Pushcart vendors and street musicians—one day a Peruvian folk band, the next a rock group—vie for space in the crowded mall. A one-man band is a permanent local fixture. ~ Corner of Washington and Summer streets.

Old City Hall, a grand French Second Empire building, was renovated in the 1970s into offices and a French restaurant. As one of the first 19th-century Boston buildings to be recycled, it helped spark the preservationist movement. In front of Old City Hall stands the **Franklin Statue**, an eight-foot bronze tribute to Benjamin Franklin. Relief tablets at the base illustrate scenes from his career as printer, scientist and signer of the Declaration of Independence. ~ 45 School Street.

Bromfield Street, a short lane located between Washington and Tremont streets, is chock-full of tiny camera shops, jewelers and watchmakers, stamp traders, pawnshops and a couple of tiny cafés. There are some interesting historical buildings sprinkled along the street, including the home of Revolutionary War hero Thomas Cushing, who held meetings here with the Adamses, Thomas Paine and other cronies.

The **Omni Parker House** is the oldest continuously operating hotel in America, first opening in 1855. Soon after, it became a hangout of the Saturday Club, a literary group whose members included Nathaniel Hawthorne, Ralph Waldo Emerson, Henry Wadsworth Longfellow, James Russell Lowell, Oliver Wendell Holmes and John Greenleaf Whittier. This little group founded the *Atlantic Monthly*. ~ 60 School Street; 617-227-8600, 800-843-6664, fax 617-227-9607; www.omniparkerhouse.com.

King's Chapel looks morosely like a mausoleum. Its steeple was never finished so its Ionic columns flank a bare, squat granite building. The inside, however, is gorgeous, with carved Corinthian columns and pewter chandeliers. The first Anglican church in New England, King's Chapel eventually became the first Unitarian church in the United States. The chapel is closed to the public Sunday, Tuesday and Wednesday from June to October; the rest of the year they're open on Saturday only. ~ Corner of

---

GREENER PASTURES

Boston Common is the first jewel in Boston's **Emerald Necklace**, a seven-mile tracery of green that loops through and around the city, all the way to Jamaica Plain, Brookline and Fenway. It was designed in the early 1900s by famed landscape architect Frederick Law Olmsted (designer of New York City's Central Park), who believed that parks could provide a psychological antidote to the noise, stress and artificiality of city life. The Emerald Necklace also includes the Public Garden, the Commonwealth Avenue Mall, the Back Bay Fens, Olmsted Park, Jamaica Pond, Franklin Park and the Arnold Arboretum. The Boston Parks and Recreation Department (617-635-7383, fax 617-635-7418) conducts periodic walking and bicycling tours of the entire Emerald Necklace.

Tremont and School streets; 617-523-1749, fax 617-227-4101; www.kings-chapel.org, e-mail kchapel@kings-chapel.org.

Beside the church is **King's Chapel Burying Ground**, the oldest cemetery in Boston. It contains the graves of John Winthrop, the colony's first governor, and William Daws, the minuteman who helped Paul Revere warn the colonists the British were coming.

Park Street Church is one of Boston's most beautiful churches, with its white Christopher Wren spire and brick exterior. It was known as Brimstone Corner during the War of 1812 because gun powder was stored in its basement. ~ Park and Tremont streets; 617-523-3383, fax 617-523-0263; www.parkstreet.org, e-mail office@parkstreet.org.

Next door is the **Old Granary Burying Ground**, which took its name from a large grain storehouse the Park Street Church replaced. Buried here are Paul Revere, Boston's Mother Goose (Elizabeth Ver Goose, who became known for her nursery rhymes) and three signers of the Declaration of Independence, including John Hancock. You can't see exactly where each is buried, however, since the headstones were rearranged for the convenience of lawn mowing. Death's heads, skeletons and hourglasses were popular headstone motifs here.

Times have changed considerably at **Boston Common**, a large tract of forested green, America's oldest public park. In 1634, its acres served as pasture for cattle, training grounds for the militia and a public stage for hanging adulterers, Quakers, pirates and witches. A few steps from the visitor kiosk is **Brewer Fountain**, brought from Paris by Gardner Brewer in 1868 for his Beacon Hill home and later donated to the city. Notable among the statuary on the Common is the **Soldiers and Sailors Monument** high on a hill, whose figures represent history and peace.

Today, downtown office workers use the crisscrossing paths as shortcuts to work, and it's a popular spot for jogging, Frisbee tossing, dog walking, concerts and community events. You might wander into **Park Street Station**, the first station built on the nation's oldest subway, which opened in 1897.

Leaving the edge of Boston Common, you can walk up Park Street, which brings you to Beacon Hill.

LODGING

A boutique luxury hotel with 201 rooms, the **Millennium Bostonian Hotel** stands right next to Faneuil Hall Marketplace. In its lobby are two exhibits on early Boston firefighting. Besides one of the city's top-rated restaurants, the Bostonian has a terraced atrium. A typical room might have a rose carpet and contemporary furnishings like glass-topped tables and white love seats. The bathroom is spacious, with double sinks and a large oval tub. Six rooms even have hot tubs and fireplaces. Complimentary use of a nearby health club is offered. ~ North and Blackstone streets; 617-523-3600, 800-343-0922, fax 617-523-2454; www.millenniumhotels.com, e-mail bostonian@mhrmail.com. ULTRA-DELUXE.

The **Boston Harbor Hotel** is simply the most visually stunning hotel to be built in Boston in many years. Set right on the harbor and designed in grand classical style, the brick structure is pierced with an 80-foot archway. The waterfront side is lined with Venetian-style piers and crowned with a copper-domed rotunda observatory. A cobblestone courtyard reaches toward the ornate marble-floored and crystal lobby. Many of the 230 guest rooms have magnificent water views and feature dark wood furniture in a green decor, marble-topped nightstands and paintings of birds. The hotel has a health club and spa, sauna and lap pool, and an award-winning restaurant and bar. ~ Rowes Wharf; 617-439-7000, 800-752-7077, fax 617-330-9450; www.bhh.com, e-mail reservations@bhh.com. ULTRA-DELUXE.

One of New England's top-rated hotels, the 274-room **Four Seasons Hotel** overlooks the Public Garden. Interiors reflect the Victorian residential character of Beacon Hill, with a grand staircase leading up from the lobby and, in the rooms, leather-topped writing desks, fresh flowers in the bathroom and marble-topped vanities. There's a spa, whirlpool, exercise room, masseur and lap pool with a view of Beacon Hill. ~ 200 Boylston Street; 617-338-4400, 800-332-3442, fax 617-351-2251; www.fourseasons.com. ULTRA-DELUXE.

The posh **Le Méridien** is one of the country's most highly acclaimed hotels. It opened in 1981 in the former Federal Reserve Bank, built in 1922, a Renaissance Revival granite and limestone structure modeled after a Roman palazzo. Many original interior architectural details remain, including elaborate repoussé bronze doors, gilded, coffered ceilings and sculpted bronze torchières. The Julien Lounge is dominated by two massive N. C. Wyeth murals depicting Abraham Lincoln and George Washington. The hotel has 326 rooms, two restaurants, a bar, an indoor lap pool and health club facilities with whirlpool and sauna. The generous-sized rooms are elegantly cozy, with varied color schemes. A matching two-toned silver embroidered sofa and club chair contrast a black lacquer writing desk, and you will find granite vanities and marble floors in the bathrooms. ~ 250 Franklin Street; 617-451-1900, 800-543-4300, fax 617-423-2844; www.lemeridienboston.com, e-mail meridien@lemeridienboston.com. ULTRA-DELUXE.

The 500-room **Swissôtel Boston** is run with legendary Swiss efficiency and hospitality. Conveniently located to everything, the hotel has every luxury you could ask for: 24-hour room service, bathroom telephones, a spa, an Olympic-size pool with outdoor terrace, a sauna, an exercise room, one restaurant and a lounge where tea and pastries are served in the afternoon. The decor mixes Colonial and European styles, with impressive antique furniture and paintings, Waterford crystal chandeliers and imported marble. Rooms are smartly finished in green, mocha or rose. ~ 1 Avenue de Lafayette; 617-451-2600, 800-621-9200, fax 617-451-0054; www.swissotel.com. DELUXE TO ULTRA-DELUXE.

Nine Zero may attract businesspeople with in-room printers and free high-speed internet access, but its location right on the Freedom Trail makes this boutique hotel a perfect choice for the vacationing traveler. A friendly staff, stylish decor and inviting ambience don't hurt, either. The 190 sleekly designed guest accommodations feature stereo sound systems with a selection of CDs, fluffy down comforters, roman shades, specialty toiletries and pre-stamped postcards to send to the folks back home. ~ 90 Tremont Street; 617-772-5800, 866-646-3376, fax 617-772-5810; www.ninezerohotel.com. ULTRA-DELUXE.

There are at least half a dozen bed-and-breakfast agencies in Boston, offering accommodations in host homes from downtown to Cambridge and the suburbs.

Bed & Breakfast Associates Bay Colony has rooms in 150 homes, most with continental breakfast and private bath, many offering Waterfront, Midtown, Back Bay or Beacon Hill locations. Accommodations range from a bow-windowed room with pine floors, antique brass bed and fireplace in a South End Victorian townhouse, to Beacon Hill and Back Bay homes close to the Public Garden. One of the best deals for the money. ~ P.O. Box 57166, Babson Park Branch, Boston, MA 02457; 781-449-5302, 800-347-5088, fax 781-449-5958; www.bnbboston.com, e-mail info@bnbboston.com. MODERATE TO DELUXE.

Breakfast is always included in rooms booked through **Greater Boston Hospitality**, which offers dozens of listings; many are in Back Bay, Beacon Hill and Cambridge. Host homes include a converted Georgian carriage house in Brookline and a classic 1890 Back Bay brownstone appointed with 18th-century mahogany

---

CELEBRITY SLEEPOVER

Omni Parker House is a fabled Boston institution. Many celebrities have stayed here, from Charles Dickens and John Wilkes Booth to former Presidents John F. Kennedy and Bill Clinton. Its lobby is decorated in the grand old style, with carved wood paneling and gilt moldings, a carved wooden ceiling, bronze repoussé elevator doors and candlelight chandeliers. In the heart of downtown, it's just steps away from Faneuil Hall Marketplace. Rooms have writing desks and wing chairs, floral spreads and marble baths. ~ 60 School Street; 617-227-8600, 800-843-6664, fax 617-742-5729; www.omniparkerhouse.com. ULTRA-DELUXE.

furniture and floors and oriental rugs. Gay-friendly. ~ P.O. Box 1142, Brookline, MA 02446; 617-277-5430, fax 617-277-7170; www.bostonbedandbreakfast.com, e-mail info@bostonbedand breakfast.com. BUDGET TO DELUXE.

DINING

Downtown dining covers a wide spectrum, from traditional Yankee bastions to sprightly outdoor cafés and inexpensive ethnic eateries.

HIDDEN ►

Haymarket Pizza fronts right on Haymarket, a weekend open-air food market, and the surrounding crowds make it hard to get in the door. But if you do, you'll find some of the best cheap pizza in Boston. Closed Sunday. ~ 106 Blackstone Street; 617-723-8585, fax 617-973-9576. BUDGET.

If you want to be treated like a local, go to **Durgin Park**. Noisy and chaotic, Durgin Park is legendary for its rude waitresses and community tables set with red-and-white-checked cloths. A Boston institution founded in 1827, it dispenses such solid and hefty Yankee fare as prime rib, corned beef and cabbage, franks and beans, corn bread and Indian pudding. ~ 30 North Market, Faneuil Hall; 617-227-2038, fax 617-720-1542; www.durgin-park.com, e-mail seanadpark30@ad.com. MODERATE TO DELUXE.

The **Commonwealth Fish & Bear** is a vast hall lined with huge copper vats, beer kegs, copper-covered tables and a brass-railed bar. The dining room is popular with sports fans from nearby FleetCenter where the Boston Celtics play. Chow down on hearty fare like three-alarm chili, steak and fish and chips. Closed Sunday, except for special events. ~ 138 Portland Street; 617-523-8383, fax 617-523-1037. MODERATE.

HIDDEN ►

Most tourists walk right by the **Marshall House** on their way to the picturesque Union Oyster House, the famous hostelry just down the street. Locals prefer this less crowded and less expensive alternative in a pocket of cobblestoned streets and brick sidewalks. Large portions of chowder, fish and chips, burgers and icy

---

AUTHOR FAVORITE

When I want to indulge myself with top-notch cooking, I reserve a table at **Radius**. Chef Michael Schlow blends seasonal goods and modern French cooking into sublime creations. You might start off with seared foie gras or sweetbreads and wild mushrooms, then proceed to a Moroccan-inspired skate or pork confit. For dessert, you can't go wrong with the classic crème brûlée. As one would expect, this epicurean delight will lighten your wallet considerably. ~ 8 High Street; 617-426-1234, fax 617-426-2526; www.radiusrestaurant.com, e-mail info@radiusrestaurant.com. ULTRA-DELUXE.

cold beer—all excellent—are served by friendly staff with thick Bahston accents. ~ 15 Union Street; 617-523-9396, fax 617-523-8163. MODERATE.

You can't beat the **Union Oyster House** for historic atmosphere. In 1742 it was a dry goods store and in 1775 it became a center for fomenting revolutionary activity. The restaurant opened in 1826, and Daniel Webster was fond of slurping down oysters at its U-shaped oyster bar, still standing today. Little alcoves with wooden booths and bare wood tables wend around the several wood-paneled dining rooms, and there are ship's models, a mahogany bar and antique wooden pushcarts in this casual and boisterous eatery. The menu features chowders, seafood and New England shore dinners. Reservations are recommended. ~ 41 Union Street; 617-227-2750, fax 617-227-6401; www.unionoyster house.com. MODERATE TO ULTRA-DELUXE.

Far above the crowded bustle of Faneuil Hall Marketplace, you can dine in removed splendor at **Seasons**, one of Boston's top-rated restaurants. Widely spaced tables, designer show plates, mocha banquettes, crisp white napery and mirrored ceilings add to the mood. A creative New American menu is served, changing seasonally, which might include seared quail with polenta and sausage or roasted monkfish with lobster roe. No dinner Sunday or Monday; no lunch on weekends. ~ 24 North Street, Faneuil Hall, in the Millennium Bostonian Hotel; 617-523-4119, fax 617-523-2454. ULTRA-DELUXE.

For nonpareil French food, make reservations at **Maison Robert**. Actually, it's two restaurants. The formal main dining room beautifully incorporates elements of the French Second Empire–style architecture with contemporary furniture. Classical French cuisine is served on the main floor, while Le Café on the ground floor offers more casual, less expensive French fare. During the summer months, there's alfresco dining along with jazz nightly from 5:30 to 7:30 p.m. ~ 45 School Street; 617-227-3370, fax 617-227-5977. ULTRA-DELUXE.

The **Boston Sail Loft** stretches back and back, out onto the harbor for some wonderful views. Some of the best potato skins in town are to be had here, along with burgers, sandwiches, pastas and fish plates, in a nautical atmosphere. ~ 80 Atlantic Avenue; 617-227-7280, fax 617-723-3467. BUDGET TO MODERATE.

The **Chart House** is one of Boston's most historic restaurants. Set on cobblestoned Long Wharf, it was built in 1760 and served as John Hancock's counting house. His black iron safe is embedded in the upstairs dining room wall. The Chart House carries a marine motif all the way, with gilt-framed black-and-white pictures of ships, as well as model ships. Famed for its dense mud pie, Chart House also dishes up hearty steaks and seafood. Dinner only. ~ 60 Long Wharf; 617-227-1576, fax 617-227-5658;

www.chart-house.com, e-mail boston@chart-house.com. DELUXE
TO ULTRA-DELUXE.

So, you want it kosher? You can get it at the **Milk Street Café**,
a cozy Financial District cafeteria that dishes up some of the best
inexpensive homemade vegetarian food in the city: soups, sandwiches, salads, muffins, bread and desserts such as homemade
brownies and cookies. No dinner. Closed weekends. ~ 50 Milk
Street; 617-542-3663, fax 617-451-5329; www.milkstreetcafe.
com, e-mail feedback@milkstreetcafe.com. BUDGET.

With its tall oak doors lettered in gold, **Tatsukichi** looks like
a foreign consulate. The food is just as impressive: almost 50 kinds
of sushi and the famed house specialty, *kushiage*, skewers of battered and fried meats and seafood. Dine Japanese-style in a light
wood and beige tatami room, or at a Western-style table. ~ 189
State Street; 617-720-2468, fax 617-742-0757. MODERATE TO
DELUXE.

Julien manages to be both sprightly and elegant with impossibly high rose-colored ceilings and massive crystal chandeliers.
Wing chairs and rose banquettes guard your privacy, and softly
shaded table lamps cast a romantic glow. When the waiter re-
moves the silver cover from your plate with a *"Voilà!"* you'll find
a light but vibrant hand has seen to the sauces. The seasonally
changing menu emphasizes regional foods, which might include
Long Island duckling with yellow root vegetables or roasted
Maine lobster with a lemon, herb, butter and mushroom soufflé.
Reservations are recommended. Dinner only. Closed Sunday. ~
Le Méridien, 250 Franklin Street; 617-451-1900, fax 617-423-
2844. ULTRA-DELUXE.

The blue glow of fish tanks and the mouth-watering smell of
spices greet you upon entering **Penang**. Located on the edge of
Chinatown, this upbeat eatery serves up spicy Malaysian dishes,
blending Thai, Chinese, Indian and Portuguese flavors. If you're
game, try an exotic dish such as sautéed frog with kung pao sauce
or chicken feet and mushroom casserole. Too wild? Tamer con-
coctions of poultry, beef, pork and seafood are available. ~ 685
Washington Street; 617-451-6373, fax 617-451-6300; www.
penangboston.com. BUDGET TO MODERATE.

HIDDEN ►   Five take-out restaurants with open kitchens surround a group
of tables at the **Chinatown Eatery**, where the same type of chaos
reigns as at a Hong Kong food market. Wall-mounted menus are
hand-printed in Chinese, Vietnamese and English, and Asians pre-
dominate among the diners (always a good sign). Open from 10:30
a.m. until 1 a.m. ~ 44–46 Beach Street, second floor. BUDGET.

HIDDEN ►   The best Chinese seafood restaurant in Boston's tiny Chinatown district is **Chau Chow**. The decor is cafeteria-minimalist, and
the well-meaning staff is practically non-English speaking, but
Bostonians of all ethnicities ignore the communication problem—

they queue up in long lines for fabulous shrimp, crab, sea bass and other delectables. ~ 52 Beach Street; 617-426-6266, fax 617-292-4646. BUDGET.

A thoroughly Chinese lobby greets diners at the **Imperial Seafood** in the heart of Chinatown, with Chinese lanterns and gold dragons. Known for its dim sum, the restaurant also serves Mandarin cuisine to lots of locals. ~ 70 Beach Street; 617-426-8439, fax 617-889-1468. BUDGET TO DELUXE.

> Taken together, the restaurants at the Chinatown Eatery offer some 400 items, covering Szechuan, Hunan, Mandarin, Cantonese, Vietnamese and Thai cuisines.

Representative of the Southeast Asian immigration to Chinatown is **Pho Pasteur**, an inexpensive Vietnamese restaurant. You can choose from noodle dishes, a variety of soups and excellent seafood entrées. ~ 682 Washington Street; 617-482-7467. BUDGET.

China Pearl specializes in Cantonese and Mandarin cuisine. Locals form long lines for their dim sum and seafood specialties. ~ 9 Tyler Street; 617-426-4338, fax 617-426-8427. MODERATE.

At **Ho Yuen Ting Seafood Restaurant**, no-frills service and decor don't diminish the excellent seafood specialties: shrimp, lobster, crab, clams, conch and snails. ~ 13-A Hudson Street, 617-426-2316. MODERATE.

Be sure to ask for a table by the window at **Aujourd'hui** so you will have a view of the Public Garden below. Tables are set with one-of-a-kind antique service plates, complemented by antique paintings and a display of porcelain. The regional American menu features game, poultry and seafood dishes. There's also a low-cholesterol menu. In addition to the regular menu, you can try the "Nightly Tasting Menu," either traditional or vegetarian, which offers five courses of the chef's evening specialties. One block from the theater district, this is a great place *après* theater. Dinner only. ~ 200 Boylston Street, in the Four Seasons Hotel; 617-451-1392, fax 617-351-2293. ULTRA-DELUXE.

A bright red railing leads upstairs to Boston's greatest culinary adventure at **Biba**, where chef Lydia Shire and co-chef Susan Regis are unafraid to create from any palette: Chinese, French, Italian, Indian. Where else would you get lobster satay with green papaya and winter mint or beef short ribs with cumin seeds and cilantro? The upstairs dining room feasts the eyes, too, with rich colors and primitive Mediterranean motifs set off by yellow walls. The menu is seasonal. ~ 272 Boylston Street; 617-426-7878, fax 617-426-9253. ULTRA-DELUXE.

SHOPPING

Located in the basement of Faneuil Hall is the nonprofit **Boston City Store**, giving you a glimpse of old Boston with its array of municipal goods. It's a great place to pick up a uniquely Boston souvenir—if you don't mind lugging home an authentic parking meter, porcelain street sign or old school banner. There's much more to see and buy, with all proceeds funding Boston neighborhood youth programs. Open by appointment only. ~ Off Congress Street in front of Quincy Market; 617-635-3911; www. cityofboston.gov/citystore.

The biggest tourist shopping bonanza in Boston continues to be **Faneuil Hall Marketplace**. A Boston institution since 1826, Quincy Market is the centerpiece of three shopping arcades filled with more than 150 shops and two dozen food stands and restaurants. Outside the market are a profusion of cheery flower and balloon stands, and under its glass-canopied sides are pushcart vendors selling novelty products.

The Boston Library System is the oldest library system in the United States.

Flanking Quincy Market are two more arcades, the North Market and the South Market.

Feel the Irish eyes smiling at **Celtic Weavers**, an importer of Irish goods. You can set yourself up with clothing, jewelry and perfume, or take home some music, pottery and food. ~ Faneuil Hall, North Market; 617-720-0750; e-mail celticweav@aol.com.

For such a small area, Chinatown has more shops than you might imagine. If you've never experienced Chinese pastries, your mouth will water for them at **Hing Shing Pastry**. ~ 67 Beach Street; 617-451-1162.

HIDDEN ►

Professional-quality Chinese cooking equipment, including traditional Chinese chopsticks and two-foot-diameter woks, is sold at **Chin Enterprises, Inc.** ~ 33 Harrison Avenue; 617-423-1725.

If there is such a thing as a vintage joke shop, **Jack's Joke Shop** is it. Open since 1922 and still run by the original family, the shop is festooned with dozens of elaborate Halloween masks and wigs, inflatable skeletons and glasses with noses and mustaches. Closed Sunday. ~ 226 Tremont Street; 617-426-9640; www.jacksjokes. com, e-mail jokeshop@world.std.com.

Downtown Crossing is the heart of downtown shopping. A brick pedestrian mall at the intersection of Washington and Summer streets, it fronts on **Macy's** (formerly Jordan Marsh). ~ 450 Washington Street; 617-357-3000. Down the street, **Filene's** has been one of its rivals since the mid-19th century. ~ 426 Washington Street; 617-357-2100.

No shopping tour would be complete without a visit to **Filene's Basement**, the country's oldest bargain store (founded in 1908), which has made a legend out of off-price shopping. In the 1940s, 15,000 women once stormed the doors to get the last dresses to leave Paris before the German occupation. Detractors say merchandise slipped during the 1980s, when the Basement opened 22 stores in six states. But the Basement is always crowded with women, who used to try on clothes in the aisles until dressing rooms were installed in 1989, and who don't mind the flaking paint and exposed piping when they can pick up designer dresses for less than ten percent of retail price after three markdowns. Or, on occasion, an $80,000 sable coat for $5000. ~ 426 Washington Street; 617-542-2011, fax 617-348-7915.

Boston's arts scene has rich centuries of history behind it and is expanding all the time. The **BosTix Booth** at Faneuil Hall Marketplace offers half-price tickets for many performance events on the day of the show, cash only, first-come, first-served. Tickets go on sale at 11 a.m. Closed Monday. ~ 617-723-5181.

NIGHTLIFE

THE BEST BARS   There's a Boston bar for everyone: young singles, bricklayers and stevedores, the State House crowd, Financial District workers, Cambridge academics, sports fans, the Irish.

The **Bell in Hand Tavern** is America's oldest tavern, opened in 1795, and retains a cozy, colonial feeling. There's live music nightly. Cover Thursday through Saturday. ~ 45 Union Street; 617-227-2098.

Irish brogues roll so thickly at the **Black Rose** that it sounds like Dublin. Irish beers, nightly Irish folk music and a rollicking good time are house specialties. Cover on the weekends. ~ 160 State Street; 617-742-2286.

Silvertone is a popular retro bar frequented by young urbanites. Fashioned after an art deco–era diner, the black-and-white photos on the wall herald the age of supper clubs and big band music. The raspberry martini is the signature drink of choice. Closed Sunday. ~ 69 Bromfield Street; 617-338-7887, fax 617-338-7890.

The **Littlest Bar** is just that—Boston's smallest tavern. There are 15 stools at the bar and a tiny bench behind them. The noise from the television is often deafening, but this is a fun place to have a quick drink before dinner; most locals haven't heard of it, either. ~ 47 Province Street; 617-523-9766.

◄ *HIDDEN*

The **Good Life** specializes in retro cocktail drinks like cosmopolitans, Manhattans and sidecars. The drab '70s decor doesn't deter large after-work crowds or music enthusiasts who enjoy live jazz downstairs Thursday through Saturday. ~ 28 Kingston Street; 617-451-2622, fax 617-292-9224.

NIGHTCLUBS AND CABARETS   You can view the city from the 33rd floor of the prosperous **Bay Tower Lounge**, where a four-piece orchestra plays on Friday and Saturday nights and live piano music is featured the rest of the week. Dress code. Closed Sunday. ~ 60 State Street, 33rd floor; 617-723-1666; www.baytower.com, e-mail contact@baytower.com.

The **Orpheum Theater** hosts nationally known rock performers. ~ One Hamilton Place off Tremont Street; 617-679-0810.

Seemingly transplanted from New York City is **Felt**, a swanky pool hall/restaurant/lounge/dance club. Early evening brings in the business-suit crowd; after 10 p.m. you'll find a younger, well-dressed clientele in their 20s and 30s. ~ 533 Washington Street; 617-350-5555.

The **Sugar Shack**, an upscale dance club, offers up a mixture of Top-40, funk and hip-hop Thursday through Saturday. Dress code, because "if you don't look good, we don't look good." Cover. ~ 3 Boylston Place; 617-351-2510.

In the basement of the Wilbur Theatre is **Aria**. Tuesday and Friday are hip-hop nights and Thursday and Saturday are Euro-house nights. Sunday features lounge music and Wednesday night is gay night. Closed Monday. Cover. ~ 246 Tremont Street; 617-338-7080.

The Roxy is a beautiful and elegant art deco–style club where people like to really dress up. Dress code. Closed Sunday through Wednesday. Cover. ~ 279 Tremont Street, in the Tremont House; 617-338-7699; www.roxyboston.com, e-mail luckydes@hotmail.com.

THEATER AND DANCE   Boston's theater district is tightly clustered on lower Tremont Street and several blocks west. Many of these host pre-Broadway tryouts and national touring companies. One such venue is the **Colonial Theatre**. ~ 106 Boylston Street; 617-426-9366; www.broadwayinboston.com. Popular contemporary plays are offered by the **Wilbur Theatre**. ~ 246 Tremont Street; 617-423-4008; www.broadwayinboston.com.

The opulent theater of the **Wang Center for the Performing Arts**, formerly a Roaring Twenties movie palace, sponsors extravaganzas in dance, drama, music and film. ~ 270 Tremont Street; 617-482-9393; www.wangcenter.org.

Also operated by the Wang Center, the **Shubert Theatre** stages broadway plays, opera and performances presented by community nonprofit organizations. ~ 265 Tremont Street; 617-482-9393; www.wangcenter.org.

The **Boston Ballet** performs classics like *The Nutcracker* and contemporary works at the Wang Center and the Shubert Theatre. ~ 19 Clarendon Street; 617-695-6950.

Musical comedies are the specialty at the **Charles Playhouse**. ~ 74 Warrenton Street. On **Stage I**, the innovative Blue Man Group wows audiences with eye-popping performance art and fun-filled escapades. ~ 617-426-6912; www.blueman.com. **Stage II** (downstairs) is home to the country's longest-running nonmusical play, *Shear Madness*, a comedy whodunit. ~ 617-426-5225; www.shearmadness.com.

Beacon Hill   Beacon Hill got its name from a beacon that stood atop it in 1634 to warn colonial settlers of danger. "The Hill" used to be much taller; it was leveled by 60 feet to make way for residential building in the 19th century.

After a building boom, Beacon Hill fast became the most elite section of the city, home to doctors, lawyers, writers and intellectuals. Oliver Wendell Holmes called it "the sunny street that holds the sifted few." The first formal residents of the neighborhood were John Singleton Copley and John Hancock. Later residents included Daniel Webster, Louisa May Alcott, William Dean Howells, Henry James and Jenny Lind.

SIGHTS

No single section of town is more elegant than Beacon Hill. This charming area still looks like a 19th-century neighborhood with its gas lamps, brick sidewalks and narrow, one-lane streets that wind up and down the hill. Its later brick rowhouses were designed in fine Federal style, with symmetrical windows, fanlight door windows, black shutters and lacy black iron grillwork. Beacon Hill residents love windowboxes and gardens, and many of the houses have beautiful hidden walled gardens. These are opened to the public during the **Beacon Hill Hidden Gardens** walking tours in late spring, sponsored by the Beacon Hill Garden Club. ~ P.O. Box 302, Charles Street Station, Boston, MA 02114; 617-227-4392; www.beaconhillonline.com, e-mail editor@beaconhilltimes.com.

The crown of Beacon Hill, at its summit, is the **Massachusetts State House,** a grand replacement for the old State House downtown. After the American Revolution, state leaders wanted a more elegant home for the prosperous new government. Charles Bulfinch designed it for them in 1795 in Federal style, with a gold

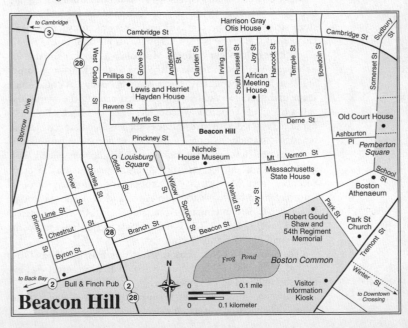

Beacon Hill

dome, brick facade, Palladian windows and white Corinthian columns and trim. A free weekday tour of the interior is well worthwhile, but be sure to make advance reservations. An impressive rotunda, floors made of 13 kinds of marble, unique "black lace" iron grillwork stair railings, stained-glass windows and decorated vaulted ceilings are all part of the appointments. Don't miss the Sacred Cod in the House of Representatives, a wooden fish hung there in 1784 to symbolize the importance of the fishing industry to Massachusetts. ~ Beacon and Park streets; 617-722-2000, fax 617-722-2897.

The **Old Court House,** now the Suffolk County Courthouse, has a grand rotunda with vaulted ceilings decorated with gilt rosettes and figures of cherubs, urns, scrolls and trumpet-blowing figures. Stone caryatids line the rotunda, representing Justice, Fortitude, Punishment, Guilt, Reward, Wisdom, Religion and Virtue. ~ Pemberton Square.

Prolific television producer David E. Kelley (Mr. Michelle Pfeiffer) grew up in the Boston area and set three of his series here: "Ally McBeal," "The Practice" and "Boston Public."

Many come to admire **Louisburg Square** for its sheer beauty. The centerpiece of the square is a serene oval park with a tall black iron fence, ringed with brick bowfront houses. Louisburg Square looks so much like London that a British film company produced *Vanity Fair* here in the 1920s. Louisa May Alcott lived at number 20. ~ Between Mt. Vernon and Pinckney streets.

Tiny one-lane **Acorn Street**—just south of Louisburg Square between Cedar and Willow streets—is one of the few old cobblestone streets left on Beacon Hill, and a very picturesque one it is. Coachmen and servants for nearby mansions used to live here.

Although the **Nichols House Museum** was not fashionable for its time, it is a fine example of the late-19th-century rowhouse. Standish Nichols was quite a personage in her day. A noted landscape architect and pacifist, she traveled around the world and was a friend of Woodrow Wilson. Designed by Charles Bulfinch, her home is filled with rare antiques such as Renaissance Flemish tapestries, statuary by noted American sculptor Augustus Saint-Gaudens and unusual imitation leather wallpaper gilded with gold. Tours run during operating hours. Open Tuesday through Saturday from May through October, and Thursday through Saturday from February through April and November through December. Closed in January. Admission. ~ 55 Mt. Vernon Street; 617-227-6993, fax 617-723-8026; www.nicholshousemuseum.org, e-mail nhm@channel1.com.

The house at **85 Mt. Vernon Street** was Harrison Gray Otis' second Bulfinch-designed home, while **45 Beacon Street** was his third, an unheard-of extravagance.

A grander library than the **Boston Athenaeum** would be hard to find. The interior features high, vaulted ceilings, pillared archways, scores of marble busts, solid wood reading tables and red-leather, brass-studded armchairs. Founded in 1807 by a group including the Reverend William Emerson, father of Ralph Waldo Emerson, it's one of the country's oldest independent libraries. Its picture gallery and sculpture hall served as Boston's first art museum, and the library still maintains an impressive collection of art today, including works by Gilbert Stuart, John Singer Sargent and Chester Harding. The library is also noted for its collections of 19th-century American prints, Confederate state imprints and books from the libraries of George Washington, General Henry Knox and Jean Louis Cardinal Cheverus. Public tours are given by appointment Tuesday through Thursday. ~ 10½ Beacon Street; 617-227-0270, fax 617-227-5266; www.bostonathena eum.org.

The **Appleton-Parker Houses,** twin Greek Revival structures alike in every detail, were built for two wealthy merchants. At number 39, Fanny Appleton married Henry Wadsworth Longfellow in 1843. Number 40 is now the home of the Women's City Club. ~ 39–40 Beacon Street.

At 63–64 Beacon Street you can see a few panes of the famous **Beacon Hill purple glass,** with hues caused by a reaction of sunlight. It acquired cachet, along with everything else traditional on "the Hill."

While most people think of Beacon Hill as a Brahmin bastion, in the 19th century its north slope was the heart of Boston's emerging free black community. Blacks arrived in Boston as slaves in 1638. By 1705, there were over 400 slaves and a few free blacks who settled in the North End. In the 19th century, most blacks lived in the West End and on Beacon Hill, between Joy and Charles streets. The free blacks worked hard to provide decent housing and education for their own, and to help end slavery.

A number of their houses and public buildings still stand, and you can see them on the 14-stop **Black Heritage Trail.** A guide leads daily scheduled trips (617-742-5415).

◄ HIDDEN

Walking-tour maps of the trail are available at the Boston Common Visitor Information kiosk, as well as at the **Museum of Afro-American History,** the last two stops on the trail. The museum is open daily in the summer; otherwise, it's closed on Sunday. ~ 46 Joy Street; 617-725-0022, fax 617-720-5225; www.afro ammuseum.org, e-mail history@afroammuseum.org.

Among the public buildings on the Black Heritage Trail is the **African Meeting House,** the oldest standing black church in America. Built in 1806, it was known in the abolitionist era as the Black Faneuil Hall. It was here, in 1832, that the New England Anti-Slavery Society was founded, with black leader Frederick Douglass and white abolitionists William Lloyd Garrison and Charles Sumner speaking from the platform. ~ 8 Smith Court.

A stirring tribute to the first black regiment recruited for the Civil War stands at the corner of Beacon and Park streets and marks the start of the Black Heritage Trail. A bas-relief sculpture by Augustus Saint-Gaudens, the **Robert Gould Shaw and 54th Regiment Memorial** shows the regiment on the march with their young white leader, Bostonian Robert Gould Shaw, and an angel flying overhead. The black military role in the Civil War won new recognition with the release of the film *Glory*, which chronicles the story of the Massachusetts 54th Regiment.

The Boston Irish gave us such political leaders as former Speakers of the House John W. McCormack and Tip O'Neill, James Michael Curley and the Kennedy clan.

The trail also takes you to one of the first schools for black children and to homes built by free blacks, among them the **Lewis and Harriet Hayden House**, which served as an Underground Railway station and was visited by Harriet Beecher Stowe. ~ 66 Phillips Street.

On an entirely different note, television history is also alive and well in Beacon Hill. Like homing pigeons, all tourists head for "Cheers," so we may as well get it out of the way. The setting for the television show was the **Bull and Finch Pub**, not to be confused with the impostor, Three Cheers, at 390 Congress Street. Even though the Bull and Finch has made such a big business out of all this—selling "Cheers" T-shirts, mugs and hats in the Hampshire House lobby upstairs—it's a bar with real atmosphere. Originally an English pub, it was dismantled and shipped here, complete with old leather and walnut paneling. ~ Downstairs at 84 Beacon Street; 617-227-9605, fax 617-723-1898; www.cheersboston.com, e-mail pubmanager@cheersboston.com.

Yet another point of television trivia can be found in Beacon Hill. Private eye Spenser of "Spenser for Hire" lived above a Boston firehouse, which he entered through a bright red door. The firehouse is right next to the Charles Street Meeting House on Mt. Vernon Street, at the corner of River Street.

LODGING   Perched atop Beacon Hill is the posh **XV Beacon**, a 1903 Beaux Arts mansion converted into a luxurious hotel. Rates are in the stratosphere, but amenities and service are unparalleled. The 61 guest rooms are richly appointed with four-poster beds, fresh flowers and marble bathrooms with mini TVs across from the, um, "facilities." On a cold evening, you can snuggle under the Italian linens and control the gas fireplace from the comfort of your bed. Reserve the complimentary chauffeured car service early—spots fill up quickly. ~ 15 Beacon Street; 617-670-1500, 877-982-3226, fax 617-670-2525; www.xvbeacon.com, e-mail hotel@xvbeacon.com. ULTRA-DELUXE.

Two mid-19th-century townhouses were renovated to create the intimate **Beacon Hill Hotel**. Twelve guest rooms and one suite are pleasingly decorated in cool shades and simple lines, and come equipped with modern-day amenities such as high-speed internet access and flat-screen TVs. The room rates include a full breakfast at the hotel's excellent first-floor restaurant. ~ 25 Charles Street; 617-723-7575, 888-959-2442, fax 617-723-7525; www.beaconhillhotel.com, e-mail stay@beaconhillhotel.com. ULTRA-DELUXE.

Beacon Hill Bed & Breakfast, a pretty six-story brick row-house, is in a quiet residential neighborhood on the lower slope of Beacon Hill, just two blocks west of Charles Street. Each of three high-ceilinged guest rooms has a decorative fireplace and a private bath. Most rooms have a view of the Charles River; some look out over the lovely Gothic Revival Church of the Advent, across the street. ~ 27 Brimmer Street; 617-523-7376; e-mail bhillbb@aol.com. ULTRA-DELUXE.

A real find, far less pricey than downtown hotels, is the **John Jeffries House.** It offers 46 spacious studio apartments and suites, most with kitchenettes, in a renovated turn-of-the-20th-century house overlooking Charles Street. Guest quarters are furnished in tasteful pastels, with dark reproduction furniture, large windows and contemporary bathrooms. There is also a large and comfortable lobby. ~ 14 David G. Mugar Way; 617-367-1866, fax 617-742-0313. MODERATE TO DELUXE.

DINING

Along with its chic boutiques, Charles Street is lined with restaurants representing many ethnic cuisines.

Don't go to **Torch** if you're ravenous. Which is not to say that the food isn't excellent: you can't argue with exquisitely prepared entrées like halibut with garlic spinach, fingerling potatoes and lemon vinaigrette. It's just that Torch is one of those eateries where presentation equals art, and with such attention to detail, the portions sometimes end up being a little skimpy. The food is rich, though, and you'll definitely have room for one of their heavenly desserts (try the chocolate mousse tart with crème chantilly). The decor is elegant but unpretentious, and the service befits the classy food. Reservations suggested. Dinner only. Closed Monday. ~ 26 Charles Street; 617-723-5939; www.bostontorch.com, e-mail info@bostontorch.com. MODERATE TO ULTRA-DELUXE.

Café Bella Vita is a great coffeehouse where you can linger over an espresso or cappuccino and feel welcome in a European way. Its café chairs are always crowded with young students munching on hearty Italian sandwiches. Specialties are desserts such as fresh gelato or chocolate cheesecake. Closed Monday. ~ 30 Charles Street; 617-720-4505. BUDGET.

Step into a Tuscan village at **Ristorante Toscano,** whose dining room has exposed brick walls hung with paintings of the Italian countryside and antique Italian cookware and pottery.

Feast on Florentine cuisine including homemade pastas and game dishes. The *tiramisu* is a dessert standout. ~ 47 Charles Street; 617-723-4090, fax 617-720-4280. MODERATE TO ULTRA-DELUXE.

Good and spicy Thai food stars over the decor at **The King and I**. Start off your meal with satay and Thai rolls, then move on to dancing squids, seafood *panang* or any number of chicken, duck, beef, tofu and noodle dishes. ~ 145 Charles Street; phone/fax 617-227-3320. BUDGET TO MODERATE.

HIDDEN ▶

Surrounded by whizzing cars in a rotary, **Buzzy's Fabulous Roast Beef** looks unsavory, to say the least. Still, this take-out stand, open 24 hours, has the best steakhouse fries in Boston, as well as cheesesteak sandwiches, chili dogs and short ribs. There's even hummus for the errant vegetarian. ~ 327 Cambridge Street; 617-242-7722, fax 617-242-0087. BUDGET.

SHOPPING

At the foot of Beacon Hill, little Charles Street is thickly lined with antique shops, art galleries and specialty stores.

Quirky bargains lie in store at the **Beacon Hill Thrift Shop**, where Beacon Hill matrons bring their best silver along with bric-a-brac. Open Tuesday and Thursday only. ~ 15 Charles Street; 617-742-2323.

On the other end of the spectrum is the chic **Wish**, where trendy clothes sell for a pretty penny. In addition to casual and formal wear, you'll find a small assortment of accessories. ~ 49 Charles Street; 617-227-4441; www.wishstyle.com.

If you stop by **Rouvalis Flowers** you can take home an exotic plant or flower. The shop has a wonderful selection of topiary trees and orchids as well as unusual seasonal varieties. Shipping is available. Closed Sunday. ~ 40 West Cedar Street; 617-720-2266, fax 617-720-2636.

The retail outlet of a local paper manufacturer, **Rugg Road Paper Co.** carries virtually every paper good you can imagine, from woodblock-printed paper to stationery to handmade books. ~ 105 Charles Street; 617-742-0002, fax 617-742-0008.

An amazing selection of beautifully colored and embroidered Western-style leather boots awaits at **Helen's Leather**, along with stylish leather coats, briefcases and belts. Closed Tuesday. ~ 110 Charles Street; 617-742-2077.

You ought to be able to find the perfect brass drawer pull at **Period Furniture Hardware**, which carries a full line of reproduction hardware. Closed Sunday from Labor Day to Memorial Day; closed Saturday and Sunday the rest of the year. ~ 123 Charles Street; 617-227-0758.

NIGHTLIFE

Despite its fame as the "Cheers" bar, **Bull and Finch Pub** is a watering hole with character. The venerable English pub features big brews, burgers and an uproarious crowd. ~ Downstairs at 84

Beacon Street; 617-227-9605; www.cheersboston.com, e-mail pub manager@cheersboston.com.

If you need more "Cheers" atmosphere, they've opened a second location: **Cheers Faneuil Hall**. The new bar features a near-perfect replica of the Hollywood set, complete with Tiffany lamps and a central island bar. ~ Faneuil Hall Marketplace; 617-227-0150, fax 617-227-8416.

The **Sevens Ale House** is a better Boston neighborhood bar than the nearby Bull and Finch Pub. Decorated in dark, mellowed wood and with photos of patrons finishing the Boston Marathon and other local events, the Sevens is small and lively, lacks tourists, and is blessed with some of the friendliest staff we've ever met. ~ 77 Charles Street; 617-523-9074.

Back Bay

Although it started life as a mud flat, Back Bay fast became a fashionable neighborhood. As the city grew, it started running out of room in its original peninsula surrounding Boston Common, so it began filling in the tidal flats of the Back Bay in 1858, the largest land reclamation project of its time. Some 450 acres of marshland were turned into usable land over 20 years.

Given all this room to plan, Back Bay is the only place in town laid out with any perceivable logic. Streets follow an orderly

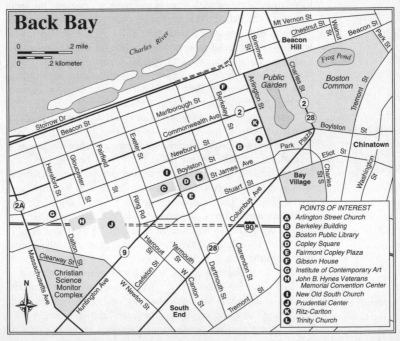

Back Bay

0 ——— .2 mile
0 ——— .2 kilometer

Charles River

Mt Vernon St · Chestnut St · Walnut St · Beacon St · Park St
Brimmer St · **Beacon Hill**
Frog Pond
Storrow Dr · Beacon St
Marlborough St
Commonwealth Ave
Newbury St
Arlington St
Berkeley St
Clarendon St
Dartmouth St
Exeter St
Fairfield St
Gloucester St
Hereford St
Ring Rd
Public Garden
Charles St
Boston Common
Tremont St
Boylston St
Chinatown
Park Plaza
Eliot St
Bay Village
Charles St S
Washington St
Newbury St
Boylston St
St James Ave
Stuart St
Columbus Ave
90
28
Harcourt St
Yarmouth St
W Canton St
W Newton St
Huntington Ave
Dalton St
Clearway St
Massachusetts Ave
Christian Science Monitor Complex
South End
Tremont St
2A
9

POINTS OF INTEREST
Ⓐ Arlington Street Church
Ⓑ Berkeley Building
Ⓒ Boston Public Library
Ⓓ Copley Square
Ⓔ Fairmont Copley Plaza
Ⓕ Gibson House
Ⓖ Institute of Contemporary Art
Ⓗ John B. Hynes Veterans Memorial Convention Center
Ⓘ New Old South Church
Ⓙ Prudential Center
Ⓚ Ritz-Carlton
Ⓛ Trinity Church

N

grid, with cross streets named alphabetically for palatial ducal mansions: Arlington, Berkeley, Clarendon, Dartmouth, Exeter, Fairfield, Gloucester and Hereford.

SIGHTS

The centerpiece of this grand reclamation project is **Commonwealth Avenue**. Patterned after the Champs Élysées, it's a wide boulevard with a grass strip mall that runs right through the heart of the Back Bay. "Comm Ave," as it's called by natives, is lined with stately brownstones and many historic buildings. Newbury, Beacon and Marlborough streets parallel Comm Ave. Stylish Newbury Street is lined with chic boutiques, expensive jewelry, fur and clothing stores, art galleries, antique stores and loads of restaurants. Back Bay crosses Massachusetts Avenue, which natives shorten to "Mass Ave," and ends at Kenmore Square.

There are two ideal times to stroll along Marlborough Street: on a snowy winter night and on a bright, warm spring morning when the magnolias are in bloom.

To the north, the Back Bay ends at the Charles River, where the wide, grassy Esplanade is a popular sunning spot in warm weather. Also on the Esplanade is the **Hatch Memorial Shell**, where the Boston Pops Symphony Orchestra performs summer concerts.

If Boston Common is Boston's Central Park, then the **Public Garden** is its Tuileries, the first botanical garden in the country. Lavishly landscaped with flowers and trees, it's home to the **swan boats**, which circle the weeping willow–draped lagoon in season. The famous boats were launched in 1877 by Robert Paget, who was inspired by the swan-boat scene in Wagner's opera *Lohengrin*. The same family continues to operate them. Also in the Public Garden is some notable statuary: George Washington on horseback and abolitionist Wendall Phillips. ~ Bordered by Beacon, Charles, Arlington and Boylston streets.

HIDDEN ▶

If you walk straight through the Public Garden gates at the corner of Beacon and Charles streets, you'll come upon **Mrs. Mallard and her brood of eight ducklings** stretched out in a row behind her, all heading for the pond. Placed here in 1987, the bronze, larger-than-life statues represent the ducks made famous in Robert McCloskey's children's story *Make Way for Ducklings*. Every Mother's Day, the ducklings are feted on Duckling Day with a parade and festival sponsored by the Historic Neighborhoods Foundation. ~ 99 Bedford Street; 617-426-1885, fax 617-426-5305; www.historic-neighborhoods.org, e-mail info@historic-neighborhoods.org.

Ever since opening in 1927, the **Ritz-Carlton** has catered to a select clientele. The 17-story brick building overlooking the Public Garden, while not particularly striking on the outside, is the epitome of old elegance inside, where the lobby is graced with a large curving staircase and antique touches such as an exquisite brass railing. The original owner would never permit a reservation without researching the client's reputation in the Social Register or business directories. Many notable people have lived at the Ritz, including Charles Lindbergh and Winston Churchill. Many more have stayed here, among them Rodgers & Hammerstein, Albert Einstein, the Duke and Duchess of Windsor, Tennessee Williams and John F. Kennedy—even Lassie and Rin Tin Tin. ~ 15 Arlington Street; 617-536-5700, fax 617-536-1335; www.ritzcarlton.com.

Down the street, the Georgian-style **Arlington Street Church** features a tall and graceful steeple fashioned in the style of Christopher Wren. ~ Arlington and Boylston streets.

The beaux-arts **Berkeley Building** looks like a wedding cake, so curlicued and beribboned is its frothy white bas-relief terracotta molding. Tiers of windows are trimmed in sea green, and a black marble entrance sign is flanked with dolphins and sea serpents. Built in 1905 and beautifully restored in 1989, it formerly housed Boston's design center. ~ 420 Boylston Street.

The **New Old South Church** is where the congregation of the Old South Meeting House moved in 1875, after they decided their Washington Street neighborhood had become too noisy to hear the sermon. The Gothic facade is dominated by a tower and carved stone rosettes. Inside the church are Venetian mosaics and 15th-century stained-glass windows depicting the Prophets, the Evangelists, the miracles and the parables. ~ Corner of Boylston and Dartmouth streets.

The heart of this area is gorgeous **Copley Square**, named for artist John Singleton Copley. Boston's religious and intellectual center at the end of the 19th century, the square is dominated by two architecturally imposing structures, Henry Hobson Richardson's Trinity Church and Charles McKim's Boston Public Library. ~ The square is on Boylston Street, located between Clarendon and Dartmouth streets.

The French-Romanesque, medieval-style **Trinity Church**, built in 1877, is visually stunning inside and out. One of Richardson's most brilliant creations, Trinity Church has an enormous tower reminiscent of the domes of Venice and Constantinople. Inside, rich colors and exquisite Moorish details cover the vaulted ceiling, rotunda and walls, and there are gorgeous John LaFarge frescoes and stained-glass windows. Public tours are available daily. ~ 206 Clarendon Street; 617-536-0944, fax 617-536-8916; www. trinitychurchboston.org, e-mail info@trinitychurchboston.org.

Much more than a library, the **Boston Public Library** houses art and architectural treasures. A wide marble staircase, Corinthian columns and frescoes grace its grand entrance hall (at the side door). Inside are murals by John Singer Sargent, paintings by John Singleton Copley, sculptures by Augustus and Louis Saint-

Gaudens and bronze doors by Daniel Chester French. Inspired by Italian Renaissance palaces, it was opened in 1895. Take time to sit in the lovely central courtyard, where you'll find a fountain and benches. ~ 700 Boylston Street; 617-536-5400; www.bpl.org, e-mail info@bpl.org.

The grande dame of Boston's vintage hotels is the **Fairmont Copley Plaza**, built in 1912 in high Victorian style. It boasts a wide stone facade, whose curving center echoes the bowfront homes of Back Bay and Beacon Hill. Inside, marble and crystal appointments set off an elegant lobby topped with a trompe l'oeil painting of the sky. The internationally known Fairmont Copley Plaza has served as a resting place for a dozen presidents and European royalty. ~ 138 St. James Avenue; 617-267-5300, fax 617-267-7668; www.fairmont.com, e-mail boston@fairmont.com.

The **Skywalk Observatory** at the Prudential Tower gives you a bird's-eye view of downtown, this time a 360° one. Commonly called "the Pru," the Prudential Center was built in the early '60s as another piece of urban renewal. It houses shops and offices, and in front of it is a cast bronze statue called *Quest Eternal*, representing man reaching for the heavens. The tower is accessible for daylight or starlight viewing, from 10 a.m. to 10 p.m. Admission. ~ 800 Boylston Street, Prudential Center; 617-859-0648, fax 617-859-0056.

The building at **314 Commonwealth Avenue** was created in the 1920s in an 1899 mansion modeled after a Loire Valley château. Its medieval-looking exterior has sculptured stone cherubs and gargoyles looking down from its battlements. Inside the building you will find spectacular bas-relief mahogany walls, gold-leaf carved ceilings, stained-glass windows and an ornately carved marble staircase.

Nowhere is the opulence of the Back Bay Victorians more amply evidenced than at the **Gibson House**, now a museum and location of the Victorian Society in America, New England chapter. Built for the prominent Gibson family in 1859, the Italian Renaissance Revival home is richly furnished with gold-embossed wallpaper and black walnut paneling, imported carpets and most of the Gibson family china and porcelain. Tours are available Wednesday through Sunday. Admission. ~ 137 Beacon Street; 617-267-6338, fax 617-267-5121; e-mail gibsonmuseum@aol.com.

Marlborough Street is Commonwealth Avenue's slimmer cousin—there's no mall running down the middle of the street. This residential street seems more lived in than Comm Ave; you'll see baby carriages and bikes chained to the cast-iron fence rails alongside the tiny, lovingly tended flower gardens that are planted around the magnolia trees.

The **Institute of Contemporary Art** has won an international reputation for its wide-ranging artistic events, held here for more than half a century. Housed in an old Boston police station, the ICA often shows experimental or controversial works, among them art exhibits, films, videos, music events, lectures and literary readings. Closed Monday and Tuesday. Admission. ~ 955 Boylston Street; 617-266-5152, fax 617-266-4021; www.icaboston.org, e-mail info@icaboston.org.

Fire Station Number 33 shares a wonderful old building with the ICA. On your way in or out of the ICA, walk slowly so that you'll have a moment to observe the contrast between the firefighters who spend a lot of time relaxing in front of their half of the building and the *très*-cool crowd that works at and visits the ICA next door.

A major convention hall, the **John B. Hynes Veterans Memorial Convention Center** was extensively renovated and rebuilt in the late 1980s. Call for a schedule of the numerous conventions and expositions, including a college-fest weekend and a bridal expo. ~ 900 Boylston Street; 617-954-2000, 800-845-8806, fax 617-954-2125; www.mccahome.com, e-mail info@mccahome.com.

LODGING

The vintage 1927 **Ritz-Carlton** sparkles. A standard room is spacious and airy, with a high ceiling, brown floral drapes and spread and French provincial furnishings. On the walls are prints of antique engravings of Boston and Bunker Hill. The bathroom has polished white marble floors and antique fixtures. Besides an in-house health and fitness facility with massage, the 293-room hotel has three restaurants, an afternoon tea lounge and a bar. ~ 15 Arlington Street; 617-536-5700, 800-241-3333, fax 617-536-1335; www.ritzcarlton.com. ULTRA-DELUXE.

For less expensive lodging in Boston, rent a furnished apartment from Comma Realty, Inc. Units with kitchens, rented weekly, have twin beds and funky bathroom fixtures. ~ 371 Commonwealth Avenue; 617-437-9200.

The grande dame of Boston hotels is the **Fairmont Copley Plaza**, built in 1912. The hotel was famed for throwing such sumptuous affairs as an "Evening in Venice," with gondolas floating on the parquet floor, converted to the Grand Canal. Every president since Taft has visited, as well as royalty from eight countries. JFK was a regular visitor. The Fairmont Copley Plaza's elegant lobby is appointed with coffered gold ceilings adorned with a trompe l'oeil painting of the sky, marble columns and floors, crystal chandeliers and French provincial furniture. The hotel has two restaurants and two bars. The 379 rooms and 28 suites are decorated with dark period furniture and warm floral patterns, while bathrooms feature vintage marble and chrome fixtures. ~ 138 St. James Avenue; 617-267-5300, 800-441-1414, fax 617-437-0794; www.fairmont.com, e-mail boston@fairmont.com. ULTRA-DELUXE.

Text continued on page 76.

Boston Area
Bookstores

Boston is a book lover's delight, brimming with bookstores full of quirky personality, charm and the imprint of history. These shops display a colorful individual stamp, with secondhand shelving, hand-lettered signs and perhaps a beat-up leather chair or two or a resident dog.

Rare and fine books are the specialty at **Peter L. Stern & Company** and the **Lame Duck Books**. Here you can get first editions, 19th- and 20th-century literature and private-press books. ~ 55 Temple Place; 617-542-2376.

The **Brattle Book Shop** claims the title of being the successor to America's oldest continuous antiquarian bookshop, dating from the 18th century. Used books sit on battered gray steel shelving and range from fiction, humor and poetry to history, genealogy and heraldry. Old *Life* magazines dating to 1936 march up the stairway and through history, covered with the faces of Tallulah Bankhead, Betty Grable and Hedy Lamarr. Closed Sunday. ~ 9 West Street; 617-542-0210, 800-447-9595, fax 617-338-1467; www.brattlebookshop.com, e-mail info@brattle bookshop.com.

Good food and good books go hand in hand, and never more so than at **Trident Booksellers & Café**. Trident claims the prize for being funky: the province of young hipsters dressed in black, a plethora of Third World, gay and alternative publications, and a menu of homemade soups and sandwiches tailored to a struggling writer's budget. It also sells bonsai trees, incense and myrrh, self-improvement videos and campy black-and-white postcards. ~ 338 Newbury Street; 617-267-8688, fax 617-247-1934.

An astonishing 25 bookshops surround Harvard Square. Established in 1856, **Schoenhof's Foreign Books, Inc.** is America's oldest comprehensive foreign-language bookstore. It carries reference books in over 500 languages and dialects, among them Swahili, Urdu, Tibetan, Navajo and classical Greek and Latin, whatever you need to complete a master's or Ph.D. Still, the shop is not too pedantic to sell children's favorites like *Le Petit Prince*, *Babar* and even *Harry Potter* in over two dozen languages.

Closed Sunday. ~ 76-A Mt. Auburn Street, Cambridge; 617-547-8855; www.schoenhofs.com, e-mail info@schoenhofs.com.

Where else but Cambridge could a poetry-only bookshop survive? The **Grolier Poetry Book Shop Inc.**, founded in 1927, is America's oldest continuously operating poetry bookshop, carrying more than 18,000 titles from all periods and cultures. Supported by friends of Conrad Aiken, who lived next door in 1929, the shop grew into a meeting place for such poets as Ezra Pound, Marianne Moore and T. S. Eliot. The shop sponsors an annual poetry prize and a reading series of unpublished poets each semester. Closed Sunday and Monday in summer. ~ 6 Plympton Street, Cambridge; 617-547-4648, 800-234-7636; www.grolierpoetrybook shop.com, e-mail grolierpoetrybookshop@compuserve.com.

Many Harvard Square bookshops specialize in rare and out-of-print books. Among them is **James & Devon Gray Booksellers**, featuring rare books—in any language or on any subject—published before 1700. Among the obscure and hard-to-find volumes are a first edition of Edmund Spenser's *The Faerie Queene* and manuscripts by John Dryden. Closed Sunday and Monday. ~ 12 Arrow Street, Cambridge; 617-868-0752; www.graybooksellers.com, e-mail nous@mindspring.com.

Seven Stars breathes New Age culture. Besides such titles as *Everyday Zen*, *The Biggest Secret* and *Passport to the Cosmos*, the shop sells tarot cards, incense and gorgeous chunks of amethyst and other crystals, which some believe have healing powers. ~ 731 Massachusetts Avenue, Cambridge; 617-547-1317.

A couple of miles out from Harvard Square, **Kate's Mystery Books** is a mecca for mystery lovers and writers. Opening on Friday the 13th in 1983, the store has a black cat logo and walls lined with several hundred black cat figurines. About 10,000 new and used titles range from Dashiell Hammett and Agatha Christie to Tony Hillerman and Robert Parker. A special section focuses on mysteries set in New England. Mystery Writers of America, New England Chapter, meets here, as does the local chapter of Sisters in Crime. Kate's hosts author readings and signings at least once a week. ~ 2211 Massachusetts Avenue, Cambridge; 617-491-2660; www.katesmysterybooks.com, e-mail katesmysbks@earthlink.net.

This is just a sampling of Boston's bookstores, large and small. In this area of scholars and writers, there's a bookstore for everyone, with almost 300 listed in the Yellow Pages. That's almost one for every 2000 inhabitants.

Built in 1891, the vintage stone **Copley Square Hotel**, completely renovated, draws lots of families and Europeans to its cozy, friendly 143 guest rooms. Though the rooms are on the smallish side, they're comfortably appointed with modern furniture and fabrics in blues, greens and mauves. ~ 47 Huntington Avenue; 617-536-9000, 800-225-7062, fax 617-267-3547; www.copley squarehotel.com. ULTRA-DELUXE.

Real working fireplaces add to the numerous vintage charms of the **Lenox Hotel**. Opening at the turn of the 20th century, the 212-room Lenox was popular with such entertainers as Enrico Caruso, who pulled his private streetcar up to the door. The lobby wears its original Gilded Age elegance of soaring white columns, gold-leaf moldings, marble fireplace and handsome wood furniture. A typical room has a Colonial-style chandelier, a rocking chair, high ceilings and a Colonial ambience. The top floor, however, has been renovated in French Provincial decor. ~ 710 Boylston Street; 617-536-5300, 800-225-7676, fax 617-267-1237; www.lenoxhotel.com. ULTRA-DELUXE.

HIDDEN ► One of the city's most charming hotels, the **Eliot Suite Hotel** was built in 1925 by the family of Charles Eliot, a Harvard president. The hotel has a warm, welcoming feeling. Its soft green-colored lobby is set with Queen Anne chairs, sofas and crystal wall sconces. It's 16 rooms and 69 suites are furnished with antique-style furniture and chintz fabric. Some have kitchenettes. ~ 370 Commonwealth Avenue; 617-267-1607, 800-443-5468, fax 617-536-9114; www.eliothotel.com, e-mail email@eliothotel.com. ULTRA-DELUXE.

The first independent luxury hotel built in Boston since the 1950s, the **Colonnade Hotel**, which opened in 1971, sparked the citywide hotel building boom a decade later. Recognized for its contemporary European atmosphere, The Colonnade has 285 rooms with classy mahogany and oak furnishings with copper or rose accents. The hotel has a restaurant as well as Boston's only rooftop pool. ~ 120 Huntington Avenue; 617-424-7000, 800-962-3030, fax 617-424-1717; www.colonnadehotel.com, e-mail reservations@colonnadehotel.com. DELUXE TO ULTRA-DELUXE.

DINING The **Ritz-Carlton Dining Room** offers one of the most serene and traditional dining spots in Boston. Overlooking the Public Garden, this sparkling, elegant place features cobalt-blue Dutch crystal chandeliers, French provincial–style furniture and blue-and-gold fringed drapes. The carving cart menu changes daily but might include such wonderful entrées as lobster in bourbon sauce, venison, pheasant or whole dover sole sautéed with pine nuts and lemon butter. There are almost 20 desserts, ranging from *bavorois à l'orange* to crêpes suzettes flambés. The **Ritz Roof Restaurant**, currently closed for renovations, will offer open-air Continental dining and dancing. ~ 15 Arlington Street; 617-536-5700, fax 617-536-1335. DELUXE TO ULTRA-DELUXE.

Though it emulates a Parisian bistro about as successfully as a McDonald's, the **Café de Paris** offers better fare than McD's: croissants, omelettes and the best chicken sandwich in Boston, with cafeteria-style service. Breakfast and lunch only. ~ 19 Arlington Street; 617-247-7121. BUDGET.

The **White Star Tavern** serves authentic global cuisine. Outstanding dishes include the shiitake and wood-ear stir-fry, chilled lobster with a bloody mary cocktail sauce and lemon Thai aioli, and a seared wintergreen salad with duck confit. No lunch on Monday. ~ 565 Boylston Street; 617-536-4477, fax 617-536-6022. MODERATE.

Skipjack's Seafood Emporium boasts one of the biggest and most varied seafood menus in Boston—over two dozen kinds of fresh fish daily, ranging from tuna, trout and salmon to lesser-known moonfish and parrot fish. The decor is far from traditional: glass block and glitzy red and blue neon, and changing exhibits by local artists. ~ 199 Clarendon Street; 617-536-3500; www.skipjacks.com, e-mail info@skipjacks.com. MODERATE TO ULTRA-DELUXE.

The beautiful people dine at **Davio's**, a stylish Italian restaurant with primo service and real panache. Brick walls, white linens and soft lighting create an intimate milieu for superb creations such as cider-glazed crispy duck with smoked apple chutney and potato cake, and Tuscan marinated chicken breast with pepperoncini, kalamata olives, tomatoes and potatoes. Upstairs there's a more casual version serving lighter fare in a sidewalk café setting. No lunch in winter. ~ 269 Newbury Street; 617-262-4810, fax 617-437-0290; www.davios.com. MODERATE TO DELUXE.

Sonsie is where you go to see and be seen. A nice perk is the food—here the elite meet to eat, and eat well. The menu has a bit of everything, from Italian pasta dishes to American staples and breakfast favorites (try the buttermilk pancakes). The service is decent, if a little uppity, and some of the tables face the win-

AUTHOR FAVORITE

If you're a fan of Indian curries but your dinner companion tends to be unadventurous, try the smallish **Bombay Café**. There will be enough spicier selections to satisfy you, and your pal will probably be pleased with the milder items, such as stuffed *nan* or chicken *tikka*. ~ 175 Massachusetts Avenue; 617-247-0555, fax 617-247-0434; www.bombaycafe. net, e-mail punjabi321@yahoo.com. MODERATE.

dows. There's sidewalk dining in good weather, the better to drape yourself around Parisian-style café tables and look elegant. Brunch on Saturday and Sunday. ~ 327 Newbury Street; 617-351-2500, fax 617-351-2565; www.sonsieboston.com. DELUXE TO ULTRA-DELUXE.

A cozy little basement restaurant, the **Kebab n' Kurry** smells of the spices of India. The tables are set with pink cloths and silk scarves embroidered with lion hunts and elephants, set under glass. Authentic curries from North India include chicken, lamb, fish and shrimp and a wide variety of vegetarian dishes. No lunch on Sunday. Closed Monday. ~ 30 Massachusetts Avenue; 617-536-9835, fax 617-536-9486. MODERATE.

SHOPPING

Back Bay is another of the city's densest shopping districts, concentrated on fashionable Newbury Street, lined from end to end with chic boutiques.

Shreve, Crump & Lowe, a Boston jeweler since 1796, has always been the place to go for fine gold and silver jewelry. Closed Sunday. ~ 330 Boylston Street; 617-267-9100.

A gold swan sculpture over the door signals the **Women's Educational and Industrial Union,** founded by a group of socially concerned women in 1877, the same year the Swan Boats set sail. Its shop sells upscale, handmade gifts, jewelry, women's accessories, stationery, cards and children's clothing. The products are made by women artists or women-owned companies, and proceeds benefit the non-profit organization. ~ 356 Boylston Street; 617-536-5651; www.weiu.org, e-mail theshop@weiu.org.

The Society of Arts and Crafts is the oldest non-profit craft organization in the United States, founded in 1897.

Alan Bilzerian is a chic shop filled with classic-style and avant-garde clothing for men and women. The store carries designs by Issei Miyake, Yoji Yamamoto and Ann Demeulemeester. Closed Sunday. ~ 34 Newbury Street; 617-536-1001, fax 617-236-4770.

Who would mind buying used men's and women's clothing when it's as fashionable and "gently worn" as that at **The Closet, Inc.** Only the latest clothes in the finest condition are accepted. ~ 175 Newbury Street, downstairs; 617-536-1919.

The **Society of Arts and Crafts** maintains two galleries where you can buy whimsical animal sculptures, ceramics, glass and furniture with real personality, as well as pottery and jewelry. ~ 175 Newbury Street, 617-266-1810; and 101 Arch Street, 617-345-0033; www.societyofcrafts.org, e-mail retailgallery@societyofcrafts.org.

London Lace specializes in reproduction Victorian lace patterns made on the only Victorian machinery left in Scotland. Items include lace curtain panels, table runners, tablecloths, antique furniture and accessories. Closed Sunday. ~ 215 Newbury Street; 617-267-3506, fax 617-267-0770.

The shopping jewel of this area is brass- and marble-bedecked **Copley Place** on upper Huntington Avenue, resplendent with indoor waterfalls and trees. The Copley Place complex also includes the Westin and Marriott hotels, and the shopping mall is in-between the two, connected to both hotel lobbies. A glass pedestrian bridge carries shoppers over Huntington Avenue to the Prudential Center.

Opened in the mid-1980s, Copley Place holds 100 upscale stores, anchored by classy Dallas import **Neiman Marcus** (617-536-3660). Copley Place also houses outlets of **Polo** (617-266-4121), **Gucci** (617-247-3000), **Bally** (617-437-1910) and **Louis Vuitton** (617-437-6519). ~ Huntington Avenue and Dartmouth Street; 617-369-5000; www.shopcopleyplace.com, e-mail info@ shopcopleyplace.com.

Vintage clothing from the 1920s to the 1990s fills **The Closet Upstairs**. ~ 223 Newbury Street; 617-267-5757; www.thecloset upstairs.com.

Step into **Selletto** for handmade products, always enhanced by piñon and cedar incense, where wares come from a world-wide network of artists. There are wreaths, dried flower arrangements and even hand-carved marble peaches from Tuscany. ~ 244 Newbury Street; 617-424-0656, fax 617-731-9475.

◀ *HIDDEN*

The best place in the city to buy new rock CDs is **Newbury Comics**, where prices are typically lower than the giant chain stores. A selection of comic books and kitschy knickknacks round out the inventory. ~ 332 Newbury Street; 617-236-4930.

Copley Place's much older cousin is the **Prudential Center**, anchored by **Saks Fifth Avenue** (617-262-8500) and **Lord & Taylor** (617-262-6000). The Pru's stylish interior includes a network of glass-roofed pedestrian streets lined with shops.

The ornate **Oak Room** was built in 1912; you can still sidle up to its original brass-and-wood bar. Cabaret and jazz are performed on Friday and Saturday. ~ 138 St. James Avenue, in the Fairmont Copley Plaza; 617-267-5300; www.fairmont.com.

NIGHTLIFE

Though a bit touristy, the Prudential Tower's **Top of The Hub** offers a breathtaking view of Boston's skyline (you are on the 52nd floor, after all). Enjoy a nightcap at the piano bar, where cocktails and appetizers are served up along with live nightly jazz. ~ 800 Boylston Street; 617-536-1775, fax 617-859-8298.

Boston nightlife doesn't get more local than the **Pour House**, where an uproarious underground bar features blues and psychedelic music. ~ 909 Boylston Street; 617-236-1767.

Your search for the classy, plush, quiet cocktail lounges of old can end now. You've found **The Red Room**, the downstairs cocktail lounge at Sonsie's restaurant. Sink into bordello-red chairs as you clink martini glasses (Godiva white-chocolate mint martinis, that is). They have an impressive list of single-malt scotches as well. Closed Sunday through Tuesday. ~ 327 Newbury Street; 617-351-2500, fax 617-351-2565; www.sonsieboston.com.

CLASSICAL MUSIC & THEATER   The **Boston Camerata**, formed back in 1954, offers medieval, Renaissance, baroque and early American music, both vocal and instrumental. ~ 140 Clarendon Street; 617-262-2092.

The **Lyric Stage Company of Boston**, Boston's oldest resident professional theater company, performs revivals and premieres. ~ 140 Clarendon Street, Copley Square; 617-437-7172; www. lyricstage.com.

Theater-goers and other performing-arts fans may purchase half-price, day-of-show tickets at **BosTix**. Shaped like an enormous webbed wooden mushroom, the booth also serves as a full-service box office and Ticketmaster outlet for performing-arts events in and around Boston. Half-priced tickets are cash only, first-come, first-served. Tickets go on sale at 11 a.m. ~ On the northwest corner of Copley Square.

The Fenway

The western side of Massachusetts Avenue edges over to the Fenway, the area surrounding the Back Bay Fens, another piece of the Emerald Necklace. Fens, from an Old English word meaning low wetlands or marshes, describes the area aptly. Along its sprawling length are several creeks and ponds, a rose garden and private garden plots, remnants of Boston's wartime "Victory Gardens."

SIGHTS   No one thinks of the Fenway without **Fenway Park**, the home of the Boston Red Sox and the Green Monster, the famous left-field wall. Fenway Park remains one of the homiest and most old-fashioned ballparks in the country. Built in 1912, it is one of the few baseball parks with a playing surface of real grass. The Green Monster is there to protect the ballfield from the Massachusetts Turnpike, and vice versa. ~ 4 Yawkey Way; 617-267-1700, fax 617-236-6640; www.redsox.com, e-mail webmaster@redsox.com.

The campuses of two well-known Boston colleges are also in the Fenway—**Boston University**, along Commonwealth Avenue, and **Northeastern University**, south of Huntington Avenue.

Visible from Kenmore Square is the brightly lit, red-white-and-blue **Citgo Sign**, a gasoline advertisement and relic of the 1950s. It is the last of six similar signs in the United States.

Housed in a 15th-century-style Venetian palazzo, the **Isabella Stewart Gardner Museum** is a little jewel of a museum. It contains the personal collection of Mrs. Isabella Stewart Gardner, amassed over a lifetime of travel to Europe. "Mrs. Jack," as she came to be called, was considered somewhat eccentric and outrageous by proper Bostonians, and she collected what she liked. Her booty includes Italian Renaissance, 17th-century Dutch and 19th-century American paintings, as well as sculpture, textiles, furniture, ceramics, prints and drawings. The museum offers weekly chamber music concerts from September through May. Closed Monday. Admission. ~ 280 The Fenway; 617-566-1401, fax 617-232-8039; www.gardnermuseum.org, e-mail membership@isgm.org.

Not far from the Gardner Museum is the **Museum of Fine Arts,** world-famous for its exceptional collections of Asian, Greek, Roman, European, Egyptian and American art. The MFA also holds impressionist paintings and works by such American masters as John Singer Sargent, John Singleton Copley and Winslow Homer. The MFA regularly attracts mega-exhibitions, such as traveling shows of Picasso and Monet works. Don't miss the Japanese gardens and the little first-floor café. Admission. ~ 465 Huntington Avenue; 617-267-9300, fax 617-236-0362; www. mfa.org, e-mail pr@mfa.org.

The lovely **Gryphon House** is a bed and breakfast set in a turn-of-the-20th-century brownstone. A curving staircase leads upstairs   **LODGING**

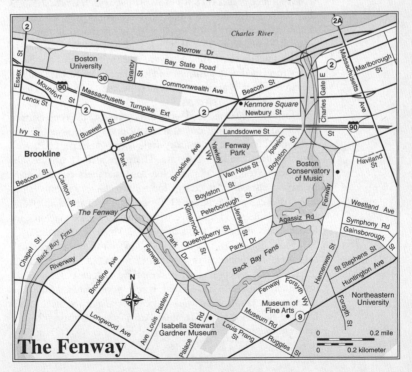

The Fenway

to the eight spacious suites, which are individually decorated with queen-sized beds, period antiques, hardwood floors, oriental rugs, wetbars and gas fireplaces. For a grand view of the Charles River, ask for the North Tower or Riverview suite. ~ 9 Bay State Road; 617-375-9003, 877-375-9003, fax 617-425-0716; www.gryphon houseboston.com, e-mail innkeeper@gryphonhouseboston.com. DELUXE TO ULTRA-DELUXE.

HIDDEN ▶   **The Buckminster,** a friendly lodging house with 100 rooms, is an inexpensive alternative to the higher-priced inns and hotels in nearby Back Bay. The hotel is on three floors of a nice old building in the heart of the vibrant Kenmore Square area. Guest rooms and suites tend to be large; all are furnished with reproduction furniture. The Buckminster's prime attraction is its thoughtful convenience to travelers who are staying for more than one night—each floor has a kitchen and full laundry facilities. If only there were hotels like this in every city! ~ 645 Beacon Street; 617-236-7050, 800-727-2825, fax 617-262-0068. DELUXE.

The Boston University Bridge on Commonwealth Avenue is said to be the only place in the world where a boat can sail under a train traveling under a car driving under an airplane.

The best deal for budget-minded travelers in Boston just has to be **Florence Frances'** 1840s brownstone, with four guest rooms that share baths. Florence has traveled around the world and decorated each room individually with an international flair. The Spanish Room, done in red, black and white, has a display of Spanish fans on the wall. The living and sitting rooms are beautifully furnished with antiques and a collection of Royal Doulton figurines. There is also a community kitchen. ~ 458 Park Drive; 617-267-2458. MODERATE.

Hostelling International—Boston represents the rock bottom of Boston accommodations in terms of price. Amenities are certainly not luxurious. Dormitory-style rooms hold six beds, with males and females kept separate. There are also 11 private, air-conditioned rooms available. Non-AYH members can stay here by paying a small extra charge for an introductory membership. The hostel can accommodate 190 people. There are laundry and kitchen facilities and a lounge with a piano, a juice machine, internet access and an ATM machine. ~ 12 Hemenway Street; 617-536-9455, 888-467-8222, fax 617-424-6558; www.bostonhostel. org, e-mail bostonhostel@bostonhostel.org. BUDGET TO MODERATE.

The **YMCA** welcomes both male and female guests. Generously appointed, the YMCA has a comfortable wood-paneled lobby, an indoor pool, laundry facilities and cafeteria. But rooms are cell-like and furnished with Salvation Army–style furniture. Rooms are available from late June to early September. ~ 316 Huntington Avenue; 617-536-7800, fax 617-536-3240; www.ymcabos ton.org. BUDGET TO MODERATE.

The **Audubon Circle Restaurant Bar**, a sleek wood-paneled space, serves notable pub grub at an affordable price. The juicy hamburgers are arguably the best in the city, while the seared tuna could rival entrées in a more upscale dining establishment. No lunch on Saturday and Sunday. ~ 838 Beacon Street; 617-421-1910, fax 617-421-1911. BUDGET TO MODERATE.

You'll halfway expect the girl from Ipanema to stroll into **Buteco**, so Brazilian and laidback is it. Framed photos of Brazil line its white walls, and tables are simply set with oilcloth covers and fresh yellow primroses. A standout is the *feijoada*—the Brazilian national dish, a stew of black beans with pork, sausage and dried beef, served with rice (available on weekends only). There is also a wide variety of chicken and vegetarian dishes. Also try the homemade soups and desserts. No lunch on weekends. ~ 130 Jersey Street; 617-247-9508, fax 617-787-4357. BUDGET TO MODERATE.

The walls of **Bangkok Cuisine** look like those in a museum, lavishly covered with elaborate framed pictures of Thai motifs in gold leaf: a peacock, villagers with elephants, Buddhist figures. Warm orange lights and crystal-and-brass chandeliers add to the exotic flair. Entrées include deep-fried whole fish, hot and sour dishes, curry dishes, and rice and noodles. ~ 177-A Massachusetts Avenue; 617-262-5377, fax 617-247-1846. BUDGET TO MODERATE.

The music of psychedelic '60s groups, '50s jazzmen and other performers of yesteryear rules at **Looney Tunes**, where you can buy used records on the cheap. ~ 1106 Boylston Street; 617-247-2238.

On the border of Brookline and Fenway sits the **Boston Book Annex**, a fine purveyor of used books. With over 100,000 volumes in stock, this funky little shop is the perfect place to while away an afternoon. ~ 906 Beacon Street; 617-266-1090.

Avalon, one of the city's largest dance clubs, plays progressive and Top-40 sounds for avid dancers, and hosts top names like Eric Clapton and Prince. Closed Monday through Wednesday. Cover. ~ 15 Lansdowne Street; 617-262-2424; www.avalonboston.com, e-mail info@avalonboston.com.

Next door, one of the trendiest dance clubs is **Axis**, which features house and techno music. Monday is gay night, though a real mixed crowd turns out at both Axis and Avalon, especially on Friday, when the doors that separate the clubs are opened up. Closed Sunday, Tuesday and Wednesday. Cover. Gay-friendly. ~ 13 Lansdowne Street; 617-262-2437, fax 617-437-7147; www.axisboston.com.

The upscale **Karma Club** accommodates a number of musical tastes. On most nights, frenzied dance music pulsates through the club; "Mod Night" is the draw on Wednesday. You can swig martinis while listening to hip-hop in the Mambo Lounge. The dress code prohibits jeans, sneakers and hats. Closed Sunday through Tuesday. Cover. ~ 9 Lansdowne Street; 617-421-9595, fax 617-351-2562; www.karmanightclub.com.

Next door is **Bill's Bar**, which specializes in loud music of all kinds, and live performances six nights a week. Sunday features reggae, Wednesday is funk and Thursday showcases new music. Cover. ~ 5½ Lansdowne Street; 617-421-9678; www.billsbar.com.

A little farther out of the neighborhood is another club. **The Paradise** draws SRO crowds for its national headliners who perform live rock music and dance. Local bands also play here. Cover. ~ 967 Commonwealth Avenue; 617-562-8800.

CLASSICAL MUSIC & THEATER   The prestigious **Boston Symphony Orchestra** presents more than 250 concerts annually. ~ 301 Massachusetts Avenue; 617-266-1492; www.bso.org.

The Symphony's **Boston Pops**, with the youthful Keith Lockhart as conductor, perform lighter favorites in spring and free outdoor summer concerts at the Hatch Shell on the Esplanade.

The **Handel and Haydn Society** is the country's oldest continuously active performing-arts group, started in 1815. They perform instrumental and choral music, including Handel's *Messiah* at Christmas. ~ 300 Massachusetts Avenue; 617-266-3605; www.handelandhaydn.org, e-mail info@handelandhaydn.org.

The **Huntington Theatre Company**, Boston University's resident company, specializes in classics, comedies and musicals. There are no summer performances. ~ 264 Huntington Avenue; 617-266-7900; www.huntingtontheatre.org

▼▼▼▼▼▼▼▼▼▼▼▼

The South End

Boston's largest neighborhood is also the least known. Like the Back Bay, it was built on filled land, preceding Back Bay by more than a decade. Victorian brick rowhouses rose apace as residences for the middle class and well-to-do. Today, the South End is listed on the National Register of Historic Places as the largest concentration of such houses in the United States.

After the panic of 1873, banks foreclosed on the area, and those who could afford to moved to Back Bay. The area was carved up into rooming houses and factories and became an immigrant ghetto of more than 40 nationalities, notably black, Syrian, Latino and Lebanese.

The South End languished for decades, but when Boston's economy rebounded in the 1960s, so did this neighborhood. Since 1965, an influx of middle-class professionals has renovated old rowhouses and partly gentrified the area. Not all of the South End has risen again, however, and there are still blighted, unsafe areas. But today the neighborhood is a vital center of creative ac-

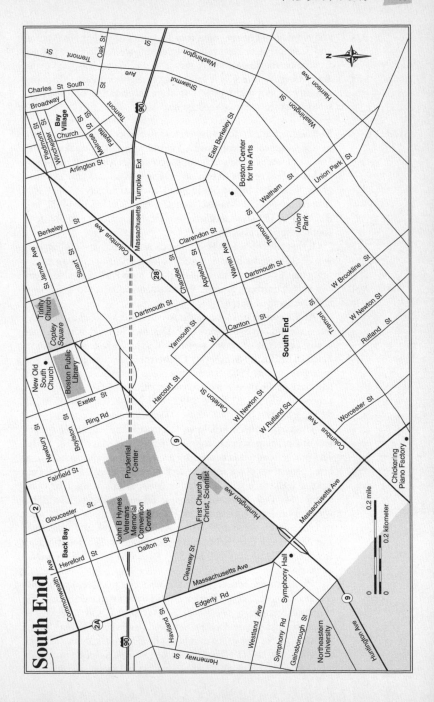

South End

tivity, and many artists live here. Fashionable shops, restaurants and nightclubs line the main thoroughfares of Columbus Avenue and Tremont Street, as well as Shawmut Avenue. The area along Columbus and Shawmut avenues between Massachusetts Avenue and Arlington Street is a largely gay neighborhood with many restaurants and nightclubs. For more information on this area, see the "Boston Gay Scene" below.

SIGHTS   The South End stretches hundreds of blocks, bounded roughly by the Southeast Expressway, Herald Street, the tracks of the MBTA's Orange Line and Huntington Avenue. Although the South End is a massive area to explore on foot, an annual house tour is given in October by the **South End Historical Society**. Call ahead. Admission. ~ 532 Massachusetts Avenue; 617-536-4445, fax 617-536-0735; www.southendhistoricalsociety.org, e-mail info@ southendhistoricalsociety.org.

If this part of South End reminds you of Beacon Hill, it's no wonder. The same hidden gardens and black iron grillwork decorate many facades. The oval-shaped **Union Park** resembles Beacon Hill's Louisburg Square. **West Rutland Square**, too, is a lovely little landscaped patch.

At the corner of Huntington Avenue and Massachusetts Avenue is the famous **Symphony Hall**. Designed in 1900, it's so acoustically perfect it's known worldwide as a "Stradivarius among halls." The Boston Symphony Orchestra celebrated its 100th anniversary here in 1981. Tours take place Wednesday and the first Saturday of the month from October through May. ~ 301 Massachusetts Avenue; 617-266-1492, 888-266-1200, fax 617-638-9436; www.bso.org.

The **First Church of Christ, Scientist** is the world headquarters of Christian Science, founded in 1879 by Mary Baker Eddy. The mother church is topped by an imposing dome and set in a brick pedestrian plaza with a reflecting pool designed by I. M. Pei. Take a walk through the echoing **Mapparium** in the Christian Science Monitor building, a unique 30-foot stained-glass globe with a footbridge through it, for a peek at how the world looked in 1935. Tours are available throughout the week and weekend; church services are also open to the public. ~ 175 Huntington Avenue; 617-450-2000, 800-288-7155, fax 617-450-3554; www. tfccs.com.

The **Boston Center for the Arts** operates the Cyclorama, the center of South End arts activity. Built in 1884 to exhibit a huge cylindrical painting, *The Battle of Gettysburg* (now in Pennsylvania), it's also where Albert Champion developed the spark plug. Its large rotunda hosts art exhibits, plays, festivals and an annual antique show. ~ 539 Tremont Street; 617-426-5000, fax 617-426-5336; www.bcaonline.org, e-mail info@bcaonline.org.

Also part of the Boston Center for the Arts is the **Mills Gallery**, which specializes in exhibits by Boston artists. These might include mixed media, sculpture and paintings, and are always intriguing. Closed Monday and Tuesday. ~ 549 Tremont Street; 617-426-8835, fax 617-426-5336; www.bcaonline.org.

Once second in size only to the U.S. Capitol, the building that formerly housed the **Chickering Piano Factory**, now a craft guild, has been a Boston landmark since 1853. The pianos made here until 1929 were played not only in Victorian drawing rooms but in the concert halls of Europe and South America. Founder Jonas Chickering was said to be just like his pianos: "upright, grand and square." The building now serves as living, work and exhibition space for artists, musicians and professionals. ~ 791 Tremont Street; 617-536-2622, fax 617-859-7794.

◄ HIDDEN

The **Berkeley Residence/YWCA** offers the most basic budget accommodations for women in the city. No men are allowed beyond the public areas. Rooms have twin beds with chenille spreads and floral decor, and bathrooms are down the hall. There are laundry facilities and a cafeteria. ~ 40 Berkeley Street; 617-375-2524, fax 617-375-2525; www.ywcaboston.org, e-mail rooms_berkeley@ywcaboston.org. BUDGET TO MODERATE.

LODGING

Ever since yuppies began moving into the South End in the 1970s and 1980s, restaurants have been springing up left and right, from small inexpensive cafés to upscale eateries.

DINING

Grillfish serves simple yet appealing seafood with a few surprises such as monkfish marsala and grilled mako shark. Glorious cathedral ceilings, sensuous wall murals, dimly lit chandeliers, and drip-laden candles behind a sturdy stone bar give the restaurant a casual, urban-gothic atmosphere. This is a popular bar stop for young professionals so expect a less-than-quiet dining experience on busy nights. ~ 162 Columbus Avenue; 617-357-1620, fax 617-357-1621; www.grillfish.com, e-mail info@grillfish.com. MODERATE.

> The first ever World Series was held in 1903 here in Beantown; the Boston Pilgrims (predecessor to the Red Sox) beat the Pittsburg Pirates in a best-out-of-nine series.

A popular, upscale eatery, **Icarus Restaurant** serves up contemporary American cuisine. There's a great bar to wet your palate, and appetizers to whet your appetite. Start with the parsnip soup or polenta with braised exotic mushrooms. The seasonal fare includes braised rabbit with porcini, leeks and red wine, pepper-crusted venison steak with pomegranate sauce, and halibut filet with stuffed lobster tail. Dinner only. ~ 3 Appleton Street; 617-426-1790; www.icarusrestaurant.com, e-mail greatfood@icarusrestaurant.com. DELUXE TO ULTRA-DELUXE.

Tourists will feel like a local insider at the **Franklin Cafe**, a warm, sophisticated eatery in the South End. The hearty, New

◄ HIDDEN

American menu may include polenta-crusted swordfish with carrot risotto, grilled sirloin with chive mashed potatoes and turkey meatloaf with fig sauce. The appetizers work well for a midnight snack (the café serves food until 1:30 a.m.). Come early or late—just nine tables, a small bar area and a no-reservations policy make the wait here ridiculously long during peak dinner hours (7 to 10 p.m.). Dinner only. ~ 278 Shawmut Avenue; 617-350-0010, fax 617-350-5115. MODERATE.

HIDDEN ▶   Don't look for silverware at **Addis Red Sea Ethiopian Restaurant**. A very African decor features authentic basketweave straw tables in a bright geometric pattern, low, carved wooden chairs, and paintings of African villagers. Platters of food cover the entire table surface. Ethiopian *injera* bread is served with chicken, lamb, beef and vegetarian dishes. The chef uses all-natural herbs and spices. No lunch on weekdays. ~ 544 Tremont Street; 617-426-8727; www.addisredsea.com, e-mail info@addisredsea.com. BUDGET TO MODERATE.

The heavenly scent of freshly baked pastries, breads, cakes and pies are the draw at **Garden of Eden**. This bakery/café was voted the Best of Boston neighborhood sandwich shop, serving scrumptious sandwiches (including the "Garden Of Eden" vegetarian sandwich) on copper-topped café tables. The full gourmet market proffers unique cheeses and pâté. ~ 571 Tremont Street; 617-247-8377, fax 617-247-8493. BUDGET.

Decorated in Christmas kitsch, Elvis busts and retro paraphernalia, the **Delux Cafe & Lounge** features a cheap, eclectic and tasty assortment of pub grub until 11:30 every night. The changing menu always features staples such as fish or sandwiches. Dinner only. Closed Sunday. ~ 100 Chandler Street; 617-338-5258. BUDGET TO MODERATE.

HIDDEN ▶   **Tim's Tavern**, a no-frills local watering hole, is known for its scrumptiously grilled half-pound burgers that satisfy a hearty appetite without a hefty tab. Steak, ribs, seafood and chicken sandwiches are also on the menu. Closed Sunday. ~ 329 Columbus Avenue; 617-437-6898, fax 617-437-1464. BUDGET TO MODERATE.

One of the South End's favorite breakfast and lunch hangouts is **Charlie's Sandwich Shoppe**. The walls are lined with photographs of satisfied patrons—local politicians, famous actors and jazz greats of decades past. Open early in the morning, it's a delightful place for homebaked muffins, pancakes, sandwiches, burgers and conviviality, since you'll be sharing a table. No dinner. Closed Sunday. ~ 429 Columbus Avenue; 617-536-7669; e-mail charlies@tiac.net. BUDGET TO MODERATE.

Anchovies is a tiny Italian restaurant with large wooden booths, murals on the walls and a bar that's very popular with the locals. The menu offers huge plates of pasta and homemade pizzas. ~ 433 Columbus Avenue; 617-266-5088. BUDGET.

The charming **Claremont Cafe** is a cozy neighborhood establishment featuring outstanding fare blending South American and Mediterranean cuisine. Entrées might include grilled marinated lamb chop with Tunisian coriander eggplant purée and braised cod with kalamata olives. The Claremont is also famous for its weekend brunch. Closed Sunday evening and Monday. ~ 535 Columbus Avenue; 617-247-9001; www.claremontcafe.com, e-mail tasty@claremontcafe.com. MODERATE TO DELUXE.

SHOPPING

You can find things to decorate your nest with at **Fresh Eggs**, a home-furnishings store that carries furniture and kitchen appliances. In addition it proffers high-end gifts handcrafted by local artists. Mexican church candles, astro resin frames, aluminum bottle stoppers, unique bath accessories and much more are sold here. Closed Monday. ~ 58 Clarendon Street; 617-247-8150, fax 617-247-2244.

Housed in an 1880 brownstone, **M. J. Berries** conveniently offers decorative advice on the spot, saving you the hassle of scheduling meetings and appointments. Along with immediate interior design consultation, it stocks flower-petal soaps from France, an extensive line of linens and furniture, and a number of other home furnishings. Closed Sunday and Monday. ~ 562 Tremont Street; 617-357-5055, fax 617-357-5204.

Candle holders, picture frames, journals and other familiar gift items receive inventive makeovers at **Tommy Tish**. Even the gift bags and wrapping paper are flecked with dried flowers. ~ 102 Waltham Street; 617-482-1111.

Right next door is **Bibelot,** an antique store stocked with decorative accessories, collectibles and handmade arts and crafts. Bring home one of many Italian vases from the '20s or '30s. Open Thursday and Saturday; extended hours in summer, but call ahead. ~ 106 Waltham Street; 617-426-8477.

◄ HIDDEN

NIGHTLIFE

Bob the Chef's Jazz Club serves up soul food with live jazz Thursday through Saturday. Closed Monday. Cover. ~ 604 Columbus Avenue; 617-536-6204; www.bobthechefs.com.

AUTHOR FAVORITE

Founded in 1947, **Wally's Café** has been showcasing local and national artists for decades. The crowded joint is everything an old-time jazz club should be—small, smoky, dark and host to lots of talented musicians, including plenty of students from the Berklee School of Music, which is just a few blocks away. ~ 427 Massachusetts Avenue; 617-424-1408.

At the **Delux Cafe & Lounge** the cool crowd consists of rockers and artists, both gay and straight. The decor is funky, the drinks are cheap and the music ranges from Frank Sinatra to the Sex Pistols. Closed Sunday. ~ 100 Chandler Street; 617-338-5258.

Boston Gay Scene

Boston's gay community is continually growing, and its collection of gay spots is always expanding. While gay activities and nightlife are found throughout Boston (like Back Bay and the Fenway), the highest concentration is found in the South End, one of the city's most diverse neighborhoods. Bounded by Columbus and Shawmut avenues, Arlington Street and Massachusetts Avenue, this area is home to an array of gay restaurants, cafés, bars and nightclubs.

SIGHTS

At the very northeast corner of the South End lies **Bay Village**, which used to be known as South Cove. This cluster of narrow little streets displays the most charmingly antique character in the area. Gaslights stand on the sidewalks outside these Victorian rowhouses decorated with black shutters and windowboxes, black iron grilled doorways and hidden, sunken gardens in backyards. ~ Bordered by Arlington, Tremont and Stuart streets and Charles Street South.

LODGING

Greater Boston Hospitality is a reservation service with dozens of bed-and-breakfast listings. It can help you find the perfect lodging in Boston, many of which are located in Back Bay, Beacon Hill and Cambridge. Gay-friendly. ~ P.O. Box 1142, Brookline, MA 02146; 617-277-5430, fax 617-277-7170; www.boston bedandbreakfast.com, e-mail info@bostonbedandbreakfast.com. BUDGET TO DELUXE.

A pretty streetside patio and stately brownstone facade greet guests of the **Newbury Guest House**. Besides its superb location on fashionable Newbury Street in the Back Bay, the restored 1882 inn offers 32 guest rooms with pine plank floors, high ceilings and reproduction Victorian furnishings. Some have bay windows, and all have private baths, televisions and telephones—rarities in a small inn. Continental breakfast included. ~ 261 Newbury Street; 617-437-7666, 800-437-7668, fax 617-670-6100; www.newburyguesthouse.com, e-mail nghdesk@aol.com. ULTRA-DELUXE.

Popular with gay visitors, **463 Beacon Street Guest House** also draws a mixed clientele. Twenty rooms, all equipped with a microwave and refrigerator, make this turn-of-the-20th-century brownstone an excellent value. The five-story walk-up also offers short-term lodging in Back Bay, business services and a laundry. ~ 463 Beacon Street; 617-536-1302, fax 617-247-8876; www.463bea con.com, e-mail info@463beacon.com. MODERATE TO DELUXE.

The circa-1860 **Oasis Guest House** caters to a gay crowd but all are welcome. Some of its 30 rooms feature antiques and queen-sized beds. Located on a quiet street in the Back Bay, the inn serves continental breakfast in the living room. ~ 22 Edgerly Road; 617-267-2262, fax 617-267-1920; www.oasisgh.com, e-mail oasis gh@tiac.net. MODERATE.

> If you're here for the world-famous Boston Marathon, bring a plastic bag and cut holes for your arms and head. You can wear it in the race if it's raining and then simply throw it away.

The **Chandler Inn** offers 56 clean, decently appointed rooms in blues and greens and oak furniture, with all the basic amenities. The bar is a popular gay hangout in the South End. ~ 26 Chandler Street; 617-482-3450, 800-842-3450, fax 617-542-3428; www. chandlerinn.com, e-mail inn 3450@ix.netcom.com. MODERATE TO DELUXE.

Also in the South End is the **Whitaker House Bed & Breakfast**, a well-run, friendly B&B. Housed in a 19th-century Victorian, the rooms are individually and beautifully decorated, walking that fine line between old-fashioned elegance and clutter. There's a common parlor room where you might run into Tucker the Golden Retriever (billed as a co-host) and you can browse their selection of guidebooks. A continental breakfast is served in the lovely kitchen or, if the weather permits, on the patio. All in all, a lovely place to stay. ~ 170 West Newton Street; 617-437-6464, fax 617-424-6833; www.whitaker-house.com, e-mail info@whitaker-house.com. DELUXE TO ULTRA-DELUXE.

DINING

Geoffrey's Cafe & Bar looks like a Parisian-style bistro with crimson walls, oversized French paintings and large picture windows looking out onto the street. Breakfast is served daily until 3 p.m. (4 p.m. on weekends), and there's a wide selection of gourmet salads, sandwiches and *tapas*. ~ 160 Commonwealth Avenue; 617-266-1122. BUDGET TO MODERATE.

At the top of the gay brunch scene is **Appetito**. The Sunday buffet includes eggs Benedict, fresh muffins, perfectly seasoned homefries, and cocktails. Reservations are recommended. ~ 1 Appleton Street; 617-338-6777, fax 617-338-1962. MODERATE.

The lesbian-owned **On the Park** is a cozy, casual American bistro that attracts both gay and straight diners with its tasty preparations of beef, seafood and poultry. Game hen stuffed with wild rice and apples, braised veal shank and mako shark are among the dishes to choose from. Dinner only; brunch on the weekends. Closed Monday. ~ 1 Union Park; phone/fax 617-426-0862. MODERATE TO DELUXE.

A local favorite for fresh, tasty food is the always-crowded **Jae's Café and Grill**. The health-conscious menu travels the Far East with selections from Korea, Japan and Thailand. Try the *kalbi* (marinated barbecued beef spareribs), crispy *pad thai* noodles or a sampling of tidbits from the downstairs sushi bar. Closed Sunday and Monday. ~ 520 Columbus Avenue; 617-421-9405, fax 617-247-6140; www.jaescafe.com. MODERATE TO DELUXE.

Gays and straights alike head over to **224 Boston Street** to nosh on sandwiches, pasta, pizzettas and salads in a lively setting. Entrées at this gay-owned restaurant include curried chicken stew; a combination of shrimp sausage, swordfish steak and salmon filet with shrimp beurre blanc; and honey-soy duck confit with butternut squash and smoked duck sausage. Dinner only. ~ 224 Boston Street, Dorchester; 617-265-1217, fax 617-825-4738. MODERATE.

SHOPPING   **We Think the World of You** is a great bookstore that carries mostly gay and lesbian titles. Come in to browse or pick up gift items like cards and music. They also have maps and information on local activities. ~ 540 Tremont Street; 617-574-5000.

Located downtown is **Calamus Bookstore**, which showcases books, videos, CDs and DVDs with a gay and lesbian theme. Look for the rainbow flag out front. ~ 92B South Street; 617-338-1931, 888-800-7300; www.calamusbooks.com.

NIGHTLIFE   For an old-style gay men's bar, head for **119 Merrimac** in the North End (they've been around since 1975). The management claims to foster "no glamour and no nonsense." For this reason, the bar attracts a slightly older crowd, but it's a friendly one. Dig out your leather and denim before you go. ~ 119 Merrimac Street; 617-367-0713; www.119merrimac.com, e-mail webmaster@119 merrimac.com.

For deejay-generated disco music in the theater district, gays head to **Chaps**. Women are also welcome at this high-energy club, which includes a separate lounge off the throbbing dancefloor. Cover. ~ 100 Warrenton Street; 617-695-9500.

The leather and Levi's crowd likes to cruise down to **The Boston Ramrod** in the Fenway. There's a special two-stepping night at this gay-only bar that also offers pool. If leather is not your scene, you can go dancing at the **Machine** (cover on weekends), which attracts all types. Cover Sunday. ~ 1254 Boylston Street; 617-266-2986, fax 617-536-1950; www.ramrodboston.com.

Club Café, an avant-garde social complex, attracts a primarily gay and lesbian crowd with its art deco style and amusing diversions. Down a few drinks in the video bar (located in the back) and catch live blues or oldies (and occasional cabaret acts) in the lounge from Thursday to Saturday. ~ 209 Columbus Avenue; 617-536-0966; e-mail clubcafe@aol.com.

Fritz, located in the Chandler Inn, is a casual gay sports bar that's usually crowded with regulars. ~ 26 Chandler Street; 617-482-4428.

You'll find buff bartenders, the latest deejay sounds and two dancefloors pulsating with sculpted bodies gleaming with sweat at **Buzz**, Boston's trendiest gay club. It's predominantly gay men on Saturday night, with a Friday-night crowd geared towards lesbians. ~ 67 Stuart Street; 617-267-8969; www.buzzboston.com.

Jacque's Cabaret has something for everyone, as long as you enjoy female impersonators mixed with your live rock. The clientele is diverse—gay, straight and lesbian couples and groups of gawkers. Cover. ~ 79 Broadway, Bay Village; 617-426-8902.

South Boston

Not to be confused with the South End, South Boston lies directly east of it. Despite its name, South Boston juts farther east into the Atlantic than any other point in the city, cut off from Boston by the Southeast Expressway and the Fort Point Channel. Everyone here calls it "Southie," especially the Irish who call it home.

The Irish poured into South Boston in the early 19th century, attracted by the work opportunities of the glass, iron and shipping industries. They stayed, and today this is the most predominantly Irish community in Boston, evidenced by the riotous St. Patrick's Day parade. The Irish are fiercely proud of their L Street Brownies, a local swim club that has won national publicity for swimming every day, even in January.

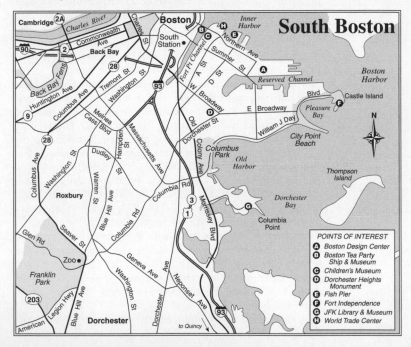

POINTS OF INTEREST
- **A** Boston Design Center
- **B** Boston Tea Party Ship & Museum
- **C** Children's Museum
- **D** Dorchester Heights Monument
- **E** Fish Pier
- **F** Fort Independence
- **G** JFK Library & Museum
- **H** World Trade Center

Though South Boston has historically been a conservative, family-oriented neighborhood, there has been a recent influx of young, single professionals to the area. Close to downtown with reasonably priced housing, this migration trend is sure to continue.

SIGHTS   Ideally positioned for shipping, the peninsula is lined with commercial fishing and shipping piers. The **Fish Pier**, near the World Trade Center and Jimmy's Harborside on Northern Avenue, is a lively scene at dawn, when the fishing boats return to port to unload their catch. The fresh catch is sold at a lively auction right off the boats to retailers.

Three bridges link South Boston with downtown: the Summer Street Bridge, the Northern Avenue Bridge and the Congress Street Bridge, with its Chinese lantern–style, wrought-iron lamps.

When you cross the Congress Street Bridge, you may not quite believe your eyes, but the first thing you'll see is a giant milk bottle. The 30-foot **Hood Milk Bottle** was a vintage lunch stand from the 1930s and sells snacks again today.

The Hood Milk Bottle signals the beginning of Museum Wharf, a mini-park of several museums. The **Children's Museum** is housed in a brick building, a former wool warehouse whose large windows and wool bays lend themselves nicely to exhibit spaces. You don't have to be a kid to enjoy this gigantic toy box filled with four floors of hands-on fun where you can make giant bubbles, scramble up a rock-climbing wall or participate in a play production at the interactive theater. There's also a water play exhibit that re-creates the Fort Point Channel. Admission. ~ 300 Congress Street; 617-426-6500, fax 617-426-1944; www.boston kids.org, e-mail info@bostonkids.org.

Also on Museum Wharf is the **Boston Tea Party Ship & Museum**, a floating museum where you can board a two-masted brig and throw your own chest of tea into the harbor (it'll be retrieved by an attached rope for another visitor to heave). Displays are lively and informative, explaining the events surrounding the 1773 dumping of 342 chests of tea overboard, a tax protest that was one of many spurs to the American Revolution. Closed January and February. The ship has suffered fire damage and is closed for renovations, so call ahead. Admission. ~ Congress Street Bridge; 617-338-1773, fax 617-338-1974; www.bostonteaparty ship.com, e-mail teapartyship@historictours.com.

A spanking white building with a flag-lined boulevard, the **World Trade Center** replaced the drab old Commonwealth Exhibition Hall in the 1980s. It hosts many of Boston's biggest trade shows, including the Boston Boat Show. ~ 200 Seaport Boulevard; 617-385-5000, fax 617-385-5491; www.wtcb.com, e-mail info@wtcb.com.

Four kinds of granite decorate the exterior of the **Boston Design Center**, New England's major design center. Architects and designers come here from miles away to search out the latest and chicest in interior designs. Outside the building stands an imposing cast of Auguste Rodin's sculpture *Cybèle*. Closed weekends. ~ 1 Design Center Place; 617-338-5062, fax 617-482-8449; www. bostondesign.com.

The work of painters, photographers, sculptors and others is on view at the **Fort Point Arts Community Gallery**. You can also visit individual artists' studios by appointment. Look for them along the 200 to 300 blocks on Summer Street. Many gallery showings are free and open to the public. Call for showings and times. Closed Sunday. ~ 300 Summer Street; 617-423-4299; www.fort pointarts.org, e-mail gallery@fortpointarts.org.

> More artists live in the old high-ceilinged, industrial buildings of the Fort Point Channel area than anywhere else in the city.

Dorchester Heights Monument is where George Washington set up his guns and forced the British to evacuate Boston in 1776, never to return. The British were astounded to see these guns, which had been dragged 300 miles by oxen from Fort Ticonderoga. A 215-foot marble tower marks the spot. The monument is open from mid-June to early September, Wednesday, Saturday and Sunday. ~ 456 West 4th Street; 617-242-5642, fax 617-367-3539; e-mail bost_email@ nps.gov.

Out at the very tip of South Boston, **Castle Island** is a windswept place of green lawns and high granite ramparts, a fine spot for picnicking and exploring. A series of eight forts has stood here since 1634, making it the oldest continuously fortified site in North America. The island was held by the British during the Revolution until Washington forced them out from his vantage point at Dorchester Heights. The current fort, the star-shaped **Fort Independence**, was built in 1851. ~ End of Day Boulevard.

On a peninsula just south of South Boston lies **Dorchester**, once the home of the country's oldest chocolate manufacturer, the Walter Baker Chocolate Factory, founded in 1780. Today Dorchester is a quiet, residential area known for its characteristic three-story houses called triple deckers.

Don't miss the **John F. Kennedy Library and Museum**, a stirring place to visit both inside and out. In a parklike setting by the ocean that JFK loved so well, the striking, glass-walled building was designed by I. M. Pei. The museum houses JFK's papers, photographs, letters and speeches, and personal memorabilia such as his desk and rocking chair, as well as an extensive exhibit on the former first lady, Jacqueline Kennedy. Also housed here are Ernest Hemingway's papers, which may be viewed by appointment. Admission. ~ Columbia Point, Dorchester; 617-929-4523, 877-616-4599, fax 617-929-4538; www.jfklibrary.org.

The **Franklin Park Zoo** was once rated one of the country's ten worst zoos by *Parade* magazine. It's made some dramatic improvements since then, most impressive of which is an African Tropical Forest. Inside the 75-foot-high bubble live tropical birds, antelopes, a pygmy hippo and gorillas, among other tropical denizens. You may also see snow leopards, lions and the Bongo Congo exhibit, as well as an exotic butterfly tent. Admission. ~ 1 Franklin Park Road, Boston; 617-541-5466, fax 617-989-2025; www.zoonewengland.com, e-mail cfisk@zoonewengland.com.

DINING

As you walk east on Northern Avenue, it becomes the Fish Pier, a crowded place of fish-processing plants and wharves. Not surprisingly, the Fish Pier is home to a spate of seafood restaurants, some of them among the city's finest.

Located right here on the Fish Pier, two of Boston's most famous restaurants, Jimmy's Harborside and Anthony's Pier 4, have waged a decades-long battle for supremacy in harborside seafood dining. Both eateries offer a long list of fresh fish, from Boston scrod to steamed, boiled or baked lobster, as well as floor-to-ceiling windows with smashing views of Boston Harbor.

Albanian immigrant Anthony Athanas started life in Boston as a shoeshine boy and built the reputation of his **Anthony's Pier 4** with backbreaking work. The smiling Anthony has posed with Liz Taylor, Red Skelton, Gregory Peck and Richard Nixon, whose photos gaze down from the walls. Despite its fame, Anthony's has its detractors, who say the seafood doesn't live up to its reputation, the expansive dining halls process guests like a factory and the wait for a table is too long. Still, Anthony's has the largest wine list in Boston, and there is outdoor seaside dining on yellow-awninged terraces. ~ 140 Northern Avenue; 617-482-6262, fax 617-426-2324; www.pier4.com, e-mail pier4@pier4.com. MODERATE TO ULTRA-DELUXE.

We much prefer **Jimmy's Harborside**, founded in 1924 by Greek immigrant Jimmy Doulos, the "Chowder King," whose first customers were fishermen at a nine-stool cafeteria. Since then, former President John F. Kennedy, his brother Bobby Kennedy, Tip O'Neill and Bob Hope have dined here, leaving their autographed photos on the wall. Today, Jimmy's grandson is the chef and his granddaughter runs the restaurant. The seafood is served in a nautical decor where the bar is a boat. No lunch on Sunday. ~ 242 Northern Avenue; 617-423-1000, fax 617-451-0669; www.jimmysharborside.com, e-mail jimmy@jimmysharborside.com. DELUXE TO ULTRA-DELUXE.

HIDDEN ►

Largely undiscovered, the cafeteria-style **International Food Pavilion** upstairs at the World Trade Center is one of the least expensive places to eat with a view in Boston. Grab a sandwich or slice of pizza to eat at the white tables overlooking the harbor. Breakfast and lunch. Closed weekends. ~ 200 Seaport Boulevard; 617-385-5611, fax 617-385-4001. BUDGET.

The **No-Name Restaurant** not only has no name, it has no decor either. Famed for the freshness of its fish bought right off the boats, the No-Name always has long lines, though we've had some complaints that the less-than-stellar service is a turn-off. ~ 15½ Fish Pier; 617-338-7539. BUDGET TO MODERATE.

SHOPPING

Looking for an Esther Williams swimsuit, a Doris Day nightgown or Stepford Wives cocktail dress? You're bound to find it at **Maude Mango Vintage Clothing**, whose owner has been rooting out one-of-a-kind fashions for years. ~ 507 East Broadway; 617-464-1180; www.maudemango.com.

NIGHTLIFE

A visit to **Lucky's Lounge** is like stepping back in time to Frank Sinatra's Vegas. Patrons sit at naugahyde booths and the long shiny bar, where they can order a whistle-wetting cocktail or a little nosh while enjoying the live entertainment Tuesday through Sunday. ~ 355 Congress Street at A Street; 617-357-5825.

Charlestown

Across the river but still considered part of Boston, Charlestown is an area that has become increasingly popular among the yuppie set. This is the oldest part of town. It was founded in 1630 by a small band of Puritans who later abandoned it, moving across the river to Boston. Much of Charlestown was destroyed by the British in the Battle of Bunker Hill, so few 18th-century houses stand today.

SIGHTS

A walk over the river on the Charlestown Bridge brings you to the Charlestown Navy Yard, the berth of the **USS Constitution**, the oldest commissioned vessel in the world. It won its nickname of Old Ironsides when British cannon fire bounced off its sturdy oak hull in the War of 1812. While you can tour the decks and down below, lines are always long; try going at lunchtime. ~ 617-242-5670, fax 617-242-2308; e-mail njps1@navtap.navy.mil.

A handsome black-and-white frigate, the USS *Constitution* once required 400 sailors to hoist its sails.

Across the yard from Old Ironsides is the **USS Constitution Museum**, which houses exhibits on Old Ironsides' many voyages and victories, memorabilia and paintings. ~ Charlestown Navy Yard, Building 22; 617-426-1812, fax 617-242-0496; www.ussconstitutionmuseum.org, e-mail info@ussconstitutionmuseum.org.

Nearby is the **Commandant's House**, a handsome Federal-style brick mansion where Navy officers lived. ~ Charlestown Navy Yard.

The **Bunker Hill Monument** actually stands atop Breed's Hill, where the Battle of Bunker Hill was in fact fought. This encounter became legend with the words of Colonel William Prescott to his ammunition-short troops: "Don't fire until you see the whites of their eyes." The cornerstone of the 221-foot Egyptian Revival granite obelisk was laid in 1825 by General Lafayette, with Daniel Webster orating. There are 294 steps to the observatory, which affords a magnificent view of the city and the harbor. ~ Monument Square; 617-242-5641, fax 617-241-2258; www. nps.gov/bost, e-mail bost_email@nps.gov.

Companion exhibits at the **Bunker Hill Pavilion** include a multimedia slide show with 14 screens re-enacting the battle. Closed December through March. Admission. ~ 55 Constitution Road; 617-241-7575, fax 617-241-4995.

DINING

Mention Charlestown to a Bostonian and chances are you'll find yourself at **Olives**. The food is New England with northern Italian and Mediterranean twists. Reservations are not taken for groups of fewer than six, so expect to wait for a table. Dinner only. Closed Sunday. ~ 10 City Square; 617-242-1999, fax 617-242-1333. DELUXE TO ULTRA-DELUXE.

> The first Boston Marathon took place in 1897 and had only 15 runners. The winner ran 24.8 miles in 2:55:10. Today, more than 13,000 participants aspire to break the current record: 2:07:15 for 26.2 miles.

Brought to you by the owners of Olive's, **Figs** offers a delectable selection of pastas, salads and wood-grilled pizzas. The modern rustic decor creates a homey, casual environment in which to load up on mushroom risotto, sweet-corn salad with fried parmesan polenta and chicken parmesan. Among the creatively topped pizzas are scallops, chicken sausage, and fig and prosciutto. Dinner only. ~ 67 Main Street; 617-242-2229, fax 617-242-1333. MODERATE.

The **Warren Tavern** dates to 1780, and the small, clapboard house with gaslights was patronized by Paul Revere and George Washington. The inside appears dark and Colonial, with a heavy beamed ceiling, wood-planked floors, candelabra wall sconces, punched-tin lights and a roaring fire. The solid fare includes steaks, seafood and a tavern burger with peddler fries. The tavern also makes homemade tavern chips. Lunch, dinner and weekend brunch. ~ 2 Pleasant Street; 617-241-8142, fax 617-242-0667; www.warrentavern.com, e-mail info@warrentavern. com. BUDGET TO MODERATE.

Outdoor Adventures

SAILING

Sailing the blue waters of the Charles on a breezy day with views of both the Boston and Cambridge skylines is an experience to be savored. **Community Boating** rents windsurfers, kayaks, sonars and more to visitors who pass a test and buy a two-day membership. Closed November through March. ~ 21 David G. Mugar Way; 617-523-1038; www.community-boating.org. You can charter captained sailboats at the **Boston Sailing Center**. Closed

November to mid-April. ~ 54 Lewis Wharf; 617-227-4198; www.bostonsailingcenter.com. Experienced sailors can rent 23- to 39-foot boats from the **Boston Harbor Sailing Club**. ~ Rose Wharf; 617-720-0049; www.bostonharborsailing.com.

Boston is within easy reach of Stellwagen Bank, a major feeding ground for whales. You can go whale watching from April through November with the **New England Aquarium**. ~ Central Wharf; 617-973-5200; www.neaq.org. **Boston Harbor Cruises** also offers day trips in the area around Stellwagen Bank. ~ 1 Long Wharf; 617-723-7800, 617-227-4321, 877-733-9425; www.bostonharborcruises.com. **A.C. Cruise Line**'s full-day whale-watching charters travel 30 miles out to sea to spot humpback and finback whales. Saturday and Sunday only. ~ 290 Northern Avenue; 617-261-6633, 800-422-8419; www.accruiseline.com. **WHALE WATCHING**

Jogging is very big in Boston, where half the population seems to be in training for the Boston Marathon. The most popular running paths are along both sides of the green strips paralleling the Charles River; these run more than 17 miles. For information, call **USA Track & Field**. ~ 2001 Beacon Street, Brookline; 617-566-7600; www.usatfne.org, e-mail office@usatfne.org. Another safe place to jog is **Breakheart Reservation**'s two- and three-mile paved roads. ~ 177 Forest Street, Saugus; 781-233-0834. **JOGGING**

Skaters have been tracing the curves of the lagoon in the Public Garden and the Boston Common's **Frog Pond** for more than a hundred years. Skate rentals are available. Closed March through October. Admission. ~ 617-635-2120. The Charles River is almost never frozen hard enough for skating, but **The Metropolitan District Commission** (MDC) maintains 20 public indoor rinks, some with rentals available. Closed mid-March to mid-November. Admission. ~ 617-727-5283; www.state.ma.us/mdc. **ICE SKATING**

  The **Skating Club of Boston** also has public skating and rentals. Call ahead for times and age restrictions. Admission. ~ 1240 Soldiers Field Road, Brighton; 617-782-5900; www.scboston.org.

Cross-country skiers have a number of options. The **Weston Ski Track** has a kilometer of gently sloping trails that are machine generated and run over a golf course; lessons and rentals (including snowshoes) are available. They operate from mid-December to mid-March. ~ 200 Park Road, Weston; 781-891-6575; www.ski-paddle.com, e-mail info@ski-paddle.com. The **Middlesex Fells Reservation** has a free six-mile trail, suiting a variety of skill levels, but you have to pay for the trail maps. ~ 4 Woodland Road, Stoneham; 781-662-5214. **Wompatuck State Park** has seven miles of fairly hilly cross-country trails, with free trail maps at the park headquarters. ~ Union Street, Hingham; 781-749-7160. **SKIING**

GOLF   You can tee up at numerous public courses. In Hyde Park, visit the 18-hole **George Wright Golf Course**. Designed by Donald Ross, the championship course rents carts and clubs. ~ 420 West Street; 617-361-8313. The par-5 **Presidents Golf Course** has 18 holes. Their signature 15th hole lands even the most experienced golfers in the water. ~ 357 West Squantum Street; 617-328-3444. The 18-hole **Braintree Municipal Golf Course** is closed January and February. ~ 101 Jefferson Street; 781-843-9781. The public **Newton Commonwealth Golf Course**'s second hole is a difficult par 5 around a creek on an elevated green. ~ 212 Kenrick Street, Newton; 617-630-1971. There are two 18-hole courses at the **Stow Acres Country Club**. ~ 58 Randall Road, Stow; 978-568-8106. A natural marsh surrounds the **Colonial Golf Club**'s course. Closed in winter. ~ 427 Walnut Street, Lynnfield; 781-245-9300.

TENNIS   The **Metropolitan District Commission** (MDC) maintains about 45 courts in the city and greater Boston. ~ 20 Somerset Street; 617-727-1680. Cambridge, too, has more than ten outdoor public courts. ~ Parks and Recreation: 617-349-6231.

There are numerous private clubs; one open to the public is the **Sportsmen's Tennis Club**, offering both indoor and outdoor courts. Fee. ~ 950 Blue Hill Avenue, Dorchester; 617-288-9092.

BIKING   Biking is popular around Boston's scenic waterways, including the Charles River, although we wouldn't recommend it in the narrow, congested downtown streets. The Charles River Esplanade, on the Boston side of the Charles River, has the well-marked, 18-mile **Dr. Paul Dudley White Bike Path**, which goes from Science Park through Boston, Cambridge and Newton, ending in Watertown. The **Stony Brook Reservation Bike Path** runs four miles through forests in West Roxbury/Hyde Park. ~ Turtle Pond Parkway, West Roxbury, Hyde Park; 617-698-1802. The **Mystic River Reservation** also has a nice bike path (3.5 miles) that runs from the Wellington Bridge in Somerville along the Mystic River to beyond the Wellington Bridge in Everett.

For information on area biking, contact the **Massachusetts Bicycle Coalition** (MassBike). ~ 59 Temple Place, Suite 669, Boston, MA 02111; 617-542-2453; www.massbike.org, e-mail bike info@massbike.org.

AUTHOR FAVORITE

If you're up for a really challenging bike route, try the 135-mile **Claire Saltonstall Bikeway**. The first segment runs from Boston to Bourne at the entrance to Cape Cod; continuing segments follow the Cape Cod Rail Trail all the way to Provincetown at the tip of the Cape.

Bike Rentals   Mountain bike and hybrid rentals (locks and helmets included) are available at the **Community Bike Shop**. ~ 496 Tremont Street; 617-542-8623. Near Copley Square, **Back Bay Bike and Board** rents mountain bikes, hybrids, cruisers and tandems and offers maps of trails. ~ 336 Newbury Street; 617-247-2336.

▼▼▼▼▼▼▼▼▼▼▼▼
Transportation

If you arrive in Boston by car, you'll have to watch closely for road markings; routes change numbers and names frequently. Also, roads will be tied up by a major project designed to construct a third harbor tunnel and to depress the Central Artery underground. This project, known as the "Big Dig," now has an estimated completion date of 2004. For more information on its current impact on traffic in the city, visit www.bigdig.com. No one in his right mind would want to bring a car to downtown Boston, where narrow, confusing streets are ruled by legendarily homicidal drivers. Save the car for touring the suburbs of Greater Boston or outlying areas.

CAR

From the north, **Route 95** follows a curving, southwesterly path to Boston, changing to **Route 128** as it forms a beltway around the city. **Route 93** runs directly north–south through Boston; its downtown portion is called the Central Artery, and it's known as the John Fitzgerald Expressway and the Southeast Expressway between Boston and Route 128 in Braintree. **Route 90**, the Massachusetts Turnpike, heads into and through Boston from the west. From the south, you can reach Boston by Route 95, **Route 24** or **Route 3**.

Logan International Airport, the busy and crowded main airport serving Boston, is two miles north of the city in East Boston. Numerous domestic and international carriers fly in and out of Logan, including Aer Lingus, Air Canada, Air France, Alitalia Airlines, America West, American Airlines, British Airways, Continental, Delta Air Lines, Icelandair, Lufthansa Airlines, Northwest Airlines, Qantas, Swissair, United Airlines, US Airways and Virgin Atlantic Airways. ~ www.massport.com.

AIR

Limousines and buses take visitors to numerous downtown locations, including **Carey Worldwide Chauffeur Services** (617-623-8700), **Commonwealth Limousine Service** (617-787-5575) and **Peter Pan Bus Lines** (800-237-8747).

You can also take the subway from the airport by taking a free Massport bus to the Blue Line stop. The slickest way to get downtown is to hop the **Airport Water Shuttle**, bypassing traffic altogether for a scenic seven-minute ride across Boston Harbor. ~ 617-330-8680.

Greyhound Bus Lines has bus service to Boston from all over the country. The main downtown terminal is at South Station. ~ 700

BUS

Atlantic Avenue; 800-231-2222; www.greyhound.com. **Bonanza Bus Lines** serves Boston from Cape Cod. ~ 700 Atlantic Avenue at South Station; 617-720-4110, 800-556-3815; www.bonanza bus.com. **Peter Pan Bus Lines** runs between Boston and New York, New Hampshire and Cape Cod. ~ 700 Atlantic Avenue; 800-237-8747; wwwpeterpanbus.com. **Concord Trailways** runs from points in New Hampshire and Maine only. ~ 700 Atlantic Avenue; 617-426-8080, 800-639-3317; www.concordtrailways.com.

TRAIN

Amtrak services many destinations from Boston including San Francisco, Chicago and New York. ~ South Station, Summer Street at Atlantic Avenue; 800-872-7245; www.amtrak.com.

CAR RENTALS

Parking grows scarcer and ever more expensive, and you can easily see Boston on foot, but if you must rent a car, you can do so in the airport terminal at **Alamo Rent A Car** (800-327-9633), **Avis Rent A Car** (800-831-2847), **Budget Rent A Car** (800-527-0700), **Dollar Rent A Car** (800-800-4000), **Hertz Rent A Car** (800-654-3131), **National Car Rental** (800-227-7368) and **Thrifty Car Rental** (800-367-2277).

Used-car rentals in the area include **U-Save Auto Rental** (617-254-1900) and **Adventure Rent A Car** (617-783-3825).

PUBLIC TRANSIT

Boston's subway system is operated by the **Massachusetts Bay Transportation Authority**, MBTA, popularly called the "T." The T has four lines, the Red, Blue, Green and Orange, which will get you almost anywhere you want to go quite handily. The basic fare is $1. Special multiple-day discount passes can be bought at many T stations and the visitor booths throughout the city.

The MBTA also operates a fleet of buses providing extensive coverage of Boston and Cambridge. Exact change is required for the 75-cent fare. ~ 617-222-3200; www.mbta.com, e-mail feed back@mbta.com.

TAXIS

Several cab companies serve Logan Airport, including **Boston Cab** (617-536-5010), **Cambridge Taxi Company** (617-492-1100), **Checker Cab** (617-497-1500) and **Town Taxi** (617-536-5000).

THREE

Outside Boston

Heady doses of history and higher education greet visitors to the small cities outside Boston. It's hard to exaggerate the importance to America of events that took place in Lexington and Concord on April 19, 1775. Although nobody knows who really pulled the trigger, "the shot heard 'round the world" was fired here that day to start the American Revolution. The two towns, where echoes of revolutionary battles can still be found beside bucolic fields, on village greens and in museums, lie within a half-hour's drive of Boston. Even closer, right across the Charles River from the city, stands Cambridge.

Everyone thinks of Cambridge and Boston together, as if they were two sides of the same coin. While Cambridge is actually a separate city, the lives of the two are very much entwined, linked by a series of foot and vehicular bridges.

Cambridge was founded in 1630, originally named New Towne, and was the colony's first capital. In 1638, two years after the founding of Harvard, the nation's oldest university, the city was renamed after the English university town where many Boston settlers had been educated. Contrasting with Harvard's ivy-covered brick eminence is the city's other major center of learning, the Massachusetts Institute of Technology, which moved across the river from Boston in 1916.

Today Cambridge remains very much an intellectual center, home to Nobel Prize winners, ground-breaking scientists and famous writers, among them John Kenneth Galbraith, David Mamet and Anne Bernays. It's a book-lover's paradise, with 25 bookstores in the Harvard Square area alone (see "Boston Area Bookstores" in Chapter Two). And Cambridge continues to be known as a site of progressive political activism.

During the 1960s and 1970s, Cambridge became the heart of what came to be nicknamed "Silicon Valley East" when high-tech companies blossomed here, as well as in outlying towns scattered along the Route 128 beltway. These think tanks and computer companies fueled a boom in the Massachusetts economy and population.

Originally, Cambridge held within its borders several villages, including the spot that's now Lexington. Along with nearby Concord, Lexington retains much of the rural flavor it had during the time of the Revolution. Surrounding the towns, cornfields lie across 17th- and 18th-century farms that are still intact. Nearby Walden Pond, although crowded with locals and tourists alike on hot summer days, reflects the spirit of Thoreau during its more peaceful moments.

But it's revolutionary history that draws most people to Lexington and Concord. Today you can visit Lexington Green, where the Minutemen gathered before the battle (when the captain commanded, "If they mean to have war, let it begin here"), and follow the path along Battle Road taken by the citizen-soldiers during that momentous day. Old stone walls, where Minutemen crouched and shelled the British with musket fire, still stand throughout the countryside.

The short journey from Boston to these now peaceful suburbs still pulls people back through the centuries, to the time of America's birth as an independent nation. Visiting them is well worth a day's sidetrip.

Cambridge

A university town since shortly after its 1630 founding, and the site of the only college in the Americas until nearly the 18th century, Cambridge remains a revered seat of learning worldwide. Nearly half of its 95,000 citizens are connected in some way to Harvard, M.I.T. or the smaller colleges that dot the city.

But not all of Cambridge is serious or intellectual. It's given life and vitality by throngs of young students, protesters handing out leaflets, cult followers and street musicians.

SIGHTS

The heartbeat of Cambridge is **Harvard Square**, where life revolves around the many bookstores, coffee shops, boutiques and newsstands. In the very center stands the **Out of Town Newspapers** kiosk, a Harvard Square landmark for many years, famous for its thousands of national and foreign periodicals. ~ 617-354-7777, fax 781-643-2622.

Right next to it you'll find the **Cambridge Office for Tourism**, which dispenses tourist information and walking maps. ~ 617-497-1630, fax 617-941-7736; www.cambridge-usa.org, e-mail info@cambridge-usa.org.

No one would come to Cambridge without taking a walk through **Harvard Yard**. A stroll of the yard's winding paths, stately trees, grassy quadrangles and handsome brick buildings is a walk through a long history of higher education. Seven U.S. presidents have graduated from Harvard.

Enter the main gate by crossing Massachusetts Avenue. On the right, you'll see **Massachusetts Hall**, built in 1718, the college's oldest remaining hall. In the quadrangle of the historic Old Yard, on the left, tucked between Hollis and Stoughton Halls, is a little jewel of a chapel. **Holden Chapel**, built in 1742, has blue gables decorated with scrolled white baroque cornices, ahead of its time in its ornateness.

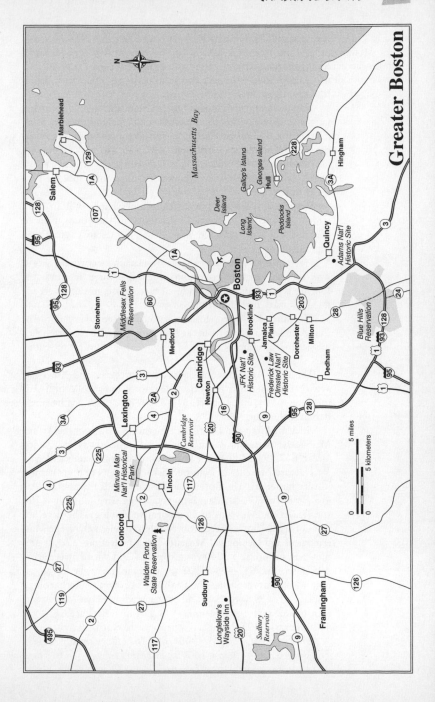

Greater Boston

Along the diagonal path that cuts across Old Yard is the **Statue of John Harvard** by Daniel Chester French, called the statue of the "three lies." Besides giving the wrong date for Harvard's founding, the statue is actually not of John Harvard at all, but of a student model instead; and John Harvard is not the college's founder but its first great benefactor.

Harvard's famed **Widener Library** stands in the New Yard, a massive building with a wide staircase and a pillared portico. With nearly three million books, Widener ranks as the third largest library in the United States, second only to the Library of Congress and the New York Public Library. Unfortunately, Widener is not open to the public, but its steps are still a popular spot for taking pictures.

Straight across from it is the **Memorial Chapel,** built in 1931 with a Bulfinch-style steeple in memory of the young men of Harvard who died in World War I. Their names are engraved on the walls.

Harvard is also home to a spate of museums known the world over for their esoteric collections, including three art museums (one fee is good for admission to all three museums; tours are offered Monday through Friday):

The **Busch-Reisinger Museum** is noted for central and northern European works of art from the late 19th and 20th centuries. Admission. ~ 32 Quincy Street; 617-495-2317; www.artmuseums. harvard.edu/busch.

The **Fogg Art Museum** showcases European and American artwork, with a particularly notable impressionist collection. Admission. ~ 32 Quincy Street; 617-495-9400; www.artmuseums. harvard.edu/fogg.

Ancient, Asian and Islamic art are the specialties at the **Arthur M. Sackler Museum.** Admission. ~ 485 Broadway at Quincy Street; 617-495-9400; www.artmuseums.harvard.edu/sackler.

Harvard Museum of Natural History consists of three natural history museums. The **Botanical Museum** holds the internationally famed handmade Glass Flowers, showcasing more than 700 species. At the **Museum of Comparative Zoology**, the development of animal life is traced from fossils to modern man. The **Mineralogical and Geological Museum** has a collection of rocks and minerals, including a 3040-carat topaz. ~ 26 Oxford Street; 617-495-3045, fax 617-496-8782; www.hmnh.harvard.edu, e-mail hmnh@oeb.harvard.edu. The **Peabody Museum of Archaeology** displays artifacts from the world over, including Mayan and American Indian relics. Admission. ~ 11 Divinity Avenue; 617-495-1027, fax 617-495-7535; www.peabody.harvard.edu.

Under the spreading chestnut tree/ The village smithy stands;/ The smith a mighty man is he/With large and sinewy hands. These words from Longfellow's famous poem "The Village Blacksmith" were written about a real blacksmith who lived in a house in Boston built in 1811. It's now the **Hi-Rise Pie Co.** with an outdoor café in warm weather and upstairs seating in cooler weather. Old World pastries and cakes are made here the same way they have been for decades. Brunch, lunch and afternoon tea are served. Closed Sunday. ~ 56 Brattle Street; 617-492-3003, fax 617-876-8761.

Harvard Lampoon Castle, a funny-looking building with a round brick turret and a door painted bright red, yellow and purple, befits its occupants: the publishers of Harvard's longstanding satirical magazine, the *Harvard Lampoon*. ~ 57 Mt. Auburn Street at Bow Street.

Christ Church Episcopal, a simple gray-and-white structure with a squat steeple, is Cambridge's oldest church. George and Martha Washington worshipped here on New Year's Eve 1775. ~ Zero Garden Street; 617-876-0200, fax 617-876-0201; www. cccambridge.org.

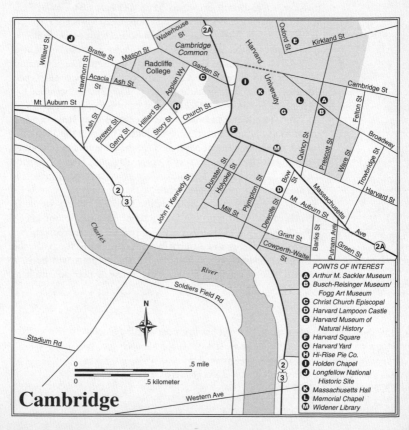

POINTS OF INTEREST
- **A** Arthur M. Sackler Museum
- **B** Busch-Reisinger Museum/ Fogg Art Museum
- **C** Christ Church Episcopal
- **D** Harvard Lampoon Castle
- **E** Harvard Museum of Natural History
- **F** Harvard Square
- **G** Harvard Yard
- **H** Hi-Rise Pie Co.
- **I** Holden Chapel
- **J** Longfellow National Historic Site
- **K** Massachusetts Hall
- **L** Memorial Chapel
- **M** Widener Library

Cambridge

Under an elm tree on the grassy **Cambridge Common**, General Washington took command of the Continental Army in 1775. A plaque and monument to Washington mark this spot. Nearby are three old black cannons, abandoned by the British at Fort Independence when they evacuated in 1776. ~ Massachusetts Avenue and Garden Street.

The **Longfellow National Historic Site** is where poet Henry Wadsworth Longfellow lived for 45 years and wrote most of his famous works. Painted a cheery yellow and accented with dark green shutters, the house was built in 1759 for a well-to-do Loyalist and years later was used by Washington as his headquarters during the siege of Boston. The house has many fine Victorian furnishings, among them Longfellow's desk, quill pen and inkstand. The house also contains Longfellow's personal 10,000-book library and his 600,000-piece collection of family papers. Closed Monday and Tuesday; closed December to mid-May. The site will be closed to the public until late 2002. Admission. ~ 105 Brattle Street; 617-876-4491, fax 617-497-8718; www.nps.gov/long, e-mail frla_superintendent@nps.gov.

A handsome, slate-blue Georgian house with black shutters, the **Hooper-Lee-Nichols House** was built by a physician named Richard Hooper. Later it was the home of Joseph Lee, a founder of Christ Church, and then the home of George Nichols. Open Tuesday and Thursday. Admission. ~ 159 Brattle Street; 617-547-4252, fax 617-661-1623; e-mail camhistory@aol.com.

The western end of Brattle Street is called **Tory Row** because of the lovely homes built there by wealthy Tories in the 18th century. A fine example is at Number 175, the **Ruggles Fayerweather House,** first the home of Tory George Ruggles, later of patriot Thomas Fayerweather. The house served as an American hospital after the Battle of Bunker Hill.

Just down the street sits **Radcliffe College**, once a women's branch of Harvard but now fully integrated into the university. The gates to **Radcliffe Yard** are entered off Brattle Street, between James Street and Appian Way. As you walk the path, the four graceful brick main buildings of the campus will be in a semicircle to your right. First is **Fay House**, a mansion built in

---

EXTRA! EXTRA!

The **Out of Town Newspapers** kiosk has been declared a National Historic Landmark. Set right in the middle of Harvard Square and surrounded by traffic, the kiosk carries more than 3000 newspapers and magazines from all over the world. ~ Zero Harvard Square; 617-354-7777, fax 781-643-2622.

1807, the administrative center. Next you'll find **Hemenway Gymnasium,** which houses a research center that studies women in society. Third is **Agassiz House,** fronted by white classical pillars, which holds a theater, ballroom and arts office. Last is the college's renowned **Schlesinger Library,** which contains an outstanding collection of books and manuscripts on the history of women in America, including papers of Susan B. Anthony, Julia Ward Howe and Elizabeth Cady Stanton.

A few miles east of Harvard Square lies Cambridge's other famous college, the **Massachusetts Institute of Technology** (M.I.T.). Offering a premier education in engineering and technology since 1865, M.I.T. draws students from all over the world, including China, Japan and Vietnam. In distinct contrast to the hallowed ways of Harvard, M.I.T. students are famed for their witty irreverence and contests they engage in to outdo each other in intellectual pranks. One of their episodes involved placing a car on top of a campus building. Fittingly, the campus looks modern and high-tech, with geometrical buildings designed by Eero Saarinen.

The **List Visual Arts Center** on campus is housed in a grid-   ◀ *HIDDEN*
like building designed by M.I.T. alumnus I. M. Pei. Its permanent collection includes work by artists such as Alexander Calder, Henry Moore, Pablo Picasso and Frank Stella. Closed Monday and the month of August. ~ 20 Ames Street; 617-253-4400, fax 617-258-7265.

Set in an office tower and shopping complex, the 293-room   **LODGING**
Charles Hotel is just steps away from Harvard Square. Rooms are styled in grays and blues, with Shaker-style beds, upholstered loveseats and armchairs, and oak armoires; many have views of the river. The gray-tiled bath has a second phone and TV along with pink-and-gray marble counters. There are two restaurants and one of the city's best jazz bars, as well as a health spa with steam room, sauna and whirlpool. ~ 1 Bennett Street at Eliot Street; 617-864-1200, 800-323-7500, fax 617-864-5715; www. charleshotel.com. ULTRA-DELUXE.

A convenient place to stay in Cambridge is the **Harvard Square Hotel.** Although some rooms are on the smallish side, this 73-room private hotel has nicely appointed digs with contemporary furniture and floral spreads. ~ 110 Mt. Auburn Street; 617-864-5200, 800-458-5886, fax 617-864-2409; www.theinnatharvard. com, e-mail reservations@theinnatharvard.com. DELUXE TO ULTRA-DELUXE.

The **Inn at Harvard** is wonderfully situated, only a couple blocks from Harvard Square. The label "inn" seems a little inappropriate, however, since it's more of a standard hotel (in fact, it's a Doubletree property). Even so, it has its charms: there's a wonderful atrium lobby area that's four stories high, open to balconies and guest rooms—very much like a Renaissance palazzo. The 113 rooms are well appointed with cherry furnishings and original artwork from the Harvard Fogg Museum. ~ 1201 Massachusetts Avenue; 617-491-2222, 800-458-5886, fax 617-491-6520; www.theinnatharvard.com, e-mail reservations@theinnatharvard.com. ULTRA-DELUXE.

Some of the least expensive, albeit plainest, accommodations are to be had at the **Irving House** near Harvard Square. This woodframe walk-up offers 44 plain but clean rooms. Your best bets are the top-floor units featuring skylights, private baths and wall-to-wall carpets. ~ 24 Irving Street; 617-547-4600, 877-574-4600, fax 617-576-2814; www.irvinghouse.com, e-mail reserve@irvinghouse.com. MODERATE TO DELUXE.

Mary Prentiss Inn was a country estate. Now, of course, it's in the middle of urban Cambridge, between the shopping areas of Porter and Harvard squares. The 20 rooms are spacious, many with high ceilings, working fireplaces and four-poster beds. All have private baths. ~ 6 Prentiss Street; 617-661-2929, fax 617-661-5989; www.maryprentissinn.com, e-mail njfandetti@aol.com. MODERATE TO ULTRA-DELUXE.

The stepped, pyramidal walls of the **Hyatt Regency Cambridge** sit right on the banks of the Charles River, offering splendid views of the Boston skyline from many rooms. The 14-story atrium lobby has a semitropical feeling, from the Australian finches in a glass cage to a large fountain and towering potted plants and trees. Lighted glass elevators whoosh you up through the atrium, past a trompe l'oeil mural of an Italian villa and a 100-foot-high glass wall. The 469-room hotel has two restaurants, a lap pool and a health club with sauna, whirlpool and steam bath. The fair-sized rooms have natural woods, contemporary furnishings and carpeting, plus marble vanities in the bathroom. ~ 575 Memorial Drive; 617-492-1234, 800-233-1234, fax 617-491-6906; www.hyatt.com. DELUXE TO ULTRA-DELUXE.

HIDDEN ►

A 20-minute walk from Harvard Square, **A Cambridge House, Bed & Breakfast Inn** is a special place to stay. A private home built in 1892 with a wide pillared porch, it's listed on the National Historic Register. Beautifully restored and richly furnished with floral print fabrics, patterned wallpapers, period antiques and oriental rugs, the living room and den offer guests luxurious spaces. Each of the 15 rooms is individually decorated with antiques and has a private bath. The room we saw had a canopied bed with a white lace duvet and a working fireplace. A full breakfast is complimentary, as are the evening hors d'oeuvres. Homemade brownies, cookies and fresh fruit are always available. No children under seven allowed. ~ 2218 Massachusetts Avenue; 617-491-6300, 800-232-9989, fax 617-868-2848; www.acambridgehouse.com, e-mail innach@aol.com. DELUXE TO ULTRA-DELUXE.

DINING

A retrofit, '50s-style decor of diner stools, neon and a black-and-white-tiled floor enlivens the **East Coast Grill & Raw Bar**. The Southern grilled ribs, pork and chicken are served with coleslaw, baked beans, corn bread and watermelon, and hot drinks to match: blue, green and gold margaritas. Grilled seafood with a tropical twist are other specialties. Appetizers are equally muscular, notably the "sausage from hell." Dinner only except for Sunday brunch. ~ 1271 Cambridge Street; 617-491-6568; www.east coastgrill.net, e-mail ecgrill@aol.com. MODERATE TO DELUXE.

It would be hard to find a friendlier place than the **Casa Portugal**, one of only a handful of Boston Portuguese restaurants. Imbibe the Latin mood set by black iron lanterns, red-vested waiters and folk-art murals of bullfights and musicians. *Chourico* arrives in a small flaming grill, followed by spicy dinners of marinated pork cubes with potatoes or mussels, *linguiça* and onions, and squid stew, all served with thickly cut Portuguese french fries. There's a good selection of Portuguese wines and beers, and espresso and cappuccino to top it all off. ~ 1200 Cambridge Street; 617-491-8880, fax 617-354-6832. MODERATE TO DELUXE.

Look for some 20 artworks from the Arts on the Line Project at the Harvard, Porter, Davis and Alewife T stations.

At **Magnolia's Southern Cuisine**, chef John Silverman, a former student of Cajun master chef Paul Prudhomme, serves up Southern-inspired creations like fried green tomatoes with tomatillo salsa and cool shrimp with hot herb vinaigrette. You can also order blackened tuna, grilled duck with orange-chipotle sauce, sweet-potato pecan pie and praline parfait. Dinner only. Closed Sunday and Monday. ~ 1193 Cambridge Street; 617-576-1971; www.magnoliascuisine.com, e-mail info@magnoliascuisine.com. MODERATE TO DELUXE.

The family-owned **La Groceria Italian Restaurant** looks like an Italian trattoria, with its striped awning, lattice ceiling and exposed brick wall. Famed for its hot antipasti and homemade pasta, La Groceria does old-style Southern Italian dishes such as lasagna, eggplant parmigiana and a seafood marinara that must be eaten to be believed. Its splendid dessert case offers cannoli, *tartufo* and *tiramisu*. ~ 853 Main Street; 617-876-4162, fax 617-864-9566; www.lagroceriarestaurant.com, e-mail lagroceria@ aol.com. MODERATE.

African folk art hangs on the walls of the green, black and white dining room of **Asmara**, one of the many Ethiopian eateries in Greater Boston. Chicken, lamb, beef, fish and vegetarian entrées are to be eaten without silverware, in the Ethiopian manner. ~ 739 Massachusetts Avenue; 617-864-7447, fax 617-628-0663. BUDGET TO MODERATE.

Upstairs at the Pudding is located at the home of a Harvard institution: the Hasty Pudding Club and Theatricals. The restau-

Text continued on page 114.

A Taste
of Somerville

Just a couple of miles northeast of Harvard Square and closer to downtown than most of Boston, Somerville—the town once known as "Slummerville"—has attracted an influx of Cambridge intellectuals, artists and young professionals trying to escape the throng of the city. And who's to blame them? This vibrant and diverse community provides a prime location, convenient access to the T, affordable housing and a plethora of hip eateries and clubs.

DINING   Just over the Cambridge–Somerville line, in a somewhat scruffy neighborhood, **Dalí** is as flamboyant as the artist it's named after. Who would've guessed that inside this vibrant blue building awaits the best Spanish food in the metropolitan area. The interior, radiant with red hues, is eccentrically decorated (the clothesline here is strung with undergarments donated by patrons). Make a meal of several different *tapas* and a bottle of hearty Iberian wine, or dig into entrées such as braised rabbit, *paella*, and shellfish stew. Dinner only. ~ 415 Washington Street; 617-661-3254; www.dalirestaurant.com, e-mail melon@concentric.net. MODERATE TO ULTRA-DELUXE.

Comfortable is the key at **eat**, where comfort food is served in a friendly, homey dining room decorated with warm lighting and mismatched tableware. The walls even bear childhood pictures of staff members. Expect such entrées as pan-seared wolf fish with lobster risotto and grilled ribeye steak with roast potatoes and Swiss chard. Dinner only. ~ 253 Washington Street; 617-776-2889; www.eatrestaurant.com. DELUXE.

Diesel Cafe is best known for its caffeinated menu, which features such jolts as the "Solid Six," six shots of espresso straight up. The café also has sandwiches, soups, salads and pastries. Two pool tables in the back make for a local hang-out. ~ 257 Elm Street; 617-629-8717. BUDGET.

Sample Southern hospitality along with barbecue ribs, chicken, fried catfish and all the fixin's at **RedBones**. Colorful paintings create a bright and airy atmosphere at this split-level restaurant. A full bar keeps several microbrews on tap. ~ 55 Chester Street; 617-628-2200, fax 617-625-5909; www.redbones.com. BUDGET TO MODERATE.

SHOPPING Black and Blues is the place to go before a night on the town. This small boutique specializes in trendy garb for a night out, though you will also find plenty of casual sweaters, T-shirts and jackets. While most of the clothing is new, there are vintage Levi's and leather coats. ~ 89 Holland Street; 617-628-0046.

NIGHTLIFE Davis Square represents the center of Somerville's nightlife scene. The **Somerville Theater**, at the corner of Holland Street and Dover Street, is a 1914 National Historic Landmark that shows second-run movies for $5.75 and doubles as a venue for popular traveling acts like the String Cheese Incident, Richie Havens and Rockapella. ~ 55 Davis Square; 617-625-5700.

Nearby, **Johnny D's Uptown Restaurant & Nightclub** presents excellent local and national rock, blues, jazz, funk, reggae and other acts every night of the week. From 4:30 to 6:30 p.m., everything on the main menu is half-price. Reservations recommended for a combination of show and dinner. Cover. ~ 17 Holland Street; 617-776-2004, 617-776-7450 (concert schedule); www.johnnyds.com.

Also in Davis Square, **The Burren** is a restaurant and pub that hosts authentic traditional Irish folk, rock and pop music. There's dancing in the back room. ~ 247 Elm Street; 617-776-6896, fax 617-776-3466.

Tír na Nóg is the quintessential small Irish watering hole with live music, a few small tables and tasty pub grub. ~ 366A Somerville Avenue; 617-628-4300, fax 617-628-1245.

rant offers one of the top contemporary American dining experiences in Greater Boston. The à la carte menu selections include fresh local seafood, rack of lamb and venison. The restaurant is currently closed while a move to a (nearby) location is planned. ~ 10 Holyoke Street; 617-864-1933, fax 617-864-4625; www. upstairsatthepudding.com, e-mail mail@upstairsatthepudding. com. DELUXE TO ULTRA-DELUXE.

HIDDEN ► Run by a group of transplanted Londoners, **Shay's** is a fairly authentic English-style pub right in the heart of Crimson territory, with a good selection of international draft beers and pub grub. ~ 58 John F. Kennedy Street; 617-864-9161. BUDGET.

The **Algiers Coffeehouse** is one of Cambridge's most bohemian eateries. With its 50-foot domed ceiling, white stucco walls and copper embellishments, it feels like a cross between a Moroccan palace and a mosque. The menu has a Middle Eastern flavor, with lentil falafel and *baba ganoosh*. There are 16 kinds of coffees and hot beverages, teas, iced drinks and Arabic pastries. ~ 40 Brattle Street; 617-492-1557. BUDGET.

The café/bar area and dining room of **Casablanca** sport murals of Rick, Ilsa and the rest of the "As Time Goes By" gang. The Mediterranean flavor continues with several exotic seating options in the café—the "love baskets" curve up to form a roof and a cocoon-like feeling. For the most part, the food is quite good. The lunch and dinner menus include lots of steak, seafood, lamb and beef dishes. ~ 40 Brattle Street; 617-876-0999, fax 617-661-1373. MODERATE TO DELUXE.

HIDDEN ► Tucked a few blocks away from busy Harvard Square, **Café Pamplona** is a tiny basement-level café that serves Spanish dishes, pastries and strong coffee. During the summer, there are a few tables outside on a brick patio. ~ 12 Bow Street; no phone. BUDGET.

Another worthwhile Southwestern restaurant, the **Border Cafe** is especially popular with Harvard students. Right in Harvard Square, the menu features Cajun, Tex-Mex and Caribbean specialties. Don't go if you're looking for a quiet place to talk, however. It's a noisy, party-like environment every evening. ~ 32 Church Street; 617-864-6100, fax 617-868-8261. BUDGET TO MODERATE.

SHOPPING Harvard Square offers a wealth of shopping, from eclectic boutiques to upscale chain stores. Most notable in this intellectual bastion are the many bookshops surrounding the square. (See "Boston Area Bookstores" in Chapter Two.)

The **Harvard Coop** holds three floors of men's and women's clothing, computer software, games and toys, and an astonishing selection of art prints, posters and books. The Coop (pronounce it as in "bird coop" to avoid student ridicule) was formed in 1882 by several Harvard students as a cost-saving measure. ~ 1400 Massachusetts Avenue; 617-499-2000, fax 617-441-2814.

The Harvard Square annex of the **Globe Corner Bookstore** is a beautiful, bright shop that's tucked into a quiet corner behind the Harvard Coop. There's a high percentage of travel books here as well as plenty of guides to the immediate area. ~ 28 Church Street; 617-497-6277, 800-358-6013; www.globecorner. com, e-mail info@gcb.com.

Wordsworth Books is Mecca in book-crazy Cambridge. Most locals check here first when they need to find a specific book. What's more, prices are discounted, browsing is expected and they're open late. ~ 30 Brattle Street; 617-354-5201, 800-899-2202. A children's bookstore, **Curious George Goes to Wordsworth Books,** is located around the corner. ~ 1 JFK Street; 617-498-0062.

Jasmine Sola is your best source for up-to-the-minute shoes that are wearable as well as fashionable. The accessories selection is extensive, too, particularly the wall stocked full of women's hosiery. They also have huge gift and jewelry departments. ~ 39 Brattle Street; 617-354-6043, fax 617-547-2057.

> Christmas wasn't a legal holiday in Massachusetts until 1856. Residents made up for lost time, however, by implementing the tradition of sending holiday cards.

Colonial Drug is like a European perfume shop, with more than a thousand kinds of fragrances. Closed Sunday. ~ 49 Brattle Street; 617-864-2222.

New Words, A Women's Bookstore carries new and used books by and about women. Along with a selection of children's books, they stock magazines and newspapers, music, jewelry, posters, T-shirts and cards, and sponsor a live reading series. ~ 186 Hampshire Street; 617-876-5310; www.newwordsbooks.com, e-mail newwords@world.std.com.

The products of Cambridge-area artists are for sale at the **Cambridge Artists Cooperative,** a treasure trove of whimsical and beautiful things: handmade paper, fiber animals, raku bowls, quilts and handpainted silk scarves. ~ 59-A Church Street; 617-868-4434; www.cambridgeartistscoop.com, e-mail info@cambridge artistscoop.com.   ◄ *HIDDEN*

Little Russia sells authentic Russian lacquered boxes and nesting dolls, jewelry, illustrated Russian fairy tales and other diverse tchotchkes. ~ 99 Mt. Auburn Street; 617-661-4928.   ◄ *HIDDEN*

Over in the Porter Square area, you will find **Iris**, with all sorts of handmade items that are reasonably priced, unusual and very creative. The pieces showcased are primarily by American artists. ~ 1782 Massachusetts Avenue; 617-661-1192, 800-869-1226; www.irisgifts.com, e-mail irisstore@earthlink.net.

Urban Outfitters features two floors of ultracool home furnishings, clothing and jewelry. Downstairs, there's a great bargain basement. ~ 11 John F. Kennedy Street; 617-864-0070.

If you're a knitter, you'll enjoy **Woolcott & Co.** There are enormous binders full of carefully organized patterns and helpful staff members who are accustomed to talking novices through knitting traumas. ~ 61 John F. Kennedy Street; 617-547-2837.

Located by Radcliffe College, **European Country Antiques** is a direct importer of antiques from England, Ireland and France, as well as a good place to look for high-quality reproductions. The owner is always happy to offer his advice. ~ 146 Huron Avenue; 617-876-7485; www.eccountryantiques.com.

In the M.I.T. neighborhood, urban trendsetters and conventional dressers alike appreciate the **Garment District**, where you can pick up the vintage '60s and '70s clothing as well as more traditional officewear. Downstairs is a room full of clothes for $1.50 a pound. ~ 200 Broadway; 617-876-5230.

Whether you're looking for estate jewelry or a Wonder Woman action figure, try the **Cambridge Antique Market**. Over 150 dealers operate out of this four-story building, where elegant furniture sits side by side with retro decorative pieces. Closed Monday. ~ 201 Monsignor O'Brien Highway (Route 28); 617-868-9655.

NIGHTLIFE   **Grendel's Den Restaurant and Bar** is a comfy pub in the basement of Grendel's Restaurant, with brick walls, plank floors, and a bar you can really lean on. Sunday brunch is served on the outdoor patio in good weather. ~ 89 Winthrop Street; 617-491-1160, fax 617-661-4107.

One of the best jazz showcases in Greater Boston, the **Regattabar** offers an intimate jazz experience in a sophisticated club environment. The Regattabar regularly features such headliners as Wynton Marsalis, Herbie Hancock and Sonny Rollins. Cover. ~ Charles Hotel, 1 Bennett Street; 617-661-5000, 617-876-7777 (performance schedule and tickets), fax 617-864-5715.

Since 1969, **Club Passim** has been going strong as a showcase for acoustic folk performers, including Tracy Chapman, Jimmy Buffett and David Bromberg, in a clean-cut, no-alcohol basement coffeehouse. Reservations for performances are suggested. Cover. ~ 47 Palmer Street; 617-492-7679; www.clubpassim.com, e-mail staff@clubpassim.com.

Harvard's professional theater company, **American Repertory Theatre** produces world premieres and classical works, often taking a nontraditional approach. Their **New Stages** initiative mounts innovative productions in more intimate venues throughout Cambridge and Boston. ~ 64 Brattle Street; 617-547-8300 (box office), 617-495-2668; www.amrep.org, e-mail info@amrep.org.

Scullers is in an unlikely place—on the second floor of the Doubletree Guest Suite Hotel in one of the uglier buildings along the Charles. Don't let the location or the architecture dissuade you—this classy jazz club (with a terrific view of the Charles, by the way) has big-name acts. Cover. ~ 400 Soldiers Field Road, Brighton; 617-562-4111; www.scullersjazz.com, e-mail jazzclub@doubletreeboston.com.

The **Plough and Stars** is that rare thing, an uncorrupted working-class bar where habitués are logo-capped, burly types who belly up for live, boisterous entertainment. Black-and-white caricatures of neighborhood regulars line a whole wall. Cover Friday and Saturday. ~ 912 Massachusetts Avenue; 617-492-9653, fax 781-641-1966.

You never know what you'll hear on open-mic nights (Sunday through Wednesday) at the **Cantab Lounge**, but the rest of the time it's soulful rhythm-and-blues or bluegrass bands in a let-it-all-hang-out playpen. Cover except on Monday and Tuesday. ~ 738 Massachusetts Avenue; 617-354-2685.

For the last several years, the coolest area in metro Boston has been in Cambridge—Harvard Square's scruffy cousin, Central Square, which is about two-thirds of the way down Massachusetts Avenue from Harvard to M.I.T. *The* nightspot in this haven of coolness is **The Middle East,** which has three venues for live music: Upstairs, Downstairs and the Corner. There's a mix of music and clientele here—from Michelle Shocked to Yo La Tengo, for example, as far as national acts go—and you're as likely to see underage high school (and college) kids as graying rock fans. Cover on most nights. ~ 472–480 Massachusetts Avenue; 617-492-1886; www.mideastclub.com, e-mail upstairs@mideastclub.com.

The **Green Street Grill at Charlie's Tap** is to Cambridge as the Bull & Finch was to Boston before *Cheers.* The friendly bartenders at this local watering hole can pour an honest pint of Guinness or mix a mean martini for the diverse crowd that frequents the well-lit bar. Entertainment ranges from live rock and

AUTHOR FAVORITE

When I'm in the mood for blues I know just where to head. Located a couple of blocks from Harvard, the original **House of Blues** looks more like a home on the bayou than a successful restaurant and club. Though several larger clubs in this chain have sprouted up all over the country, the Cambridge venue maintains its genuine Southern feel. The intimate stage offers national acts nightly. Bring the family to the Sunday gospel brunch and you'll find yourself breaking into song. Reservations recommended. ~ 96 Winthrop Street; 617-491-2583, 617-497-2229 (box office); www.hob.com, e-mail hobmarketca@postman.hob.com.

jazz on most nights to comedy and even live magic shows. ~ 280 Green Street; 617-876-1655, fax 617-492-7944.

An industrial dance club with a flair for art, **Man Ray/Campus** serves up progressive and alternative music. Wednesday is goth night and Thursday is gay night. Creative attire is encouraged, but when in doubt wear black. Cover. ~ 21 Brookline Street in Central Square; 617-864-0400; www.manrayclub.com.

TT the Bear's Place is another *très*-cool place to hear good live music in Central Square. The low ceilings and paintings showcased on purple and mauve walls make for a hip atmosphere. Past performers include Sunvolt, Smashing Pumpkins and the Indigo Girls. There isn't much dancing, just lots of listening by people who make a habit of following Boston's hopping music scene. Cover. ~ 10 Brookline Street; 617-492-2327, 617-492-0082, fax 617-661-6752; www.ttthebears.com.

Named for the carved wooden amphibians overlooking the bar, **Toad** teems with music lovers of all ages enjoying live bands seven nights a week. Aimee Mann (formerly of 'Til Tuesday) has even been spotted in this tiny no-cover hotspot. ~ 1920 Massachusetts Avenue; 617-497-4950, fax 617-497-7950.

Pat Metheny got his start at **Ryles**, which features nightly jazz, rhythm-and-blues, Latin music and Big Band nights in a casual atmosphere. Closed Monday. Cover. ~ 212 Hampshire Street; 617-876-9330; www.rylesjazz.com.

PARKS

HIDDEN ▶

MIDDLESEX FELLS RESERVATION 🏃 🚴 🏇 🛶 ⛵ "Fells" is a Scottish word meaning wild, hilly country, which aptly describes the 2000-plus-acre terrain of this reservation. These rugged highlands were first explored in 1632 by Governor Winthrop, first governor of the Massachusetts Bay Colony. They were acquired as public parkland in 1893, and a 19th-century trolley line brought in droves of picnickers. The region has been used for logging, granite quarrying, ice harvesting and water power for mills that manufactured the first vulcanized rubber products. Fifty miles of hiking trails and old woods roads run through the Fells. For anglers, Fellsmere, Doleful, Dark Hollow and Quarter Mile ponds hold sunfish, catfish, perch, pickerel and bass. Horses are allowed, though there are no stables. Biking trails are seasonal. Facilities include picnic areas, a skating rink and a swimming pool. ~ Six miles north of Boston, off Exits 33 and 34 from Route 93; 617-727-5380, fax 617-727-8228.

Outlying Areas

Although many tourists never leave the bounds of Boston and Cambridge, there is much of interest in the surrounding towns, many of which serve as bedroom communities for Boston workers and have rich colonial histories, too.

Hiking Boston's Backroads

Scant miles outside the urban clatter of downtown Boston, Massachusetts turns to rolling green hills, river valleys and pine and hardwood forests. A surprising number of parks and wildlife sanctuaries are to be found in these rural country towns, where you can hike scenic trails, short or long.

Quincy Quarries Footpath (2.5 miles) leads past steep quarry walls, the first commercial railway in America and an 1898 turning mill, used to cut and polish the Quincy granite columns and slabs that went into many famous buildings in America.

The main path at **World's End** (4.5 miles) winds uphill and down over a little peninsula extending north from Hingham into Massachusetts Bay. Its beautifully landscaped, gently curving roads were laid out by famed landscape architect Frederick Law Olmsted for a housing development that was never built. The wide, grassy path meanders through meadows and marshland, past rocky glacial drumlins, through avenues of English oaks, pine and red cedars, and up a steep knoll, where your reward is a knockout view of the Boston skyline, one of the best on the South Shore.

The **Ponkapoag Trail** (3.5 miles) in the Blue Hills Reservation circles Ponkapoag Pond, passing through wetlands and a golf course. From it, the Ponkapoag Log Boardwalk crosses a floating bog, filled with highbush blueberries, blue flag iris and Atlantic white cedar.

Little known and little used, Stony Brook Reservation allows you to walk in solitude among peaceful woods along the **Bearberry Hill Path** (3 miles). The trail leads into the woods toward Turtle Pond, then returns via the east boundary asphalt bicycle path leading past a swampy thicket and a golf course.

The **Skyline Trail** (6.8 miles), in the Middlesex Fells Reservation, is a strenuous trail that climbs many rocky knobs running between two observation towers. Scenery varies considerably along the way, from a pond with water lilies and frogs to volcanic-rock hills, wild hardwood forests, an old soapbox derby track, carpets of Canada mayflower and swampy areas.

Although you will be accompanied by crowds of others, you can walk the shores Thoreau walked at **Walden Pond** in Concord. A 1.7-mile circuit trail winds through woods along the crystal-clear waters of the pond. At the cabin site where Thoreau lived for two years, travelers from all corners of the globe have piled up stones in memoriam.

SIGHTS Due west of the city and bordering the Fenway, **Brookline** is one of the more prestigious and wealthy residential surrounding towns. The architect of Boston's Emerald Necklace lived and worked in a little house in a quiet Brookline neighborhood, where he often took his work outside to a landscaped hollow.

At the **Frederick Law Olmsted National Historic Site**, you can tour the house and grounds and see many of his landscape plans, memorabilia and photographs. The grounds are open daily; tours are offered Friday through Sunday. ~ 99 Warren Street, Brookline; 617-566-1689, fax 617-232-3964; www.nps.gov/frla, e-mail frla_superintendent@nps.gov.

President John F. Kennedy was born in Brookline in 1917, in a little house now restored to its period appearance as the **John F. Kennedy National Historic Site**. The house holds much JFK memorabilia, including his crib and some of his books. Open Wednesday through Sunday from mid-April to mid-November. Admission. ~ 83 Beals Street, Brookline; 617-566-7937, fax 617-730-9884; www.nps.gov/jofi.

South of Brookline lies **Jamaica Plain**, which is technically part of Boston. The star of Jamaica Plain is the **Arnold Arboretum of Harvard University**, one of the more remarkable green strands in Boston's Emerald Necklace. The 265-acre preserve was established in 1872, and growing here are more than 15,000 scientifically labeled trees and plants from around the world. The arboretum has one of the oldest and largest lilac collections in North America, 200-year-old bonsai trees and rare specimens from China. A two-mile walk along a nature trail takes visitors through meadows and over valleys and hills, offering serene and secluded vistas in any season. Maps are available for $1. ~ 125 Arborway, Jamaica Plain; 617-524-1718, fax 617-524-1418; www.arbore tum.harvard.edu, e-mail arbweb@arnarb.harvard.edu.

To the southeast, the working-class city of **Quincy** may look uninteresting, but it happens to be the "City of the Presidents"—birthplace of John Adams and his son John Quincy Adams, the second and sixth U.S. presidents. There are several sights surrounding the Adams family history. But before you make a trip through history, be sure to stop at the **Visitors Center** or call ahead to make necessary tour arrangements. ~ 1250 Hancock Street, Quincy; 617-770-1175, fax 617-472-7562; e-mail adam_visitor_ center@nps.gov.

At the **Adams National Historic Site** stands an elegant gray Colonial house built in 1731; it's home to four generations of Adamses. The house is set on several acres strikingly set off with formal gardens that create a beautiful profusion of color in spring and summer. Inside the house are many original furnishings, including portraits of George and Martha Washington, Waterford candelabra and Louis XV furniture. There is also a cathedral-ceilinged library with 14,000 original volumes. As the Adams family prospered, John and his wife Abigail, who moved into the house in 1787, enlarged it from 7 to 20 rooms. The National Park Service gives excellent tours of this dwelling. Closed mid-November to mid-April. Admission. ~ 135 Adams Street, Quincy; 617-773-1175, fax 617-472-7562; www.nps.gov/ adam, e-mail adam_visitor_center@nps.gov.

Nearby and part of the same site are the **John Adams** and **John Quincy Adams Birthplaces,** a pair of simple saltbox houses where the two presidents were born, built in 1663 and 1681. Closed mid-November to mid-April. Admission. ~ 133 and 141 Franklin Street, Quincy; 617-773-1175, fax 617-472-7562; www.nps. gov/adam, e-mail adam_visitor_center@nps.gov.

East of the Adams National Historic Site lies the **Quincy Homestead,** home to four generations of Edmund Quincy's, the family of Dorothy Hancock. The fourth Quincy daughter, Dorothy, married John Hancock, who was born in Quincy. A Colonial-style herb garden and authentic period furnishings embellish the 1686 house, and one of Hancock's coaches is displayed. The homestead is currently closed to the public, but regular hours will be established. Call ahead. ~ 1010 Hancock Street, Quincy; 617-773-1177.

The 1872 Gothic Revival **Adams Academy** was founded by John Adams and is home to the **Quincy Historical Society.** Exhibits show the city's industrial history. Winter hours vary so call ahead. Closed weekends. ~ 8 Adams Street, Quincy; 617-773-1144, fax 617-472-4990; e-mail qhist@ci.quincy.ma.us.

Dominating downtown Quincy Square is a beautiful granite church, **United First Parish Church,** designed by Alexander Parris and built in 1828. The church crypt holds the remains of John Adams, John Quincy Adams and their wives. ~ 1306 Hancock Street, Quincy; 617-773-0062, fax 617-773-7499.

sights

AUTHOR FAVORITE

If, like me, you find a certain thrill in lying down with literary lions, then curl up with a volume of Henry Wadsworth Longfellow's poetry at **Longfellow's Wayside Inn**. Built around 1700, the inn was made famous by Longfellow's cycle of poems, *Tales of a Wayside Inn*, which includes "Paul Revere's Ride." Historic structures include an 18th-century grist mill and the little red schoolhouse of "Mary Had a Little Lamb" fame. Restored in 1923, it's a fully functioning inn and restaurant. ~ 72 Wayside Inn Road, Sudbury; 978-443-1776, 800-339-1776, fax 978-443-8041; www. wayside.org, e-mail info@wayside.org.

Across the street is **City Hall**, designed in 1844 in Greek Revival style by Bunker Hill architect Solomon Willard. Near City Hall is the **Hancock Cemetery**, dating to about 1640, where John Hancock's father is buried, as are Quincy and Adams ancestors.

Surrounding the Route 128 beltway are several more towns of interest to the traveler. A large and urbanized town about 20 miles west of Boston, **Framingham** offers a lovely respite within the **Garden in the Woods**, the largest collection of native plants in the Northeast. You can meander along 45 acres of woodland trails, planted with some 1700 varieties of flora. There are specially designed garden habitats, including woodland groves, a lily pond, bog, limestone garden, pine barrens and meadows. Closed November to mid-April. Admission. ~ 180 Hemenway Road, Framingham; 508-877-7630, fax 508-877-3658; www.newfs.org, e-mail newfs@newfs.org.

HIDDEN ►

A few miles north of Framingham lie the endearing green Colonial towns of **Sudbury** and **Lincoln**, still quite rural in character.

Walter Gropius, founder of the Bauhaus school of art and architecture in Germany, had his family home in the rolling green hills of Lincoln. The first house he designed upon his arrival in the United States in 1938, **Gropius House** embodies those principles of function and simplicity that are hallmarks of the Bauhaus style. The house has works of art and Bauhaus furnishings. Closed Monday and Tuesday; open weekends only from mid-October through May. Admission. ~ 68 Baker Bridge Road, Lincoln; 781-259-8098, fax 781-259-9722; www.spnea.org.

Great Blue Hill, the highest point on the Massachusetts coast south of Maine, is the site of the oldest weather station in North America.

Set in a wooded, green, 35-acre park, the **DeCordova Museum and Sculpture Park** has a collection of 20th-century American art, including paintings, sculpture, graphics and photography. A café serves light fare. The museum is closed on Monday. Admission. ~ 51 Sandy Pond Road, Lincoln; 781-259-8355, fax 781-259-3650; www.decordova.org, e-mail info@decordova.org

LODGING There's a great deal of historic ambience to **Longfellow's Wayside Inn**, which the poet made famous in his *Tales of a Wayside Inn*. The innkeepers have kept a number of the original rooms furnished with period items. Of the inn's ten rooms, only two are in the older part of the inn. Eight are in a modern addition and feature Colonial reproduction furniture (as well as original pieces), traditional colors of cranberry and green, and oak floors. The two rooms in the original inn have wide-planked floors and hand-hewn ceiling beams, but they have tiny bathrooms with cramped showers. The inn has a wonderful restaurant that serves traditional country fare. A full breakfast is included in the rates. ~ 72

Wayside Inn Road, Sudbury; 978-443-1776, 800-339-1776, fax 978-443-8041; www.wayside.org. MODERATE TO DELUXE.

If you're looking for a funky, East Village–esque night on the town, give **Bella Luna** a try. The pizza parlor is loud and energetic and the food's pretty good, although service can be slow. But there's plenty to look at, from the eclectic patrons to the rotating art exhibits to the open kitchen. And if your patience wears thin, pop downstairs to the nightclub/bowling alley and knock over a few pins. ~ 405 Centre Street, Jamaica Plain; 617-524-6060.

DINING

Don't be deterred by the strip-mall surroundings of **La Paloma in Quincy,** complete with laundromat, sub shop and package store. La Paloma has won several awards from *Boston* magazine, including six "Best Mexican Restaurant" awards. People line up outside the doors on weekends for the first-rate food, including beef and chicken fajitas, Mexican paella and *gorditos* (fried tortillas topped with homemade sausage and sour cream). The dining room feels as warm and festive as a Mexican village, with peachy-colored walls, dim lantern light, airy latticework, tiled floors and Mexican paintings and folk art. Closed Monday. ~ 195 Newport Avenue, Quincy; 617-773-0512, fax 617-376-8867. BUDGET TO MODERATE.

Even Southerners recommend **Tennessee's** for some of the best barbecue in the area. Beef brisket, baby-back ribs, chicken wings and pulled pork are all smoked then dry-rubbed with a blend of spices. Platters come with barbecued beans, cucumber salad, corn bread and watermelon. Collard greens, dirty rice and sweet potato pie round out the Southern selections. ~ 341 Cochituate Road, Framingham; 508-626-7140; www.tennbbq.com. MODERATE TO DELUXE.

Visions of Longfellow will come to mind immediately when you enter **Longfellow's Wayside Inn.** Before lunch or dinner, you can tour the period rooms of the original inn and several historic buildings on the grounds. Ask for a table in the small and intimate Tap Room, which has a truly Colonial ambience with two fireplaces, ladderback chairs and brown-and-white-checked tablecloths. The menu features hearty game and seafood dishes such as those an 18th-century wayfarer might have dined on: prime rib, rack of lamb, roast duckling, goose and sole. For dessert, there are deep-dish apple pie and baked Indian pudding. ~ 72 Wayside Inn Road, Sudbury; 978-443-1776, fax 978-443-8041; www.waysideinn.org. DELUXE.

You'll find plenty of fun cards, gifts, clothing, shoes, accessories and more at the incense-imbued **Pluto.** ~ 603 Centre Street, Jamaica Plain; 617-522-0054.

SHOPPING

Shop for a good cause at **Boomerangs,** a fundraising venue for the AIDS Action Committee that's chock-full of recycled housewares and clothing. Brand-name quality goods are also donated by such retailers as Filene's Basement and Urban Outfitters. ~ 716 Centre Street, Jamaica Plain; 617-524-5120; www.aac.org, e-mail boomerangs@acc.org.

NIGHTLIFE   Locals flock to the **Midway Cafe** for everything from country to jazz to metal to reggae. The very eclectic schedule includes Thursday's "Dyke Nyte," with a deejay and dancing. Cover for some shows. ~ 3496 Washington Street, Jamaica Plain; 617-524-9038; www.midwaycafe.com.

If you've ever thought a nightclub in a bowling alley would be a great idea, someone beat you to it. **The Milky Way Lounge & Lanes**, downstairs from the Bella Luna pizza parlor, is a big room split in half; you can bowl on one side, or sit at the bar or on sofas on the other. There's pool; live bands entertain some nights, deejays on others. ~ 405 Centre Street, Jamaica Plain; 617-524-3740.

Once a hash house for shipyard workers, the **Yard Rock Cafe** now serves up live blues nightly. Tuesday night is open mic for all ages and Sunday afternoon is youth open mic. ~ 132 East Howard Street, Quincy; 617-472-9383; www.yardrock.com.

Ballroom dancers from 18 to 80 love **Moseley's on the Charles** for its large ballroom and '40s ambience, complete with sparkling ceiling globe. Closed Saturday through Tuesday; Wednesday is open ballroom, Thursday and Friday are reserved for private functions. Cover. ~ 50 Bridge Street, Dedham; 781-326-3075, fax 781-326-9862; www.moseleysonthecharles.com.

BEACHES   **BOSTON HARBOR ISLANDS** 🏃 🚣 ⚓ 🚤 ⛵ Over 30 is-
& PARKS   lands lie in Boston Harbor, scattered along the coast from Boston south to Quincy, Hingham and Hull, with 10 of them comprising
HIDDEN ►   a state park. Each island has a unique flavor and character.

Peddocks Island, a 188-acre preserve of woodlands, salt marsh, rocky beaches and open fields, has a turn-of-the-20th-century fort, a wildlife sanctuary and an old cottage community, as well as a visitors center with displays detailing the island's history.

Peaceful and primitive **Lovells Island** is characterized by long beaches and diverse wildlife, rocky tidepools and sand dunes. This is the only island where swimming is allowed.

The smaller **Georges Island**, the most developed in the park, is dominated by Fort Warren, a National Historic Landmark built between 1833 and 1869. Construction was overseen by Sylvanus Thayer, the "Father of West Point."

Other islands in the park system include **Gallop's**, **Grape** and **Bumpkin**. (Gallop's is currently closed to the public.) Swimming is permitted on Lovells Island only. Fishing is good from the rocky shores and public piers on all the islands except Peddocks;

you'll find lots of flounder, cod, haddock, pollack and striped bass. Picnic areas, restrooms, park rangers, nature trails, fort tours, historical programs, boat docks and a concession stand are available on Georges Island. Georges Island also serves as the entrance to the park and provides free inter-island water taxis from Memorial Day to Labor Day. (The islands are also accessible through **Boston Harbor Cruises.** ~ 1 Long Wharf; 617-227-4321. **The Friends of the Boston Harbor Islands** sponsors special boat trips and tours. ~ 349 Lincoln Street, Building 45, Hingham; 781-740-4290.) Closed Labor Day to Memorial Day. ~ 617-223-8666, fax 617-223-8671; www.bostonislands.com.

> The Puritans used the Boston Harbor Islands for pastureland and firewood, and there are tales of buried pirate treasure and ghosts haunting old Civil War forts.

▲ There are primitive sites on Peddocks and Lovells islands (free MDC permit required), and on Grape and Bumpkins islands ($5 per night; reservations required). No water or electricity; outhouses available. ~ 877-422-6762 (Grape and Bumpkin islands), 617-727-7676 (Peddocks and Lovells islands).

BELLE ISLE MARSH 🏃 🌿 This preserve holds 241 acres of one of the largest remaining salt marshes in Boston. Typical of the wetlands that once lined the shores of the Massachusetts Bay Colony, Belle Isle Marsh is a special place where you can see lots of wildlife and salt marsh plants, a rare experience in an urban area. Facilities include nature trails and an observation tower. ~ At Bennington Street in East Boston; 617-727-5350, fax 617-727-8228; www.state.ma.us/mdc, e-mail wood5@mediaone.net.   ◄ HIDDEN

NANTASKET BEACH 🚣 🏖 🌊 💧 Once a classy mid-19th-century resort with grand hotels rivaling those in Newport, the Nantasket Beach area later declined into a tacky strip of bars, fast-food stands and Skeeball arcades. Still, this three-and-a-half-mile barrier beach is one of the nicest in the area, with clean white sand and a wide open vista of the Atlantic Ocean. The water is always good for swimming, and after a storm there's enough surf to go bodysurfing or windsurfing. There are picnic areas, restrooms, lifeguards, shade pavilions, a boardwalk, a carousel, restaurants and snack stands. Parking fee, $3. ~ On Nantasket Avenue, at the terminus of Route 228 in Hull; 781-925-1777, fax 617-727-8252.

WOLLASTON BEACH RESERVATION 🌊 💧 Come high tide, the beach virtually disappears, so narrow is this two-mile stretch of sand. The beach is backed by a wide seawall and a parking strip along its entire length. Here people like to sunbathe in lawn chairs or draped across the hoods of their cars, and to walk their dogs, giving this beach a distinctly urban feel. The sand here is gravelly and often crowded, but the beach does have a splendid view of the Boston skyline. You'll find picnic areas, restrooms, bathhouses and a playground; snack bars and restaurants with great fried clams are across the street. ~ On Quincy Shore Drive, south on Route 3A from Neponset Circle, Quincy; 617-727-1680, fax 617-727-9905.

BLUE HILLS RESERVATION 🏃 🚲 🐎 🎿 🏛 ⚓ 🚣 ⛵ This 7000-acre park is the largest open space within 35 miles of Boston. The reservation comprises dozens of hills, forested land and also several lakes and wetlands, as well as 150 miles of hiking, ski touring and bridle trails. There's the **Trailside Museum** (admission), a natural-history museum with live animals and exhibits, and 16 historic sites, including the 1795 Redman Farmhouse. ~ 1904 Canton Avenue, Route 138, Milton; 617-333-0690, fax 617-333-0814.

Houghton's Pond, with its calm waters and sandy bottom, offers particularly good swimming for children. Ponds are stocked with trout, bass, bullhead, perch and sunfish. Facilities include picnic areas, restrooms, lifeguards, a snack bar, tennis courts, a golf course, a small downhill ski run with rentals and ballfields. ~ Reservation headquarters are on Hillside Street next to the police station in Milton, where maps are available; 617-698-1802, fax 617-727-6918.

▲ The Appalachian Mountain Club operates 20 cabins and 2 campsites on Ponkapoag Pond (781-961-7007 for reservations); camping rate is $10 per night, cabin rates are $83 to $112 per week (there are only weekly rentals in the summer). Reserve these well ahead of time. There are outhouses; no water or electricity. ~ 617-523-0655, fax 617-523-0722; www.outdoors.org.

▼▼▼▼▼▼▼▼▼▼▼▼▼
Lexington & Concord

Just outside Cambridge, the two towns of Lexington and Concord are forever linked by the historical events of April 19, 1775, when the first battle of the Revolutionary War took place. The British planned to advance on Concord from Boston to seize the colonials' stash of military supplies. Warned by Paul Revere the night before, farmer/soldier Minutemen had mustered early before dawn on the Lexington Green.

About 77 men at Lexington Green, and hundreds more at Concord, fought off 700 highly trained British regulars. With heavy casualties, the British retreated back to Boston. "The shot heard 'round the world" had been fired, launching the American Revolution.

SIGHTS   Between the two towns you can spend a couple of days visiting battle sites and monuments. When you arrive in Lexington, a few miles north of Lincoln off Route 128, stop first at the **Lexington Visitors Center** for maps and brochures, and to see a diorama of the battle. Closed weekends from April through November. ~

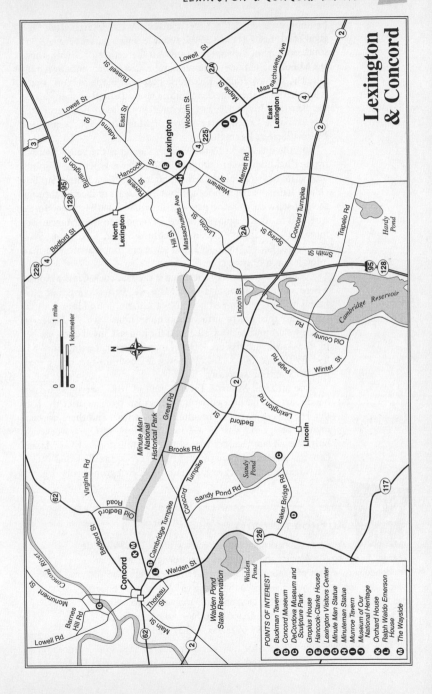

Lexington & Concord

POINTS OF INTEREST

- Ⓐ Buckman Tavern
- Ⓑ Concord Museum
- Ⓒ DeCordova Museum and Sculpture Park
- Ⓓ Gropius House
- Ⓔ Hancock-Clarke House
- Ⓕ Lexington Visitors Center
- Ⓖ Minute Man Statue
- Ⓗ Minuteman Statue
- Ⓘ Munroe Tavern
- Ⓙ Museum of Our National Heritage
- Ⓚ Orchard House
- Ⓛ Ralph Waldo Emerson House
- Ⓜ The Wayside

Lexington Green, 1875 Massachusetts Avenue, Lexington; 781-862-2480, fax 781-862-5995; www.lexingtonchamber.org.

Across from Lexington Green, in the center of town, stands the **Minuteman Statue,** a simple bareheaded farmer holding a musket. The statue's rough, fieldstone base was made of stone taken from the walls the American militia stood behind as they shot at the British. This statue has become symbolic of Lexington history. ~ Battle Green, intersection of Massachusetts Avenue and Bedford Street, Lexington.

On the green next to the Visitors Center is the yellow, wood-frame **Buckman Tavern,** built in 1709. This is where the Minutemen gathered to await the British after Revere's warning. Smiling elderly ladies wearing mobcaps and long skirts guide you through the house, with its wide-planked floors and 18th-century furniture and musket displays. Closed December to mid-March. Admission. ~ Lexington Green, 1 Bedford Street, Lexington; 781-862-5598, fax 781-862-4920; www.lexingtonhistory.org, e-mail info@lexingtonhistory.org.

A short walk north of the green is the **Hancock-Clarke House,** where Samuel Adams and John Hancock were staying that fateful night. Revere stopped here to warn them. John Hancock's father built this pretty little woodframe house with 12-over-16 windows around 1700. Call ahead for hours. Closed late October to mid-April. Admission. ~ 36 Hancock Street, Lexington; 781-861-0928, fax 781-862-4920; www.lexingtonhistory.org, e-mail info@lexingtonhistory.org.

The little red **Munroe Tavern,** built in 1695, served as British headquarters and housed wounded British soldiers after the battle. The tavern has been maintained as it was, and there are mementos of a 1789 visit by George Washington. Open weekends only. Closed late October to mid-April. Admission. ~ 1332 Massachusetts Avenue, Lexington; 781-862-1703, fax 781-862-4920; www.lexingtonhistory.org, e-mail info@lexingtonhistory.org.

sights

AUTHOR FAVORITE

A trip to Concord should include a visit to **The Wayside**. Former home to the Alcotts and Nathaniel Hawthorne, this historical residence is now part of Minute Man National Historical Park. The Alcotts lived there for several years when Louisa was a girl. Hawthorne bought the house in 1852 and wrote his biography of Franklin Pierce here. Closed Wednesday and from late October to May. Admission. ~ 455 Lexington Road, Concord; 978-369-6975, fax 978-371-2483; www.nps.gov/mima/wayside.

The **Jonathan Harrington House**, now a private residence, was the home of Minuteman fifer Jonathan Harrington, who died in his wife's arms after being fatally wounded in the battle. ~ Harrington Road, Lexington.

The **Museum of Our National Heritage** has changing exhibits on American history in four galleries. Past programs have included retrospectives on Ben Franklin, Paul Revere and the USS *Constitution*, plus exhibits of clocks, furniture and swords from different periods. There are also permanent exhibits on the American Revolution and Masonic lodges. There's also a small café in an airy, bright room featuring light sandwiches, snacks and coffee. ~ 33 Marrett Road, Lexington; 781-861-6559, fax 781-861-9846; www.monh.org, e-mail info@monh.org.

Within the 970-acre **Minute Man National Historical Park** are several more sites involved in the Battle of Lexington and Concord. In this peaceful, sylvan spot, it's hard to picture the bloody carnage of the historic battle. A wide, pine-scented path leads to the site of the **Old North Bridge** spanning the Concord River, a 1956 replica of the bridge where Concord Minutemen held off the British. Another **Minute Man Statue** stands across the river, made of melted 1776 cannon, designed by Daniel Chester French. This one shows a farmer with gun and plow in hand. ~ 174 Liberty Street, Concord; 978-369-6993, fax 978-371-2483; www.nps.gov/mima.

At the **Minute Man Visitor Center** are a film and exhibits. ~ Route 2A, Lexington; 781-862-7753; www.nps.gov/mima.

Concord is also famed as the home of four great literary figures of the 19th century: Nathaniel Hawthorne, Ralph Waldo Emerson, Henry David Thoreau and Louisa May Alcott.

The **Old Manse** was home not only to Emerson but also to Hawthorne, who lived there with his wife for two years while writing *Mosses from an Old Manse*. The restored house is filled with Emerson and Hawthorne memorabilia. Closed November to mid-April. Admission. ~ 269 Monument Street, near North Bridge, Concord; 978-369-3909, fax 978-287-6154; www.the trustees.org, e-mail oldmanse@ttor.org.

The Alcott family lived at **Orchard House** for almost 20 years. Here Louisa May Alcott wrote her most famous novels, *Little Women* and *Little Men*. Closed the first two weeks in January. Admission. ~ 399 Lexington Road, Concord; 978-369-4118, fax 978-369-1367; www.louisamayalcott.org, e-mail info@louisamayalcott.org.

Ralph Waldo Emerson House is where Emerson lived for almost 50 years, with Thoreau, Hawthorne and the Alcotts as his frequent guests. Almost all furnishings are original. Closed Monday through Wednesday and from mid-October to mid-April. Admission. ~ 28 Cambridge Turnpike, Concord; 978-369-2236.

The **Concord Museum** contains Revolutionary War artifacts, literary relics and other historic items associated with Concord. Emerson's study was reconstructed and moved here, and the Thoreau Room holds the simple furniture Thoreau made for his cabin at Walden Pond. Admission. ~ Cambridge Turnpike, Concord; 978-369-9763, fax 978-369-9660; www.concordmuseum. org, e-mail cm1@concordmuseum.org.

Few places have been more indelibly stamped by the presence of one individual than **Walden Pond State Reservation**. "I went to the woods because I wished to live deliberately, to front the essential facts of life, and see if I could not learn what it had to teach, and not, when I came to die, discover that I had not lived," wrote Thoreau in his famous account of his two years spent in a little cabin in these woods, beginning in 1845. Thoreau occupied himself studying nature, fishing and hoeing his bean crop. Today, Walden Pond offers less solitude—it's almost always crowded. But you can swim or fish in the pond, or perhaps try a little rowboating. Nature trails wind around the pond. You can also visit the little cairn of stones that marks the cabin site, and see a replica of the house. Parking fee, $5. ~ Route 126 off Route 2; 978-369-3254, fax 978-371-6438.

> Among other things, Concord is known for Concord grapes, developed and cultivated here by Ephraim Wales Bull.

LODGING   If you're looking for an inexpensive place to stay right in the middle of Lexington, you might stop at the **Battle Green Inn**. The 96 rooms in this L-shaped motel surround two courtyards graced with tropical plants and a heated swimming pool. Inside, guest rooms sport blond furniture and Colonial decor. ~ 1720 Massachusetts Avenue, Lexington; 781-862-6100, 800-343-0235, fax 781-865-9485; www.battlegreeninn.com. BUDGET TO MODERATE.

Concord is greener and more rural than Lexington, making it a more restful place to stay. You can't stay there without stumbling over history.

The **Hawthorne Inn**, built around 1870, is situated on land that once belonged to Emerson, the Alcotts and Hawthorne, and stands right across the street from the Hawthorne and Alcott houses. This homey inn has seven rooms, three furnished with canopied, antique four-poster beds covered with handmade quilts, as well as Colonial-patterned wallpaper and oriental rugs. The private baths are large and nicely redone. Rates drop significantly during the off-season. Continental breakfast and afternoon tea are included. No smoking. ~ 462 Lexington Road, Concord; 978-369-5610, fax 978-287-4949; www.concordmass.com, e-mail inn@concord mass.com. DELUXE TO ULTRA-DELUXE.

Right on the town green, the **Colonial Inn** dates to 1716. The original part of the house was owned by Thoreau's grandfather.

Although the inn has 49 rooms, few are in the historic old inn. Thirty-two rooms are in a newer wing added in 1961 and are comfortable but bland. The 15 rooms in the original part of the house are larger and have a more historic ambience, with wide-planked floors, hand-hewn beams and four-poster beds. The inn has two restaurants and two taverns. ~ 48 Monument Square, Concord; 978-369-2373, 800-370-9200, fax 978-371-1533; www. concordscolonialinn.com, e-mail colonial@concordscolonialinn. com. DELUXE TO ULTRA-DELUXE.

In nearby Bedford, the contemporary **Renaissance Bedford Hotel** occupies 24 piney acres, offering a bit of a resort experience. The 285 rooms are all decorated with modern furnishings. Facilities include indoor and outdoor tennis courts, a fitness center, a whirlpool and sauna. The hotel works well both as a family-friendly accommodation (rooms are child-proof) and as a business hotel (there are meeting rooms and a business center). ~ 44 Middlesex Turnpike, Bedford; 781-275-5500, 800-228-9290, fax 781-275-8956; www.renaissancehotels.com. DELUXE TO ULTRA-DELUXE.

DINING

Yangtze River Restaurant specializes in Polynesian cuisine as well as Szechuan and Cantonese favorites. The dining room is noisy and casual, with a jungle of greenery and exposed brick walls. ~ Depot Square, Lexington; 781-861-6030, fax 781-861-0410. MODERATE.

Styled after a Colonial country inn, the **Hartwell House** is actually two dining establishments in one. The casual bistro features familiar fare such as clam chowder, pizza and chopped sirloin burgers along with a limited choice of more elaborate chef's specials that change monthly. The more formal restaurant, where "smart" attire is required, serves a range of seafood, beef, fowl and pasta dishes including macadamia-crusted scrod, steak *au poivre* and grilled boneless maple leaf duck breast with brandied cherry glaze. No lunch on weekends. Closed Sunday. ~ 94 Hartwell Avenue, Lexington; 781-862-5111, fax 781-862-7501; www. thehartwellhouse.com, e-mail info@thehartwellhouse.com. MODERATE TO DELUXE.

For some traditional Yankee fare in a historic setting, try the **Colonial Inn**. Built in 1716, the original part of the house was owned by Thoreau's grandfather. There are two restaurants, each with its own Colonial-inspired decor. The menu includes prime rib, steak, scrod and lobster. ~ 48 Monument Square, Concord; 978-369-9200; www.concordscolonialinn.com, e-mail colonial@ concordscolonialinn.com. MODERATE TO ULTRA-DELUXE.

Wandering in the pretty but sleepy suburban community of Concord, I was not expecting to find innovative cuisine. But **Aïgo Bistro** proved a pleasant surprise from start to finish. It's located in the old Concord train depot. The menu is full of French- and Mediterranean-inspired delights arranged and served with quiet flair. Dinner only. Closed Sunday and Monday. ~ 84 Thoreau Street, Concord; 978-371-1333, fax 978-371-1703. ULTRA-DELUXE.

SHOPPING   At **Verrill Farm**, shoppers can find apples, pears, strawberries, heirloom tomatoes and other fruits in season, as well as honey, maple syrup, cheese and beef, all produced on site or at local New England farms. Don't forget to pick up one of their popular pies; last year the farmstand made 800 pies for Thanksgiving. ~ 11 Wheeler Road, Concord; 978-369-4494; www.verrillfarm. com, e-mail info@verrillfarm.com.

NIGHTLIFE   The **Colonial Inn** features live blues, jazz and folk music nightly by a host of regular performers. Monday nights are open mic. ~ 48 Monument Square, Concord; 978-369-9200.

Outdoor Adventures

For information on participatory sports in the areas around Boston, see Chapter Two.

Transportation

Visitors generally come to Cambridge, Lexington and Concord via Boston. See Chapter Two for information on air, bus and train transportation as well as rental cars.

FOUR

Cape Cod and the Islands

Every year starting in June, close to 3.5 million people invade this foot-shaped peninsula, grappling with horrendous traffic and crowded beaches just to be on their beloved Cape Cod. It's easy to understand why.

The Cape has it all: silver-gray saltbox cottages, historic villages, sports, seafood, art, first-rate theater and more. But those attributes aren't the real reason people come here. It's the land itself. With its ethereal light, comforting woodlands and 300 miles of majestic, untamed shoreline, Cape Cod reaches deep into the soul. Formed 12,000 years ago from an enormous glacier that left in its wake a unique and magical landscape of sand dunes, moors, salt marsh and ocean vistas, the Cape has a staggering number of utterly beautiful beaches and natural parks.

Linked to the Cape in the minds of many travelers (although definitely *not* in the minds of residents) are the nearby islands of Martha's Vineyard and Nantucket, wealthy enclaves where celebrities find retreat and make their homes along quiet or dramatic seascapes, beside purple heath or in museum-perfect villages dotted with historic buildings. Following in the footsteps of Lillian Hellman and Dashiell Hammett, folks like Walter Cronkite have moved to Martha's Vineyard. Smaller Nantucket has one lovely town filled with museums, galleries and history, plus great wild beaches and backroads. Everyone calls Nantucket and Martha's Vineyard "the Islands"—except the people who live there. Don't even *suggest* that the "islanders" are connected to the Cape unless you want to start a row.

The Cape's first visitors were the Pilgrims, who landed near Provincetown just long enough to write the Mayflower Compact before heading off to Plymouth. As Massachusetts thrived after the Revolution, Nantucket and Martha's Vineyard joined other coastal areas as major whaling ports.

In the 1800s, artists and writers such as Henry David Thoreau discovered the Cape. Tourists were soon to follow, and these once-isolated fishing communities were never the same again.

Tourism has taken its toll. The Cape has a commercial side, complete with tired-looking shopping malls, pizza parlors, video arcades, tract houses and ugly motels. But it's easy to avoid all that if you know where to go.

The 70-mile-long Cape projects out into the ocean in an east–west direction for about 35 miles, then becomes narrower and turns northward. Practically everything worth seeing here lies along the shore, so an ideal way to explore is to follow the northern coast along Cape Cod Bay to the tip in Provincetown, then go back down along Nantucket Sound to Falmouth and Woods Hole. This is the route we will take.

We have labeled the first segment the North Cape, which follows scenic Route 6A along the north shore past some of the Cape's most charming historic villages. Route 6A eventually joins with busy Route 6 and soon arrives at Eastham. Here begins the Outer Cape area, the region known for sand dunes, rolling moors, impressive beaches and the bohemian and tourist enclave of Provincetown. Route 28 runs back along South Cape past a couple of attractive villages and some of the region's less scenic commercial areas (including Hyannis, home to the Kennedy clan). This section ends at the scientific community of Woods Hole, noted for its oceanographic institute. We then journey to those two pearls off the Cape's southern coast, Martha's Vineyard and Nantucket.

Touring this area, perhaps you'll understand what inspired Thoreau to write *Cape Cod*. There's something here, though, that can't be put into words—a special chemistry and charisma that draw people back year after year, generation after generation.

▼▼▼▼▼▼▼▼▼▼▼▼
The North Cape

Hugging Cape Cod Bay along Route 6A are the beautiful historic villages of Sandwich, Barnstable, Yarmouth, Dennis and Brewster. Once known as Olde Kings Highway, Route 6A is a tree-lined road that dips and turns past lovely old homes, sweeping lawns, stone walls, duck ponds, museums, elegant restaurants and antique stores.

SIGHTS

Sandwich, the first town we reach, is very green, woodsy and English looking. It dates back to 1639 and has a 17th-century grist mill. Sandwich has more sights than any town on the Cape except Brewster. Maps are available at the **Cape Cod Canal Region Chamber of Commerce**. The information booth is closed mid-October to mid-April. ~ 70 Main Street, Buzzards Bay; 508-759-6000, fax 508-759-6965; www.capecodcanalchamber.org, e-mail canalreg@capecod.net.

Near the heart of the village stands the **Hoxie House**, one of the oldest houses in Sandwich. Built around 1675, this modest saltbox structure has furnishings that are impressive in their simplicity and ingenuity. A 1701 Connecticut blanket chest with inlay is spectacular; chairs turn into tables and benches into beds. Closed mid-October to mid-June. Admission. ~ Water Street (Route 130), Sandwich; 508-888-1173.

Heritage Plantation has a 1912 carousel, an antique car collection (including a stunning Dusenburg once owned by actor Gary Cooper), an American history museum and an art museum. If cars, folk art or military history interest you, you'll be impressed. The American history museum has 2000 handpainted miniatures and all sorts of replica flags and firearms. The art museum includes an impressive collection of antique weathervanes, early American primitive and Western art, and cigar-store carved figures. The plantation's 76 acres of gardens are so perfectly manicured they look artificial. Admission. ~ 67 Grove Street, Sandwich; 508-888-3300, fax 508-888-9535; www.heritageplantation. org, e-mail heritage@heritageplantation.org.

In the heart of Sandwich village is the **Sandwich Glass Museum**. In 1825 Deming Jarves, a Bostonian, built a glass factory in Sandwich because of its convenient water access to Boston and abundant wood supply for the furnaces, and also because he thought his employees wouldn't squander their money on city temptations, as they had in Boston. His formula worked, and in no time Sandwich became renowned for its glass.

The museum's collection includes everything from jars, nursing bottles and tableware to saucers, vases and candlesticks. A

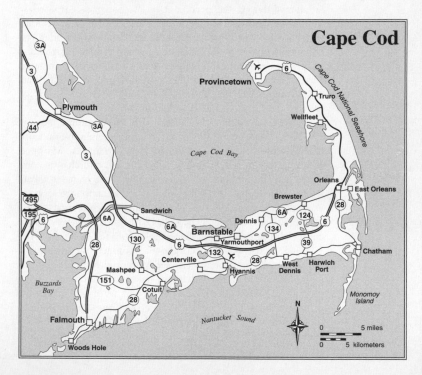

lot of the glass is displayed on shelves in front of large picture windows. Sun illuminates the glass, and it lights up the museum in a kaleidoscope of sparkling colors. Closed Monday and Tuesday from February through March; closed in January. Admission. ~ 129 Main Street, Town Hall Square, Sandwich; 508-888-0251, fax 508-888-4941; www.sandwichglassmuseum.org, e-mail glass@sandwichglassmuseum.org.

The **Green Briar Nature Center and Jam Kitchen** and the **Old Briar Patch Conservation Area** are east of the center of town. "'Tis a wonderful thing to sweeten the world which is in a jam and needs preserving," wrote Thornton W. Burgess to Ida Putnam. As a boy Burgess roamed the woods around Ida's jam kitchen. Today, the Burgess Society produces natural jams, pickles and jellies from Ida's recipes (you can observe the process from April to December only). Nestled deep in the woods next to a pond, the old-fashioned kitchen looks like an illustration from one of Burgess' books. Peter Rabbit and his animal friends would have loved it here. The Jam Kitchen is closed from January through March; the Nature Center is closed Sunday and Monday from January through March. ~ 6 Discovery Hill Road, Sandwich; 508-888-6870, fax 508-888-1919; www.thorntonburgess. org, e-mail tburgess@capecod.net.

East of Sandwich lies the popular resort town of **Barnstable**, where some of the Cape's most beautiful inns and tempting restaurants and shops are located. For information on local sights and happenings, contact the **Hyannis Area Chamber of Commerce**. Closed Sunday from mid-October to Memorial Day. ~ 1481 Route 132, Hyannis; 508-362-5230, 877-492-6647, fax 508-362-9499; www.hyannis.com, e-mail chamber@hyannis.com.

In West Barnstable, the **West Parish Meetinghouse**, built in 1717–19, is the second-oldest surviving meetinghouse on Cape Cod (its senior, the 1684 Old Indian Meeting House in Mashpee, is but a 20-minute drive away). The present church was completed in 1719, and the bell tower went up four years later. Paul Revere cast the bell in 1806; it still rings to announce services, weddings and special events. The building is open every day from Memorial Day to Labor Day. ~ 2049 Meetinghouse Way, at the corner of Route 149, West Barnstable; 508-362-4445, fax 508-375-6431; www.westparish.org, e-mail contact@westparish.org.

You'll find the **Donald Trayser Memorial Museum**, a brick structure built in 1856, which was once a custom house, then a post office. Named after a local patriot and historian, the museum includes a potpourri of artifacts related to Cape Cod life and history, such as Indian tools and ships in bottles. Next to the museum stands the oldest wooden jail in the United States (circa 1690), whose walls are covered with graffiti written by seamen. Closed

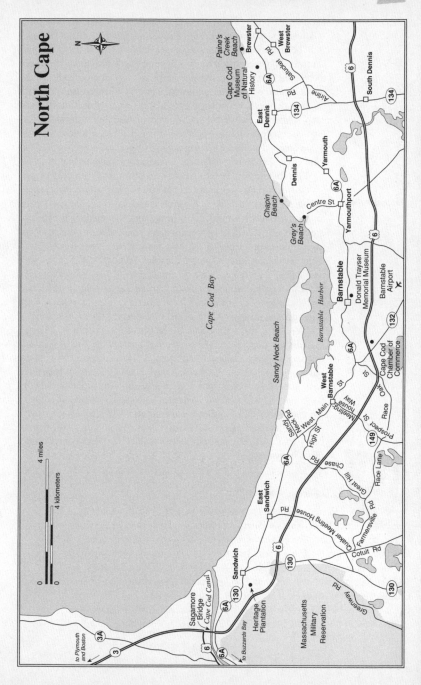

North Cape

N

Cape Cod Bay

Sandy Neck Beach

Barnstable Harbor

Paine's
Creek
Beach

Brewster   West
Brewster

Cape Cod
Museum
of Natural
History

Satucket Rd

6A

Airline Rd

East
Dennis

134

134

South Dennis

6

Yarmouth

Dennis

6A

Yarmouthport

Chapin
Beach

Centre St

*Grey's
Beach*

6

Barnstable

Donald Trayser
Memorial Museum

Barnstable
Airport

6A

132

Cape Cod
Chamber of
Commerce

West
Barnstable

Meeting-
house
St

149

Main
St

Prospect St

Race

Oak
St

High St

Sandy
Neck Rd

West
Main
St

Chase Rd

Race Lane

Great Hill
Rd

Farmersville
Rd

6A

East
Sandwich

Quaker Meeting House Rd

6

130

Cotuit Rd

130

Greenway
Rd

Sandwich

130

6A

Heritage
Plantation

Massachusetts
Military
Reservation

Sagamore
Bridge

Cape Cod Canal

6
6A

to Buzzards Bay

3A

3

*to Plymouth
and Boston*

0   4 miles

0   4 kilometers

Monday through Wednesday, and from mid-October to mid-June. ~ Route 6A, Barnstable; 508-362-2092, fax 508-862-4725.

The original part of the **Sturgis Library** is the birthplace of Captain William Sturgis, who deeded the building to the town to be used as a library. Built in 1644, it's now the oldest building in the country to house a library. Aptly, the library holds one of the finest collections of accessible genealogical information about early Cape Cod settlers. There's a fee to use the research collection, free access to the public library. Closed Sunday. ~ 3090 Main Street (Route 6A), Barnstable; 508-362-6636, fax 508-362-5467; www.sturgislibrary.org, e-mail sturgislib@attbi.com.

HIDDEN ▶
Even during the height of the tourist season, the North Cape isn't a hustle-and-bustle kind of place, but plenty of locals come to the pastoral **St. Mary's Church Gardens** to escape the traffic and tourists on Route 6A. In the spring, the gardens are full of crocus, tulips, daffodils and lilies. A small stream, crisscrossed with tiny wooden bridges, flows through the property. ~ 3055 Main Street (Route 6A), Barnstable; 508-362-3977, fax 508-362-8286.

HIDDEN ▶
Ancient slate headstones are scattered across the little hillock that's topped by **Lothrop Hill Cemetery**. This is where John Lothrop and many of the other founders of Barnstable rest. ~ On Route 6A just to the east of the center of Barnstable Village.

HIDDEN ▶
Farther along Route 6A, **Yarmouthport** is the site of two historic homes with impressive antiques. A white Greek Revival home with black shutters, **Captain Bangs Hallet House** is furnished with elegant settees, tables and chairs, and many classic old toys such as a rocking horse with real animal hide and hair. Open Thursday through Sunday from June to mid-October; group appointments available during off-season. Admission. ~ 11 Strawberry Lane, Yarmouthport; 508-362-3021; www.hsoy.org, e-mail info@hsoy.org.

sights

AUTHOR FAVORITE

Even during my first visit to Cape Cod, I felt an air of nostalgia evoked by the **Thornton W. Burgess Museum**. Dedicated to the author of *Old Mother West Wind* and other children's tales, this shrine to childhood is filled with the children's books that my grandparents read to my parents. The three-quarter Colonial building overlooking the idyllic Canadian geese and swan-friendly Shawme Pond contains a large collection of books by Burgess, beautiful old book illustrations and a gift shop with children's books. Closed November through March. ~ 4 Water Street, Sandwich; 508-888-4668, fax 508-888-1919; www.thorntonburgess.org, e-mail tburgess@capecod.net.

The 1780 **Winslow Crocker House,** a shingled Georgian with handsome wood paneling and an impressive walk-in fireplace, has a rare 17th-century wooden cradle and blanket chest, a Windsor writing chair and many more valuable antiques. Tours available. Open weekends only. Closed mid-October through May. Admission. ~ 250 Route 6A, Yarmouthport; 508-362-4385; www.spnea.org.

Brewster has a couple of sights for children and history buffs. The **New England Fire and History Museum** displays hand- and horse-drawn fire equipment that makes you wonder how they ever put out fires, and a full-scale model of Ben Franklin's first Philadelphia firehouse. Kids like all the bells and fire alarms that are constantly sounding off here. Also on the premises are a blacksmith and an apothecary. Open daily from mid-June to Labor Day. Open weekends only from Labor Day to Columbus Day. Admission. ~ 1439 Main Street (Route 6A), Brewster; 508-896-5711; www.nefiremuseum.org.

The **Cape Cod Museum of Natural History** hosts guided walks through the salt marsh behind the museum, as well as kayaking trips, lectures and overnight stays at Monomoy Island. The hands-on exhibits are popular with both children and adults. Admission. ~ Main Street (Route 6A), Brewster; 508-896-3867, fax 508-896-8844; www.ccmnh.org, e-mail info@ccmnh.org.

LODGING

◄ *HIDDEN*

Located in the heart of Sandwich Village, the **Village Inn** is a renovated 1830s Federal-style house. Without sacrificing historic details, the owners have made everything look fresh and new. The eight soothing, uncluttered guest rooms have lace swag curtains, Colonial armoires and pickled four-poster beds. All of the wood furniture is custom made. A wraparound front porch is a good spot for people watching. They also operate an adjacent art studio that houses art workshops for all levels of expertise. Lodging/workshop packages are offered. Breakfast included. ~ 4 Jarves Street, Sandwich; 508-833-0363, 800-922-9989, fax 508-833-2063; www.capecodinn.com, e-mail capecodinn@adelphin.net. MODERATE TO DELUXE.

The **Dan'l Webster Inn** is a full-service hotel on Main Street. The Federal-style, 54-room inn is so much bigger than most of the other buildings in Sandwich, it looks a little out of whack. But the inside is very warm and cozy. Guest rooms are done in muted shades like smoke and rose, and are decorated with reproduction Colonial furniture and wingback chairs; some beds have canopies, and some of the rooms have fireplaces and whirlpool tubs. Brick paths lead through graceful flower gardens to a gazebo and pool area. The hotel has four dining rooms, an informal tavern, a gift shop and a bar. Rates available with or without breakfast and dinner. ~ 149 Main Street, Sandwich; 508-888-3622, 800-444-

3566, fax 508-888-5156; www.danlwebsterinn.com, e-mail info@ danlwebsterinn.com. DELUXE TO ULTRA-DELUXE.

The **Seth Pope House 1699 B&B** is a three-room bed and breakfast thoughtfully run by owners Beverly and John Dobel, two Midwestern transplants. Unlike many bed and breakfasts, there's a sense of privacy here since all three guest rooms have their own baths. Each room is individually decorated with beautiful antiques, including a pencil-post bed in the Colonial Room— sneak a peek at it if you can. Comfort is important here; the beds are big with an abundance of pillows. A full breakfast is served by candlelight each morning in the keeping room. Closed late October through March. ~ 110 Tupper Road, Sandwich; 508-888-5916, 888-996-7384; www.sethpope.com, e-mail info@sethpope.com. MODERATE.

The **Charles Hinckley House**, a fine example of early Federal architecture, was built in 1809 by Charles Hinckley, a shipwright and the great-great-grandson of the last governor of Plymouth Colony. Guests linger in the homey living room with its deep, soft couches and comfortable wing chairs. Each of the four rooms has a four-poster bed, a private bath, a working fireplace, views of wildflower gardens and carefully chosen antique furniture. Artistic details abound in the bedrooms: two walls of the Library are stuffed with books, and the Summer Kitchen is a delightful cathedral-ceilinged haven with whitewashed walls and soft golden highlights. The innkeeper serves exquisite breakfasts in the lovely Colonial-style dining room. Closed Christmas week. ~ 8 Scudder Lane, Barnstable Village; 508-362-9924, fax 508-362-8861. DELUXE.

The **Beechwood** is one of the prettiest inns on Route 6A. An ancient weeping beech tree shades a good portion of this buttery yellow, gabled Queen Anne Victorian and its lovely wraparound porch. The entire house is furnished with fine antiques. In the Cottage Room you'll find a rare 1860 handpainted bedroom set, in the Marble Room a graceful marble fireplace and 19th-

LIVE LIKE A NATIVE

The Cape has some of the most beautiful inns in the country, plus hundreds of other accommodations in every price range, location and style imaginable. If you plan to stay for at least a week, think about renting a house, apartment or condo; it's usually less expensive than a hotel. Contact the **Cape Cod Chamber of Commerce** for names of realtors handling rentals in a particular area. ~ Junction of Routes 6 and 132, Hyannis, MA 02601; 508-862-0700, 888-332-2732, fax 508-862-0727; www.cape codchamber.org, e-mail info@capecodchamber.org.

century brass bed. The Garret Room on the third floor has steeply angled walls and a half-moon window overlooking Cape Cod Bay, while the popular Rose Room features a fainting couch at the foot of an antique canopy bed and a working fireplace. It doesn't matter where you stay—all six guest rooms are wonderful. They all have private baths and air conditioning. A full breakfast is served in the wood-paneled dining room and tea on the porch. ~ 2839 Main Street, Barnstable Village; 508-362-6618, 800-609-6618, fax 508-362-0298; www.beechwoodinn.com, e-mail info@beechwoodinn.com. DELUXE TO ULTRA-DELUXE.

We'd heard from friends that innkeeper Evelyn Chester runs an unusual bed and breakfast, but nothing prepared us for how unique **Cobb's Cove** truly is. Guests follow a path of phosphores-   ◄ *HIDDEN* cent crushed white seashells up a slope, where they enter another world. Beds of lilies, wildflowers and herbs border the patio. Painted pottery, bird feeders and a zoo of birds vie for attention. Thick, rough timbers form a sparse wooden web overhead. The common areas are furnished with furniture and art from all styles and periods. In the winter, radiant heat under the tiled floors makes every room cozy. The six rooms (all with private baths) have magnificent views of the north side of the Cape and Cape Cod Bay. The Cobb's Cove experience is definitely a relaxing getaway for Cape visitors. ~ Powder Hill Road, Barnstable Village; phone/fax 508-362-9356, 877-378-5172; www.cobbscove.com, e-mail evelyn@cobbscove.com. DELUXE TO ULTRA-DELUXE.

Built in 1812, the **Wedgewood Inn** sits on a little hill overlooking historic Route 6A. Surrounded by stately elm trees and stone walls, the Colonial inn makes a lasting impression. Nine air-conditioned guest rooms sport handcrafted cherry wood pencil-post beds, antique quilts, private baths and wideboard floors; some have private decks and working fireplaces. The decor is an elegant interpretation of formal country style. A full breakfast, afternoon tea and fresh fruit in each room are included in the rate. ~ 83 Main Street (Route 6A), Yarmouthport; 508-362-5157, fax 508-362-5851; www.wedgewood-inn.com, e-mail info@wedge wood-inn.com. DELUXE TO ULTRA-DELUXE.

Located in Yarmouthport's historic district is **Gull Cottage**, a guest house that has a predominantly gay male clientele. The three guest rooms with shared bath are on the lower level of this 1790s house and are decorated mostly with antiques. The cottage is a mile from the beach and five miles from the boat docks. Closed January through March. ~ 10 Old Church Street, Yarmouthport; 508-362-8747, fax 508-362-5488; e-mail mario@ ccsnet.com. BUDGET.

A rambling white 1875 Victorian close to the beach, the **Four Chimneys Inn** is the kind of place where you can plop down on the living room couch in front of the fire and settle in for a good read. Homey and low-key, the seven guest rooms (three with decorative fireplaces) are large and airy with high ceilings; all have private baths. A large yard with gardens surrounds the house, which sits well back from the road. Breakfast is included. ~ 946 Main Street, Dennis; 508-385-6317, 800-874-5502, fax 508-385-6285; www.fourchimneysinn.com, e-mail barry@fourchimneys inn.com. MODERATE TO DELUXE.

The **Isaiah Clark House**, an 18th-century sea captain's home, is surrounded by five acres of gardens, fruit trees and wild berry patches. Impeccably appointed with Shaker and Colonial antiques, many of the seven guest rooms have stenciled walls, canopy beds, sloping pine floors and fireplaces. Breakfast is served in an appealing room with an enormous fireplace—guests linger here all morning. Pre-dinner get-togethers are included. ~ 1187 Main Street, Brewster; 508-896-2223, 800-822-4001; www.isaiahclark. com, e-mail innkeeper@isaiahclark.com. DELUXE.

A large turn-of-the-20th-century gray-and-white-trimmed house, the **Old Sea Pines Inn** used to be a girls' finishing school. The spacious lobby and 24 guest rooms are comfortably furnished with antique wicker, slipcovered chairs and sofas; 19 rooms have private baths. Each of the five suites can accommodate a family of four. A wraparound porch with rockers, perfect for reading or snoozing, overlooks a yard canopied by pine and beech trees. Breakfast is served on a bright sunporch with many skylights or on the canopied side deck. Several gardens are open for meandering. Closed January through March. ~ 2553 Main Street, Brewster; 508-896-6114, fax 508-896-7387; www.oldseapines inn.com, e-mail info@oldseapinesinn.com. MODERATE TO DELUXE.

DINING

The **Dan'l Webster Inn** is so Colonial looking, you expect it to serve traditional New England fare, but the food is rather diverse. While the menu changes yearly, specials change every four to six weeks and cover a wide range of tastes. The award-winning restaurant boasts an extensive wine cellar. Meals are served in the very formal Webster Room with peach walls, mahogany chairs and brass chandeliers; in the intimate Heritage Dining Room with brass chandeliers; the light and airy Music Room with a fireplace and grand piano; or in the Conservatory overlooking the garden and gazebo. The **Tavern at the Inn Grille & Winebar** offers casual, reasonably priced meals that include wood-grilled pizzas, sandwiches, burgers and salads. Breakfast is also available. ~ 149 Main Street, Sandwich; 508-888-3622, 800-444-3566; www. danlwebsterinn.com, e-mail info@danlwebsterinn.com. BUDGET TO DELUXE.

The place to go for breakfast in Sandwich is **Marshland**. A diner-cum-bakery, it's locally famed for its reasonably priced, hearty and reliably good food. It has all the customary breakfast dishes plus lots of daily specials like pancakes, omelettes and hash. Be sure to order a homebaked muffin; they're celestial. No dinner on Sunday and Monday from September through May. ~ 109 Route 6A, Sandwich; 508-888-9824. BUDGET.

Barnstable Tavern serves traditional lunch and dinner fare such as mussels marinara, shrimp scampi and pasta. Located in a small complex of shops, the restaurant creates a pleasant Early American feeling with Windsor chairs, folk art and brass light fixtures. The friendly bar is a good place for a drink, and different varieties of wine are served by the glass. ~ 3176 Main Street (Route 6A), Barnstable; 508-362-2355, fax 508-362-9012. MODERATE TO DELUXE.

Mattakese Wharf, a quintessential summer resort eatery that   ◄ HIDDEN
is literally on the wharf in Barnstable Harbor, is a bit overpriced, but the million-dollar view will be well worth the cost of a meal. Try to get here before sunset and linger over cocktails while you watch fishermen and waterskiing families come and go in this quiet, lovely harbor. Entrées include large swordfish steaks, burgers, generous portions of mussels and boiled lobster, naturally. Closed November through April. ~ 271 Mill Way, Barnstable; 508-362-4511; www.mattakeese.com, e-mail mattakeese@aol. com. MODERATE TO ULTRA-DELUXE.

Abbicci serves contemporary Mediterranean cuisine in an 18th-century Cape Cod cottage on one of the prettiest stretches of historic Route 6A. A good spot for a special lunch or dinner, the restaurant has an imaginative, occasionally changing menu. Dishes have included grilled beef tenderloin with a truffle madeira sauce, pistachio-crusted rack of lamb, and pan-seared halibut with fresh tomatoes, white wine and olives. Cozy yet sophisticated and contemporary, it has a number of small dining rooms with low ceilings, Windsor chairs and white tablecloths. ~ 43 Main Street

AUTHOR FAVORITE

The **Bramble Inn** is one of those restaurants people (including me) always rave about. Housed in a Greek Revival farmhouse on scenic Route 6A, the place offers a prix-fixe menu that changes every three weeks. Dinner is served in five small dining rooms complete with Queen Anne chairs, fresh flowers and antiques. Innovative dishes have included grilled seafood in curry sauce, smoked bluefish pâté, and rack of lamb with garlic and rosemary. Dinner only. Closed January to mid-April. ~ 2019 Main Street (Route 6A), Brewster; 508-896-7644, fax 508-896-9332; www.brambleinn.com. DELUXE.

(Route 6A), Yarmouthport; 508-362-3501; www.abbiccirestau
rant.com, e-mail abbicci@attbi.com. DELUXE TO ULTRA-DELUXE.

Seafood is the speciality at **Oliver's**, where you can start off
with crab-stuffed mushrooms or clams casino then proceed to
broiled scrod or shellfish linguine. Veal parmigiana, grilled sirloin and chicken cordon bleu are options for meat eaters. ~
Route 6A, Yarmouthport; 508-362-6062; www.oliverscapecod.
com, e-mail cameron1@capecod.net. MODERATE TO DELUXE.

HIDDEN ▶   **Gina's By The Sea**, a sweet little white-shingled restaurant located within walking distance of Chapin Beach, is far more sophisticated than it looks. The predominantly Italian menu features
daily specials and includes entrées like shrimp scampi, mussels
marinara, chicken, veal and pasta dishes. Ruffled curtains, white
tablecloths and plain wooden chairs create a casual elegance.
Dinner only. Closed December to April. ~ 134 Taunton Avenue,
Dennis; 508-385-3213. MODERATE TO DELUXE.

The food is hearty and predictable, the service fast and friendly
HIDDEN ▶   at **Marshside Restaurant**, a casual restaurant popular with locals. Omelettes, bagels, pancakes and french toast are some of
the breakfast offerings. Lunch items include lobster salad, quesa-
dillas and fried clams. At dinner it's fried clams, stuffed shrimp,
steak, chicken piccata and daily specials. The decor is kitchen-
cute with bentwood chairs and ruffled curtains. The back room
has a spectacular view of a salt marsh meadow. ~ 28 Bridge
Street, East Dennis; 508-385-4010, fax 508-385-4038. BUDGET
TO MODERATE.

Located in a bustling shopping area, **Cafe Alfresco** is the perfect place to start the day or take a lunch break from sightseeing.
The breakfast menu includes homemade pastries and breakfast
sandwiches, such as egg and bacon on toast. Sandwiches are the
specialty at lunch, including many made on the panini press. You
can also opt for soup, chowder or a salad. A gelato bar provides
a refreshing dessert. This café is very popular with both locals
and tourists, so expect a crowd. ~ 1097 Main Street, Brewster;
508-896-7771. BUDGET.

The painted wood floors, linen drapes, ceiling fans and cloth
HIDDEN ▶   napkins of the **Brewster Fish House Restaurant** creates a quaint
and casual atmosphere. Its small, imaginative menu features
dishes such as calamari with tomato-red aïoli and grilled Atlantic
salmon with prosciutto and a mild dijon mustard sauce. Closed
mid-December through March. ~ 2208 Main Street (Route 6A),
Brewster; 508-896-7867, fax 508-896-7344. MODERATE TO ULTRA-
DELUXE.

Elegant and expensive, **Chillingsworth** has been repeatedly
praised by the *New York Times* and *Esquire*. The menu changes
daily, utilizing seasonal and fresh ingredients. The food is French
American, with dishes such as loin of veal with white-truffle risotto,

and grilled chicken with mascarpone polenta, snow peas and chanterelles. Located in a tree-shaded 1689 Colonial house, the restaurant has dining areas combining modern and traditional decorative touches such as contemporary artwork, antique mirrors and white tablecloths. Lunch, brunch and bistro dinners are served in the greenhouse room. After lunch, browse in the restaurant's adjacent antique and pastry shop. The seven-course dinner is served at two seatings. The main dining room, closed on Monday, is ultra-deluxe. Bistro dining in the garden is moderate to deluxe. Closed Monday and Tuesday from Labor Day to late November, and from Thanksgiving through Memorial Day. ~ 2449 Main Street (Route 6A), Brewster; 508-896-3640, 800-430-3640; www.chillingsworth.com, e-mail webchill@chillingsworth.com. MODERATE TO ULTRA-DELUXE.

SHOPPING

Some of the Cape's best shopping is along Route 6A, which is lined with antique stores and artists' studios selling pottery, weavings, handcrafted furniture and more.

With its sloping wood floors and wainscotting, **The Brown Jug** looks like an old general store. Along with antique glass and china from the late-18th through early-20th centuries, it sells high quality, hand-pressed glass. Many of the pieces were made in Sandwich in the 19th century. Closed November through May. ~ 155 Main Street, Sandwich; 508-833-1088.

The Cape Cod Antique Market, a large gathering of antique and collectibles dealers, takes place year-round at the First Congregational Church in Barnstable.

The **Black's Handweaving Shop** has beautiful hand-woven coverlets, throws, place mats, hats, gloves and wallhangings in lush colors. The store is in a large barn-like room where you can watch owners/designers Bob and Gabrielle Black working at one of the many looms. ~ 597 Main Street (Route 6A), West Barnstable; 508-362-3955.

Design Works specializes in antique Scandinavian pine armoires, mirrors, chairs, settees, and white linen and lace napkins, tablecloths and bed accessories. ~ 159 Main Street (Route 6A), Yarmouthport; 508-362-9698.

Originally a general store that also housed a church on its second floor, **Parnassus Book Service** has a wealth of marine and Cape Cod book titles. ~ 220 Old King's Highway (Route 6A), Yarmouthport; 508-362-6420.

One of the nicest sights on Route 6A is the vibrant display of fresh produce and flowers at **Tobey Farm Country Store**. Stop here in the summer for fresh native corn, peaches and plums, and in the fall for pumpkins and apples. The white clapboard farm also sells reasonably priced dried wreaths made from German statice, rose hips, lavender, yarrow, dried pink rosebuds, baby's-breath, purple statice and eucalyptus. In October, the store sponsors "scary" and "not-so-scary" hayrides. Hours vary; call ahead.

Closed January to mid-April. ~ 352 Main Street (Route 6A), Dennis; 508-385-2930, fax 508-385-4666.

Even if you can't afford anything at **Kingsland Manor**, stop and browse through its labyrinth of beautiful rooms and gardens filled with exquisite American and European antiques. ~ 440 Main Street (Route 6A), West Brewster; 508-385-9741, fax 508-385-8379.

NIGHTLIFE   **Heritage Plantation Concerts** offers a diverse program on Wednesday evenings and Sunday afternoons, including jazz, ethnic and folk music, banjo music, Scottish pipe bands, chorale groups and big bands. ~ Pine and Grove streets, Sandwich; 508-888-3300; www.heritageplantation.org, e-mail programs@heritage plantation.org.

Barnstable Comedy Club Community Theater, founded in 1922, is the oldest amateur theater group on the Cape. Throughout the year it gives major productions and workshops. Kurt Vonnegut, an alumni of the Club, acted in many of its earlier productions. ~ Route 6A, Barnstable Village; 508-362-6333.

> A pleasant spot for walks along the shore, the thin, slightly curved, dune-backed Chapin Beach has soft, white sand ideal for clean, comfortable sunbathing.

Established in 1927 and America's oldest professional summer theater, **The Cape Playhouse** presents well-known plays and musicals such as *The Sound of Music, Ain't Misbehavin'* and *Noises Off*, performed by Hollywood and Broadway stars. Lana Turner, Gregory Peck and Henry Fonda have been on stage here; Bette Davis, an usher, was plucked from her job to fill a small role as a maid in a play here. Nostalgic and romantic-looking, the Playhouse is in an 1838 meetinghouse surrounded by graceful lawns, gardens and a Victorian Gothic ticket booth. On Friday morning, the group presents children's theater. Closed mid-September to mid-June. ~ Route 6A, Dennis; 508-385-3911, 877-385-3911, fax 508-385-8162; www.capeplayhouse.com.

The Cape Museum of Fine Arts' **Reel Art**, on the grounds of The Cape Playhouse, shows quality films—new, old, foreign, independent—such as *Henry V* with Laurence Olivier, *Ginger and Fred* and *House of Games*. Films are shown all year long. ~ Route 6A, Dennis; 508-385-4477; www.cmfa.org.

BEACHES & PARKS   North Cape beaches are on protected Cape Cod Bay. They tend to be quiet and calm, with gentle surf and scenic vistas of soft sand dunes and salt marsh.

SANDY NECK BEACH & THE GREAT MARSHES 🏃 🛶 This area has all the ecological treasures for which the Cape is known. Very straight and long, beautiful Sandy Neck Beach offers a 360-degree view of the ocean and rippling sand dunes bordered by the Great Marshes, 3000 acres of protected land harboring many species of marine life and birds. The sand is ideal for beachcombing, and trails meander through the dunes and marsh. Facilities are limited to restrooms and a snack bar. Parking fee, $10 (Memorial Day to Labor Day only). ~ Take Sandy Neck Road off Route 6A in Sandwich to the beach in Barnstable; 508-362-8300.

GREY'S BEACH This small, quiet beach is perfect for children. But the main reason people come here is to stroll along the long, elevated walkway stretching across the marsh that skirts the beach. The walkway permits a close-up view of marsh flora and fauna, and from a distance it appears to be floating in grassy water. This area is quite beautiful, especially at sunset. Facilities here include picnic tables, a playground, restrooms, lifeguards and a pier for fishing and watching the sunset. ~ Off Route 6A on Centre Street, Yarmouth; for information, call the Yarmouth Chamber of Commerce, 508-775-7910.

CHAPIN BEACH The sand-strewn road leading to Chapin Beach passes gentle sand dunes and small, unpretentious, summer cottages. During nesting season, dogs are not allowed on the beach. Occasionally, daredevils (armed with the proper permits) ride their four-wheel buggies on the beach (riding on the dunes is illegal). Chase Garden Creek at the back of the beach is fun for canoers; you can shore fish for striped bass. Facilities are limited to portable toilets. Parking fee, $10 (from mid-June to Labor Day only). ~ Off Route 6A on Chapin Beach Road, Dennis; 508-394-8300, fax 508-394-8309.

PAINE'S CREEK BEACH There are better beaches nearby ◄HIDDEN for sunning and swimming, but Paine's Creek is ideal for quiet walks through timeless scenery bathed in golden light. Weatherbeaten skiffs are moored along the shore, and Paine's Creek, a gentle slip of a stream, winds through a salt marsh meadow down to a narrow strip of soft beach surrounded by tiny coves and inlets. Children love the tidepools that form when the water recedes almost two miles into the bay. Parking fee, $8 (mid-June to Labor Day only); parking stickers are only available at the Brewster Visitor Center (2198 Main Street). Be prepared for a miniscule parking lot at the beach. ~ Off Route 6A on Paine's Creek Road, Brewster; for information, call the Brewster Chamber of Commerce at 508-896-3500, fax 508-896-1086; www.brewstercape cod.org.

NICKERSON STATE PARK This 2000-acre park looks more like the Berkshires than Cape Cod. Dense pine groves, meadows and jewel-like freshwater ponds with beaches are home to abundant wildlife including red foxes and white-tailed deer. There is so much to do here— hiking, biking, motor boating, canoeing—it gets very crowded in the summer. Quiet beaches and hiking trails can be found around

Little Cliff and Flax ponds. In winter there's cross-country skiing and ice-skating on the ponds. Catch-and-release fishing is excellent at Higgins Pond, which is stocked annually with trout; salmon can be caught for keeps at Cliff Pond. You can swim in the freshwater ponds. You'll find canoe rentals, picnic areas, restrooms, showers, a ranger station and interpretive programs. ~ On Route 6A, Brewster; 508-896-3491.

▲ There are 418 tent/RV sites (no hookups); 168 are available on a first-come, first-served basis; 250 require reservations six months in advance; $12 to $15 per night. Five yurt-style buildings that accommodate four to six adults rent for $25 to $30 per night. Winter camping is allowed for self-contained RVs; $6 per night. Call 877-422-6762 for reservations; www.reserve america.com.

The Outer Cape

Route 6A ends at Orleans, where it intersects with Route 6 and leads to Eastham. At this point the character of the landscape changes dramatically. The woods disappear and the sky opens up to reveal towering sand dunes, miles of silver marsh grass and windswept moors. At the very tip is Provincetown, one of the Cape's largest communities.

About 50 percent of the Outer Cape is under the jurisdiction of the Cape Cod National Seashore, a natural playground with miles of bicycle paths, hikes and the Cape's most dramatic beaches (see the "Beaches & Parks" and "Hiking" sections in this chapter).

SIGHTS

Fort Hill in Eastham offers a mesmerizing view overlooking Nauset Marsh that's so beautiful it doesn't seem real. Once productive farmland, the marsh today is laced with wavy ribbons of water that wind through downy, soft green-gold marsh grass past old farmhouses, stone walls and ponds complete with adorable ducks. Trails meander through this area, which is a special resting place for blue herons. This private residence is surrounded by the Cape Cod National Seashore. ~ 75 Fort Hill Road, Eastham; 508-240-2870; www.forthillbedandbreakfast.com.

After Eastham is **Wellfleet**, an unpretentious, wiggle-your-toes-in-the-sand kind of place with a surprising number of good art galleries and gourmet restaurants. On Saturday nights in the summer, many galleries have openings that feel like neighborhood block parties. Wellfleet has many year-round residents, and they all seem to know each other.

Before heading into town, stop at the **Wellfleet Chamber of Commerce** for a gallery guide. Closed Monday through Thursday from mid-May to late June and from Labor Day to mid-October; closed mid-October to mid-May. ~ Route 6; 508-349-2510, fax 508-349-3740; www.wellfleetchamber.com, e-mail info@wellfleet chamber.com.

On the way to Wellfleet is **Uncle Tim's Bridge**, a low wooden
boardwalk that goes over a field of silvery marsh grass to a small
wooded hill. A dreamy sort of place shrouded in delicate mist in
the morning and soft mellow light in the afternoon, it's perfect
for a picnic or quiet walk.

◀HIDDEN

North of Wellfleet lies magnificent **Truro**, a vast treeless plain
of rolling moors surrounded by water and some of the state's
most impressive sand dunes. Named after an area of Cornwall,

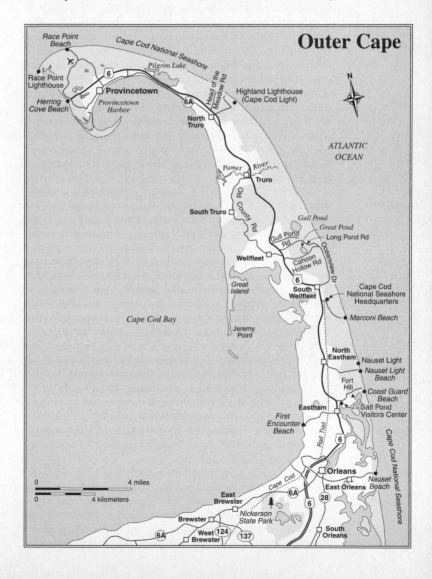

Outer Cape

England, that's similar in appearance, Truro is a wonderful area for picture taking.

LODGING

HIDDEN ►

To capture the essence of Wellfleet, stay at the **Holden Inn**, a long, white farmhouse-style building. There's nothing fancy about the place, but like Wellfleet, it has an easy, casual feeling. Located on a shady country lane five minutes from the wharf, the inn offers 27 well-kept rooms (some with shared bath) with ruffled white curtains and floral wallpaper or wood paneling. Closed late October to early May. ~ 140 Commercial Street, Wellfleet Bay; 508-349-3450; www.theholdeninn.com, e-mail info@theholden inn.com. BUDGET TO MODERATE.

Housed in an 1871 sea captain's home, the **Stone Lion Inn** offers three guest rooms with queen-sized beds and private baths, as well as an apartment with private entrance and kitchenette. Also available is a cottage with three bedrooms and a full kitchen. The owners are happy to answer questions about the surrounding area. An extensive breakfast is included. ~ 130 Commercial Street, Wellfleet; 508-349-9565, fax 508-349-9697; www.stone lioncapecod.com, e-mail info@stonelioncapecod.com. MODERATE TO ULTRA-DELUXE.

DINING

Restaurants on the Cape fall into three categories: expensive French/nouvelle cuisine, surf and turf, and coffee shop fare. If you crave variety, head for the Outer Cape. Wellfleet has a surprising number of excellent, imaginative restaurants.

Right on Wellfleet's pretty harbor, the **Bookstore Restaurant** lets you browse through regional titles while you wait for a table. The fare is almost entirely seafood, ranging from Cajun shrimp and steamed littleneck clams to boiled lobster and charbroiled swordfish. Breakfast, lunch and dinner. ~ 50 Kendrick Avenue, Wellfleet; 508-349-3154; www.wellfleetoyster.com, e-mail bookst re@cape.com. MODERATE.

The Lighthouse is a Wellfleet institution. If you want to mingle with the locals, come here in the morning for breakfast. The ambience is strictly coffee shop, as is the food, which includes french toast, bacon and eggs, fried seafood, sandwiches, hamburgers and the like. Located in the center of town, it has a kitschy miniature lighthouse on its roof that is impossible to miss. Breakfast, lunch and dinner are served. ~ 317 Main Street, Wellfleet; 508-349-3681, fax 508-349-1411. MODERATE.

Sweet Seasons is an exceptionally pretty restaurant overlooking an idyllic duck pond surrounded by rushes, flagstone paths, locust trees and woods. The pale gray and apricot restaurant serves dishes such as grilled tuna and figs, seafood stew, shrimp with feta cheese, tomatoes and ouzo, petite rack of lamb and lobster marsala. Dinner only. Closed Monday and from mid-September

to late June. ~ The Inn at Ducke Creeke, 70 Main Street, Wellfleet; 508-349-9333, 508-349-6535; www.innatduckcreek.com,
e-mail info@innatduckcreek.com. DELUXE.

FIRST ENCOUNTER BEACH This is where the Pilgrims first
encountered the Wampanoag Indians, who were not exactly happy
to see them. Six years earlier an English slave dealer had kidnapped
some of them to sell in Spain. When the Pilgrims arrived a mild skir-
mish broke out, but no one was hurt and the Pilgrims made a hasty
retreat. Sandy paths lead through dense green grass to this striking
beach bordered by a vast marsh meadow and brilliant sky. The
long, wide beach attracts a relatively quiet crowd in the summer.
Facilities are limited to restrooms. Day-use fee, $10. ~ Take Samo-
set Road off Route 6, Eastham; 508-240-5972, fax 508-240-6687.

**BEACHES
& PARKS**

CAPE COD NATIONAL SEASHORE This 27,000-acre ecological wonderland includes endless
stretches of unbelievably beautiful beaches, 60-foot sand dunes,
steep cliffs, wind-bitten moors, salt marsh, freshwater ponds and
woodlands. Undisturbed and undeveloped, the area runs from
Chatham to Provincetown and is laced with some of the Cape's
finest hiking and bicycle trails (see "Cape Cod by Bike" and the
"Hiking" section in this chapter). There's great fishing offshore
and in the ponds. Canoe, kayaks and paddleboats can be rented
in Provincetown and Eastham. There are lifeguards and restrooms
in beach areas (summer only). Parking fee, $10, $30 for a season
pass (mid-June to Labor Day only).

What follows are some of the National Seashore's most re-
nowned beaches and ponds. For more information visit the **Salt
Pond Visitors Center.** ~ Route 6, Eastham; 508-255-3421. The
Cape Cod National Seashore Headquarters is also helpful. ~ 99

AUTHOR FAVORITE

My idea of camping tends more towards lazing than hiking. Lucky for me,
Paine's Campground has wooded campsites just a few minutes' walk
from Cape Cod National Seashore and the ocean. Nearby, crystal-clear
kettle ponds offer freshwater swimming. Toward the front are trailer and
RV sites with water and 30-amp electric hookups. A family section has
hookups and room for multiple tents or a tent and a camper. Quiet couples, singles and young couples sections have tent sites without hookups.
There are central restrooms, and water is available throughout the
camp. Reservations are recommended during the summer. ~ 180 Old
County Road, South Wellfleet; 508-349-3007, fax 508-349-0246; www.
campingcapecod.com. BUDGET.

Marconi Site Road, Wellfleet; 508-349-3785, fax 508-349-9052; www.nps.gov/caco.

COAST GUARD BEACH ⚓ ♨ "On its solitary dune my house faced the four walls of the world," wrote Henry Beston of the place he built in 1927 on this extraordinary beach. In 1978 the house washed away in a storm, but Beston's experiences are chronicled in *The Outermost House*, available at most Cape Cod bookstores. Rugged and wild, Coast Guard Beach goes on for as far as the eye can see. Bordered by cliffs, marsh grass and tributaries, an abandoned red-and-white coast guard station sits on a bluff overlooking the beach. The beach is ideal for long walks, sunbathing, swimming (although the sea can be rough at times) and surfing. Among the amenities are restrooms, showers and lifeguards (summer only). A shuttle bus runs between the parking area and the beach (summer only). Parking fee, $10 (mid-June to Labor Day, and weekends from Memorial Day to mid-October). ~ Take Doane Road off Route 6 near Eastham; 508-349-3785, fax 508-349-9052.

NAUSET LIGHT BEACH & MARCONI BEACH ⚓ ♨ ⚓ These impressive beaches are bordered by towering, shrub-covered cliffs. Long, steep wooden stairways descend to the clean, white-sand beaches. The imposing cliffs and expansive vistas make you feel very small and in awe of it all. Walk north along the shore for a quiet spot in the summer, when the beaches get crowded. Swimming is excellent in the protected area, but watch the undertow; swimmers are urged to make sure a lifeguard is on duty before taking the plunge. On the road to Nauset Beach is Nauset Light, a classic red-and-white lighthouse, one of the most photographed sights on Cape Cod. There are restrooms, showers and summer lifeguards. Day-use fee, $10 per vehicle or $30 for a season pass. ~ Nauset Light is off Route 6 at the end of Cable Road and along Nauset Light Beach Road in Eastham. Marconi is off Route 6 on Marconi Beach Road, Wellfleet; 508-349-3785, fax 508-349-9052.

HIDDEN ▶ **GREAT POND & GULL POND** ⚓ Wellfleet has some of the most idyllic freshwater ponds on the Cape. Less than a mile from wild-looking shoreline, these two offer a completely different nature experience. Densely wooded and pine-scented, they look like mountain ponds. The sparkling water is fresh and invigorating. Gull Pond has a lovely shaded grassy area with picnic tables, a small sand beach and a float in the water. Great Pond is approached via wooden steps leading down from the parking lot overlooking the pond. It has a pretty sandy beach. Half-hidden houses lie along some of the shore. You must live or be staying in Wellfleet to park at either pond, and nonresidents must purchase a permit and furnish proof of stay; there are paddleboat concessions at

Gull Pond (508-349-9808). Restrooms and picnic tables are available to visitors. ~ To reach Great Pond, take Calhoon Hollow Road off Route 6 in Wellfleet; for Gull Pond, take Gull Pond Road off Route 6 in Wellfleet; for information (late June through Labor Day only), call the Beach Sticker House, 508-349-9818; or call Wellfleet Chamber of Commerce, 508-349-2510, fax 508-349-3740.

▼▼▼▼▼▼▼▼▼

Provincetown

Provincetown, at the Cape's outer tip, is nestled on a hill overlooking the bay. Everything good and bad about Cape Cod can be found here: elegant sea captains' mansions, a honky-tonk wharf, dazzling beaches, first-rate museums, schlocky galleries, hamburger joints and gourmet restaurants.

The people are equally diverse. Provincetown has a large gay population, as well as artists and writers, Portuguese fishermen, aristocrats, beer-guzzling rabble-rousers and plenty of tourists. Similarly, Provincetown's many attractions draw all types of visitors, but the town is particularly popular among gay travelers. The gay scene is everywhere, ranging from the beaches to the boulevards to the bars. Every hotel and restaurant in the area welcomes gays and lesbians and in many cases caters primarily to them, as is noted in the listings below.

> Provincetown is so small (and parking is such a hassle) that everything is (luckily) within walking distance.

Of all the towns on the Cape, Provincetown has the most interesting history. The Pilgrims landed here in 1620 before going to Plymouth, and in the 18th and 19th centuries it was a prominent whaling and fishing port, attracting many Portuguese settlers who still fish the waters today.

Around the turn of the 20th century, artists and writers, such as Eugene O'Neill, started moving to Provincetown, and it became one of America's most renowned artists colonies. A renaissance period flourished until about 1945, when tourism evolved and many artists scattered for quieter parts of the world.

SIGHTS

To immerse yourself in Provincetown's artistic past, get a map of the town from the **Provincetown Chamber of Commerce** and ask for the names and addresses of the famous writers and artists who lived here. Their former homes aren't open to the public, but it's fun to walk by 577 Commercial Street and imagine what it was like when O'Neill rented a room there. Call ahead for off-season operating hours. ~ 307 Commercial Street, MacMillan Wharf; 508-487-3424, fax 508-487-8966; www.ptownchamber.com, e-mail info@ptownchamber.com.

Walk east on Commercial Street, the main drag, to the **Provincetown Art Association and Museum** for the best art on the Cape. The museum exhibits work by noted Provincetown artists. In the winter (November through April) the museum is open on weekends only. Admission. ~ 460 Commercial Street; 508-487-1750, fax 508-487-4372; www.paam.org, e-mail paam@capecod.net.

The nonprofit **Fine Art Works Center** offers residency programs for young writers and artists, as well as gallery shows, lectures, workshops and exhibits throughout the year. Closed Saturday and Sunday. ~ 24 Pearl Street, Provincetown; 508-487-9960, fax 508-487-8873; www.fawc.org, e-mail info@fawc.org.

For a picture-postcard view of Provincetown and the surrounding seashore and sand dunes, visit the **Pilgrim Monument and Provincetown Museum**. The 252-foot granite tower was copied from the Torre del Mangia tower in Siena, Italy. The museum houses an eclectic collection that includes everything from antique dolls, Wedgwood china, primitive portraits and scrimshaw to figureheads and a captain's cabin from a whaling ship. Closed December through March. Admission. ~ High Pole Hill; 508-487-1310, fax 508-487-4702; www.pilgrim-monument.org, e-mail info@pilgrim-monument.org.

LODGING

The **Outermost Hostel** offers dorm-style accommodations in five cottages. Amenities are standard hostel: common kitchen and lounge. One unique feature is the hostel's key system, which allows entry to your room during the day. Closed mid-October to mid-May. Gay-friendly. ~ 28 Winslow Street; 508-487-4378. BUDGET.

Set in a carefully restored 18th-century sea captain's home, the **Fairbanks Inn** comprises a charming building and fairly extensive amenities (working fireplaces in most and air conditioning in all of the rooms, for example). There are 13 guest rooms, two with a kitchen. Wide plank floors and wainscoting, large, airy rooms and four-poster beds complete the picture. An extended continental breakfast is offered in the dining room. Gay-friendly. ~ 90 Bradford Street; 508-487-0386, 800-324-7265, fax 508-487-3540; www.fairbanksinn.com, e-mail info@fairbanksinn.com. DELUXE TO ULTRA-DELUXE.

HIDDEN ►

With its dark wood shingles, sky-blue shutters and nursery-rhyme garden, the **Snug Cottage** looks like an illustration from a Mother Goose book. One of the most inviting cottages in Provincetown, the Bradford has eight guest rooms, six with working fireplaces and all with private baths. An apartment on the side of the house with its own entrance has a sitting room, brick fireplace and garden view. A buffet breakfast is served in the dining room. Gay-friendly. ~ 178 Bradford Street; 508-487-1616, 800-432-2334, fax 508-487-5123; www.snugcottage.com, e-mail info@snugcottage.com. DELUXE TO ULTRA-DELUXE.

The lesbian-owned **Heritage House** offers great people watching and harbor views from the upper veranda. This centrally located Cape Cod–style home, which dates from 1856, has seven

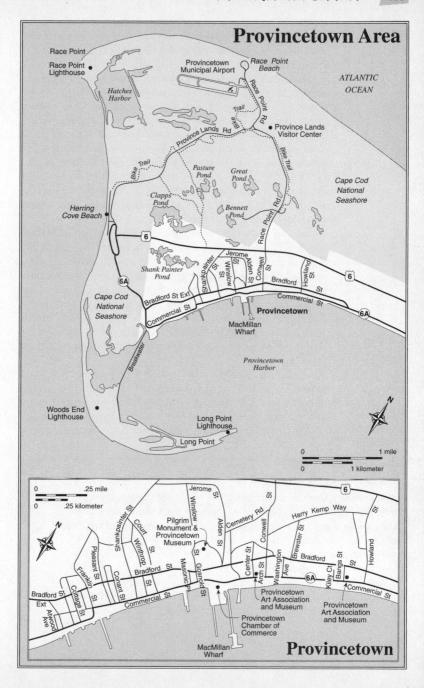

Provincetown Area

Race Point
Race Point Lighthouse
Hatches Harbor
Provincetown Municipal Airport
Race Point Beach
ATLANTIC OCEAN
Trail
Bike
Race Point Rd
Province Lands Rd
Province Lands Visitor Center
Bike Trail
Bike Trail
Pasture Pond
Great Pond
Cape Cod National Seashore
Clapps Pond
Bennett Pond
Herring Cove Beach
6
Race Point Rd
Shank Painter Pond
6A
Shankpainter St
Jerome St
Winslow St
Alden St
Cornell
Bradford
Howland St
6
Cape Cod National Seashore
Bradford St Ext
Commercial St
Commercial St
Provincetown
6A
Breakwater
MacMillan Wharf
Provincetown Harbor
Woods End Lighthouse
Long Point Lighthouse
Long Point
N

0 ———— 1 mile
0 ———— 1 kilometer

Provincetown

0 —— .25 mile
0 —— .25 kilometer
N
Jerome St
Winslow St
Alden St
Cemetery Rd
Cornell St
6
St
Harry Kemp Way
Shankpainter St
Court St
Winthrop
Pilgrim Monument & Provincetown Museum
Brewster St
Bradford
Bangs St
Howland St
Pleasant St
Franklin St
Conant St
Bradford St
Masonic Pl
Gosnold St
Center St
Arch St
Washington Ave
Kiley Ct
6A
Commercial St
Bradford St Ext
Cottage St
Commercial St
Provincetown Art Association and Museum
Provincetown Art Association and Museum
Atwood Ave
Provincetown Chamber of Commerce
MacMillan Wharf

rooms furnished with an eclectic assortment of antiques. Expanded continental breakfast buffet included. ~ 7 Center Street; 508-487-3692, fax 508-487-5694; www.heritageh.com, e-mail info@heritageh.com. MODERATE TO DELUXE.

Built in 1820, the **Watership Inn** is popular with gay men and women. Located on a quiet street yet close to everything, the inn features 15 guest rooms with arched beamed ceilings and antiques and two ultra-deluxe-priced two-bedroom apartments. Some have private decks. Continental breakfast is served on an outdoor deck or in an attractive living room with vaulted ceilings, a wood stove and a bank of french doors leading out to a yard where volleyball and croquet are played in the summer. The inn offers terrific off-season bargains. ~ 7 Winthrop Street; 508-487-0094, 800-330-9413; www.watershipinn.com, e-mail info@watershipinn.com. MODERATE TO ULTRA-DELUXE.

Located in the heart of Provincetown, the **Beaconlight Guesthouse** was home to a local sea captain in the 1850s. This charming, gay-friendly inn offers guests an eclectic setting, mixing modern and antique furnishings to create a cozy, friendly atmosphere. Common areas include a roof deck, a hot tub, a living room with a fireplace and grand piano and an open kitchen where a continental breakfast is served each morning. ~ 12 Winthrop Street; phone/fax 508-487-9603, 800-696-9603; www.beacon lightguesthouse.com, e-mail info@beaconlighthouse.com. DELUXE TO ULTRA-DELUXE.

Within easy reach of all of P-Town's attractions, yet a bit removed, is the **Ampersand Guesthouse**. Catering to a mostly gay male clientele, it's a Greek Revival house whose nine guest rooms and one studio are decorated with a combination of antique and contemporary furnishings; all have private baths. Some have views

AUTHOR FAVORITE

The **Brass Key Guesthouse** is one of the area's best gay-friendly inns. The owner's background in the high end of the hotel trade shows in his attention to the details that count—elegant yet comfortable furniture, sparkling clean bathrooms, meticulous landscaping and friendly staff. The Brass Key comprises 33 rooms in a sea captain's home and two other Victorian buildings, as well as three cottages. The large courtyard features a pool and hot tub. All rooms have private baths and air conditioning; many have private whirlpool baths and gas fireplaces. Closed November through April (but open New Year's weekend). ~ 67 Bradford Street; 508-487-9005, 800-842-9858, fax 508-487-9020; www.brasskey.com, e-mail ptown@brass key.com. ULTRA-DELUXE.

of the water. There's a great sundeck with a view of the bay. ~ 6 Cottage Street; 508-487-0959, 800-574-9645, fax 508-487-4365; www.ampersandguesthouse.com, e-mail info@ampersandguest house.com. MODERATE TO DELUXE.

The Oxford Guesthouse is within walking distance to Provincetown's beach, shops, bars and restaurants, but retains a secluded English country feel. Perhaps this is because this 1850 Greek Revival house is owned by a pair of British innkeepers, who also maintain the surrounding gardens. In the morning, continental breakfast can be served inside or on the garden patio or veranda. Six rooms offer private bath, and one suite has a fireplace. Complimentary glass of sherry or port in the evening. Gay-friendly. ~ 8 Cottage Street, Provincetown; phone/fax 508-487-9103; www.oxfordguesthouse.com. DELUXE TO ULTRA-DELUXE.

Especially during the off-season, the 102-room, two-story **Provincetown Inn** is an excellent place to spend a weekend, if you're not tied to the idea of staying in a quaint inn that's right in the middle of town. The inn overlooks salt marshes, sand dunes and the town's picturesque harbor. Rooms are pretty run-of-the-mill, but given the lovely view, this is certainly more than simply an adequate lodging choice. Continental breakfast is included. ~ 1 Commercial Street; 508-487-9500, 800-942-5388, fax 508-487-2911; www.provincetowninn.com, e-mail info@provincetown inn.com. DELUXE.

If you're in the mood for a splurge during your visit to the Outer Cape, the beautiful Federal-style **Red Inn** is your best choice. The six rooms and two efficiency apartments are carefully furnished with lovely antique furniture and original artwork, and each room has a spectacular view of Provincetown Harbor and Cape Cod Bay. The inn's fabulous restaurant is a treat, too. ~ 15 Commercial Street; 508-487-7334, fax 508-487-5115; www. theredinn.com, e-mail info@theredinn.com. ULTRA-DELUXE.

A short walk through the artsy East End brings you to and from **Windamar House**, a peaceful white clapboard guesthouse that caters mainly to women. Right across the road from Cape Cod Bay, the six rooms and two efficiency apartments (some with shared bath) vary from attractive to elegant, but the inn's prettiest areas are its spectacular gardens. Continental breakfast is provided in the common room, where guests are also welcome to watch television and videos or use the microwave to prepare snacks. Closed January to mid-April. ~ 568 Commercial Street; 508-487-0599, fax 508-487-7505; www.provincetown.com/wind amar, e-mail windamarhouse@aol.com. MODERATE TO DELUXE.

Just off of Commercial Street is the **Grand View Inn**, offering 12 reasonably priced rooms with shared or private baths. Mingle with others and enjoy the views from two outdoor patio decks where continental breakfast is served. Four-night minimum from mid-June to mid-September. ~ 4 Conant Street; 508-487-9193, 888-268-9169, fax 508-487-2894; www.grandviewinn.com, e-mail grandviewinn@attbi.com. MODERATE.

DINING

Provincetown restaurants serve everything from Italian, French, vegetarian and Continental to nouvelle, meat-and-potatoes and bistro-style fare.

Ciro & Sal's is one of Provincetown's most legendary restaurants. Established in 1951 as a coffeehouse for artists, it grew into a full-fledged restaurant serving classic northern Italian food. In 1959 Sal left and opened his own restaurant (described below), and in 2000 the place was bought by two former employees who continue the traditions begun by its founders. Dripping with atmosphere, the basement dining room resembles an Italian wine cellar with a low ceiling, slate floor and candle-lit tables. An upstairs dining room overlooks a garden. Popular dinner entrées include linguine with seafood in a plum tomato sauce and veal tenderloin with mozzarella and prosciutto. Dinner only. Closed Monday through Thursday from November through May. Closed in January. ~ 4 Kiley Court; 508-487-6444; www.ciroandsals.com, e-mail info@ciroandsals.com. MODERATE TO ULTRA-DELUXE.

For a free directory of gay- or lesbian-owned hotels, restaurants, bars, shops and services, stop by the Provincetown Business Guild. ~ P.O. Box 421-94, Provincetown, MA 02657; 508-487-2313, 800-637-8696; www.ptown.org, e-mail pbguild@capecod.net.

Red Inn is so close to the water, you can't see any land below the large picture windows that run the length of the restaurant. Built in 1805, the inn serves traditional American fare, with a sprinkling of newer dishes—vegetable spring roll, seafood pasta, pepper-crusted filet mignon, and grilled duck breast. The beautiful bar has a magnificent fireplace, antique chairs and large-paned windows with expansive ocean views. ~ 15 Commercial Street; 508-487-7334, fax 508-487-5115; www.redinn.com. DELUXE TO ULTRA-DELUXE.

Sal's Place is cozy and intimate, with Italian ambience: Chianti bottles hang from the low-beamed ceiling, bay windows are draped with lace curtains and a Modigliani poster adorns a wall. The southern Italian menu includes pasta, veal dishes and inventive seafood entrées such as *brodetto* (seafood medley) and broiled salmon with balsamic vinegar and capers. Try the homemade *tiramisu* or chocolate mousse for dessert. Dinner only. Closed November through April. ~ 99 Commercial Street; 508-487-1279, fax 508-349-6243; www.salsplaceprovincetown.com, e-mail sirrocco@attbi.com. MODERATE.

With its white cloths, salmon-colored walls and casablanca ceiling fans, **Gallerani's Café** attracts locals and out-of-towners alike. The prices are reasonable, the food is down to earth and so is the crowd. The room is bright and airy, and the long bar in back is a pleasant place for a drink. Gallerani's serves dishes such as baked stuffed lobster, filet mignon and a variety of pastas. Dinner only. Closed Monday and Tuesday from late September to mid-May; closed Wednesday from January to May. ~ 133 Commercial Street; 508-487-4433. MODERATE TO DELUXE.

Whimsically decorated with cherubs and other fanciful creatures, **Spiritus** has terrific pizza, is open late ('til 2 a.m.) and attracts a colorful crowd. Closed December through March. ~ 190 Commercial Street; 508-487-2808. MODERATE.

Café Heaven is located on a part of Commercial Street away from the touristy hoopla. Housed in an old storefront with large picture windows, the restaurant is bright and uncluttered, with white wooden tables and wooden floors. Colorful paintings by nationally known artist John Grillo adorn one wall. The food is hearty and all-American—bacon and eggs, Portuguese french toast, omelettes, tasty scones, lusty sandwiches, gourmet burgers and salads such as chicken tarragon. This popular hangout for gays and lesbians is open for breakfast, lunch and dinner. Closed January through March. ~ 199 Commercial Street; 508-487-9639. MODERATE.

A brick-walled place that's almost always crowded, **Front Street Restaurant** is one of the most reliable restaurants in town. One menu is Italian, while the other is best described as "Mediterranean fusion" (interesting combinations of vegetables, fruits and meats), and both change frequently, but the quality is consistently high. Rack of lamb, smoked duck and soft-shell crab are popular. Dinner only. Closed Tuesday from mid-September to mid-May; closed January through May. ~ 230 Commercial Street; 508-487-9715; www.capecod.net/frontstreet, e-mail frontst@capecod.net. MODERATE TO ULTRA-DELUXE.

Café Blasé features an eclectic mix of international dishes, plus some classic American fare. The sidewalk café is perfect for people-watching. Gay-friendly. ~ 328 Commercial Street, Provincetown; 508-487-9465.

Sitting right on the water, boasting picture windows galore and dripping with seaside ambience, **The Dancing Lobster** attracts tourists, locals and celebrities who love to devour red crustaceans and other seafood. Closed Monday and from late November through March. ~ 371 Commercial Street; 508-487-0900. MODERATE TO ULTRA-DELUXE.

The **Mews Restaurant & Café** has two levels of dining right on the waterfront. Elegant dinners and brunches are served downstairs, while upstairs is more casual. The cuisine is intercontinental, the fresh seafood especially good. Entertainment some nights; open-mic coffeehouse on Monday from November to mid-May, and brunch on Sunday (mid-February to early December).

~ 429 Commercial Street; 508-487-1500; www.mews.com, e-mail info@mews.com. MODERATE TO ULTRA-DELUXE.

SHOPPING   At **Norma Glamp's Rubber Stamps** you may find a necessity that you never knew you needed—a stamp with your name on it, a stamp with your child's name on it, a stamp with a reclining Marilyn Monroe, and thousands of other designs. Pair 'em up with several ink pads in bright or even shocking colors and your correspondence will never be the same. Closed January through March. ~ 212 Commercial Street; 508-487-1870; e-mail nglamp@aol.com.

Marine Specialties sounds like a straightforward place, but it's not. Housed in a barnlike room, this eclectic shop is jammed with all sorts of reasonably priced oddball nautical and military items such as antique brass buttons, old-fashioned oars, bells, baskets, antique diving gear, fog horns, vintage shoe carts, Army and Navy clothing, flags, bicycle lights, shells and fishing nets. Even people who hate to shop love this place. Closed weekdays in January and February. ~ 235 Commercial Street; 508-487-1730; www.thearmynavy.com, e-mail shop@thearmynavy.com.

Remembrances of Things Past is fun to explore even if you aren't in the mood to buy. It's full of nostalgic memorabilia from the '20s to the '50s—phones, jewelry, sports memorabilia and vintage photographs of Elvis, Marilyn and Lucy. Closed weekdays from November through March. ~ 376 Commercial Street; 508-487-9443; www.thingspast.com, e-mail shop@thingspast.com.

NIGHTLIFE   Provincetown has first-rate gay and lesbian entertainment—everything from afternoon tea dances, cabaret and ministage productions to piano bars, discos, you name it. Here are some of the most popular hotspots, a few of which draw straights and gays alike.

The hottest gay bar and disco in town is the **Atlantic House**. You can join in on the "manhunt" on Thursday or a specialty theme on Friday. There are three bars: a dance bar, a small jukebox bar and a leather bar. Cover for dance bar only. ~ 4–6 Masonic Place; 508-487-3821.

TIME FOR A TEA DANCE

During the summer a popular activity for gays is the afternoon tea dance at **The Boatslip Beach Club**, a full-service resort on the beach. The afternoon dances run daily through Labor Day and Saturdays only in September and October. Closed November to mid-April. Cover. ~ 161 Commercial Street; 508-487-1669.

The **Pied Piper** is a mixed gay bar with a waterfront deck and a big, open dancefloor. Locals say the best time to go is after 6 p.m. for the after-tea dances. Closed November through March. Cover from June 15 through September 15 and weekends in May, September and October. ~ 193-A Commercial Street; 508-487-1527; www.thepied.com, e-mail info@thepied.com.

Drag shows are a hit at the **Crown and Anchor Inn**, housed in a historic waterfront building. This place attracts gays, lesbians and straights. Cover. ~ 247 Commercial Street; 508-487-1430.

The Post Office Cabaret is the spot for lesbians in the summer, when it presents noted female performers such as Teresa Trull. The café, located downstairs, is a good place to hang out. Cover. ~ 303 Commercial Street; 508-487-2234.

RACE POINT BEACH & HERRING COVE BEACH 🏃 🚲 🏊 ⛵

"Here a man may stand, and put all America behind him," wrote Thoreau in his book *Cape Cod*. Located at the end of the Cape, both beaches have magnificent 360° views of brilliant sky, ocean, dunes and a silver sea of beach grass. On cloudy days, the winds shift, the colors change and a minimalist environment unfolds. When the sun shines, everything shimmers. Both beaches offer long stretches of clean white sand surrounded by acres of untouched land. Bicycle paths and hiking trails are everywhere. There are restrooms, showers and lifeguards, as well as a snack bar at Herring Cove. Day-use fee, $10 per vehicle (mid-June through Labor Day only). ~ To reach Race Point, take Race Point Road off Route 6; for Herring Cove, go to the end of Route 6 and follow the signs; 508-487-1256.

The South Cape

This part of the Cape is a hodgepodge of scenic villages, inexpensive motels, mini-malls and gas stations. To explore it from Provincetown, head back on Route 6 to Route 28 in Orleans, a pleasant yet unassuming residential area. At Chatham, Route 28 swings around to the west and runs along the south shore of the Cape along Nantucket Sound.

Chatham, one of the most stylish towns on the Cape, has exquisite inns, good restaurants and beautiful shops. It's a very Ralph Lauren kind of place where everyone looks as though they play tennis.

Chatham's **Information Booth** is in the middle of town. Closed mid-October to mid-May. ~ 533 Main Street, Chatham; 508-945-5199, 800-715-5567; www.chathamcapecod.org, e-mail chamber@chathamcapecod.org. For year-round information, you can stop by the **Bassett House.** ~ Intersection of Route 137 and Route 28.

At the end of Main Street, you run into **Shore Road**, lined with graceful oceanfront homes and a classic lighthouse across from the Coast Guard station.

The beacon of the **Chatham Lighthouse**, on Main Street between Bridge Street and Shore Road, is visible 15 miles out to sea. The parking area across the street is rarely empty, even in the wee hours of the foggiest morning. Along the edge of the lot, perched on the short cliff above the beautiful beach, are coin-operated telescopes that allow visitors to take a closer look at the famous, startling **Chatham Break**, the result of a ferocious storm in 1987 that forced a channel through the offshore sandbar that protects Chatham from the open sea. The Break has made boating through Chatham's tricky waters more treacherous than ever.

At the corner of Shore Road and Bar Cliff Avenue on Aunt Lydia's Cove, the **Chatham Fish Pier** is a fascinating spot at any time of the day or night. To observe the fishermen returning from their day's work, arrive at the Pier after 2 p.m. and you'll see them unloading their catch. While you're at the Pier, stop at the **Fisherman's Monument**, an interesting example of contemporary sculpture that suits its location perfectly.

HIDDEN ►   The **Old Atwood House Museum** is an unassuming 1752 shingled house exhibiting antiques, seashells and Sandwich glass. Right next to the house, a barn displays compelling murals by realist painter Alice Stallknecht. The murals depict Chatham townspeople of the 1930s in religious settings, such as Christ preaching from a dory below the Chatham lighthouse. There's also a maritime exhibit and autobiographical material of Chatham's 19th-century sea captains. Open Tuesday through Friday from mid-June to late September. Admission. ~ 347 Stage Harbor Road, Chatham; 508-945-2493; www.atwoodhouse.org, e-mail chs2002@msn.com.

Monomoy National Wildlife Refuge includes Morris and two other sandy islands immediately off the coast of Chatham, and is home to over 300 species of birds, many on the threatened and/or endangered species list. Harbor and gray seals also thrive here; over 3000 gray seals inhabit this area. The islands, which were actually one island before it split in 1978, are accessible by private boat (North and South islands) or by car (headquarters). Parts of them are off limits to the public. ~ Morris Island, Chatham; 508-945-0594, fax 508-945-9559; monomoy.fws.gov.

West of Chatham is Harwich Port, a lovely residential area, followed by Dennis Port, West Dennis, West Yarmouth and Hyannis, considerably less attractive spots. This stretch of Route 28 is mostly gas stations, coffee shops and cheap motels. But if you've had it up to here with history and quaint villages, this area is great for slumming. There are 11 miniature golf courses in the region, and one of the best is **Pirates Cove**. The Trump Tower of miniature golf, it has an elaborate pirate ship in a lagoon surrounded by terraced rock cliffs, gushing waterfalls and caves populated with animated pirates. Closed November to mid-April.

Admission. ~ 728 Main Street, South Yarmouth; 508-394-6200, fax 508-394-7575.

Solemnly perched on the edge of what was once a Wampa-noag-only cemetery, the tiny **Old Indian Meetinghouse**, is the oldest surviving meetinghouse on the Cape. Colorful, large-block quilts hang on the walls between the enormous windows. The church's only decorations, the quilts commemorate the glorious dead rather than the living members of the tribe who made them. Climb up the narrow stairs into the choir loft where you'll see some lighthearted graffiti—several masterful carvings of multi-masted ships, carefully carved during lengthy sermons sometime in the last century. Tours are given Monday, Wednesday and Friday from May through October; by appointment only the rest of the year. ~ Old Meetinghouse Road near the Route 28 intersection, Mashpee; 508-477-0208, fax 508-477-1218.

◄ *HIDDEN*

Because the Kennedys live in **Hyannis**, people usually expect it to be glamorous and beautiful, but most of the town is very commercial. The Kennedys live in the one nice area. People come to Hyannis for three reasons: the airport, ferries to the Islands, and spying on the Kennedys.

At the western end of the South Cape is **Falmouth**, a large and bustling town with a beautiful village green surrounded by some of the Cape's loveliest historic homes. One of these, which houses the **Falmouth Historical Society**, is a creamy yellow, hip-roofed 1790 Colonial building with a widow's walk. ~ 55 Palmer

South Cape: Chatham to Hyannis

Avenue (across from Village Green), Falmouth; 508-548-4857, fax 508-540-0968; www.falmouthhistoricalsociety.org, e-mail fhsoc@juno.com.

HIDDEN ►   Six miles north of town, **Ashumet Holly & Wildlife Sanctuary** offers tours as well as self-guided nature trail walks through its 45 acres. A variety of holly and wildlife abound. Admission. ~ Off Route 151 and Currier Road, East Falmouth; 508-362-1426; www.massaudubon.org, e-mail longpasture@massaudubon.org.

The rest of downtown Falmouth isn't as scenic, but it does have a number of beautiful, high-quality clothing and home furnishing stores. The **Falmouth Chamber of Commerce**, right off Main Street, can provide more information. ~ 20 Academy Lane, Falmouth; 508-548-8500, 800-526-8532, fax 508-548-8521; www. falmouth-capecod.com, e-mail info@falmouth-capecod.com.

Immediately south of Falmouth is **Woods Hole**, a small, deeply wooded, hilly village that's home to the **Woods Hole Oceanographic Institution**. The Institution isn't open to the public; it's strictly a research facility ranked in stature alongside Scripps Institute of Oceanography in California.

However, the nearby **National Marine Fisheries Service Aquarium** is open to the public year-round. In its effort to preserve regional species, everything in its 16 major display tanks is native to the area: cod, lobster, flounder. The aquarium also has a seal tank. Proof of identification is required at the door. Closed Sunday and Monday in summer, weekends the rest of the year. ~ Corner of Water and Albatross streets, Woods Hole; 508-495-2001, fax 508-495-2258; www.nmfs.noaa.gov.

HIDDEN ►   **Spohr's Garden** is a spectacular five-acre private garden that's open to the public. You'll share the wide paths with geese, ducks and the occasional squirrel. ~ 45 Fells Road, off Oyster Pond Road, between Falmouth and Woods Hole; 508-548-0623.

Built in 1828, the fixed beacon of **Nobska Light** is visible to the 30,000 ships that pass here annually. The building itself is one of the most-photographed lighthouses on the Cape; you'll probably recognize it. There are spectacular views of the nearby Elizabeth Islands and the north shore of Martha's Vineyard. ~ Nobska Point, just to the east of Woods Hole Harbor.

HIDDEN ►   To keep his colleagues from being too caught up in the earthly details of their work, a student at the Marine Biological Laboratories designed the Romanesque **St. Joseph's Bell Tower** and tiny chapel in the 1880s, then arranged to have the bells ring twice a day to remind the scientists and townspeople of God. These days, the bells ring at 7 a.m., noon and 6 p.m. The tower and chapel are surrounded by the beautifully kept, peaceful **St. Mary's Garden**. Come here to see how many varieties of plants include the name of St. Mary, or just to look out over pretty **Eel Pond**, where locals are nearly always busy with their fishing and pleasure boats. ~ Millfield Street, Woods Hole.

One of the prettiest harbors on the Cape is **Quissett**, north of Woods Hole. Traveling north from Woods Hole on Route 28, turn left onto Quissett Harbor Road. Follow this road to **Quissett Harbor**. Park the car, then walk around the edge of the water toward Buzzards Bay and up the path that goes up over the hill of **The Knob**, an outcrop that's one-half wooded bird sanctuary and one-half rocky beach. This is a favorite picnic spot for locals; it's also a great place to watch a sunset, when the breezes off Buzzards Bay aren't too chilly.

◄ HIDDEN

A romantic, dark brown 1810 farmhouse, the **Nauset House Inn** is within walking distance of beautiful beaches. One of the inn's most memorable features is a magnificent 1907 conservatory with white wicker furniture, exotic plants and grapevines. Each of the 14 guest rooms is individually decorated, and may feature tiny floral-print wallpaper, stenciling and antiques such as a handpainted Victorian cottage bed. Most of the guest rooms in the main house and carriage house have private baths. Full breakfast included. Closed November through March. ~ 143 Beach Road, East Orleans; 508-255-2195, 800-771-5508, fax 508-240-6276; www.nausethouseinn.com, e-mail info@nauset houseinn.com. MODERATE TO DELUXE.

LODGING

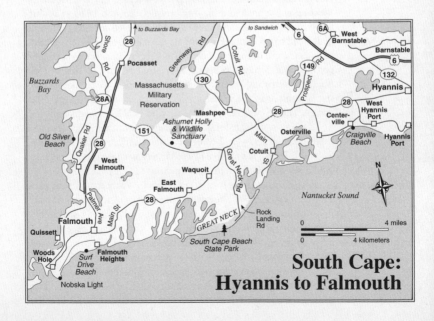

South Cape:
Hyannis to Falmouth

If tennis is your game, and the resort community idea appeals to you, you'll probably enjoy your stay at the **Wequassett Inn**. It's actually more of a small village than an inn, comprising 20 separate buildings, a swimming pool, a beach on Pleasant Bay and four carefully tended tennis courts. Try to stay in the Tennis Villa buildings 16 and 17, adjacent to the courts. The large rooms, all with views of pretty piney woods and carefully tended lawns, are tastefully decorated. On-site amenities include a tennis pro shop, fitness center, sailing lessons, boat rentals and babysitting services. A boat shuttle delivers guests to the Cape Cod National Seashore. Closed December through March. ~ Route 28 and Pleasant Bay Road, East Harwich; 508-432-5400, 800-225-7125, fax 508-432-1915; www.wequassett.com, e-mail reservations@ wequasett.com. ULTRA-DELUXE.

Motels aren't known for beautiful landscaping, but **Pleasant Bay Village Resort's** will be a welcome surprise. It boasts impeccably maintained rock and flower gardens that are so lush you hardly notice the 58 nondescript guest rooms and apartments. It is, however, only one-eighth of a mile away from a warm-water bay beach and there are guest laundry facilities. Closed November through April. ~ 1191 Orleans Road, Route 28, Chatham Port; 508-945-1133, 800-547-1011, fax 508-945-9701; www.pleasant bayvillage.com, e-mail pbv@cape.com. DELUXE TO ULTRA-DELUXE.

Chatham Bars Inn, one of Cape Cod's most luxurious grand resorts, looks like the kind of place where everyone should be wearing white linen and playing croquet. Built in 1914 as a hunting lodge, the horseshoe-shaped gray-shingled inn sits high on a gentle hill overlooking Pleasant Bay. An expansive brick veranda runs the length of the inn. The inviting lobby, luxurious rooms and comfortable cottages reflect the original beauty of this historic building with antique reproductions and period pieces like Vanderbilt Casablanca fans, authentic Victorian mantels and Hitchcock chairs. The 25-acre resort has a private beach, heated swimming pool, tennis courts, fishing, golf, magnificent theme gardens and three restaurants. ~ 297 Shore Road, Chatham; 508-945-0096, 800-527-4884, fax 508-945-6785; www.chathambarsinn.com, e-mail welcome@chathambarsinn.com. ULTRA-DELUXE.

HIDDEN ► **Port Fortune Inn** is located two blocks away from the historic Chatham Lighthouse. The small, attractive, nonsmoking inn stands in an exclusive residential neighborhood of winding streets and impeccably restored oceanfront homes. Chatham village is about a five-minute walk. The twelve rooms and one suite are decorated with traditional touches such as four-poster beds and antique furnishings. All have private baths and air conditioning; some have ocean views. A continental breakfast buffet is served in the private dining room. ~ 201 Main Street, Chatham; 508-945-0792,

800-750-0792; www.portfortuneinn.com, e-mail portfor@cape
cod.net. DELUXE TO ULTRA-DELUXE.

Since 1860, the **Chatham Wayside Inn** has set the casually
elegant tone of the busiest part of Main Street. Each of the inn's
56 rooms has air conditioning, a private bath and reproduction
period furniture. Some rooms have a can-
opied or four-poster bed. If you're planning to be in Chatham on a Friday night during the summer, try to reserve a suite with a
private deck overlooking Kate Gould Park,
where Chatham's famous band concerts are held.
~ 512 Main Street, Chatham; 508-945-5550,
800-242-8426, fax 508-945-3407; www.wayside
inn.com, e-mail info@waysideinn.com. DELUXE TO
ULTRA-DELUXE.

> Woods Hole is primarily a scientific
> community, and it looks and feels
> like a small university town, with
> a good bookstore, craft gal-
> leries and cafés. This is also
> where you can catch a ferry
> for the islands—Martha's
> Vineyard and Nantucket.

Another nearby option is **The Bradford of Chatham**. The 38 guest rooms and suites (all with private baths)
are cheerfully decorated; many have balconies or fireplaces.
There's an outdoor heated pool. A continental breakfast is included. Children over 12 only. ~ 26 Cross Street, Chatham; 508-
945-1030, 800-562-4667, fax 508-945-9652; www.bradfordinn.
com, e-mail info@bradfordinn.com. DELUXE TO ULTRA-DELUXE.

Most of Chatham's hotels are expensive, but not the **Bow Roof
House**. Located in the heart of the high-rent district, a five minute
drive from the beach, this cozy late-18th-century sea captain's
house feels comfortable and casual. A patio overlooking a scenic,
winding road makes an ideal spot for afternoon tea or cocktails.
The six guest rooms are appointed with Colonial bedspreads and
furniture, but they're far apart and private. ~ 59 Queen Anne
Road, Chatham; 508-945-1346. MODERATE.

One of the best places for families in Chatham, the 24-room
Ridgevale Beach Inn Resort Motel provides plenty of space for
kids and parents, as well as an outdoor pool, barbecues and widely spaced picnic tables. Eight condos and two cottages rent by the
week. Closed November to mid-April. ~ 2045 Main Street, Chatham; 508-432-1169, 800-244-1169, fax 508-432-1877; www.
capecodtravel.com/ridgevalebeachinn. MODERATE TO DELUXE.

Accommodations in Harwich Port are limited and expensive,
but **Harbor Walk Guest House** is an exception. The white 1880
bed and breakfast with gingerbread trim is within walking distance of the town's exclusive beaches. Six guest rooms (two with
shared bath) are decorated with new and antique furnishings. A
porch runs the length of this house overlooking the yard. A full
breakfast is included. Call for hours between November and April.
~ 6 Freeman Street, Harwich Port; 508-432-1675. MODERATE.

◀ HIDDEN

Augustus Snow House is one of the most beautiful inns in New
England. Every inch of this magnificent Queen Anne Victorian is

flawless. It's known for its fabulous wallpapers—some have ceiling borders of antique roses or clusters of fall flowers that look hand-painted. Then there are the unbelievable bathrooms—one has an antique Victorian mahogany sink, another a black-and-white diamond tile floor and claw-footed tub. The dazzling public rooms are appointed with thick oak and mahogany paneling, moreen drapes, etched-glass french doors and period antiques. Located in a quiet, affluent town, the inn has five guest rooms and a suite, all with private baths, fireplaces and ceiling fans. A full breakfast is included. ~ 528 Main Street, Harwich Port; 508-430-0528, 800-320-0528; www.augustus snow.com, e-mail info@augustussnow.com. DE-LUXE TO ULTRA-DELUXE.

Even though the Kennedy compound (near Ocean Street in Hyannis) is surrounded by tall hedges, all day long tour buses prowl this area, hoping to catch a glimpse of one of the clan. Their efforts are almost always in vain.

On a very quiet street, with its own mile-and-a-half stretch of Nantucket Sound beach, **Dunscroft By The Sea**, a 1920 Dutch Colonial inn, offers eight rooms plus a cottage. All are romantically decorated in designer linens and each room has its own bath. Some feature fireplaces and jacuzzis. There's a sitting room and screened porch to be enjoyed by all. Children over 12 only. A full breakfast is included in the room rate. ~ 24 Pilgrim Road, Harwich Port; 508-432-0810, 800-432-4345, fax 508-432-5134; www.dunscroftbythe sea.com, e-mail info@dunscroftbythesea.com. ULTRA-DELUXE.

HIDDEN ►

Route 28 from Dennis Port to Hyannis is dotted with one indistinguishable motel after another. However, if you head south toward the beach you will find some nice alternatives, like **The Lighthouse Inn**. This sprawling, 61-room, Old World resort is remarkably affordable for Cape Cod. Located on the ocean, the inn is formed around a lighthouse that stood at nearby Bass River during the 19th century. The ambience is friendly and unpretentious. Activities include shuffleboard, horseshoes, miniature golf, tennis, hiking in nearby woods, swimming in the pool or ocean and nightly entertainment. A children's director provides daily family activities, as well as day and evening babysitting. Guest rooms in the main inn are simply furnished, and separate cottages are also available. Full breakfast is included in the rates. Closed November through April. ~ 1 Lighthouse Inn Road, West Dennis; 508-398-2244, fax 508-398-5658; www.lighthouseinn. com, e-mail inquire@lighthouseinn.com. ULTRA-DELUXE.

Located in elegant Hyannis Port, the **Simmons Homestead Inn** was once a country estate. Built in 1820, this gracious inn is furnished with quality antiques, canopy beds, white wicker and brass. Sweeping porches overlook gardens leading down to Simmons Pond. The inn also has ten-speed bikes for guest use, a hot tub, a billiards room and a collection of 54 classic red sports cars.

Unlike those in most old inns, the twelve rooms and one two-bedroom suite here are fairly large. Full breakfast and evening wine are included in the rates, which drop on weekdays. ~ 288 Scudder Avenue, Hyannis Port; 508-778-4999, 800-637-1649, fax 508-790-1342; www.simmonshomesteadinn.com, e-mail simmonshomestead@aol.com. ULTRA-DELUXE.

Craigville Realty rents a wide variety of homes within a mile of Craigville Beach in Centerville. The houses, available by the week, are clean, well equipped and situated in quiet neighborhoods. ~ 648 Craigville Beach Road, West Hyannis Port; 508-775-3174, fax 508-771-5336; www.craigvillebeach.com, e-mail martinclay@attbi.com. DELUXE TO ULTRA-DELUXE.

Centerville Corners is a pleasant motel of 48 spacious rooms, all with two double beds and private bath. The decor and furnishings are rather ordinary, but the place is clean, comfortable and quiet. The attraction of Centerville Corners, other than the reasonable rates, is its location in the peaceful center of Centerville, half a mile from Craigville Beach and directly across the street from Four Seas Ice Cream. Other amenities include an indoor pool and a lawn that's perfect for croquet and badminton. Closed November to mid-April. ~ 369 South Main Street, Centerville; 508-775-7223, 800-242-1137, fax 508-775-4147; www. centervillecorners.com, e-mail ccorners@cape.com. DELUXE.

New Seabury is more of a town onto itself than a part of Mashpee. Scattered across the resort's 2300 acres of shorefront property, 13 groups or "villages" of small gray-shingled buildings offer a variety of configurations. All apartments and condos are furnished with kitchens. Facilities include three restaurants, sixteen tennis courts, two golf courses, a well-equipped health club, two outdoor pools, a three-and-a-half-mile-long private beach on Nantucket Sound, bike rentals and trails, a small shopping area, miniature golf and activities for children. Sound like Disneyland on the Cape? Believe me, you're not far off. Three-night minimum stay during the summer, two-night minimum off-season. ~ Great Neck Road, Mashpee; 508-477-9111, 800-999-9033, fax 508-477-9790; www.newseabury.com. ULTRA-DELUXE.

It may look more like a suburban home for a large family than a bed-and-breakfast inn, but **Bed & Breakfast of Waquoit Bay** is a pleasant surprise all around. The four bedrooms and bathrooms are large, furnished in floral fabrics and hung with fine paintings by the innkeepers' talented daughter. Request the room with the very private roof deck. During the summer, breakfast is served on the back porch, where there's a terrific view over the Child's River. You can also canoe and kayak from an on-site dock. ~ 176 Waquoit Highway, Waquoit; phone/fax 508-457-0084, 866-457-0084; www.bbwaquoitbay.com, e-mail bbwaquoit@hotmail.com. DELUXE.

Sea Shell Guest House and Weekly Apartments distinguish it from the otherwise indistinguishable strip of shingled guest houses along East Falmouth's Ocean Beach. The five rooms and apartments are individually decorated and boast bracing seaside views and breezes from the open windows; one apartment is furnished in a funky beach house motif, decorated with fishnets, road signs and peculiar paintings. It's a great place to spend a barefoot seaside vacation. Closed November through April. ~ 88 Menauhant Road, East Falmouth; 508-548-6941, 800-878-8024; www.seashellinn.com, e-mail seashell@gis.net. DELUXE.

Shore Haven Inn is steps from the beach and a ten-minute walk to the center of town along one of Falmouth's prettiest residential streets. The studios, rooms and efficiency apartments are relaxing, comfortable, unfussy seaside apartments—and we do mean seaside. ~ 321 Shore Street, Falmouth; 508-548-1765, 800-828-3255; www.shorehaven.net. MODERATE TO ULTRA-DELUXE.

The **Village Green Inn**, a white clapboard house with green shutters and a picket fence, is typical of many of the homes in Falmouth's historic district. Guest rooms are decorated with antiques. Two of the five rooms have working fireplaces; all rooms have air conditioning, private bath and cable TV. One room has impressive wood inlay floors. Full gourmet breakfast included. Closed January through March. ~ 40 Main Street, Falmouth; 508-548-5621, 800-237-1119, fax 508-457-5051; www.village greeninn.com, e-mail vgi40@aol.com. MODERATE TO DELUXE.

In 1849 Captain Albert Nye built **La Maison Cappellari Mostly Hall** for his Southern bride, who refused to live in a traditional Cape Cod house. Typical of houses in New Orleans' garden district, this raised Italian-style Greek Revival mansion (aptly named for its 35-foot center hall) has ten-foot windows, louvered shutters, a wraparound veranda and a wrought-iron fence. Only steps away from Falmouth's village green, this elegant inn is set well back from the road and hidden from view by trees and bushes. The six rooms are spacious and airy, furnished with antiques, including canopied, four-poster beds. Bikes are available for guest use. No smoking. A full breakfast is included. Closed January to mid-April. ~ 27 Main Street, Falmouth; 508-548-3786, 800-682-0565, fax 508-548-5778; www.mostlyhall. com, e-mail mostlyhall@aol.com. DELUXE TO ULTRA-DELUXE.

Sippewissett Cabins and Campground is a well-run campground with large sites for tents, trailers and RVs and clean, pleasant bathrooms and showers. Twelve cabins rent by the week. Closed mid-October to mid-May. ~ 836 Palmer Avenue, Falmouth; 508-548-2542, 800-957-2267; www.sippewissett.com, e-mail campcapecd@aol.com. BUDGET TO MODERATE.

As one of the jewels of New England's seaside inns, **The Inn at West Falmouth** is the place to splurge on. The turn-of-the-20th-century inn, once one of the largest private homes in New England, is steeped in glorious details, such as riotous arrangements of fresh flowers and an enormous buffet breakfast. The six rooms are all exquisitely furnished with antique furniture, art and wall-coverings, and each has its own private whirlpool bath. ~ 66 Frazar Road, West Falmouth; 508-540-7696, fax 508-540-9977; www.innatwestfalmouth.com, e-mail info@innatwestfalmouth. com. ULTRA-DELUXE.

Woods Hole Passage is full of colorful splashes, from the raspberry-pink walls in the huge front room to the carefully refinished painted antiques and wonderful paintings and photographs that are sprinkled throughout the inn. The five bedrooms are large, warm and thoughtfully laid out. A delicious home-cooked breakfast is served either at the formal dining table or more casually on individual café tables set out on the porch, which looks out over two acres of spectacular gardens and lawn. ~ 186 Woods Hole Road, Woods Hole; 508-548-9575, 800-790-8976, fax 508-540-4771; www.woodsholepassage.com, e-mail inn@woodsholepassage.com. DELUXE.

◄ HIDDEN

A popular local hangout, especially on Saturday nights, **Land Ho** is a fish and chips place. The white clapboard restaurant has red-and-white checked tablecloths, dark wood walls and nautical decorative touches. The menu offers classic Cape Cod fare—fried and broiled seafood, hearty salads, fries and burgers. The bar is a friendly watering hole. ~ Route 6A and Cove Road, Orleans; 508-255-5165, fax 508-240-2621; www.land-ho.com, e-mail goodtimes@land-ho.com. BUDGET TO MODERATE.

DINING

On their days off, chefs from the Cape's most noted restaurants often dine at **Nauset Beach Club**, on the road to beautiful Nauset Beach. The small gray-shingled restaurant offers consis-

◄ HIDDEN

AUTHOR FAVORITE

It took some searching among the trendy nouveau cuisine and northern Italian restaurants that are Cape Cod's norm, but I finally found timeless New England cooking in an equally classic setting. Housed in an 18th-century, red-and-white inn on the edge of a duck pond, the **Coonamesset Inn** serves seafood Newburg, oysters on the half shell, quahog chowder, Indian pudding and other classic native New England dishes. The Cahoon Room, one of three dining rooms, features primitive paintings by artist Ralph Cahoon depicting life on Cape Cod. The inn and restaurant are tastefully decorated with Shaker and Colonial furnishings. ~ Jones Road and Gifford Street, Falmouth; 508-548-2300, fax 508-540-9831. MODERATE TO ULTRA-DELUXE.

tently good, reasonably priced Northern Italian fare such as roasted local oysters with herbed crust, or lobster ravioli; ingredients are usually local and always fresh. They also have an excellent wine selection. Dinner only. ~ 222 Main Street, East Orleans; 508-255-8547; www.nausetbeachclub.com, e-mail info@nausetbeach club.com. MODERATE.

The **Impudent Oyster** is the place to go for traditional or exotic seafood in an informal setting next to a park. The menu changes seasonally. Many of the dishes have Chinese or Mexican ingredients, such as Szechuan beef and shrimp satay. There are also some excellent non-seafood items, such as the chicken enchiladas *rojas* and steak *au poivre*. The cheerful restaurant has skylights, a cathedral ceiling and stained-glass panels. Prices are much lower in the winter. ~ 15 Chatham Bars Avenue, Chatham; 508-945-3545, fax 508-945-9319. MODERATE TO DELUXE.

In historic Chatham village, **Christian's** draws an attractive tennis and yachting crowd. The bar, a regular watering hole for many locals, does as much business as the two restaurants combined. A semi-formal, nonsmoking dining room on the ground floor, appointed with oriental rugs, dark wood floors and linen tablecloths, serves dishes such as salmon and vegetables baked in a puff pastry, seafood sauté, pan-seared chicken breast and filet mignon topped with lobster meat. In addition to the downstairs menu items, the informal, wood-paneled restaurant and piano bar on the second floor serves appetizers, hamburgers and pizzas. The upstairs dining room is closed Tuesday from October through April. ~ 443 Main Street, Chatham; 508-945-3362, fax 508-945-9058; www.christiansrestaurant.com. MODERATE TO DELUXE.

Everyone is comfortable at the **Chatham Squire**, from retired folks who have just finished a round of golf to college kids just

REPAST AT THE ROADHOUSE

A great find in Hyannis is the **Roadhouse Café**. With four dining rooms, all with fireplaces, it can seat 200, but the restaurant has a small, intimate feel with lots of antiques, hardwood floors and oriental rugs. The menu features local seafood (whatever's in season), plus beef, veal medallions, chops and pasta dishes. Diners can choose from the regular dinner menu or a lighter bistro menu, for salads, sandwiches and thin-crust pizza. There's an impressive wine list and over three dozen types of beers, plus desserts—all made on the premises. There's live jazz on Monday and piano on Friday and Saturday. Dinner only. ~ 488 South Street, Hyannis; 508-775-2386, fax 508-778-1025; www.roadhousecafe.com, e-mail contact@road-housecafe.com. MODERATE TO ULTRA-DELUXE.

back from the beach. Paisley carpeting, exposed beams and a pool table (winter only) give the Squire the feeling of a family rec room. Good burgers, chowder and other family-type foods, along with fresh swordfish, are served by a friendly staff. ~ 487 Main Street, Chatham; 508-945-0945; www.thesquire.com, e-mail info@thesquire.com. MODERATE.

The **Chatham Bars Inn**, one of the Cape's most luxurious resorts, also boasts an excellent restaurant. The food, service and location are superb, the crowd elegant old money. The large dining room overlooking the water is decorated in soothing shades of beige, rose and navy. In the summer the restaurant offers a menu of healthful dishes such as steamed halibut, plus a regular dinner menu—grilled swordfish and roast loin of veal. Reservations are required if you aren't a guest at the inn. Breakfast and dinner served from mid-May to mid-November; breakfast only from mid-November to mid-May. ~ 297 Shore Road, Chatham; 508-945-0096; www.chathambarsinn.com, e-mail welcome@ chathambarsinn.com. MODERATE TO ULTRA-DELUXE.

It looks like something out of a Popeye cartoon. Half of **The Lobster Boat Restaurant** is a gray-shingled Cape Cod cottage with cheerful red window boxes, and the other half is an enormous red, white and blue lobster boat that seems to have grown out of the restaurant's side. The dining room overlooks a small harbor, and the decor is very yo-ho-ho with captains chairs, dark wood and rope. The atmosphere is free and easy, and the menu features lobster as well as a variety of fried, sautéed and broiled seafood. Dinner only. Closed November through April. ~ 681 Main Street, West Yarmouth; 508-775-0486, fax 508-778-6110. MODERATE TO DELUXE.

Best known for their award-winning clam chowder, **Captain Parker's Pub** has a wide range of seafood options, including a raw bar, as well as grilled pork chops, London broil and baked stuffed chicken. Sunday brunch is also available. ~ 668 Main Street, West Yarmouth; 508-771-4266; www.captainparkers.com, e-mail info@captainparkers.com. MODERATE

At **Mildred's Chowder House** you'll find a crowd of fanatical   ◄ HIDDEN
regulars. All the favorites are available: thick chowders, fish and chips, steamers and scrumptious lobster rolls. The restaurant looks like a coffee shop, but that's not the point. ~ 290 Iyanough Road (Route 28), Hyannis; 508-775-1045, fax 508-771-2196. BUDGET TO MODERATE.

Penguins Sea Grill and Steakhouse serves classic New England–style dishes, such as baked stuffed lobster and grilled salmon, as well as Italian favorites, sushi and New York sirloin. Brick walls, mahogany chairs, linen napkins and waiters outfitted in long, black, bistro-style aprons contribute to the upscale ambience. Dinner only. Closed Monday during the winter and from January to mid-February. ~ 331 Main Street, Hyannis; 508-775-2023, fax 508-778-6999. MODERATE TO DELUXE.

Founded in 1934, **Four Seas** serves traditional sandwiches such as peanut butter and jelly, lobster salad and tuna salad, but is best known for its ice cream. Owner Doug Warren, son of the original owner Dick Warren, insists on using only the freshest ingredients in the ice cream; for example, he won't make his famous peach flavor (reportedly the favorite of the Kennedy clan, who live down the street) until the fruit is ripe enough. The small dining area is decorated with photos of the all Ameri-can–looking summer crews, newspaper articles about Four Seas and framed odes from its many fans. Closed September to May. ~ 360 South Main Street, Centerville; 508-775-1394, fax 508-775-6964; www.fourseasicecream.com, e-mail dugger@fourseas icecream.com. BUDGET.

HIDDEN ▶   **The Flume** is run by Earl Mills, who is a Wampanoag Indian, a native of Mashpee and the chef. His Wampanoag upbringing provided the unusual recipes and combinations that attract food lovers to this small, casual restaurant that's built right over a herring run in the quiet village of Mashpee. Antique beadwork and artifacts hang from the walls. Sample menu items include salt codfish cakes, marinated herring and genuine Indian pud-ding. Mills enjoys meeting his guests, but he's most content when he sees his peers—other Wampanoags—cleaning their plates. Apparently, they do enjoy his food; the Flume is popular with locals as well as tourists who are interested in something out of the ordinary. Dinner only. Closed late November through March. ~ 13 Lake Avenue, Mashpee; 508-477-1456. MODERATE TO DELUXE.

Pizza Prima is the place to go for good, honest Italian food and lots of it. Generous portions of pasta are popular with lo-cals, as is the pizza. ~ 22 Falmouth Road, Mashpee; 508-477-4113. BUDGET.

The Regatta of Cotuit is considered one of the top restau-rants on the Cape. Housed in a Federal-style mansion that dates back to 1790, it specializes in New American cuisine with Euro-pean and Asian touches. Dinner selections, served in one of the eight candlelit dining rooms, include a lobster and scallop ravi-oli, pan-seared filet mignon with Great Hill bleu cheese and a sesame-encrusted tuna sashimi with wasabi vinaigrette and veg-etable potstickers. They also do wonderful things with striped bass and shrimp. A dessert not to miss is the Chocolate Seduction Cake with sauce *framboise* and *crème anglais*. Dinner only. ~ Route 28, Cotuit; 508-428-5715; e-mail regatta@cape.com. DELUXE TO ULTRA-DELUXE.

HIDDEN ▶   At **Moonakis Cafe** delicious food is served, and plenty of it. If you have your breakfast or lunch at Moonakis Café, it's likely that you won't feel any hunger pangs until well into the afternoon. Indulge in fluffy omelettes stuffed with sausage, onions, bacon or Brie. Or try a stack of fresh blueberry pancakes, thick french toast or eggs Benedict. Lunch favorites include the homemade corned beef hash and clam chowder. No lunch on Sunday. ~ 460 Route 28, Waquoit; 508-457-9630. BUDGET.

Pat's Pushcart, which offers homegrown Italian fare, is an offshoot of Pat's in Boston's North End. The red sauce is fabulous, the portions of everything are enormous and the staff is brash, fun and enthusiastic about the food they serve. Dinner only. Closed from January through the first week of April. ~ 339 Main Street, East Falmouth; 508-548-5090. BUDGET TO MODERATE.

◄ HIDDEN

Located on a winding country road, **Peach Tree Circle** is the perfect place for lunch on a lazy summer day. A combination restaurant, farm stand, gourmet health food store and bakery, it is shaded by large graceful trees. Fresh flowers and vegetables are sold in front of the small gray building with nasturtiums climbing its walls. Lunch offerings include big, healthy sandwiches, quiche, chowder, garden salad, fruit and cheese. Open for breakfast and lunch. ~ 881 Old Palmer Avenue, Falmouth; 508-548-2354. BUDGET.

The Clam Shack serves fantastic seafood in genuine seaside ambience. Unfortunately, there's not enough room to sit down inside; the tiny place is taken up with cooking vats. That's OK—walk around the building to the back deck, have a seat on a bench and watch the fishing and sailing vessels coming and going from Falmouth's Inner Harbor. Closed Labor Day to Memorial Day. ~ 227 Clinton Avenue, Falmouth; 508-540-7758. BUDGET.

Locals come to **Fishmonger's Café** because it isn't as touristy as some of the other Woods Hole restaurants. The café serves California food—avocado tostada, garden vegetable salad, tabbouleh—and Cape Cod classics like fried clams, grilled fish and chowder. The atmosphere is casual, the decor salty dog. Paned windows overlook the harbor, and there's a counter where you can have lunch or a beer while you're waiting for the ferry.

AUTHOR FAVORITE

Looking for a little joie de vivre? I recommend **Tony Andrew's Farm Stand**, a wonderful spot to be alive during strawberry season (late May to early June). Pick your own berries and pick up some other produce, too; all are reasonably priced (especially the fruit you pick yourself). ~ 394 Old Meeting House Road, East Falmouth; 508-548-4717, fax 508-548-3675.

Breakfast, lunch and dinner are served. Closed Tuesday from Labor Day through Memorial Day; closed early December through February. ~ 56 Water Street, Woods Hole; phone/fax 508-548-9148. MODERATE TO DELUXE.

Pie in the Sky is a great source of strong coffee, scrumptious pastries and pies and thick deli-style sandwiches. ~ 10 Water Street, Woods Hole; 508-540-5475; e-mail etgura@aol.com. BUDGET.

The place to go for a raw bar in Woods Hole is **Shuckers Raw Bar**. It's a bustling little spot, on the water, with table service provided by college students. In addition to raw bar offerings, you can choose from a tempting selection of seafood dishes and lobster rolls that just hit the spot. Shuckers serves its own home-brewed beer, Nobska Light. Closed Monday through Friday from mid-September to mid-October; closed mid-October to mid-May. ~ 91-A Water Street, Woods Hole; 508-540-3850; e-mail shuckersrb@aol.com. MODERATE.

SHOPPING   Aptly named **Bird Watcher's General Store** sells anything having to do with birds—field guides, binoculars, 25 kinds of birdbaths, bath heaters, birdfeeders and carving kits. It also has coffee mugs, T-shirts, floor mats and pot holders adorned with birds. ~ 36 Route 6A, Orleans; 508-255-6974, 800-562-1512; www.birdwatchers generalstore.com, e-mail bwgs.capecod@verizon.net.

HIDDEN ►   The Odells—Tom and Carol, metalsmith and painter, respectively—run a gallery out of the lovely old house that they live and work in. Carol's colorful abstract oils are an interesting and flattering complement to the jewelry, small sculptures, and vases that Tom makes out of precious metals and alloys. Closed Sunday. ~ 423 Main Street, Chatham; 508-945-3239, fax 508-945-4591; www.odellarts.com.

At **The Mayflower**, the painted sign reads "Newspapers from Boston and New York." This genuine old-time general store also sells other reading material, sunblock, toys, T-shirts and souvenirs, local preserves and jams, greeting cards and stationery. ~ 475 Main Street, Chatham; 508-945-0065, fax 508-945-0033.

HANDSOME HANDWORKS

Woods Hole Handworks is a tiny crafts shop that juts out over the water next to the drawbridge to Eel Pond. The exceptionally high quality of the goods sold here—jewelry, clothing and home furnishings—and the skillful layout and discreet lighting make it seem more like an art gallery than a shop. Closed weekends in the fall; closed late December through April. ~ 68 Water Street, Woods Hole; 508-540-5291.

Mark, Fore, & Strike is a Cape Cod institution for men's and women's fashions. ~ 482 Main Street, Chatham; 508-945-0568.

There are countless stores on Cape Cod selling nautical decorative items, but few are as classy as **The Regatta Shop**. Here you find silver nautical jewelry, sleek hand-carved house signs, baskets, racing-yacht models, painted furniture and a wide collection of museum-quality maritime posters by New England artists. Closed December through April. ~ 483 Main Street, Chatham; 508-945-4999, fax 508-945-8706; www.regattashop.com.

The Spyglass is a wonderful salty-dog store filled to its dark brown rafters with antique telescopes, microscopes, opera glasses, barometers, nautical antiques, paintings and tools. Closed Sunday during winter. ~ 618 Main Street, Chatham; 508-945-9686, fax 508-945-2033.

If you've always had a hankering to buy a Nantucket lightship basket, but don't have the time or the inclination to visit the island itself, **Oak and Ivory** is just the place for you. The baskets are expensive (from about $700 to several thousand dollars), reflecting the fine craftsmanship that goes into each delicate piece. Even if you're not a prospective buyer, you will probably enjoy your visit here; the more intricate baskets are truly works of art. Closed Sunday from Christmas to Memorial Day. ~ 1112 Main Street, Osterville; 508-428-9425, fax 508-428-3259; www.oakandivory.com, e-mail sales@oakandivory.com.

Isaiah Thomas Books has an enormous selection of first edition and slightly used books collected in a peppermint-pink Victorian house. A sampling of categories: bodice rippers, thesauri, military shipping, and children's books, divided by age group and interest. The dealer, a highly knowledgeable antique-book enthusiast, also offers appraisals, restoration and repair services. There are occasional lectures on book collecting and the store's namesake. Hours vary by season; call ahead. ~ 4632 Falmouth Road, Cotuit; phone/fax 508-428-2752.

Ben & Bill's Chocolate Emporium is an old-fashioned sweets shop that surrounds patrons with glass walls chock-full of candy in clear bins—chocolate, yes, but lots of other goodies, too. Treat yourself even more with a cone of the store-made ice cream. Closed Sunday from September through May. ~ 209 Main Street, Falmouth; 508-548-7878; e-mail benandbills@cs.com.

Named for one of Louisa May Alcott's lesser-known works, **Eight Cousins Children's Books** has lots of presents for young readers. ~ 189 Main Street, Falmouth; 508-548-5548; www.eight cousins.com, e-mail cousins8@eightcousins.com.

If you're the kind of person who always finds a treasure at a thrift shop, you probably won't go wrong at the **Falmouth Hospital Auxiliary Thrift Shop**. A particularly well-organized example of its kind, it's a great source of very inexpensive second-

◄ *HIDDEN*

hand sweaters, jackets and other clothes for the entire family. ~ 702 Palmer Avenue, Falmouth; 508-547-3992, fax 508-457-3675.

NIGHTLIFE   Musical acts, comedies and plays are presented at the **Academy Playhouse**, in a former town hall built in 1837. ~ 120 Main Street, Orleans; 508-255-1963.

Duval Street Station draws a gay and lesbian crowd for dancing to deejay music Thursday through Sunday nights. During the summer you can gather around the baby grand and sing along to your favorite showtunes. Cover on Friday and Saturday. ~ 477 Yarmouth Road, Hyannis; 508-771-7511.

The Monomoy Islands were formed by sand from Cape Cod's eroding shoreline. Carried by ocean currents, the sand initially formed shoals that eventually graduated into today's islands.

The **College Light Opera Company**'s energetic college-student company has risen to the challenge of providing live entertainment for area visitors. Music and theater-arts students from across the country audition by cassette tape. Those who are accepted perform nine shows in nine weeks, from Gilbert and Sullivan operettas to American musical comedies, from mid-June to late August. Box office is closed the rest of the year, and on Sunday. ~ 58 Highfield Drive, at the top of Depot Avenue next to Highfield Hall, Falmouth; 508-548-0668; www.collegelightopera.com.

BEACHES & PARKS   South Cape beaches are usually big and wide with huge parking lots and ample facilities. Located in residential neighborhoods, they're popular with college students and families. Because this is the ocean side of the Cape, the water tends to be rougher than on the North Cape.

NORTH MONOMOY ISLAND, SOUTH MONOMOY ISLAND AND SOUTH BEACH 🏃 ⛵ 🚣 🚤 🎣 Although these are public beaches, North Monomoy Island and South Monomoy Island are usually deserted for a very good reason—they're difficult to reach. South Beach, once completely cut off from the mainland, is now joined and accessible by foot—and more congested as a result. Still, all three areas will greet you with an expanse of pristine beauty. Throw a pair of binoculars into the picnic basket; you'll have plenty of opportunities to watch dozens of species of birds on these long, wide, clean and sandy beaches. Finned creatures and shellfish are abundant. Monomoy is known as the East Coast's largest "haul out" (resting site) for gray seals. There are no facilities. ~ Your only realistic mode of transportation to either North or South Monomoy Island is by boat. Several operators run out of Chatham and Harwich to the islands. Call Stage Harbor Marine (508-945-1860), Outermost Harbor Marine (508-945-2030) or Monomoy Island Ferry (508-945-5450) for information or to arrange a ride to either place. For information on the Monomoy Islands, contact the Monomoy National Wildlife Refuge at

508-945-0594, fax 508-945-9559; for South Beach information, call 508-945-5185, fax 508-945-5121.

HARDINGS BEACH 🏊 ⛴ Big, straight and long, this popular beach attracts a gregarious crowd of kids. Expensive houses on a hill overlook Hardings, a spot good for swimming, sunning and hanging out with the neighbors. You can surf fish for blue fish and striped bass. Modest little sand dunes with paths running through them lead down to the beach. There are restrooms, showers, lifeguards and a snack bar open from July to Labor Day. Parking fee, $10 per vehicle (July to Labor Day only). ~ Take Barn Hill Road off Route 28 to Hardings Beach Road, Chatham; 508-945-5158, fax 508-945-3550.

WEST DENNIS BEACH 🏊 🚣 ⛴ The view at the end of this sprawling beach, where the Bass River empties into the Atlantic, is of old summer houses with green lawns spilling down toward docks dotted with boats. West Dennis Beach attracts big summer crowds; its parking lot can accommodate 1600 cars. Popular with surfers, families and teens, this wheelchair-accessible beach is bordered by flat salt marsh laced with tributaries from the river. Surf fishing is good for bass and bluefish. There are restrooms, showers, a boardwalk, lifeguards, swings and a snack bar. Day-use fee, $10. ~ Take School Street off Route 28 to Lighthouse Road, West Dennis; 508-398-3568, 800-243-9920, fax 508-760-5212; e-mail denniscc@gis.net.

CRAIGVILLE BEACH 🏊 🏃 Dubbed "Muscle Beach" by the locals, this crescent-shaped beach is popular with college crowds and families alike, and there's plenty of room for both. The beach is edged with parking lots, tiny motels and clam shack–style lunch places. Swimming is good—the water warms up early in the summer, and the waves are gentle. There are restrooms, changing rooms, outdoor showers and lifeguards. You can park at the public beach, or across the street in a private lot. ~ Located on Craigville Beach Road, Centerville; 508-790-9888.

SOUTH CAPE BEACH STATE PARK 🏃 🏊 ⛴ This 432-acre park on the south side of Waquoit Bay has an incredible two-mile-long barrier beach with fragile sand dunes that provide protection against the ocean. The beach serves as a nesting ground for the endangered piping plover as well as a foraging ground for the endangered roseate tern. There's great surf casting for bluefish and striped bass, and swimming is very good. Facilities include restrooms, nature trails, a large parking lot and lifeguards in the summer. Dogs are not allowed on the beach. Parking fee, $7 (Memorial Day to Labor Day only). ~ At the end of Great Oak Road in Mashpee, you'll see a sign for the park on the left; 508-457-0495, fax 617-727-5537; www.waquoitbayreserve.org, e-mail waquoit.bay@state.ma.us.

HIDDEN ▶

ASHUMET HOLLY & WILDLIFE SANCTUARY 🏃 A treat for bird-watchers and botany enthusiasts, this 45-acre reserve abounds with many varieties of holly grown by the late Wilfred Wheeler, who donated the land to the Audubon Society. You're definitely out in the wilds here, and nothing looks manicured or fussed over. An easy-to-maneuver trail goes past a pond, forest, dogwoods, rhododendrons and a grove of Franklinia, an unusual, fall flowering shrub discovered in Georgia in 1790. Wildlife includes catbirds, so named because they make a meowing sound, belted kingfishers and pond critters such as ribbon snakes, catfish and painted turtles with bright yellow heads and dark shells. Since 1935, a barn on the property has been a nesting site for swallows. Every spring up to 44 pairs arrive to nest, then depart in late summer. Day-use fee, $4. ~ 286 Ashumet Road, East Falmouth; 508-362-1426; www.massaudubon.org, e-mail longpasture@massaudubon.org.

WAQUOIT BAY NATIONAL ESTUARINE RESEARCH RESERVE 🏃 This area comprises 2500 acres of protected estuary and barrier beaches around lovely Waquoit Bay in East Falmouth. Visit the headquarters to pick up a trail map and to inquire about guided nature walks and evening talks offered in the summer. You'll find restrooms and trails. ~ Driving east out of Falmouth on Route 28, the entrance is on the right just after Seacoast Boulevard and just before Barrows Road; 508-457-0495, fax 617-727-5537; waquoitbayreserve.org, e-mail waquoit.bay@state.ma.us.

SURF DRIVE BEACH 🚣 🏖 This narrow, curved beach attracts sea kayakers, walkers and swimmers who want to escape the crowded beaches in downtown Falmouth. Parts of the beach are quite rocky and unsafe for swimming or kayaking, but other areas are perfect for all water sports (swimming is fine outside of the rocky areas). Facilities are restrooms, showers, picnic areas, a snack bar and lifeguards. Parking fee, $10. ~ In Falmouth, drive west along Surf Drive. From Woods Hole, drive south along Church Street. You can also get there by bike on the Shining Sea Path; 508-548-8623.

OLD SILVER BEACH 🏊 This spot, popular with a college-aged crowd and locals, doesn't look like a typical Cape Cod beach. A large, modern resort is situated on the north end, and most of the beach houses in the immediate area are fairly new. A lovely cove to the south is protected by wooded cliffs jutting down to the shore. Swimming is calm; lessons are available. You'll find restrooms, showers, lifeguards, and a snack bar. Parking fee, $10. ~ Located off Route 28A on Quaker Road, Falmouth; 508-548-8623, fax 508-457-2511.

With its museum-perfect villages, Gothic Victorians and scenery that mimics the coast of Ireland, it isn't any wonder this enchanting island swells from

Martha's Vineyard

around 14,000 year-round residents to more than 100,000 in the summer months.

Discovered in 1602 by the English explorer Bartholomew Gosnold, it was named by him for its proliferation of wild grapes. Who Martha was is anybody's guess, but legend has it she may have been Gosnold's daughter or his mother.

An active whaling port in the 19th century, "the Vineyard," as it's often called, became a popular summer resort in the 20th century. Today it is a summer home to an impressive number of celebrities fiercely protected from ogling tourists by proud locals. Vacationing notables such as former President Bill Clinton, Spike Lee and Michael J. Fox have also spent time on the Vineyard.

One way not to impress the natives is to rent a moped. In the summer these noisy (but fun to drive) motorized bicycles sound like swarms of angry bees. They're considered a menace on the road, and bumper stickers that read "Outlaw Mopeds" are everywhere.

Only 20 miles long and 10 miles wide, the Vineyard can easily be toured in a day. Ferries dock at Oak Bluffs or Vineyard Haven, or you can fly in (see the "Transportation" section at the end of this chapter). The Vineyard's three major towns—Vineyard Haven, Oak Bluffs and Edgartown—are on the northeast side of the Island. The western end, known as "up-island," comprises bucolic farmland, moors and magnificent beaches.

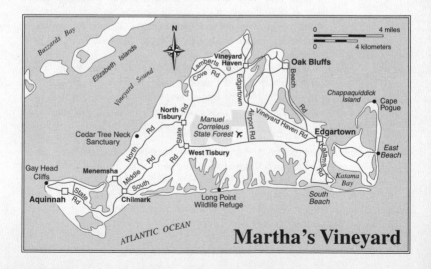

Martha's Vineyard

SIGHTS   In the '30s, Lillian Hellman and Dashiell Hammett spent their summers in **Vineyard Haven**, and ever since writers have been coming to this friendly, unpretentious town. Vineyard Haven has never attracted tourists like Edgartown, the island's main resort town, and therein lies its charm. It has the best bookstore (Bunch of Grapes), attractive shops, restaurants and a handful of wonderful inns. It's also home to the **Martha's Vineyard Chamber of Commerce**. ~ Beach Road; 508-693-0085, fax 508-693-7589; www.mvy.com, e-mail mvcc@mvy.com.

One historical sight of note here is the **Martha's Vineyard Seafaring Center**, established in 1893 to provide spiritual guidance to seamen and a refuge to shipwreck victims. Today it is part of a larger organization, the Boston Seaman's Friend Society that still offers social services and ministry to seafarers. A small museum houses a collection of seafaring artifacts. Call for hours. ~ 110 Main Street, Vineyard Haven; 508-693-9317, fax 508-693-1881.

Oak Bluffs is only a couple of miles away. A must-see here is the **Martha's Vineyard Camp Meeting Association**, also known as **Cottage City**, right off the main drag through town. In 1835, Methodist church groups started holding annual summer meetings in Oak Bluffs, with hundreds of families living in tents for the occasion. Over time the tents were replaced by tiny whimsical cottages with Gothic windows, turrets, gables and eaves dripping with gingerbread and painted in a riot of colors—pink, green and white; peach, yellow and blue. Called "campground Gothic Revival," this is the only architecture native to the Vineyard. In mid-August, on Illumination Night, a custom dating back to 1870, hundreds of colorful glowing oriental lanterns are strung up all over the cottages, creating a dazzling display of light. ~ Off Circuit Avenue, Oak Bluffs; 508-693-0525, fax 508-696-8661.

With the exception of Cottage City and Ocean Park—a genteel neighborhood of Queen Anne Victorians overlooking the water on the road to Edgartown—most of Oak Bluffs is ham-

WINERIES IN MASSACHUSETTS?

From Menemsha head back to Vineyard Haven via North Road and State Road, which goes by **Chicama Vineyards**. Massachusetts' first winery, it offers guided tours and winetastings in an appealing shop that sells wine, homemade jam, mustard and herb vinegar. Tour availability and hours vary. ~ Stoney Hill Road, West Tisbury; 508-693-0309, fax 508-693-5628; www.chicamavineyards.com, e-mail info@chicamavineyards.com.

burger restaurants and T-shirt and souvenir shops. It has a funky, saltwater-taffy kind of charm. In the center of town is the **Flying Horses Carousel**, an antique, hand-carved wooden carousel (the oldest in the country) still in operation. In the glass eye of each horse is a replica of a small animal. The carousel is closed from mid-October to Easter Sunday. Admission. ~ Lake Street at Circuit Avenue, Oak Bluffs; 508-693-9481.

Not far from Oak Bluffs is elegant **Edgartown**. With its narrow streets, brick sidewalks, graceful yachts and pristine Greek Revival and Federal-style architecture, it looks like a living museum. Prim, proper and perfect, Edgartown can sometimes appear a bit too perfect.

Edgartown has always been a town of considerable wealth and power. Prosperous whaling captains retired here, building magnificent homes along **North Water Street** that can still be seen today. Today's residents include many Boston Brahmin families. Life revolves around the formidable yacht club, where expert sailor Walter Cronkite reigns supreme.

The main thing to do in Edgartown is walk along its tree-lined streets window shopping and admiring the homes. The **Martha's Vineyard Historical Society**, tucked away on a beautiful side street, comprises several buildings, including the 1765 **Thomas Cooke House**. This fine example of pre-Revolutionary architecture once served as a customs house. The house, which has undergone little renovation since the mid-19th century, contains a small collection of relics from the Vineyard's whaling days. The 1854 Fresnel lens from the Gay Head Lighthouse is housed here; it's illuminated for a few hours each night. The historical society also maintains a **museum** with a maritime exhibit of scrimshaw, ship models, period costumes and whaling gear such as harpoons. Closed Sunday and Monday from mid-June to mid-October, and Sunday through Tuesday the rest of the year. Admission. ~ Cooke and School streets, Edgartown; 508-627-4441, fax 508-627-4436; www.marthasvineyardhistory.org, e-mail info@marthasvineyardhistory.org.

With exquisitely preserved details that include an enclosed cupola, roof and porch balustrades, shallow hipped roof, large window panes and a portico, the 1840 **Dr. Daniel Fisher House** is the Vineyard's best example of Federal-period architecture. Dr. Fisher was Martha's Vineyard's 19th-century Renaissance man—he was a doctor, whaling magnate, banker, merchant and miller. The house is now the headquarters of the Martha's Vineyard Preservation Trust, which saves, restores, and makes self-sufficient any important island buildings that might otherwise be sold for commercial purposes or radically remodeled. Dr. Fisher's house is open (and tours are conducted) daily from mid-June to mid-October.

Admission. ~ 99 Main Street, Edgartown; 508-627-4440, fax 508-627-8088; e-mail mvpt@vineyard.net.

Right off the coast of Edgartown is **Chappaquiddick Island.** Called "Chappy" by locals, it is accessible by ferry (see the "Transportation" section at the end of this chapter). There's not much to do here except go to the beach and take long walks. The island, of course, is noted for the tragic auto accident involving Senator Edward Kennedy that resulted in the death of a young woman. Chappaquiddick Road ends at Dyke Bridge, site of the mishap, which has now fallen apart and is off limits to cars and people. The island's only other road, Wasque Road, leads to Wasque Point, a beautiful natural area.

The up-island section of the Vineyard includes West Tisbury, Chilmark and Aquinnah, bucolic rural areas sporting lush green farms, meadows and scenic harbors. To explore this area from Edgartown, take the Edgartown–West Tisbury Road, which cuts through the middle of the island.

HIDDEN ▶   About the only thing in West Tisbury is **Alley's General Store,** where locals sit on the front porch drinking coffee and glaring at tourists. It's the oldest running store in Martha's Vineyard, first opened in 1858. ~ State Road, West Tisbury; 508-693-0088, fax 508-693-3315.

HIDDEN ▶   On Saturday mornings, the big social event is the outdoor produce market at **Grange Hall,** down the road from Alley's. Don't be fooled by the casual way the locals are dressed. Look closely and you'll see Rolex watches, $600 cowboy boots and maybe, if you're lucky, James Taylor. This area of the island is where many accomplished writers, musicians and artists make their homes.

From West Tisbury, follow the road to **Chilmark.** At the center of Chilmark, **Beetlebung Corner** is an intersection of the main up-island roads: Middle Road, South Road, State Road and Menemsha Cross Road. The intersection was named for a grove of beetlebung trees, the New England name for tupelo trees, which are unusual in the northeastern United States. A very tough wood, tupelo proved to be excellent for making wooden mallets, or beetles, and plugs, or bungs, that stopped up the holes of the wooden barrels used to store whale oil.

At Beetlebung Corner, bear left onto South Road, heading toward Aquinnah. After a mile, you'll pass over a bridge. Nashaquitsa Pond, or Quitsa, depending on who's talking, will be on your right, and Stonewall Pond on your left. About one-tenth of a mile farther, the road heads up a hill. Halfway up the hill, pull over to the wide spot on the side of the road. This is called the

HIDDEN ▶   **Quitsa Overlook.** Step out of the car to look out over Quitsa and Menemsha ponds. Past the ponds is the tiny village of Menemsha, then Vineyard Sound, the Elizabeth Islands and Woods Hole and Falmouth on the mainland.

About half a mile farther along on the road to Aquinnah, there's another wide spot in the road with room on both sides for two or three cars to pull over safely. This is where the locals park their cars and bikes, then walk over to drink from a fresh, sweet **aquifer**. This water is considered an antidote for various afflictions, from stress to the common cold to the occasional hangover.

◄ HIDDEN

The road ends at **Gay Head Cliffs**, towering ocean cliffs formed by glaciers over 10,000 years ago. Laced with multicolored bands of rust, lavender, wheat and charcoal, constant erosion over the millennia has washed away most of the vibrant hues. This popular tourist attraction is approached by a path lined with chowder and gift shops owned by the native Wampanoag people.

The Aquinnah Wampanoag tribe and the town of Gay Head voted to change the town name back to Aquinnah in 1998.

Leave the Gay Head Cliffs area via Lighthouse Road, then turn left onto State Road. When you get to Beetlebung Corner, turn right onto Menemsha Cross Road, which takes you out to **Menemsha Creek** and **Dutcher's Dock**, a lovely fishing village of simple, weathered gray shingled houses and short, sturdy docks. The channel seems to be impossibly narrow to be a working harbor, yet it's nearly constantly used by hardworking fishing folks.

LODGING

Crocker House Inn is tucked away on a quiet side street within walking distance of Vineyard Haven and the harbor, and dotted with gardens, patios and cobblestone walkways. The eight country-cozy, air-conditioned guest rooms in this shingled Victorian are masterfully decorated; all feature private baths, entrances and decks. For serious getaways, try a room with gorgeous harbor views and a balcony. An expanded continental breakfast is served, as well as cookies in the afternoon. ~ 12 Crocker Avenue, Vineyard Haven; 508-693-1151, 800-772-0206, fax 508-693-1123; www.crockerhouseinn.com, e-mail crockerinn@aol.com. ULTRA-DELUXE.

A classic 1918 Craftsman-style main house, a Cape Cod–style shingled carriage house, and a private cottage make up the **Thorncroft Inn**, which rests on a quiet, tree-lined residential street. There is nothing very craftsman-like about the decor, which leans toward country Colonial. Catering to couples on romantic getaways, most of the 14 guest rooms have working fireplaces and four-poster lace-canopy beds; some have jacuzzis and hot tubs. One of the best things about Thorncroft is its enormous breakfast of buttermilk pancakes, bacon, french toast, quiche, Belgian waffles, stuffed croissant sandwiches and more. If you don't mind the crumbs, they'll serve it to you in bed. ~ 460 Main Street, Vineyard Haven; 508-693-3333, 800-332-1236, fax 508-693-5419; www.thorncroft.com, e-mail info@thorncroft.com. ULTRA-DELUXE.

◄ HIDDEN

The front lawn of **Martha's Place Bed and Breakfast** overlooks Vineyard Haven harbor and a small beach. Guests enjoy their continental breakfast on a terrace overlooking this pretty vista. The six pleasant guest rooms vary in their amenities—all have private baths, some have working fireplaces, some have jacuzzis and some have fine views of the harbor. ~ 114 Main Street, Vineyard Haven; 508-693-0253; www.marthasplace.com, e-mail info@marthasplace.com. ULTRA-DELUXE.

Just up the road from the center of Oak Bluffs is the **Admiral Benbow Inn**. What makes it stand apart from many inns is that it has all the New England touches, but not a don't-put-your-drink-on-this-table attitude. The 1870s house is a beauty. All seven rooms are attractively furnished with some antique pieces, big comfortable beds and private baths. A continental breakfast is served. ~ 81 New York Avenue, Oak Bluffs; 508-693-6825, fax 508-693-7820; www.admiral-benbow-inn.com, e-mail abi@vineyard.net. DELUXE TO ULTRA-DELUXE.

Right across the street from busy, picturesque Oak Bluffs Harbor, the **Wesley Hotel** is the last of the seven large oceanfront hotels that graced Oak Bluffs during the turn of the 20th century. The Carpenter Gothic–style building, a traditional Gothic design elaborately constructed with wood, is wrapped with a wide, welcoming veranda. The hotel's 96 fairly large bedrooms are comfortably furnished. Closed mid-October through April. ~ 70 Lake Avenue, Oak Bluffs; 508-693-6611, 800-638-9027, fax 508-693-5389; www.wesleyhotel.com, e-mail wesleyhotel@aol.com. ULTRA-DELUXE.

At the top of Circuit Avenue, you can't miss the **Oak Bluffs Inn**—it's the pink building on the left with an enormous cupola atop the third story. Guests are encouraged to climb (escorted)

AUTHOR FAVORITE

One look at the **Captain R. Flander's House** and I understood why it was featured in Martha Stewart's *Wedding Book*. The rambling, 18th-century farmhouse sits on a grassy knoll overlooking ancient stone walls, rolling meadows, grazing horses, a sparkling pond, ducks and woodlands. Chilmark is so peaceful and bucolic, it's no wonder the rich and famous have chosen to live here. The inn is simply furnished, but with scenery like this who needs decoration? Guest accommodations (some with shared bath) are comfortable and sparsely appointed with antiques and country-style furnishings. Two ultra-deluxe-priced cottages are available. Continental breakfast is served. Closed November through May. ~ North Road, Chilmark; 508-645-3123; www.captainflanders.com. ULTRA-DELUXE.

up to the cupola to take in the view of Oak Bluffs' rooftops and the ocean beyond. The inn's guest rooms and common areas are filled with fine examples of cottage-style furniture, prints and wall coverings. All nine accommodations have private baths, bright bathrooms, air conditioning and views of charming Oak Bluffs. Continental breakfast served. Closed November through April. ~ Corner of Circuit and Pequot avenues, Oak Bluffs; 508-693-7171, 800-955-6235, fax 508-693-8787; www.oakbluffsinn. com, e-mail bmyguest@oakbluffsinn.com. ULTRA-DELUXE.

The shingled, gingerbreaded 1872 **Oak House** is appropriately named—there's oak, oak everywhere, from the walls to the ceilings to the fine examples of antique oak furniture. The large wraparound veranda has wonderful rocking chairs and swings where many guests spend a lot of time relaxing and looking out across Seaview Avenue to the ocean. Many rooms have private balconies. All eight guest rooms and both suites have private baths and air conditioning. Continental breakfast and afternoon tea are provided. Closed mid-October to mid-May. ~ Corner of Seaview and Pequot avenues, Oak Bluffs; 508-693-2966, 800-245-5979, fax 508-696-7293; www.vineyard.net/inns, e-mail inns@vineyard.net. ULTRA-DELUXE.

The **Arbor Inn** is a quintessential New England cottage, fresh and white with a winsome vine-clad arbor, brick path and English garden. Located a couple of blocks away from Edgartown's shopping district, the inn offers ten guest rooms simply but attractively appointed with antiques and fresh cut flowers, as well as a one bedroom house that is available for rent on a weekly basis. A continental breakfast is served in the old-fashioned formal dining room or in the garden. Closed November through April. ~ 222 Upper Main Street, Edgartown; 508-627-8137, 888-748-4383, fax 508-627-9104; www.mvy.com/arborinn. DELUXE TO ULTRA-DELUXE.

Built in 1840 by Edgartown's leading physician, Dr. Clement Frances Shiverick, the **Shiverick Inn** is a fantastic example of the high Greek Revival style. Inside, the common areas and ten guest rooms are furnished with fine antiques and pieces of art of the same period. All guest rooms have private baths and air conditioning; six have fireplaces. The library on the second floor has a terrace that looks out over the Old Whaling Church. In the backyard, there's a small flagstone terrace and flower garden. A full gourmet breakfast is served in the airy Garden Room. Gay-friendly. ~ 5 Pease's Point Way, Edgartown; 508-627-3797, 800-723-4292, fax 508-627-8441; www.shiverickinn.com, e-mail shiverickinn@vineyard.net. ULTRA-DELUXE.

Edgartown Commons has 35 comfortably furnished efficiencies, from studios to one- and two-bedroom apartments. Outside, there are grills and picnic tables, a play area for the kids and an outdoor swimming pool. Closed late October to early May. ~ 20 Pease's Point Way, Edgartown; 508-627-4671, fax 508-627-4271. DELUXE TO ULTRA-DELUXE.

The **Harbor View Resort** is Edgartown's only waterfront resort with conference facilities. Its 124 rooms, suites and cottages all have private bath, telephone and cable TV. Rooms are generously proportioned, and decorated with four-poster beds, armoires, antique prints and watercolor landscapes by local artists. The hotel's gazebo is one of the most-photographed structures on the Edgartown waterfront. True to its name, the Harbor View does indeed have some of the best views of the harbor. ~ 131 North Water Street, Edgartown; 508-627-7000, 800-225-6005, fax 508-627-7845; www.harbor-view.com. ULTRA-DELUXE.

It is believed that humans first came to the Vineyard after the Ice Age but before melting glaciers raised the sea level, separating it from the mainland. Remains of Indian camps from around 2270 B.C. have been discovered on the Island.

The **Tuscany Inn at the Captain Fisher House** reflects the innkeepers' flair for balancing color, space and magnificent furniture. The result is an inn with an elegant, airy feeling. The eight guest bedrooms are all doubles with private bath (one is detached), and many have whirlpool baths. Breakfast is served in the tile-floored dining room or, in warm weather, on the flagstone terrace. Closed mid-December through March. ~ 22 North Water Street, Edgartown; 508-627-5999, fax 508-627-6605; www.tuscanyinn.com, e-mail tuscany@vineyard.net. ULTRA-DELUXE.

If you want to stay in a Vineyard classic, choose the **Daggett House**'s four 17th-century buildings. Located on the water, this inn has 31 rooms furnished with numerous antiques; some have wonderful water views while others have kitchenettes. The main house has its own dock and a Chimney Room (circa 1660), said to have been Edgartown's oldest tavern; it's now used as a dining room for breakfast (open to the public). ~ 59 North Water Street, Edgartown; 508-627-4600, 800-946-3400, fax 508-627-4611; www.thedaggetthouse.com, e-mail innkeeper@thedaggetthouse.com. DELUXE TO ULTRA-DELUXE.

For an inn with such a prestigious address, the **Shiretown Inn** has pretty good prices. Some rooms are furnished with antiques and have private entrances and air conditioning; others, especially those in the carriage houses in the back of the inn, are quite plain, rather than quaint. A cottage rents weekly and features a full kitchen. All have private bathrooms. ~ 44 North Water Street, Edgartown; 508-627-3353, 800-541-0090, fax 508-627-8478; www.shiretowninn.com, e-mail paradise@shiretowninn.com. DELUXE TO ULTRA-DELUXE.

HIDDEN ►   With its elaborate windows and dormers, the **Victorian Inn** looks formal from the outside, but it's an easygoing place located one block from Edgartown harbor. Guests enjoy the cool, private garden in the summer. The 14 guest rooms are sweet and tidy with canopy beds, floral wallpaper, antiques and some antique reproductions; a few rooms have private balconies. Full breakfast included. Closed January to mid-February. ~ 24 South Water Street, Edgartown; 508-627-4784; www.thevic.com, e-mail victorianinn@vineyard.net. ULTRA-DELUXE.

The **Charlotte Inn** is one of the most elegant and luxurious inns in America. A sparkling white 1860 sea captain's house, it is nestled amid a profusion of flowers, lawns, wisteria and latticework. Guests check in at a gleaming English barrister's desk. Twenty-five meticulous guest rooms are appointed with fine English antiques, handpainted china and equestrian prints. Suites, located in separate buildings, are quite extravagant—one has its own English cottage garden, another a bedroom balcony and palladium window. A continental breakfast is served in the inn's dining room. ~ 27 South Summer Street, Edgartown; 508-627-4751, fax 508-627-4652; e-mail charlotte@relaischateaux.com. ULTRA-DELUXE.

The homey, unpretentious **Summer House** is a place for vacationers who enjoy staying in a B&B that really is someone's home. There's a big, beautiful, very private front yard with a wonderful ivy-covered wall as a backdrop. The two large guest bedrooms have king-sized beds. Full continental breakfast is served. Closed October to mid-May. ~ 96 South Summer Street, Edgartown; 508-627-4857; www.mvsummerhse.com. DELUXE.   ◄ HIDDEN

Hostelling International—Martha's Vineyard is an ideal place to stay on the Vineyard if you want to spend a lot of time biking. It's on the edge of the Correleus State Forest, which is crisscrossed with bike paths. The hostel was the first purpose-built youth hostel in the U.S. when it was built and opened in 1955. Sleeping areas are dormitory-style bunk beds and are separated by sex. All linen is provided and no sleeping bags are allowed. Bathrooms are large, as they are shared by all (also segregated by sex). There's also a fully equipped kitchen as well as a common room with a fireplace. Hostels aren't for everyone, but if you know what to expect, this is a good one. Reservations recommended. Closed mid-November through March. ~ 525 Edgartown–West Tisbury Road, West Tisbury; 508-693-2665, 888-901-2097, fax 508-693-2699; www.usahostels.org, e-mail mvh@yahoo.com. BUDGET.

Talk about off the beaten path. **Lambert's Cove Country Inn** is down a long country road deep in the woods. Surrounded by vine-covered stone walls, expansive lawns and apple orchards, the white clapboard inn is appointed with Shaker- and Colonial-style antiques. Some of the 15 guest rooms have private decks, and one has a greenhouse sitting room. Guests have access to Lambert's Cove Beach, one of the Vineyard's most beautiful private beaches.   ◄ HIDDEN

Full breakfast included. Three-night minimum stay required in summer. ~ Lambert's Cove Road, West Tisbury; 508-693-2298, fax 508-693-7890; www.lambertscoveinn.com, e-mail lambinn@gis.net. DELUXE TO ULTRA-DELUXE.

The nice folks at **Flanders Up-Island Real Estate** rent properties seasonally, bi-weekly or monthly for homeowners all over Aquinnah, Menemsha, Chilmark and West Tisbury from April through October. They have houses and prices to suit nearly everyone. ~ 59 State Road, Chilmark; 508-645-2632, fax 508-645-3346; www.flandersrealestate.net, e-mail flandersre@flandersreal estate.net. MODERATE TO ULTRA-DELUXE.

The emphasis is on the luxury of spare decorations and peaceful surroundings at **Menemsha Inn and Cottages,** which is situated on 14 acres of tranquil forest in beautiful Menemsha. There are six luxurious rooms in the Carriage House, nine smaller, bright and lovely rooms in the inn's main building, and twelve fairly spartan housekeeping cottages. There's also a two-bedroom, two-bath suite, complete with kitchen. All rooms and cottages have private bath, and each cottage has a screened-in porch, fully equipped kitchen, outdoor shower, barbecue and wood-burning fireplace. There's a tennis court and fitness room. Closed late October to late April. ~ North Road between Menemsha Cross Road and Menemsha Harbor, Menemsha; 508-645-2521, fax 508-645-9500; www.menemshainn.com. ULTRA-DELUXE.

HIDDEN ► **Duck Inn** is a health-oriented B&B that offers a variety of luxuries, including massages, post-massage relaxation in the inn's outdoor hot tub, all-natural fibers on the comfortable beds, and delicious breakfasts that accommodate vegetarians, vegans and flesh-eaters alike. Some of the island's most spectacular beaches are but a few minutes' walk through the waving beach grass. The five guest rooms are furnished eclectically with a duck motif, oriental prints and funky old calendars and posters. The suite in the basement has a large fireplace; all rooms have private baths. Gay-friendly. ~ 10 Duck Pond Way, Aquinnah; 508-645-9018, fax 508-645-2790. DELUXE TO ULTRA-DELUXE.

The Outermost Inn is on a 20-acre piece of land that has the island's second-most spectacular ocean view. (For the best, walk a few hundred yards up the hill to the Aquinnah lighthouse.) The inn has six guest rooms and one suite, all with private bath and one with a private whirlpool. Teal-blue carpets in the halls, unpainted furniture, subdued colors and natural fabrics suit the inn's location perfectly; nothing detracts from the location or the views. This is one of the most romantic inns in coastal New England; it's worth the splurge. Closed October through April. ~ 81 Lighthouse Road, Aquinnah; 508-645-3511, fax 508-645-3514; www.outermostinn.com, e-mail inquiries@outermostinn.com. ULTRA-DELUXE.

Only Edgartown and Oak Bluffs serve liquor, but you can bring your own when you dine in other towns.

A gray-shingled saltbox overlooking the harbor, rustic **Black Dog Tavern** is a Vineyard institution popular with the yachting crowd. The best place to sit in the summer is an enclosed porch with beautiful ocean views. The changing menu is traditional—clams casino, codfish, roast duckling—with an emphasis on fresh seafood. Breakfast, lunch and dinner are served. ~ Beach Street Extension, Vineyard Haven; 508-693-9223; www.theblackdog.com, e-mail info@theblackdog.com. ULTRA-DELUXE.

Chef/owner Jean Dupon prepares a terrific selection of classic French cuisine at the classy **Le Grenier**, from vichyssoise to escargots to frogs' legs provençale. Dinner only. ~ 82 Main Street, Vineyard Haven; 508-693-4906; www.legrenierrestaurant.com, e-mail info@legrenierrestaurant.com. DELUXE TO ULTRA-DELUXE.

Cephrus, a trendy establishment with deco light fixtures, gray industrial carpeting, and a Lambert's Cove beach-scene mural, attracts a young, stylish crowd. The menu includes grilled meat, poultry and seafood with different sauces such as Mediterranean or marinara. Other dishes include rack of lamb, pan-seared lemon-pepper salmon, and grilled halibut with risotto. An awning-covered outdoor patio in front is a good spot for people watching in the summer. ~ 9 Main Street, Vineyard Haven; 508-693-3416, fax 508-693-4095; www.tisburyinn.com. MODERATE TO DELUXE.

It's a bit off the beaten track in busy Vineyard Haven, but maybe that's why the locals go to **Louis'** for pizza and take-out salads and pasta dishes. ~ 350 State Road, Vineyard Haven; 508-693-3255, fax 508-696-7436. BUDGET TO MODERATE.

◄ *HIDDEN*

Giordano's is a classic family-style restaurant, and yes, there usually are a lot of large families here, with diners gobbling up what some people insist are the Vineyard's best fried clams. There's also an Italian restaurant on the premises, serving up traditional fare. Closed late September to late May. ~ Lake and Circuit avenues, Oak Bluffs; 508-693-0184; www.giosmv.com, e-mail gio@giosmv.com. MODERATE.

◄ *HIDDEN*

AUTHOR FAVORITE

For me, walking along the beach trying to eat an ice cream cone before it melts just about epitomizes summer. The island's best homemade ice cream is at **Mad Martha's**, a bright, noisy, crowded spot that's full of families and college kids from spring through fall. ~ 12 Circuit Avenue, Oak Bluffs; 508-693-9151; e-mail mvmad@aol.com. BUDGET.

The homey **Linda Jean's** serves fantastic, thick pancakes and other delicious breakfast items, as well as such lunch and dinner fare as baked stuffed chicken, pork chops, fresh fish and meatloaf. Check the blackboard for daily specials. ~ 34 Circuit Avenue, Oak Bluffs; 508-693-4093. BUDGET TO MODERATE.

HIDDEN ►   Small, casual **Jimmy Sea's Pan Pasta** has enormous portions of delicious pastas ranging from raviolis, tortellonis, to flat pastas—all cooked to order and served in the pan. The *frutti di mare* is for those who can't get enough of shellfish (all types of shellfish with red sauce over linguini). If you're only moderately hungry, you may be able to get two meals out of one dinner—many people carry doggy bags out of Jimmy's. Dinner only. ~ 32 Kennebec Avenue, Oak Bluffs; 508-696-8550, fax 508-696-0282. MODERATE TO DELUXE.

David Ryan's Restaurant is the kind of place where you stop for a drink and end up staying for hours. It's a restaurant/bar where you can order anything from a burger to clams to a big bowl of pasta topped with tasty sauce. Downstairs is informal with high stools situated around tall tables and a bar; upstairs has a selection of booths and tables and an intimate martini bar. Closed in January. ~ 11 North Water Street, Edgartown; 508-627-4100, fax 508-627-5475; www.davidryans.com. MODERATE TO ULTRA-DELUXE.

The Coach House serves European and American classics with an Asian influence. Breakfast might include a spicy omelette of smoked turkey and chipotle or eggs poached in a baked tomato. For lunch, try the chicken salad with sweet and hot mustard sauce; for dinner, you can choose from yellowfin tuna with braised baby bok choy or osso buco with sautéed winter greens, and cannellini beans. Each week there's an Asian night. ~ 131 North Water Street, Edgartown; 508-627-3761; www.harbor-view. com/coach_house. DELUXE TO ULTRA-DELUXE.

The **Charlotte Inn's L'étoile**, one of the finest dining establishments in New England, is perfect for a special occasion. An incredibly beautiful restaurant, it's in a 19th-century conservatory with skylights, bowed windows, a flagstone floor and lush plants. In this romantic, fantasylike environment, contemporary French cuisine is served. The prix-fixe menu offers fresh game and seafood entrées. Sauces are light and aromatic, flavored with fresh herbs, exotic fruit, shiitake mushrooms and shallots. Dinner only. Limited hours during the off-season. ~ 27 South Summer Street, Edgartown; 508-627-5187, fax 508-627-4652. ULTRA-DELUXE.

Even if you're not knocked out the by the prix-fixe surf-and-turf menu (steak, salad, lobster, etc.) at **Home Port**, come here for the mesmerizing view. The rustic, brown-shingled restaurant overlooks sand dunes, rolling green pastures and idyllic Menemsha harbor. An outdoor patio is available for summer dining.

Dinner only. Closed mid-October through April. ~ 512 North Road, Menemsha; 508-645-2679, fax 508-645-3119. DELUXE TO ULTRA-DELUXE.

Small, exclusive **Beach Plum Inn** is easy to miss. A tiny sign points the way down a dirt road to a building without a sign that looks like a private home with a terraced rock and flower garden. Once you've figured out where to go, you'll be glad you came. The intimate dining room has large picture windows overlooking Menemsha Harbor. The cuisine features items such as steamed lobster, duck with honey-curry sauce and rack of lamb. Breakfast and dinner served. Closed January through April. ~ North Road, Menemsha; 508-645-9454, 877-645-7398, fax 508-645-2801; www.beachpluminn.com, e-mail info@beachpluminn.com. ULTRA-DELUXE.

> Carly Simon, James Taylor, Caroline Kennedy Schlossberg, Diana Ross, Beverly Sills, Walter Cronkite, Mike Wallace and Art Buchwald all have homes on "the Vineyard."

The view of the sunset at the Outermost Inn Restaurant is unforgettable and distracting—don't forget to eat. Perched next to the cliffs at Gay Head, the **Outermost Inn Restaurant** serves dinner only; it's extremely popular, and reservations are essential. The prix-fixe meals, a variety of gourmet and home-style American and French-inspired foods, are scrumptious. Closed mid-October to mid-May. ~ 81 Lighthouse Road, Aquinnah; 508-645-3511; www.outermostinn.com, e-mail inquiries@outermostinn.com. ULTRA-DELUXE.

The **Aquinnah Restaurant**, a slightly shabby establishment that's perched on top of the highest of the Gay Head Cliffs, has a breathtaking view of the cliffs, the ocean, Noman's Land and the Elizabeth Islands. The food varies from good—chowder, lobster and scallops—to uninspired, but you may not notice what you're eating as you indulge in the view. Closed Columbus Day to Easter. ~ On the Cliffs, Aquinnah; 508-645-3867, fax 508-645-2427. DELUXE TO ULTRA-DELUXE.

Bunch of Grapes Bookstore is a writers' hangout. The best bookstore on the island, it has shelves well-stocked with quality fiction and poetry. The store regularly hosts autograph parties. ~ 44 Main Street, Vineyard Haven; 508-693-2291, fax 508-693-2263.

SHOPPING

Timeless Treasures is a tiny shop that's full of antiques, pine furniture and hand-knit sweaters from Ireland, Victorian and Edwardian silverware and much more. ~ Main and Spring streets, Vineyard Haven; 508-696-7637.

Linen, antique English pine furniture, handpainted coffee mugs and nubby hand-knit sweaters can be found at **Bramhall & Dunn**. ~ 23 Main Street, Vineyard Haven; 508-693-6437.

Housed in an old barn, **Bowl & Board** is full of useful household items, such as picture frames, kitchen utensils, small carpets and candles for your living room, dining room and porch. ~ 35 Main Street, Vineyard Haven; 508-693-9441.

If you want to advertise your vacation destination on your clothes, be cool and buy a T-shirt, sweatshirt or cap at the one-and-only **Black Dog General Store.** ~ 716 Water Street, Vineyard Haven; 508-696-8182.

In the Woods, a cavernous red brick room, sells handsome hand-crafted wooden spoons, plates, bread platters, bowls, cutting boards, Christmas ornaments, tables and benches. Prices are reasonable, and the craftsmanship is superb. Closed Monday through Friday from November through April. ~ 55 Main Street, Edgartown; 508-627-8989.

The Great Put-On has the Vineyard's most stylish line of clothing for men and women. Closed mid-April to mid-October. ~ 1 Dock Street, Edgartown; 508-627-5495.

HIDDEN ►   **Penumbra Photographs** has a fascinating selection of top-quality vintage photographs spanning from the 1850s to the 1950s that will interest amateurs and collectors alike. Open July, August and September; closed Monday. ~ 33 North Summer Street, Edgartown; 508-627-9002.

Granary Gallery's best wares are photographs by the superb local photographer Alison Shaw and adopted Vineyarder Alfred Eisenstadt, one of *Life* magazine's best-known photographers. Also on display and for sale are antiques and McAdoo hand-hooked rugs. ~ 636 Old County Road, West Tisbury; 508-693-0455, 800-472-6279.

The **Field Gallery** is known for the field of dancing white figures that have become one of the icons of the Vineyard's contemporary cultural life. It also has three rooms that showcase local and national talent. Open April to December and off-season by appointment. ~ 1050 State Road, West Tisbury; 508-693-5595; e-mail fieldgallery@adelphia.net.

Pandora's Box carries wonderfully comfortable women's clothing that suits the laidback to dressy Vineyard lifestyle. ~ Basin Road, Menemsha; 508-645-9696.

NIGHTLIFE   Throughout the year, the **Vineyard Playhouse**, the Island's only professional theater, presents an interesting selection of new works and classics. ~ 24 Church Street, Vineyard Haven; 508-693-6450, 508-696-6300 (summer box office).

Island Theatre Workshop is the Vineyard's oldest theater. Year-round it presents a wide range of plays, musicals and children's theater performed by Vineyard actors. With no permanent home, it stages productions at different locations throughout the island. ~ P.O. Box 1893, Vineyard Haven, MA 02568; 508-693-5290.

Seasons Atlantic Connection, a hopping dance and music club, has year-round live bands and entertainment. Deejay dancing happens on Friday and Saturday. Cover. ~ 19 Circuit Avenue, Oak Bluffs; 508-693-7129.

The Island House is a restaurant featuring live music several nights a week. The styles run the gamut from blues to rock. Open during summer. ~ 11 Circuit Avenue, Oak Bluffs; 508-693-4516.

Old Whaling Church Performing Arts Center offers cultural lectures, classic films, concerts and plays throughout the year. Located in an 1843 Greek Revival church, the center has featured stars such as Patricia Neal, Andre Previn and Victor Borge. Folk artists such as Arlo Guthrie have also graced the stage. ~ Old Whaling Church, 89 Main Street, Edgartown; 508-627-4440.

Keep the wooden nickel the bartender hands you along with your beer at **The Newes from America**. When you've collected 500 of them, you'll get a Newes glass engraved with your name. When you present your second 500 nickels, the Newes will engrave your name on one of their bar stools. Don't get on the wagon now—in order to keep your bar stool, you have to keep up a 500-nickels-a-year minimum. ~ 23 Kelley Street, Edgartown; 508-627-4397 or 508-627-7900, fax 508-627-8417.

Popular with the under-30 set, **Hot Tin Roof**, owned by Carly Simon and others, has live rock-and-roll bands, comedy nights and a jumping dancefloor in the summer. Open Memorial Day through Columbus Day. Cover. ~ Martha's Vineyard Airport Road; 508-693-1137, fax 508-693-9320.

FELIX NECK WILDLIFE SANCTUARY 🏃 A 350-acre haven for wild animals, birds, flora and fauna, the sanctuary has four miles of easy walking trails through salt marshes, thick forests and open meadows of wildflowers. The area is managed by the Massachusetts Audubon Society. There are activities for children and adults, including guided nature walks and bird-watching trips geared toward novices and experts alike. You'll find restrooms, an interpretive exhibit center and a gift shop. Admission (free for Massachusetts Audubon Society members). ~ Three miles from the center of Edgartown on the Edgartown–Vineyard Haven

BEACHES & PARKS

◆◆◆

BEACH TIPS

Beaches in rural West Tisbury, Chilmark and Aquinnah are dramatic, untamed and less crowded than beaches near the Vineyard's three towns. But the parking lots are for residents only, and in the summer guards check to see if cars have resident stickers. Nonresidents ride bikes to these beaches. Shore fishing is excellent from all south shore beaches.

Road, off State Road, between Oak Bluffs and Edgartown; 508-627-4850, fax 508-627-6052.

NANTUCKET SOUND BEACHES Strung together along protected Nantucket Sound are Oak Bluffs Town Beach, Joseph A. Sylvia State Beach, Bend-in-the-Road Beach and Lighthouse Beach. Swimming lessons are offered at some of the beaches, and bicycle paths run alongside the shore, which is bordered by ponds, salt marsh and summer homes. A stately lighthouse overlooks Lighthouse Beach. You can expect lifeguards but not much else. ~ Along Beach Road between Oak Bluffs and Edgartown.

The beaches of the Nantucket Sound are where the movie *Jaws* was filmed, but don't panic—this isn't shark country. The narrow, gently curved shoreline has clean sand and calm water.

SOUTH BEACH Also called Katama South, this popular, mile-long, Atlantic-facing beach runs into Norton Point Beach on one end and a privately owned beach on the other. Wide, expansive and flat, it is surrounded by heath dotted with 20th-century homes—a rare sight in Martha's Vineyard. In the summer the air is soft and warm from southwesterly winds. The beach allows swimming (watch out for the undertow), and fishing is excellent; you might be able to surf or windsurf if the waves or wind show up. You'll find restrooms, changing rooms and lifeguards. ~ Off Katama Road, south of Edgartown. You may take a shuttle bus from the center of town; 508-627-6145.

FULLER STREET BEACH A favorite among the many young folks who spend the summer in Edgartown, it's a quick bike ride away and a great place to take a break from Edgartown's other, more crowded beaches. There are no facilities or lifeguards. ~ At the end of Fuller Street near Lighthouse Beach; 508-627-6165, fax 508-627-6123.

HIDDEN ▶ **CAPE POGE WILDLIFE REFUGE & WASQUE RESERVATION** If you want to get away from it all, take the two-minute car and passenger ferry from Edgartown to these wilderness areas on Chappaquiddick Island, an undeveloped peninsula of vast, empty beaches and moors. (Be prepared: There are often long ferry lines.) The refuge and reservation are adjacent to each other and form the northeastern tip of the Vineyard. Both offer an assortment of low dunes, ponds, tidal flats and cedar thickets. Wildlife abounds, including noisy least terns, piping plovers, common terns and American oystercatchers. East Beach, part of the Cape Poge Wildlife Refuge, is the best spot for swimming (although it is sometimes rough), and is a great spot to catch blue fish. Wasque Point is a world-renowned fishing area that teems with bonito, striped bass and more. Motorized boats are prohibited. There are restrooms. Day-use fee, $3 per person; parking fee, $3. ~ Cape Poge is at the end of Chappaquiddick Road on the other side of Dyke Bridge. Wasque Point is at the end of Wasque Road; 508-693-7662, fax 508-693-7717.

MANUEL CORRELEUS STATE FOREST 🏃 🚲 🐎 🏕 Right in the center of the Vineyard lie over 5000 acres of towering evergreens and scrubland. Laced with bicycle and horseback-riding paths, as well as hiking trails carpeted with soft, thick pine needles, the cool, hushed forest offers a peaceful respite from the Vineyard's wind-bitten moors and wide-open beaches. Beware of ticks. ~ Off Barnes Road between West Tisbury and Edgartown; phone/fax 508-693-2540.

LONG POINT WILDLIFE REFUGE 🏃 🏊 ⚓ A never-ending, loosen-your-teeth dirt road is the only way to get to this mystical, magical wildlife refuge. The road forks here and there; just follow the signs and eventually you come to a small parking lot (seasonal parking with a fee). Shortly beyond lies an endless grass and huckleberry-covered heath that looks like a prairie with two enormous ponds. Tisbury Great Pond and Long Cove are home to black ducks, bluebills, ospreys, canvasbacks and swans. Beyond the ponds you'll discover a sea of silver beach grass and a white sand beach. Swimming and fishing are good, although the waters can get rough and there are no lifeguards on duty. Facilities are limited to portable toilets and a freshwater pump. Day-use fee, $3 per person; parking fee, $9. ~ This place is very difficult to find. It's one mile west of Martha's Vineyard Airport off Edgartown–West Tisbury Road on Waldrons Bottom Road, a deeply rutted dirt road without a sign; look for ten mailboxes in a row and the sign for Long Point. It's best to ask locals for directions; 508-693-7392, fax 508-696-0975; e-mail longpoint@ttor.org.

MOSHUP BEACH 🏊 🎣 ⚓ Adjacent to the multicolored Gay Head Clay Cliffs, a national landmark off-limits to the public, this long, flat, sandy beach is extremely popular in the summer. Land Bank is great for sunning, fishing, swimming and beachcombing, but be cautious of the surf. You can pay a hefty fee to park at the lot behind the dunes (508-693-7662), but you may be better off taking the Up Island Shuttle Bus that runs in the summer. There are restrooms and snack bars nearby. Parking fee, $15. ~ At the western tip of the Vineyard at Moshup Trail; 508-627-7141, fax 508-627-7415.

CEDAR TREE NECK SANCTUARY 🏃 The raucous chirping of   ◄ HIDDEN
kingfishers, osprey, terns and Carolina wrens is the first thing to greet you at this 300-acre preserve. This is their kingdom, and what a spectacular place it is. Follow one of several well-marked paths through hilly woods of beech, sassafras, red maple, hickory oak and beetlebung. Soon the sky opens up, and, out of nowhere, extraordinary vistas appear of deep ponds, rolling sand dunes and the ocean

beyond. Paths lined with ferns, moss and mushrooms lead down through the woods to an elevated catwalk and the shore. Unfortunately, picnicking is not allowed, and swimming and fishing are prohibited in the sanctuary. ~ From State Road in West Tisbury, take Indian Hill Road to a dirt road with a Cedar Tree Neck sign. The road goes down a hill to the parking lot; 508-693-5207, fax 508-693-0683; e-mail info@sheriffsmeadow.org.

Nantucket

Thirty miles out to sea from Cape Cod, this magical, fog-shrouded island is a study in contrasts. With its historic homes and cobblestone streets, Nantucket looks like storybook land, circa 1800. Yet it has quite a number of sophisticated New York City/San Francisco–style restaurants and Madison Avenue shops. Outside town, Nantucket is a bittersweet world of rolling moors, wild roses and windswept saltbox cottages that appear to have sprouted from the earth itself.

Nantucket was first sighted in 1602 by Captain Bartholomew Gosnold on his way to Martha's Vineyard. English settlers and Quakers farmed the land until the 1830s, when it was one of the busiest whaling ports in the world, a fact noted by Herman Melville in *Moby Dick*. In the 1870s, when kerosene started to replace whale oil as a fuel source and whales were becoming scarce, the industry started to decline. As a result, Nantucket lost 60 percent of its population. A depression followed, but around the turn of the century tourism blossomed and the island prospered once again.

Nantucket is so small and flat you can zip across it on a bicycle in about two hours or by car in 30 minutes. There are almost as many bicycle paths as roads, and bicycle rental shops abound on the wharf where the ferries dock. Like Martha's Vineyard, the only way to get here is by ferry or plane (see the "Transportation" section at the end of this chapter). If you come here in summer, you *must* have reservations beforehand—competition is intense, and anti-camping laws are actively enforced.

SIGHTS

There is only one town, Nantucket, but it can occupy you for hours or days if you enjoy historic homes, museums, fine restaurants, shopping and gallery hopping.

At the **Nantucket Island Chamber of Commerce**, you can pick up the 288-page color guidebook, *Official Guide to Nantucket*, a comprehensive resource guide. Benches abound, so you can sit and map out an itinerary or just people watch. During summer the town is packed with tanned college kids, prosperous-looking couples, families on vacation and some wide-eyed daytrippers from the Cape and nearby Martha's Vineyard. Tail-wagging dogs wander about, and the local gentry stand on corners sipping coffee and chatting. Closed weekends. ~ 48 Main Street; 508-228-

1700, fax 508-325-4925; www.nantucketchamber.org, e-mail info@nantucketchamber.org.

The **Nantucket Historical Association** maintains a number of historical properties, including the Jethro Coffin House and the Old Mill. A handy visitor's pass can be purchased from them, as well as from individual sites. Closed mid-October to mid-June. ~ P.O. Box 1016, Nantucket, MA 02554; 508-228-1894; www.nha. org, e-mail nhainfo@nha.org.

If you walk up Main Street past the shops, you'll find many elegant mansions built during the heyday of whaling.

Nearby stands the **Maria Mitchell Science Center**. Mitchell, a Nantucket native, was the first American woman to discover a comet with a telescope, and the first female member of the American Academy of Arts and Sciences. The center, named in her honor, includes a natural science museum with an impressive insect and bird collection, an aquarium, and the house in which Mitchell was born. Their library and observatory are both open year-round. The center conducts summer field trips, as well as bird and marine walks. Call for hours. Closed October to mid-June. Admission. ~ Vestal and Milk streets; 508-228-9198, fax 508-228-1031; www.mmo.org.

For a heady dose of Nantucket country life, visit **Siasconset**, a doll-sized hamlet of 17th-century pitched-roofed cod fisher shan-

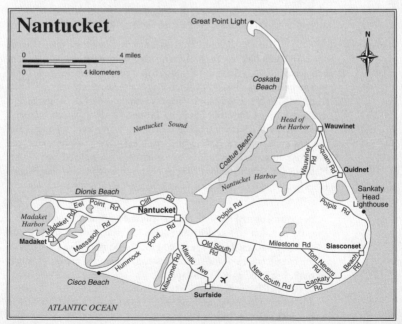

Historic Nantucket

This easy walk through the streets of old Nantucket takes in more than a dozen historic sites from the town's 18th- and 19th-century whaling heyday. It takes about two and a half hours to walk.

THOMAS MACY WAREHOUSE   Start your walk at the Thomas Macy Warehouse (c. 1846) on the waterfront. Originally a storehouse for whaleship supplies, it now houses the Nantucket Historical Association Visitor Center. Buy a handy visitors' pass covering the sites on this tour. All are open daily May through September. ~ Straight Wharf; 508-228-1700.

BROAD STREET   Walk one block west to South Water Street, then north (right) two blocks to Broad Street and the **Whaling Museum**. A former candleworks with enormous cross beams, this rustic old building contains a 40-foot finback whale skeleton, a lighthouse lens, a whaleboat, a scrimshaw collection and relics from the *Essex*, the ship rammed by an enraged sperm whale that inspired Herman Melville's *Moby Dick*. Admission. Closed Sunday through Friday from December through May. ~ 5 Broad Street; 508-228-1736. Next door, the **Peter Foulger Museum** traces Nantucket's human history from American Indian habitation to the present. ~ 15 Broad Street; 508-228-1894.

MAIN STREET   Leaving the museums, walk one block west on Broad Street and turn south (left) on Federal, then west (right) onto the picturesque, cobblestoned Main Street. A fire destroyed most of the town in 1846, and some buildings, such as the public library, have only recently been restored. Two blocks up on Main, turn south (left) on Fair Street and go one block to the **Friends Meeting House** (c. 1838), which has been preserved by the historical society for more than a century and is still used as a house of worship by the island's Quakers. An annex to the meeting house, the **Fair Street Museum** originally housed the Whaling Museum and now contains changing historical exhibits. ~ 7 Fair Street. Returning to Main Street, turn west (left) again and continue for another

ties transformed into beguiling summer homes. In spring and early summer this endearing village looks as though it's been attacked by roses. Everywhere you look wild pink roses are climbing over fences, up sides of houses and over roofs, creating a dusty pink, gray and sage landscape.

Called "Sconset" by nearly everyone, the village lies seven and a half miles from Nantucket town on Milestone Road, which is bordered by a smooth, flat bicycle path. There isn't much to do here except enjoy the scenery and go to the beach. Sconset has a block to Walnut Street. Turn north (right) and go one block to Liberty Street to the **Macy-Christian House** (c. 1740), a pre-Revolutionary merchant's home where a guided tour takes you through rooms of period furnishings. ~ 12 Liberty Street. Returning to Main Street, walk two more blocks west to tour the **Hadwen House** (c. 1845), one of the most elegant mansions on the island; the local garden club maintains period-style gardens here. ~ 96 Main Street.

MILLS AND MOORS   Turn south (left) on Pleasant Street and go four blocks to South Mill Street, then turn west (right) and climb the hill to the corner of Prospect Street to see the **Old Mill** (c. 1746), a Dutch-style sailed windmill with wooden gears. It still grinds corn into meal, which is offered for sale to visitors. ~ Mill and Prospect streets. Returning north on Pleasant Street, turn west (left) on Mill Street. Passing the private **Moor's End** mansion (c. 1839) and the **1800 House** (c. 1801, closed for restoration), continue one block to New Dollar Lane.

GARDNER STREET   Turning north (right), walk one block and turn west (left) onto Vestal Street. Continue for one and a half blocks to the **Old Gaol** (c. 1805), used to incarcerate prisoners for nearly 130 years before a rash of escapes prompted the town council to build a new jail. ~ Vestal Street. Returning the way you came, turn north (left) onto Gardner Street and walk two blocks, past the **Civil War Monument** at the corner of Main Street, to the **Hose-Cart House** (c. 1886), the last of several fire stations housing hand-pumped fire carts that were built throughout town after the devastating fire of 1846. ~ 8 Gardner Street.

JETHRO COFFIN HOUSE   From the corner of Gardner and Main, you can return to your starting point at the visitor center by walking six blocks east on Main Street. For a longer walk—ten minutes each way—continue north on Gardner Street, which becomes North Liberty Street; turn east (right) on West Chester Street, then north (left) onto Sunset Hill Lane to see the Jethro Coffin House (c. 1686), Nantucket's oldest house. It's a classic saltbox, characteristic of late-17th-century Massachusetts Bay Colony homes. ~ Sunset Hill; 508-228-1894. West Chester becomes Centre Street and returns you to Main Street three blocks from the visitor center.

couple of restaurants, including renowned Chanticleer, and Summer House, one of Nantucket's prettiest inns.

On the way back to town, take scenic Polpis Road. It goes past **Sankaty Head Lighthouse** and **The Moors**, magnificent, wind-bitten low-lying land that resembles a Persian carpet in the fall.

The road also passes the windswept **cranberry bogs**, where ◄ HIDDEN you can watch cranberries being harvested in the fall (see "Exploring Cranberry Country" in Chapter Five for information about cranberry growing on the South Shore).

The rest of Nantucket is all huckleberry-covered heath dotted with houses surrounded by spectacular beaches (see "Beaches & Parks" below).

LODGING   Nantucket has an astonishing number of inns and bed and breakfasts, but perhaps the most well-known is the **Jared Coffin House**. Built in 1845 by wealthy shipowner Jared Coffin, it features guest and public rooms appointed with antiques, oriental rugs, crystal chandeliers, period wallpaper, marble fireplaces and canopy beds. All guest rooms have private baths; some are air-conditioned. A busy, festive establishment, it feels like a big city hotel of the 19th century. Sixty guest rooms span four different buildings. There are two on-site restaurants. ~ 29 Broad Street; 508-228-2400, 800-248-2405, fax 508-325-7752; www.jared coffinhouse.com, e-mail jchouse@nantucket.net. ULTRA-DELUXE.

Right down the street from the Jared Coffin House is one of the island's few bargain spots, the **Nesbitt Inn**. The white Victorian was built in 1872 and most of the original furniture still remains. One room has a wood-rimmed bath tub that accommodates two. There are 12 guest rooms, each with a sink and shared bath. The inn's front porch is a great place for people watching. Closed January and February. ~ 21 Broad Street; 508-228-0156, fax 508-228-2446. MODERATE.

HIDDEN ►   Nearby in the historic district, the **Martin House Inn** has 13 very different guest rooms, from tiny, charming single-occupant-only cubicles with shared baths to much larger, spacious rooms with queen-sized canopy beds, fireplaces and private porches. Everyone shares a wonderful large living room, where the complimentary seated breakfast is provided. You may also dine out on the veranda if you wish. ~ 61 Centre Street; 508-228-0678; www.nantucket.net/lodging/martinn, e-mail martinn@nantucket.net. ULTRA-DELUXE.

AUTHOR FAVORITE

The Summer House, a rose-covered structure overlooking the ocean, is quintessential Nantucket, the kind of place you dream about but rarely find. Not surprisingly, it once graced the cover of *New York* magazine. Quaint little low-slung, vine-clad cottages surrounding the main house look as though they were designed by and for elves. But they're much bigger and lighter than they seem, and the decor blends just the right mix of rustic country charm. Rooms have features such as fireplaces, jacuzzis, rough-hewn beams, painted wood floors and hand-painted borders. There is a lively restaurant, as well as an oceanfront pool. Closed November through March. ~ 17 Ocean Avenue, Siasconset; 508-257-4577, fax 508-257-4590; www.thesummer house.com. ULTRA-DELUXE.

Right next door is the **Centerboard Guest House**, a restored 1885 Victorian residence with seven rooms, all decorated with period furnishings. At an inn of this sort, it's surprising to find modern amenities such as air conditioning and refrigerators in each guest room. Continental breakfast included. ~ 8 Chester Street; 508-228-9696; www.nantucket.net/lodging/centerboard, e-mail centerbo@nantucket.net. ULTRA-DELUXE.

Anchor Inn, a narrow gray clapboard house with green shutters and window boxes, is typical of Nantucket's many bed and breakfasts. Old and quaint, with narrow halls and sloping wood floors, it offers 11 cozy guest rooms, some hidden under dormers and eaves in small irregular spaces. Each has a private shower and air conditioning and some have canopy beds. Once the home of the Gilbreth family (of Frank Gilbreth's *Cheaper by the Dozen*), the Anchor is furnished with Colonial- and Shaker-style antiques. A continental breakfast is served in a cheerful blue-and-white breakfast room, or out on a brick patio. Closed January and February. ~ 66 Centre Street; 508-228-0072; www.anchor-inn.net, e-mail anchorin@nantucket.net. DELUXE.

Located in Nantucket's historic district, the **Summer House Fair Street** has ten rooms and two suites decorated in English country manner. All have private baths; some boast antique fireplaces. Three times a day a jitney carries guests to the beach and pool in Sconset. A continental breakfast is included. ~ 27 Fair Street; 508-257-4577, fax 508-257-4590; www.thesummerhouse. com, e-mail summerhouse@nantucket.net.

The **Woodbox Inn** is one of Nantucket's oldest and most delightful inns. Built in 1709, it exudes New England charm, with low-beamed ceilings, wood-paneled walls and walk-in fireplaces. The three guest rooms and six suites are furnished entirely in period antiques; all have private baths. Located in a quiet part of town away from all the hoopla, it has an excellent restaurant that can get a little noisy on weekends. Closed January to Memorial Day. ~ 29 Fair Street; 508-228-0587, fax 508-228-7527; www.woodboxinn.com, e-mail woodbox@nantucket.net. ULTRA-DELUXE.

The **Wauwinet**, a lavish resort outside town, is decorated to the hilt with country pine antiques, green wicker, primitive folk art, Victorian carpet runners, white wainscotting and pickled floors. The 25 guest rooms sport gentle sea-breeze colors like pale smoke, sage and cream; five cottages sleep up to six people each. White wicker furniture sits prim and proper on a vast lawn overlooking Nantucket Bay, and cushioned wicker furniture lines a bayside porch. Guests are transported to and from town in a shuttle bus. The Wauwinet is one of the most expensive inns on the island, attracting a well-heeled young crowd. There's a full-service restaurant on the premises. Closed November to early May.

~ 120 Wauwinet Road; 508-228-0145, 800-426-8718, fax 508-228-6712; www.wauwinet.com. ULTRA-DELUXE.

HIDDEN ▶

If you haven't stayed in a youth hostel since you gave up your backpack, you might want to try it again when you see **Hostelling International—Nantucket.** Located across from Surfside Beach, this historic wooden A-frame building looks like a cross between a Swiss chalet and a church. Originally a lifesaving station, it today attracts a lot of young people, Europeans, senior citizens and cycling groups. Volleyball is played in a large yard in back bordered by sand dunes. The rows of bunk beds inside remind most people of camp. As with most youth hostels, Nantucket's is closed to guests during the day. The dormitory-style rooms and restrooms are segregated by sex; there is a good-sized kitchen, dining room and common room. Closed mid-October to mid-April. ~ 31 Western Avenue; 508-228-0433, fax 508-228-5672; www.usahostels.org, e-mail nantuckethostel@juno.com. BUDGET.

DINING

Among Nantucket's astonishing number of sophisticated restaurants, one of the best is **Le Languedoc.** Elegant and hushed, the upstairs has bistro-style dining with yellow walls, contemporary art and dark carpeting that are strictly big-city, yet its navy-and-white checked tablecloths and Windsor chairs add a touch of French country; the downstairs resembles a pied-à-terre. Lobster hash, Boston glazed jumbo shrimp and jambalaya risotto may be found on the moderate-to-deluxe bistro menu, while the deluxe-to-ultra-deluxe downstairs menu may include pan-roasted lobster with garlic-thyme potatoes, soft-shell crab and porcini-dusted lamb tenderloin. A lot of care goes into the presentation. Advance reservations suggested for upstairs; no reservations accepted for downstairs. Dinner is served nightly. Closed Monday. ~ 24 Broad Street; 508-228-2552; www.lelanguedoc.com, e-mail langudoc@nantucket.net. DELUXE TO ULTRA-DELUXE.

The Tap Room at the Jared Coffin House is a comfortable place to enjoy a hearty lunch or dinner. Their most popular dish is the roast prime rib *au jus*, but others enjoy the baked scallops or the seafood platter (deep-fried scrod, shrimp, scallop and calamari). ~ 29 Broad Street; 508-228-2400; www.jaredcoffinhouse.com, e-mail jchouse@nantucket.net. MODERATE TO DELUXE.

American Seasons serves American regional cuisine such as mesquite-smoked sweetbreads and herb-crusted tuna with root-vegetable gratin. The restaurant is in a white, two-story building with window boxes spilling a variety of seasonal blossoms. The interior is romantically lit with hurricane lamps, and jazz plays softly in the background; the outdoor patio has copper tables to dine on. The crowd is young, happy and casual. Dinner only. Closed mid-December to mid-April. ~ 80 Centre Street; 508-228-

7111, fax 508-325-0779; www.americanseasons.com. ULTRA-DELUXE.

The **Atlantic Café** is on a street that should be called Hamburger Row. Every restaurant on this block serves the same thing—burgers, beer and rock-and-roll. You can smell the fried food before you get here. The restaurant attracts families with small kids. The Atlantic is a clean-looking establishment with white walls, wood beams and a bar in the middle surrounded by wooden chairs and tables. Steak and seafood specials round out the menu. Closed mid-December to early January. ~ 15 South Water Street; 508-228-0570, fax 508-228-8787; www.atlanticcafe.com, e-mail theac@nantucket.net. BUDGET TO DELUXE.

One of Nantucket's most beautiful and versatile restaurants, the **Boarding House** has a shady brick patio that's perfect for people watching and a lovely bar and café with floor-to-ceiling windows. (A woman could come to the bar alone and feel totally at ease.) A formal dinner is served in the cellar, a grottolike, candlelit room with cream-colored arched walls. Dishes change frequently. Popular offerings, many served in both the café and dining room, include seared yellowfin tuna with wasabi aïoli and soy ginger glaze, and twin lobster tails grilled with champagne beurre blanc and mashed potatoes. A comprehensive wine list is featured. Dinner only. Closed Sunday and Monday from November through April. ~ 12 Federal Street; 508-228-9622, fax 508-325-7109. DELUXE TO ULTRA-DELUXE.

Woven lightship baskets and carved scrimshaw items were crafts created in the 18th century by lighthouse keepers and sailors with idle time on their hands.

Tiny **Sconset Café** has an enticing menu any time of day. The café's patrons are the lucky taste-testers of new recipes and variations on old favorites, which are best termed New American. Try the lamb Dijon or the baby vegetable risotto. Closed mid-October through April. ~ Post Office Square, Siasconset; 508-257-4008; www.sconsetcafe.com, e-mail rc@sconsetcafe.com. DELUXE TO ULTRA-DELUXE.

The **Chanticleer** is one of New England's most romantic restaurants. In spring, the many-windowed, gray-shingled house is covered with climbing roses, and the garden is a riot of pink, white and lavender flowers. The menu features traditional French cuisine—foie gras, lobster soufflé, fresh figs in sweet white wine and herbs, trout with salmon mousse and lobster ginger sauce. Many locals prefer the restaurant for lunch in the rose garden. Closed Monday and from November to mid-May. ~ 9 New Street, Siasconset; 508-257-6231; www.thechanticleerinn.com, e-mail info@thechanticleerinn.com. ULTRA-DELUXE.

Hoorn-Ashby Gallery, one of Nantucket's most beautiful galleries, sells American and European contemporary paintings, antique

SHOPPING

handpainted blanket chests, French-country porcelain and more in a sun-filled room with wood-paneled walls, tall columns, wainscoting and high ceilings. Closed Monday through Wednesday after Columbus Day, closed Monday through Friday in November, closed mid-December to May. ~ 10 Federal Street; 508-228-9314, fax 508-228-6178.

Many shops in Nantucket sell handwoven goods, but at **Nantucket Looms** the blankets, throws and shawls are a cut above the rest. Popular designs include voluminous, fluffy white throws with thin navy stripes, and blankets in all colors of the rainbow. Closed Sunday from late December through March. ~ 16 Main Street; 508-228-1908, fax 508-228-6451; www.nantucketlooms.com, e-mail acklooms@nantucket.net.

Four Winds Craft Guild specializes in the island's two oldest crafts: antique and new lightship baskets and scrimshaw. The former are tightly woven, bowl-shaped baskets used as purses or decorative items; scrimshaw are items decoratively carved from whale bone and teeth. Lightship purses are a status symbol among the island's conservative ladies. The older the basket, the better. ~ 15 Main Street; 508-228-9623, fax 508-228-8958; www.sylvia antiques.com.

Brimming with hidden delights, **Vis-A-Vis** offers an eclectic mix of goods ranging from hand-knit sweaters, bathing suits and antique hooked rugs, to quilts and jewelry. Women can find something to wear to the beach, a wedding or an evening on the town. Closed Sunday through Thursday in January and February. ~ 34 Main Street; 508-228-5527; e-mail visavis@nantucket.net.

NIGHTLIFE In summer, **Nantucket Musical Arts Society** gives classical concerts in the First Congregational Church located at 62 Centre Street. ~ P.O. Box 897, Nantucket, MA 02554; 508-228-1287.

Throughout the year, **The Theatre Workshop of Nantucket** stages plays such as *Arsenic and Old Lace*, *Pantomime* and *Don't Dress for Dinner*. ~ Bennett Hall, 62 Centre Street; 508-228-4305.

Actors Theatre of Nantucket has something for everyone: serious drama, light comedy (like Neil Simon's *Lost in Yonkers*), original youth theater productions and comedians. Watch for their summer benefit concerts, which have featured Judy Collins and Joan Baez in the past. Closed Columbus Day to Memorial Day. ~ Methodist Church, 2 Centre Street; 508-228-6325; www. nantuckettheatre.com, e-mail actors@nantucket.net.

For evening cocktails in a comfortable old tavern, try the **Tap Room at Jared Coffin House**. ~ 29 Broad Street; 508-228-2400.

The Rose and Crown carries 14 beers on draught, plus a full bar and nightly entertainment. Live rock and R&B music can be heard Thursday through Saturday, with karaoke and deejays the rest of the week. Closed mid-December to mid-April. Cover. ~ 23 South Water Street; 508-228-2595.

Fun, funky and informal, **The Chicken Box**, a bar with live entertainment, presents a variety of bands—rock-and-roll, reggae, rhythm-and-blues and others. They perform nightly in the summer, on weekends only in the winter. Cover for bands. ~ 4 Daves Street; 508-228-9717, fax 508-228-4714; www.thechickenbox.com.

BEACHES & PARKS

Bicycle paths go to Madaket, Dionis, Surfside and Siasconset beaches, and fishing is great from those on the south shore. Nantucket doesn't have parks, per se, but the **Nantucket Conservation Foundation** owns and manages more than 8500 acres (28 percent of the island's land area) of undeveloped land open to the public to explore. Foundation land is identified by roadside maroon posts topped with a wave and seagull logo. If you want to know more, stop in and talk to the foundation folks, a friendly group of people who are happy to discuss the island's flora and fauna. They'll also commiserate about the rapid growth on the island, and the frightening amounts being paid for land. ~ Larsen-Sanford Center, 118 Cliff Road; 508-228-2884. The **Nantucket Park and Recreation Commission** oversees Dionis, Madaket, Surfside and Siasconset beaches. ~ 2 Bathing Beach Road; 508-228-7213, fax 508-325-5347.

Surfers take note: surfing is *not* permitted in lifeguarded areas. Furthermore, lifeguarded areas are subject to frequent change. Before dragging your gear out, you might want to call **Upperdeck and Indian Summer Surf Shop** (508-228-3632, fax 508-228-4211) and ask where people are surfing.

DIONIS BEACH 🚲 🚶 If it weren't for a white rock on which the word Dionis is painted, you'd never find this beach, which faces the bay and is ideal for swimming, picnics and cookouts (fire permits available from the Nantucket fire station). Beyond the

---

AUTHOR FAVORITE

I can't help but gush about **Madaket Beach**. One of Nantucket's most beautiful bicycle paths ends at this spectacular western-facing beach. Everything about this long, wide beach is just right. The sand is white and clean, the surf fantastic, the sunsets the best on the island. It's also one of the best spots on Nantucket to fish. You'll find lifeguards, portable toilets and a shuttle service, all in summer only. ~ At the end of Madaket Road, Madaket; 508-228-7213, fax 508-325-5347; e-mail parkrec@townnantucket.net. 🚲 🚶 ⚓

large dirt parking lot, a path leads through tall sand dunes to the beach. These are dunes protected from natural erosion and people by a fence. The beach has some rocks and seaweed. During low tide, a sand bar stretches out into the water quite a distance. There are restrooms and lifeguards in summer. ~ Three miles west of town off Eel Point Road, Dionis; 508-228-7213, fax 508-325-5347; e-mail parkrec@town.nantucket.net.

HIDDEN ►   **CISCO BEACH** 🏊 🏄 🚶 The road to this out-of-the-way beach goes past scenic Hummock Pond and rolling heathlands. The wide-open beach is a free and easy place where you can walk for miles on white sand. It's popular with seasoned beach rats and young surfer types. Lifeguards are not always available, so call ahead to check. ~ At the end of Hummock Pond Road in Cisco, four miles southwest of town; 508-228-7213, fax 508-325-5347; e-mail parkrec@town.nantucket.net.

Nantucket is an island, a county and a town. As if that weren't enough, it's also the only place in the United States with the same name for all three distinctions.

SURFSIDE 🚲 🏊 🏄 🚶 Narrow sand paths lace the moors leading to this massive beach. Because Surfside is only three miles from town, it gets very crowded in the summer. But it's a great beach—big, long and wide with the best surf on the island. Surfside attracts families and college students. To get away from the crowds, walk east along the shore toward Siasconset and soon you'll discover long stretches of blissfully empty beach. There's a bike path. Summer facilities include restrooms, showers, lifeguards, a snack bar and a shuttle service. ~ At the end of Surfside Road, three miles south of town; 508-228-7213, fax 508-325-5347; e-mail parkrec@town.nantucket.net.

SIASCONSET BEACH 🚲 🏊 This lovely eastern-facing beach seven miles from town is in the village of Siasconset. People make a day out of bicycling or driving here to explore the beach and the village; you can catch a shuttle bus from town in summer. Part of the beach is surrounded by grassy cliffs and dunes, then the land dips and becomes flat. To the left of the beach is Sankaty Lighthouse and the summer community of Quidnet. Walk south along the beach for an empty spot. Because of the wind, seaweed can be a problem. Keep an eye on small children: this beach gets very deep about 20 feet out. There are lifeguards in summer. ~ Seven miles east of town at the end of Milestone Road, Siasconset; 508-228-7213, fax 508-325-5347; e-mail parkrec@town.nantucket.net.

HIDDEN ►   **GREAT POINT, COSKATA & COATUE BEACHES** 🏊 🚶 If you really want to leave civilization, consider exploring this narrow stretch of uninhabited land that wraps around Nantucket Harbor. It's like one giant sand dune surrounded by water. Driving through this desertlike landscape is an adventure, and those who make the trek can swim in calm waters lapping a deserted white-sand beach and view a nesting ground for piping plovers, clam and oyster ponds, the remains of a shipwreck, a century-old cedar forest and the Great Point Lighthouse. There's fantastic shore fishing for fluke, Spanish mackerel, bluefish and bass at Great Point, the northernmost point of land; swimming is calm on Nantucket Sound but not recommended on the Atlantic side, where the current and undertow are rough. Driving in this area requires an expensive ($20 per day for rental vehicles; $85 for private vehicles for the year) permit and a four-wheel-drive vehicle equipped with everything you need to dig yourself out of a deep sand rut. Permits are available at the Wauwinet Gate House on Wauwinet Road (508-228-5646). Tours and fishing excursions are advertised in the local paper. ~ The end of Wauwinet Road off Polpis Road, at the island's northeast end.

SANFORD FARM 🏃 🚲 Owned by the Nantucket Conservation Foundation, this former dairy farm consists of 779 acres of classic Nantucket countryside. A magical place for quiet walks and private picnics, it has 6.6 miles of trails meandering through rare maritime heathlands that look like Scotland. Follow the trail past long and winding Hummock Pond down to the empty beach on the island's south shore. In spring and summer Sanford Farm is lush with wildflowers, but its most beautiful time is fall, when the land is a tapestry of burgundy, sage, rose, gold and ivory. Deer can be spotted early in the morning and at dusk. Turtles live in the pond. To minimize damage, visitors are urged to stay on trails and roadways. Motorized vehicles are prohibited. ~ West of town off Madaket Road near the intersection of Cliff Road and Madaket; 508-228-2884, fax 508-228-5528; e-mail info@ nantucketconservation.org.

◄ HIDDEN

Cape Cod, Martha's Vineyard and Nantucket offer a staggering number of opportunities for fishing, boating and other water sports, as well as cycling, golf, tennis and more.

Outdoor Adventures

Bluefish, striped bass, tuna, cod and flounder are abundant. No license is required to fish, and tackle shops are everywhere. For detailed information on what to catch when, where and how, check the website of the **Massachusetts Division of Marine Fisheries**. ~ www.mass.gov/marinefisheries.

FISHING

NORTH CAPE Among the hundreds of charter and party boat outfits on Cape Cod, one of the most reputable is the 52-foot **Albatross**. ~ Sesuit Harbor, East Dennis; 508-385-3244. The 60-foot **Naviator** also comes highly recommended; sea bass and blackfish are common catches. ~ Wellfleet town pier; 508-349-6003. **Teacher's Pet** has a good reputation, offering bluefish and striped bass excursions. Closed November to mid-May. ~ Hyannis Harbor; 508-362-4925.

MARTHA'S VINEYARD **Larry's Tackle Shop** has shore guides and charter services. The five-hour trips can be small (three people) or large (six people). ~ 258 Upper Main Street, Edgartown; 508-627-5088, fax 508-627-5148.

NANTUCKET The **Albacore** will take you out for bluefish, bass, shark or tuna. Private charters only. Closed November to May. ~ Slip 17, Straight Wharf, Nantucket; 508-228-5074. **Surf & Fly Fishing** with Mike Monte offers guided fishing tours. Closed November to May. ~ 508-228-0529.

WATER SPORTS

Cape Cod abounds with marinas and harbors where you can rent sailboats, windsurfing equipment, canoes and more. The bay and ponds around the area are good for canoeing and kayaking, while the ocean whips up fine surfing waves.

OUTER CAPE **Jack's Boat Rental** has four locations for canoe, kayak, boogieboard and surfboard rentals. Closed Labor Day to mid-June. ~ Route 6, Wellfleet, 508-349-9808; Gull Pond, Wellfleet, 508-349-7553; Flax Pond, Brewster, 508-896-8556, Nickerson State Park, Brewster, 508-896-8556.

PROVINCETOWN **Flyer's Boat Rental** can outfit you with powerboats, sailboats and kayaks. Closed mid-October to mid-May. ~ 131-A Commercial Street; 508-487-0898.

SOUTH CAPE **Cape Water Sports** rents Hobie cats, canoes and kayaks. ~ Route 28, Harwich Port; 508-432-5996. They also have beachfront locations at Pleasant Bay in East Harwich and Ridgevale Beach in Chatham. The Pleasant Bay location offers sailing lessons.

MARTHA'S VINEYARD For sailboat rentals, as well as kayaking and windsurfing rentals or lessons, there's **Wind's Up**. ~ 199 Beach Road, Vineyard Haven; 508-693-4252. **Ayuthia Charters**

JUST PLANE FUN

The public 18-hole **Fairgrounds Golf Course** on the South Cape features a driving range, a pro shop, and a restaurant and lounge. A large sign at the driving range warns players to "Stop driving when planes approach." If you wait around for a while, you'll see why; the course is close to an airport that launches gliders. Sometimes the planes fly so low you can wave to the passengers. ~ 1460 Route 149, Marstons Mills; 508-420-1142.

offers half-day sails on a 48-foot ketch. Closed October through April. ~ Coastwise Wharf, Vineyard Haven; 508-693-7245.

NANTUCKET **Nantucket Island Community Sailing** rents windsurfing gear, kayaks and sailboats, and gives lessons. ~ North Beach Street; 508-228-5358.

April through October is the season to catch sight of humpbacks and minkes. Among the many excursions departing from Cape Cod is **Hyannis Whale Watcher Cruises.** Whale spotting is guaranteed, which takes 400 passengers out on a 138-foot triple decker boat. ~ Millway Marina, Barnstable Harbor, Barnstable; 508-362-6088. In Provincetown, **Dolphin Fleet Whale Watch** also guarantees whales. A naturalist from the Center for Coastal Studies is on board one of the three 100-foot boats to provide insight. ~ MacMillan Pier; 508-255-3857.

WHALE WATCHING

Lobsters, starfish, crabs and skates are common sights when diving in Cape Cod waters. Cape Cod Bay and Sandwich Town Beach are recommended spots.

SCUBA DIVING

NORTH CAPE Clientele primarily consists of resort guests at the 18-hole **Ocean Edge,** but everyone is welcome. Carts are required. ~ 832 Village Drive, Brewster; 508-896-5911.

GOLF

OUTER CAPE Located on the Cape Cod National Seashore, **Highland Golf Links** is a nine-hole public course that requires tee times. You'll get views of Cape Cod Lighthouse as well as the seashore. ~ Lighthouse Road, Truro; 508-487-9201.

SOUTH CAPE The **Harwich Port Golf Club** has a nine-hole course. ~ Forest and South streets, Harwich Port; 508-432-0250.

MARTHA'S VINEYARD **Mink Meadows Golf Club** is a semiprivate, nine-hole course featuring wooded, rolling terrain. ~ Golf Club Road off Franklin Street, Vineyard Haven; 508-693-0600. The 18-hole, semiprivate **Farm Neck Golf Course** offers beautiful scenery. ~ County Road, Oak Bluffs; 508-693-2504.

NANTUCKET The nine-hole, semiprivate **Miacomet Golf Club** has a driving range and a practice putting green. ~ 15 West Miacomet Road; 508-325-0333. Or play your nine holes at **Siasconset Golf Club,** one of the oldest courses in the country. This public links-style course resembles Scotland Yard. ~ Milestone Road, Siasconset; 508-257-6596.

Most Cape Cod towns have tennis courts in schools and resorts.

TENNIS

NORTH CAPE A privately owned club, **Mid-Cape Racquet & Health** has nine courts, all lighted. They rent racquets and offer lessons. ~ 193 White's Path, South Yarmouth; 508-394-3511.

Text continued on page 214.

Cape Cod by Bike

Cape Cod, Martha's Vineyard and Nantucket are a cyclist's paradise. The flat landscape is laced with miles of smooth, paved bicycle paths that meander past sand dunes, salt marsh, woods and pastures. What follows is a modest sampling of some of the best rides. Local chambers of commerce can provide more comprehensive information. *Short Bike Rides*, by Edwin Mullen and Jane Griffith (Globe Pequot Press) is a handy little book that describes 31 bike rides on Cape Cod, Nantucket and Martha's Vineyard.

NORTH CAPE   The **Cape Cod Rail Trail**, an eight-foot-wide bicycle path, runs about 30 miles along the old Penn Central Railroad tracks from Route 134 in South Dennis to six miles off Locust Road in Eastham, past classic Cape Cod scenery—ponds, forest, saltwater and freshwater marsh, cranberry bogs and harbors.

OUTER CAPE   **Head of the Meadow**, a moderately hilly bicycle path in the Cape Cod National Seashore in Truro, traverses some of the Cape's most dramatic scenery, including The Highlands' vast expanses of grassy knolls. The two-mile path starts at Head of the Meadow Road off Route 6 and ends at High Head Road.

PROVINCETOWN   Talk about dramatic scenery. The **Province Lands Bike Trail** dips and turns past towering sand dunes, silvery mounds of wavy beach grass, two magnificent beaches and the Province Lands Visitors Center. The five-mile loop starts at Herring Cove Beach parking lot at the end of Route 6 and includes many places where you can stop and picnic.

SOUTH CAPE   The **Shining Sea** bicycle path between Falmouth and Woods Hole is popular with experienced cyclists because it's hilly in some areas and very scenic. The 3.3-mile path runs along Palmer Avenue in Falmouth, then down a hill past deep woods and historic homes, ending at Woods Hole harbor.

MARTHA'S VINEYARD   The **Oak Bluffs–Edgartown–Katama Beach** bike path on Martha's Vineyard is smooth and easy, even though it's nine miles long. Departing from Oak Bluffs, the flat path runs along the shore past lovely old homes, beaches, ponds and salt marsh to historic Edgartown, then through heathland dotted with occasional houses to magnificent Katama Beach.

From Vineyard Haven, the hale and hearty can bicycle to **Menemsha** and **Aquinnah** via State Road to West Tisbury, then Middle Road to the end.

The ride is hilly in parts, but the scenery is breathtaking. The beaches in this area have residents-only parking lots, so bicycling is the only way a non-resident can enjoy them.

NANTUCKET   Aside from the downtown hazards of cobblestone streets, narrow roads and heavy traffic, bicycling on Nantucket is a snap. Smooth, flat bike paths parallel the island's two main roads. The 6.2-mile **Madaket** bicycle path is the more scenic, dipping and winding past moors and ending at Madaket Beach, the western tip of the island. The 8.2-mile **Siasconset** path is a straight, flat line that goes past barren scrub pine and sandy scenery, ending at the village of Siasconset on the eastern end of the island.

A 3.5-mile bike path leads to the ever-popular **Surfside Beach** and offers lovely scenery. The ten-mile **Polpis Bike Path**, an alternate route to Siasconset, features views of Nantucket Harbor.

Bike Rentals   Practically every town on Cape Cod has a couple of bike rental shops. Most are closed November through April.

In South Yarmouth, **The Outdoor Shop** can outfit you with mountain or hybrid bikes, as well as helmets and locks. They also sell and repair bikes. ~ 50 Long Pond Drive; 508-394-3819. Along with sales and service, **The Little Capistrano Bike Shop** rents cruisers, hybrids and mountain bikes; helmets and locks cost extra. ~ 341 Salt Pond Road, Route 6, Eastham; 508-255-6515. In Provincetown, check out **Arnold's** for repairs, sales or rentals (hybrids, kids' bikes, mountain bikes). Locks are included; helmets are extra. ~ 329 Commercial Street; 508-487-0844. Falmouth Heights' **Holiday Cycles** rents seven-speed cruisers, hybrids, mountain bikes, quadracycles, recumbent bikes, tandems and kids' bikes, as well as four-wheeled surreys. Repairs and sales are undertaken, and knowledgeable staff will direct you to a suitable bike path. ~ 465 Grand Avenue; 508-540-3549.

Martha's Vineyard has **Anderson's Bike Rentals** in Oak Bluffs. Choose from mountain and kids' bikes, hybrids and tandems; helmets and locks are included. Free road service for broken bikes is provided. You can also get the necessary repairs done here, or just buy a new bike. ~ 23 Circuit Avenue Extension; 508-693-9346. In Edgartown, there's **R. W. Cutler Bicycle Shop**. Rental bikes (mountains and hybrids) come with locks and helmets. They sell and repair bikes as well. ~ 1 Main Street; 508-627-4052.

Nantucket's wharf has many bicycle rental shops; one of the biggest outfits is the full-service **Young's Bicycle Shop**, whose rental bikes (tandems, hybrids, mountain, full-suspension) include helmets and locks. ~ 6 Broad Street, Steamboat Wharf; 508-228-1151.

PROVINCETOWN   Bissell Tennis Courts is a privately owned facility with five clay courts. Pros here can show you the swing of things. ~ 21 Bradford Street Extension; 508-487-9512.

MARTHA'S VINEYARD   Tennis is very popular on Martha's Vineyard. Municipal courts are at Church Street in Vineyard Haven, Niantic Park in Oak Bluffs, Robinson Road in Edgartown, Old Country Road in West Tisbury and the Chilmark Community Center on South Road.

NANTUCKET   The **White Elephant Tennis Center** has nine outdoor clay courts and tennis pros ready to teach. They rent racquets and sell balls. Closed mid-October to mid-May. Fee. ~ 48 North Beach Street; 508-228-4044. Right near town, **Jetties Beach Tennis Courts** have six courts and plenty of lessons. Walk-ins are allowed during the off-season; reservations accepted. ~ Bathing Beach Road; 508-325-5334.

RIDING STABLES   Liability insurance has gotten so high that only a few stables still rent horses.

MARTHA'S VINEYARD   **Crow Hollow Farm** is surrounded by 20 acres of gorgeous countryside, providing the ideal terrain for meandering rides. Lessons and rides of varying size and length are available. Advance reservations are wise. ~ Tiah's Cove Road, West Tisbury; 508-696-4554; www.crowhollowfarm.com.

BIKING   For biking listings see "Cape Cod by Bike" in this chapter.

HIKING   Otherworldly sand dunes, heaths that recall those across the Atlantic, sheltering forests and salt marshes are just a few of the environments available to hikers on Cape Cod and the Islands. You can trek through wilderness areas or stick to spots close to town. For more information on hikes throughout the state, contact the **Massachusetts Department of Environmental Management Trails Program.** ~ 251 Causeway Street, Boston; 617-626-1250. All distances listed for hiking trails are one way unless otherwise noted.

NORTH CAPE   **Talbot's Point Salt Marsh Trail** (1.5 miles), off Old Country Road in Sandwich, offers excellent views of the Great Marsh. The trail winds through red pine forest, along the fern-filled marsh, and past cranberry bogs and the state game farm, where thousands of quail and pheasant are raised.

OUTER CAPE   **Nauset Marsh Trail** (1-mile loop) offers some of the Cape's lushest scenery. The trail starts at the Salt Pond Visitors Center in North Eastham and goes past the shoreline of Salt Pond and Nauset Marsh, then rises through pastoral farmland filled with beach plums, bayberries and cedars.

A mesmerizing view of salt marsh and the ocean beyond greets you at **Goose Ponds Trail** (1.4-mile loop) in the Wellfleet Bay

Wildlife Sanctuary. The path leads through forest down a slight grade past Spring Brook to marshlands covered with wild lupine. A wooden boardwalk leads to secluded tidal flats. Among the many species of bird life are white-bottomed tree swallows nesting in bird houses throughout the sanctuary. ~ 508-349-2615.

Great Island Trail (3 miles), a wind-bitten wilderness, is best in the morning when the sun isn't too intense. Starting at the end of Chequesset Neck Road in Wellfleet, this challenging trail borders tidal flats, grassy dunes, pitch pine forest, the ocean and meadows where purple marsh peas and fiddler crabs flourish. Great for solitary beachcombing, the trail offers a number of spectacular views. Sections are occasionally submerged, depending on the tide.

PROVINCETOWN You'll find hikers and bikers on the moderately difficult **Beech Forest Trail** (1 mile), which winds to the Cape's most monumental sand dunes. Most of the trail wanders through cool beech forests and past freshwater ponds, and at one point it opens up to reveal the desertlike sand dunes. It starts on Race Point Road in Provincetown. ~ 508-487-1256.

MARTHA'S VINEYARD **Felix Neck Wildlife Sanctuary Trail** (1.5 miles), off the Edgartown–West Tisbury Road, provides habitat for animals such as ducks, swans, otters, muskrats, egrets, harrier hawks and other wildlife. The easy trail winds past waterfowl ponds, salt marsh, the tip of a peninsula, wetland vegetation and oak forest. It ends at the sanctuary's exhibit building, which has aquariums, wildlife displays, a library and a naturalist gift shop. Admission. ~ 508-627-4850.

NANTUCKET The island's only marked hiking trail is the **Sanford Farm–Ram Pasture Walking Trail**, offering 15 miles of wilderness. The Nantucket Conservation Foundation also owns parcels of wilderness the public can explore. For more on this, see the "Beaches & Parks" sections in this chapter. Following are two of the most scenic areas in which to hike:

Tupancy Links, off Cliff Road immediately west of town, is laced with paths that overlook Nantucket Sound. A former golf

---

TRANSPORTATION TIPS

For information on every conceivable way to get to Martha's Vineyard, Nantucket and Cape Cod short of walking on water, call the **Massachusetts Office of Travel and Tourism** and order a free *Getaway Guide*. In addition to transportation details, the guide lists outdoor adventure possibilities, lodging choices and sightseeing highlights. ~ 10 Park Plaza, 4th floor, Boston; 617-973-8500, 800-227-6277; www.mass-vacation.com.

course, today this marked trail system traverses a big, open, grassy field offering dramatic views.

Alter Rock, off Polpis Road in the central moors, is criss-crossed by unmarked paths and rutted dirt roads. Dotted with kettle hole ponds, rocks and scrub oak thicket, the scenery is classic heathland. A four-wheel-drive is required if driving.

For more information on hiking trails on Nantucket, call the chamber of commerce at 508-228-1700.

Transportation

CAR

Route 6 cuts through the middle of Cape Cod, ending at Provincetown. **Route 6A** runs along the north side of the Cape, and **Route 28** runs along Nantucket Sound. Both routes connect with Route 6 in Orleans.

AIR

Five airports serve Cape Cod and the Islands: **Logan International Airport** (800-235-6426) in Boston, Barnstable Airport and Provincetown Municipal Airport on Cape Cod, Martha's Vineyard Airport and Nantucket Memorial Airport.

Barnstable Airport in Hyannis is served by Cape Air, Colgan Air, Island Air, Nantucket Airlines and US Airways Express.

Cape Air services **Provincetown Municipal Airport** (508-487-0241).

Flying into **Martha's Vineyard Airport** (508-693-7022) are Cape Air and US Airways Express.

Nantucket Memorial Airport (508-325-5300) is serviced by Cape Air, Colgan Air, Continental, Delta Connection, Island Air, Nantucket Airlines and US Airways Express.

For ground transportation from Barnstable Airport to Logan Airport and areas throughout southern Massachusetts, contact **King's Airport Coach** (508-747-6622).

Taxis and car rentals listed below provide ground transportation to all other airports except Logan.

FERRY & BOAT

Ferries and boats between Boston, Cape Cod, Martha's Vineyard and Nantucket require reservations during the summer. Throughout the year, the **Steamship Authority** transports cars and passengers from Route 28 to Woods Hole to Oak Bluffs and Vineyard Haven, as well as from Hyannis to Nantucket. ~ 509 Falmouth Road, Mashpee; 508-477-8600.

The following ferries and boats operate seasonally and do not transport cars: **Hy-Line Cruises** takes passengers to and from Hyannis, Nantucket (year-round) and Oak Bluffs on Martha's Vineyard. ~ Ocean Street Dock, Hyannis; 508-775-7185; www.hy-line cruises.com. **Martha's Vineyard Ferry** operates between New Bedford and Oak Bluffs on Martha's Vineyard. ~ 1494 East Rodney French Boulevard, Billy Woods Wharf, New Bedford; 508-997-1688. **The Island Queen** goes between Falmouth and Oak Bluffs on Martha's Vineyard. ~ 75 Falmouth Heights Road, Pier 45, Falmouth; 508-548-4800. The **Chappaquiddick Ferry**, universally known as the "Chappy ferry," travels between Edgartown and Chappaquiddick Island year-round. ~ Dock and Daggett streets, Edgartown, Martha's Vineyard; 508-627-9427.

BUS

Greyhound Lines offers frequent service to Newburyport and Boston. ~ 700 Atlantic Avenue, South Station, Boston; 617-526-1801, 800-229-9424; www.greyhound.com.

Bonanza runs buses to and from Logan Airport, Hyannis, Woods Hole, Falmouth, Bourne, New Bedford, Fall River, Connecticut, Rhode Island and New York. ~ 59 Depot Avenue, Falmouth; 508-548-7588, 888-751-8800.

Plymouth and Brockton Street Railway Company has year-round express service to and from Boston's Logan Airport and local service along Route 6 on Cape Cod from Sagamore to Provincetown. ~ The Plymouth terminal is at 8 Industrial Park Road, Plymouth, 508-746-0378; the Hyannis terminal is at 17 Elm Avenue, Hyannis, 508-775-6502.

Peter Pan Bus Lines offers service to Springfield, Newton and Worcester. ~ 700 Atlantic Avenue, Boston; 800-343-9999.

CAR RENTALS

Car-rental agencies at Barnstable Airport include **Avis Rent A Car** (800-331-1212), **Hertz Rent A Car** (800-654-3131) and **National Car Rental** (800-227-7368).

Thrifty Car Rental (800-847-4389) serves the airport in Provincetown.

Martha's Vineyard has **Thrifty Adventure Car and Moped Rentals** (508-693-1959, 800-367-2277), **Budget Rent A Car** (800-527-0700) and **Hertz Rent A Car** (800-654-3131).

Nantucket Memorial Airport agencies include **Budget Rent A Car** (800-527-0700), **Hertz Rent A Car** (800-654-3131) and **Nantucket Windmill Auto Rental** (800-228-1227).

PUBLIC TRANSIT

Cape Cod Regional Transit Authority offers door-to-door minibus service (reservations required) and makes six daily round-trips between Barnstable and Woods Hole, Hyannis and Orleans, and Hyannis and Barnstable Harbor. ~ Old Chatham Road, South Dennis; 508-385-8326.

Nantucket doesn't have public transportation. Most people get around with rental cars or bicycles.

TAXIS

Taxis serving airports on the coast are as follows: Barnstable Airport, **Hyannis Taxi** (508-775-0400) and **Town Taxi of Cape Cod** (508-771-5555); Provincetown Airport, **Mercedes Cab** (508-487-3333); Martha's Vineyard Airport, **Adam Cab** (508-627-4462); Nantucket Memorial Airport, **A-1 Taxi** (508-228-3330).

FIVE

Massachusetts Coast

Immortalized by Herman Melville in *Moby Dick*, the Massachusetts coast today remains fertile territory for the imagination. This magnificent stretch of windswept coast abounds with historic seaside villages, vintage lighthouses, glorious beaches and history that reads like an adventure story complete with witches and pirates, authors and artists, Pilgrims and American natives, sea captains and Moby Dick.

An ethnic melting pot of Portuguese fishermen, Yankee blue bloods, old salts and the Irish (who seem to be everywhere), coast residents are very proud of where they live. North Shore loyalists wouldn't think of moving to the South Shore, and vice versa. What unifies everyone is the sea. Rich and poor alike have mini weather stations on their roofs to determine wind direction, and everyone reads tide charts. Kids learn how to fish, sail and dig for clams when they're five years old.

That all-encompassing sea is, of course, what lured Europeans to these shores in the first place. One hundred years before the Pilgrims stepped foot on Plymouth Rock, English adventurers fished the waters around the Massachusetts coast. Between 1600 and 1610, explorers Samuel de Champlain and Bartholomew Gosnold sailed to Gloucester.

Aboard the *Mayflower*, 102 Pilgrims landed in Plymouth in 1620, establishing the first permanent settlement in New England. By 1640, about 2500 of the new settlers lived in eight communities. Although they came to America to seek religious freedom, the Pilgrims persecuted Quakers and anyone else who didn't adhere to their strict Puritan religion. Their intolerant thinking helped fuel one of the most infamous pieces of American colonial history—the Salem witch trials of 1692. Salem had been founded six years after Plymouth. Here the Puritans tried to impose their religious laws on rowdy fishermen who lived in nearby Marblehead, but adultery and drunkenness won out. The Puritans were more successful in their witch hunt—20 people, most of them women, were executed for practicing "witchcraft" in a single year.

The gruesome trials took place during a time when witchcraft was thought to be the cause for any unexplained event. Similar trials and executions occurred throughout New England and Europe, but Salem had the dubious distinction of executing the most women in the shortest amount of time.

Fortunately by the 1700s the focus was more on commerce than religion. Salem sailing vessels had opened routes to the Orient, thus establishing the famous China trade and Salem's reputation as a major port.

For the next 150 years, shipbuilding, the China trade and commercial fishing flourished along the Massachusetts coast, particularly in the towns north of Boston. Concurrently, New Bedford, near Rhode Island, became a leading whaling port.

All this maritime activity brought great prosperity to the coast. Fortune and adventure lay in wait for any man willing to risk his life on a whale boat or ship bound for the Orient to obtain ivory, spice, silver and gold. It was an exciting, swashbuckling time, filled with tall tales and tragedy. The widows' walks on many historic homes in towns such as Newburyport are a sad reminder of the men who never returned from the sea.

Evidence of the wealth gleaned during these years is apparent in the amazing number of 18th- and 19th-century mansions built by sea captains that dot the coast. Impeccably restored by a people in love with the past, these coast homes make up an architectural feast bulging with Greek Revival, Federal, Queen Anne, Victorian Gothic, Colonial and classic saltbox structures. Historic villages and buildings throughout the area enable visitors to see the evolution of America's unique architectural style. Many sea captains' homes are now inns, allowing travelers to experience the structures as well.

By the mid-1800s everything along the Massachusetts coast started to change. Salem's prominence as a seaport was over. Its harbor was too shallow for the new, faster clipper ships, and railroads provided cheaper and more rapid shipping service. The whaling industry also started to decline as petroleum replaced whale oil and whales became scare. Eventually the entire industry vanished, plummeting New Bedford and other whaling ports into serious depressions.

The Industrial Revolution came along in the nick of time, and manufacturing businesses started to sprout along the Massachusetts coast and throughout New England. In the late 1800s, New Bedford and Fall River became leading textile manufacturers, but this prosperity was short lived. Prior to the Depression, union problems and cheaper labor in the South wiped out the textile industry.

While the coast economy was transforming itself in the mid-1800s, two other developments were evolving that would change the flavor of the coast forever. Tourism began to bloom on Cape Cod, and artists and writers discovered the inspirational charms of the coast.

Rudyard Kipling and Winslow Homer lived north of Boston in Rocky Neck, one of the country's oldest artist colonies. Nathaniel Hawthorne wrote about Salem, which he called home, in the *House of the Seven Gables*. Melville immortalized whaling in New Bedford. To this day, creative people are drawn to the Massachusetts coast, now supported by light industry, fishing and a tourist industry that just keeps growing.

We have divided the coast into two geographic areas. The North Shore (everything above Boston to the New Hampshire border) and the South Shore (Plymouth and the area from Cape Cod to the Rhode Island border). Cape Cod and the

Islands have always attracted the lion's share of tourists, but the North Shore and South Shore offer more opportunities to discover hidden villages, inns, restaurants, beaches and more.

The North Shore wears many faces. Immediately north of Boston are the affluent commuter towns of Magnolia, Manchester and Marblehead, where prep schools, yachts and turn-of-the-20th-century seaside mansions are a way of life.

Beyond these towns are Salem, known for architecture, witches and maritime museums; Gloucester, a major fishing port; Rockport, an artist-colony-turned-resort; Essex and Ipswich, pastoral areas with antiques and seafood; and Newburyport, a scenic 19th-century town near the New Hampshire border.

The South Shore is a patchwork of wealthy commuter towns, Portuguese neighborhoods, blue-collar communities and cranberry farms. Its three main towns include Plymouth, "America's Home Town," New Bedford and Fall River. You'll find Pilgrim lore, factory outlets, whaling museums, scenic ports, winding rivers and coastal pastures.

The coast has milder weather than the rest of the state. Summer temperatures range from the 60s to the 80s. Humidity can be a problem, especially along the North Shore, although ocean breezes keep things from getting too unbearable. In the fall temperatures range from the around 45° to 65°. Rain is unpredictable and can happen any time of year.

Traditionally the Massachusetts coast has been a summer destination, but more people are starting to visit in the fall, when prices decline along with the crowds. But no matter when you visit you're bound to be impressed. The scenery is unparalleled, the architecture magnificent, the history fascinating, the seafood plentiful.

The North Shore

The North Shore is a real sleeper. Unspoiled and relatively uncommercial, it's a place where you can still discover hidden inns, restaurants, beaches and parks. An explorer's destination, it's perfect for people who like to go it on their own.

From Marblehead immediately north of Boston to Newburyport on the New Hampshire border, this craggy stretch of coast offers tremendous diversity. Marblehead has magnificent yachts; Salem means witches and maritime history; gritty Gloucester is filled with old salts; Rockport has art and beautiful inns; Essex offers antiques; Ipswich has the best seafood; and Newburyport displays 19th-century elegance.

The North Shore is a vacation area and bedroom community to Boston populated by investment bankers, Yankee blue bloods, fishermen, artists and history buffs. In the 18th and 19th centuries, the country's most magnificent ships were built in North Shore towns, bringing great wealth to the area.

SIGHTS

HIDDEN ►

In Marblehead, head directly to the Old Town historic district, where you'll find **Abbot Hall,** the Victorian town hall that houses the famous historic painting The Spirit of '76 by Archibald

Willard. Visitors are free to wander in and view this dramatic work of art. Closed weekends from November through Memorial Day. ~ 188 Washington Street, Marblehead; 781-631-0000, fax 781-631-8571; www.marblehead.com.

Right down the street is the **Jeremiah Lee Mansion,** a Georgian home built in 1768 for Colonel Lee, a Revolutionary War patriot. The guided tour is packed with trivia and entertaining anecdotes: We learn, for example, that the extra-wide stairway and the entrance hall were the largest in New England. There are lovely historic gardens for wandering. Closed Monday, and mid-October to June. Admission. ~ 161 Washington Street, Marblehead; 781-631-1768, fax 781-631-0917.

Salem is so civilized and proper looking, it's hard to believe the 1692 witchcraft trials ever took place here. This macabre piece of American history began in a very innocent way. A group of teenage girls, who had learned black magic from a West Indian woman named Tituba, were diagnosed as bewitched. All hell broke loose, and everyone started accusing everyone else of being a witch. In the nine months to follow, 14 women (and 5 men) were hanged and 150 imprisoned. The hysteria came to an end when the wives of prominent men were accused of being witches.

When the Revolutionary War broke out in 1775, America didn't have a Navy, so Salem sea captains armed their merchant vessels and fought the British.

Salem's three witch exhibits are somewhat commercial, but kids love them. Every day in the summer, children wearing pointed black hats and capes purchased at nearby witch boutiques stand in long lines waiting to get in. The saving grace of the exhibits is that they are in historic buildings—not re-creations of haunted houses.

Salem Witch Museum is an audio-visual sound-and-light show. Life-size dioramas are spotlighted during the show to illustrate the events of the 1692 witch trials. They also have a more cerebral exhibit that examines the new views and multiple meanings of "witch." Closed one week in mid-January. Admission. ~ 19½ Washington Square North, Salem; 978-744-1692, fax 978-745-4414; www.salemwitchmuseum.com, e-mail facts@salemwitchmuseum.com.

Witch House is the restored 1642 home of witch trial judge Jonathan Corwin, and the only structure still standing in Salem with direct ties to the witch trials. A narrated tour describes the style of life during this era and examines the process of the witch trials. Closed December to mid-March. Admission. ~ 310½ Essex Street, Salem; 978-744-0180, fax 978-740-9299.

Witch Dungeon Museum re-enacts the witch trials. Admission. ~ 16 Lynde Street, Salem; 978-741-3570, fax 978-741-1139; www.cityofsalem.com.

A tourist information booth is located at the **Central Wharf Warehouse** on Derby Wharf.

To understand the real story of Salem, which was a major port in the 18th and 19th centuries, visit the **Peabody Essex Museum**. The Liberty Street site houses a treasure trove of objects acquired during Salem's active China trade days, such as an elaborate, moon-shaped, hand-carved wooden Chinese bed. A genealogy research library and original witch trial documents are some of the highlights. The Essex Street site consists of a history museum and four impeccably restored homes and gardens dating from 1684 to 1818. The houses are fascinating, especially if toured in chronological order, and the architecture and craftsmanship are superb. Anyone who has ever renovated an old house will appreciate a special exhibit about the painstaking efforts that go into museum restoration work. Since bright colors were a sign of wealth in the 19th century, the 1804 Gardner-Pingree House, a fine neoclassical building, holds a few surprises. The kitchen is deep salmon and green; one bedroom wears a vivid peacock-blue hue, while another sports canary yellow. Closed Monday from November through March, though the museum will be closed until June 2003 for renovations. Admission. ~ East India Square, Salem; 978-745-9500, fax 978-745-7750, 800-745-4054; www.pem.org.

Chestnut Street is one of the most architecturally significant avenues in America. Many of its mansions were designed by Salem's famed Federal-period architect and woodcarver, Samuel McIntire. These brick-and-wood houses are simple in their design, yet the overall effect is graceful and elegant.

Pickering Wharf, a short walk from Chestnut Street, is a new but made-to-look-old commercial development of tourist shops and chain restaurants. About a block east stands **Derby Wharf**— a good area for strolling along the harbor.

Even though it's often crowded with tourists, there's something romantic and compelling about the **House of Seven Gables**, located down the street from Derby Wharf. Built in 1668, the dark, almost black house is framed by ocean and sky. The tall, imposing gables look a bit like witch hats (although this thought probably wouldn't come to mind in another town). Inside, a labyrinth of cozy rooms with low ceilings, narrow passageways and secret stairs add to the ancient feeling of the place. Year-round guided tours are available. Closed the first two weeks in January. Admission. ~ 54 Turner Street, Salem; 978-744-0991, fax 978-741-4350; www.7gables.org.

Northeast of Salem on scenic Route 127, which hugs the coast, are the residential towns of **Manchester** and **Magnolia**, known for their old money, private schools and magnificent mansions.

HIDDEN ►   Right off Route 127 is **Hammond Castle Museum**, a popular spot for weddings. Built by John Hays Hammond, Jr., creator of the radio remote control, the house features an eccentric collection of medieval artifacts. Closed Monday through Thursday from Labor Day to the end of September; closed in October; open weekends only from November to Memorial Day. Admission. ~ 80 Hesperus Avenue, Gloucester; 978-283-2080, fax 978-283-1643; www.hammondcastle.org.

The **Beauport Museum**, a sprawling oceanfront English manor   ◄ *HIDDEN* formerly owned by noted decorator Henry Davis Sleeper. From 1907 to 1934 Sleeper spent a fortune decorating all 40 rooms with a vast collection of American and European antiques, tapestries, wood pancling from abandoned old homes and much more. An informal pale green dining room has a worn brick floor and two long wooden tables set with a beautiful collection of colored glassware that reflects the light coming in from a bank of ocean-facing windows. Surprisingly, the overall effect is of an intimate English cottage. Closed mid-October to mid-May, and weekends from mid-May to mid-September. Admission. ~ 75

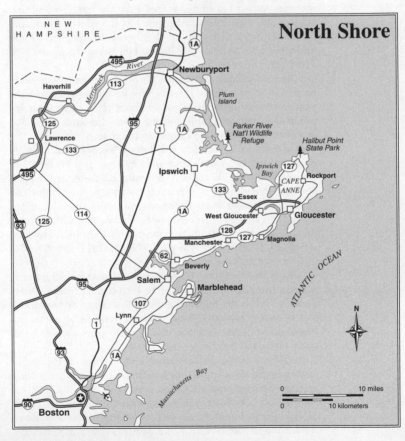

North Shore

Eastern Point Boulevard, Gloucester; 978-283-0800, fax 978-283-4484; www.spnea.org, e-mail beauporthouse@spnea.org.

Bearskin Neck, a narrow peninsula jutting out into the ocean, is one of Rockport's main tourist attractions. It is lined with Lilliputian-sized wooden fishermen's shacks transformed into restaurants, shops and galleries selling everything from T-shirts and seascapes in every style imaginable to model ships made of cut-up beer cans. Overlooking the harbor, off Bearskin Neck, is **Motif #1**, a red lobster shack so named because it has been painted by so many artists.

About two miles south of downtown Rockport is the **Rockport Chamber of Commerce**. ~ 22 Broadway, Rockport; 978-546-6575, fax 978-546-5997, 888-726-3922; www.rockportusa.com, e-mail info@rockportusa.com.

The folks here can point out the local sights, such as the eccentric **Paper House**. At first it looks like a normal cottage, but it's made entirely out of newspaper. Even the furniture and fireplace mantle piece are rolled paper. Elis F. Stedman, its creator, started the house in 1920; it took 20 years to complete. Closed mid-October to March. ~ 52 Pigeon Hill Street, Rockport; 978-546-2629.

The rural villages of **Essex** and **Ipswich** are about 30 minutes north of Rockport. Essex is famous for its antique stores (see the "Shopping" section below), Ipswich for its clams. A pleasant day can be spent antiquing and enjoying fresh, affordable seafood at one of the many roadside eateries in this area.

This route takes you right past **John Whipple House**, a steeply pitched-roofed house built circa 1655 and occupied by the Whipple family for over 200 years. As did many colonists, the Whipples built their home in the post-Elizabethan style popular in England at the time. It has a lovely Colonial-style garden and is located in a semirural area close to other historic buildings. Closed Monday and Tuesday and from November through April. Admission. ~ 1 South Village Green, Ipswich; 978-356-2811, fax 978-356-2817; e-mail ihs@cove.com.

Just before the New Hampshire border, about 30 minutes north of Ipswich, lies the handsome 19th-century town of **Newburyport**. When the fog rolls in and the smell of brine and fish fills the air, you can walk along narrow streets bearing names like Neptune and imagine what it was like 100 years ago when this was a major shipbuilding center.

In the late 1970s the downtown area overlooking the harbor was renovated from top to bottom. Today, Newburyport's 19th-century brick buildings are so spit-and-polish clean, the town literally sparkles. As in many European towns, there's a central plaza overlooking the harbor where you can sit and watch the world go by. The shops and restaurants are quite tasteful; T-shirt and souvenir shops are the exception. **Greater Newburyport Chamber of Commerce** is in the heart of downtown. Closed weekends from Memorial Day to Columbus Day. ~ 38R Merrimac Street, Newburyport; 978-462-6680, fax 978-465-4145; www.newburyport chamber.org, e-mail info@newburyportchamber.org.

High Street (Route 1A) offers a view of every architectural style from the pilgrim era to the present. It is lined with immaculate 19th-century Federal-style mansions built by sea captains and includes houses built from the 1690s to the 1850s. For a peek inside, visit **Cushing House Museum,** home of the Historical Society of Old Newbury. It has 19th-century antiques, plus a genealogical library, a 19th-century garden and a carriage house. Closed Sunday and Monday and from November through April. Admission. ~ 98 High Street, Newburyport; 978-462-2681, fax 978-462-0134; www.newburyhist.com, e-mail hson@greennet.net.

Many of the North Shore's accommodations are in the resort town **LODGING** of Rockport. A sprinkling of motels can be found along Route 127, but they're short on charm and expensive.

The **Marblehead Inn,** an 1872 Victorian, is located on a historic street surrounded by other impressive homes. A grand staircase leads to ten two-room suites and sets off wide hallways, tall ceilings and fireplaces. Each suite has a kitchenette and air conditioning. ~ 264 Pleasant Street, Marblehead; 781-639-9999, 800-399-5843, fax 781-639-9996; www.marbleheadinn.com. ULTRA-DELUXE.

A modest-looking green clapboard house, **The Nautilus Guest** ◀ HIDDEN **House** doesn't have a sign outside. "People just know about it," says the owner. Four plain and simple guest rooms with quaint furnishings occupy the second floor (no private baths). The house stands on a narrow street across from the busy harbor and the Driftwood, a colorful, sea shanty–style restaurant popular with fishermen and locals. ~ 68 Front Street, Marblehead; 781-631-1703, fax 781-631-6204. MODERATE.

If you can't live without a telephone, color TV, air conditioning and room service, stay at **The Hawthorne Hotel.** One of

"HOW DRY AM I . . ."

Rockport is a dry town, thanks to Hannah Jumper, a temperance supporter. In 1856 after a raucous Fourth of July celebration, Hannah convinced town fathers to outlaw liquor. Even today you can't buy it in a store or order it in a restaurant. But you can buy liquor in Gloucester, which is only ten minutes away, and bring it to any Rockport restaurant.

The North Shore

This 80-mile day trip from Boston provides a chance to explore the North Shore in all its diversity and quiet charm. Start by taking the Callahan Tunnel (Route 1A) north through the suburbs, where it becomes the McClellen Highway, then North Shore Road, and finally Lynnway before the divided roadway ends at East Lynn, a distance of ten miles.

MARBLEHEAD Take the east fork in the highway and follow Route 129 for six miles to **Marblehead**, a small village of clapboard houses, hollyhocks and cobblestone streets. Marblehead is sailboat country. All summer long the harbor is alive with some of the most sophisticated racing vessels in America. A good place to picnic and watch them is high on a hill in **Crocker Park** at the western end of Front Street. Marblehead's **Old Town**, which surrounds the harbor, dates back to before the Revolution and is a pleasant place to stroll, with interesting shops and casual restaurants. The **Marblehead Chamber of Commerce** maintains a visitor information booth at Pleasant and Spring streets. ~ 62 Pleasant Street, Marblehead; 781-631-2868; www.marbleheadchamber.org.

SALEM Salem, the largest North Shore town, is only ten minutes away from Marblehead on Route 114, which rejoins Route 1A just south of town. People come here for architecture, maritime museums, Nathaniel Hawthorne and, of course, witches. Tourist information is available at the **National Park Service Visitor Center**. ~ 2 New Liberty Street, Salem; 978-740-1650. Or contact the **Chamber of Commerce**. ~ 63 Wharf Steet, Salem; 978-744-0004; e-mail scc@salemchamber.org. An easy way to see historic sights is to follow **Salem's Heritage Trail**, a self-guided walking tour indicated by a red line painted on the street.

GLOUCESTER Northeast of Salem, turn off Route 1A again onto scenic Route 127, which hugs the coast and takes you through the residential

the few real hotels on the North Shore, this impeccably restored Federal-style building is located across from Salem Common. Eighty-nine guest rooms are tastefully decorated with reproduction Colonial antiques. Elegant public rooms have wood paneling, brass chandeliers and wingback chairs. ~ 18 Washington Square West, Salem; 978-744-4080, 800-729-7829, fax 978-745-9842; www.hawthornehotel.com, e-mail info@hawthorne hotel.com. DELUXE TO ULTRA-DELUXE.

Within easy reach of Singing Beach is the **Old Corner Inn**, a small, unpretentious and very casual inn in a building that dates towns of Manchester and Magnolia, known for their old money, private schools and magnificent mansions. Right off Route 127, about 14 miles north of Salem, you'll spot **Hammond Castle** perched on the edge of a steep, windswept cliff, looking like the setting for a Gothic novel. Three miles beyond the castle is Gloucester, the oldest seaport in the United States. Home port to approximately 200 fishermen, it has a salty-dog ambience that brings you back to the real world after the castle. Overlooking the harbor stands the town's famed **Gloucester Fisherman** statue, *Man at the Wheel*, commemorating "They that go down to the sea in ships." There's not much to do in Gloucester; information on the town and local services is available at the **Cape Ann Chamber of Commerce**, the largest tourist information center on the North Shore, in the center of town. ~ 33 Commercial Street, Gloucester; 978-283-1601; www.cape-ann.com.

ROCKPORT   A short hop from Gloucester off Route 127 is **Rocky Neck Art Colony**, one of the country's oldest artist colonies, dating back to the 18th century. Winslow Homer and Rudyard Kipling lived here. Today it is a quainter than quaint seaside village with tiny houses, restaurants and galleries. Ten minutes farther along on Route 127 is Rockport, the quintessential New England seaside village and the North Shore's only resort town. Until the mid-19th century, Rockport was a quiet fishing village. Then artists discovered its scenic charm, and the proverbial seascape was born. Today tourists flock to Rockport in the summer. The town is rather commercial, but the beautiful harbor and windswept rocky coast that originally attracted artists are still here to enjoy.

BACK TO BOSTON   From Rockport, continue on Route 127 for nine more miles as it loops around the peninsula and joins Route 128, a divided freeway that connects to Routes 1 and 95 and can put you back in downtown Boston in less than an hour. Or, to extend your North Shore outing, leave Route 128 after four miles at Exit 14, detour through **Essex** and **Ipswich** (page 221) on Route 133, and return to Boston via Route 1A.

back to 1865. The nine rooms (six with private baths) are simply but comfortably furnished with some antiques. A couple of rooms have four-poster beds and working fireplaces; the bathroom of room number one has a ball-and-claw bathtub. Advance reservations are a must in the summer months since it's the only inn in Manchester. ~ 2 Harbor Street, Manchester; 978-526-4996, 800-830-4996, fax 978-526-7671; www.theoldcornerinn.com, e-mail theoldcornerinn@aol.com. MODERATE TO ULTRA-DELUXE.

There is something inexpressibly lovable about the **White House**, a cross between an inn and a motel. Surrounded by a well-coifed lawn steps away from the heart of little Magnolia, it has a total of 16 rooms, six seasonal ones fitting beautifully into the charming-inn category (antique furnishings and all sorts of little Victorian touches), and another ten rooms that are traditional motel accommodations. The latter are actually quite comfortable, most with two big double beds, a television, a private entrance, a private bath and a parking spot—a welcome change from the inns that sometimes compromise on privacy. A continental breakfast is included. ~ 18 Norman Avenue, Magnolia; 978-525-3642; www.whitehouseofmagnolia.com. MODERATE TO DELUXE.

Beach lovers enjoy the **Blue Shutters Inn,** a lovely old house across the street from Good Harbor Beach, one of the North Shore's most beautiful strips of sand. It's situated on the outskirts of a secluded, affluent residential area overlooking the ocean and a vast expanse of scenic salt marsh. Blue and white throughout, the inn offers ten rooms and four individual apartments, all with ocean views and sporting furnishings that are homey, simple and sparkling clean. Breakfast included. ~ 1 Nautilus Road, Gloucester; 978-283-1198. MODERATE TO ULTRA-DELUXE.

Only a ten-minute walk from Gloucester's famed fisherman statue, **The Manor Inn** has economical accommodations to satisfy all tastes. The main guest house, a lovely Victorian built in 1900, has 11 B&B-style guest rooms, some with turret-shaped ceilings and oversized beds. Next to the guest house are one-story motel units, some of which overlook the Annisquam River, a salt marsh and estuaries. The decor is plain and unobtrusive. ~ 141 Essex Avenue, Gloucester; 978-283-0614, fax 978-283-3154; www.themanorinnofgloucester.com, e-mail themanorinn@prodigy.net. MODERATE TO DELUXE.

A 1791 Colonial bed and breakfast, **The Inn on Cove Hill** is a five-minute walk from Bearskin Neck, Rockport's main tourist attraction. Eight guest rooms have wide pine-plank floors, beautiful restored moldings, antiques, queen-sized canopy beds, coun-

AUTHOR FAVORITE

Witches aside, one of the best reasons I can think of to visit Salem is the **Stephen Daniels House**, which is like a trip back in time. Built in 1667 by a sea captain, it is one of the few bed and breakfasts around here furnished entirely with museum-quality antiques. The four guest rooms have enormous walk-in fireplaces, low beamed ceilings and age-worn pine floors. It's located on a quiet, historic street within walking distance of everything, although the sign outside is small and easy to miss. ~ 1 Daniels Street, Salem; 978-744-5709. MODERATE TO DELUXE.

try quilts and Laura Ashley–style wallpaper. In summer a continental breakfast is served in the garden; in spring and fall it's served indoors. Shared bath, budget; private bath, moderate to deluxe. No smoking on the premises. ~ 37 Mount Pleasant Street, Rockport; 978-546-2701, 888-546-2701, fax 978-546-1095; www.innoncovehill.com, e-mail beck@ziplink.net. MODERATE TO DELUXE.

The **Old Farm Inn** looks like the original Sunny Brook Farm.   ◄ HIDDEN
Built in 1779, the barn-red inn is shaded by glorious weeping willow trees. Only ten minutes from downtown and within walking distance of Halibut Point State Park, it's a good place for getting away from it all without going to extremes. Four guest rooms in the main house (some featuring sitting rooms) have gun stock beams, wide pine-plank floors, fireplaces and antique quilts. Four large guest rooms in a newer building (some with kitchenettes) are decorated with country-style prints, but they lack the charm of the other rooms. ~ 291 Granite Street, Rockport; 978-546-3237, 800-233-6828, fax 978-546-5190; www.oldfarminn.com, e-mail oldfarm@shore.net. DELUXE TO ULTRA-DELUXE.

JFK and Jackie once slept at the **Yankee Clipper Inn**, one of Rockport's finest hostelries. The main inn, a stately white art-deco oceanfront mansion, has magnificent wood-paneled public rooms appointed with model ships, oriental rugs, paintings and elegant yet comfortable furniture. The Quarterdeck, a separate building built in 1960, has panoramic ocean views and a traditional look. The inn has a saltwater swimming pool, a gazebo and nature paths. Breakfast is included. Closed December through March. ~ 96 Granite Street, Rockport; 978-546-3407, 800-546-3699, fax 978-946-9730; www.yankeeclipperinn.com, e-mail info@yankeeclipperinn.com. ULTRA-DELUXE.

The **Peg Leg Inn**, a white clapboard Colonial, is only steps away from the beach. One of the inn's two buildings is on the ocean and commands the highest rates, but it has spectacular views, a large, sweeping lawn and a granite gazebo. The 16 guest rooms are furnished with chenille bedspreads, braided rugs and reproduction Colonial furnishings and wallpaper. A continental breakfast is included in the rates. Closed mid-December to mid-February. ~ 2 King Street, Rockport; 978-546-2352, 800-346-2352; www.pegleginn.com. MODERATE TO DELUXE.

Located on a quiet street in the center of town, the **Linden Tree Inn** has 18 rooms with private baths. Twelve antique-furnished rooms are in the main house; the rest are motel-style accommodations in the carriage house. The inn is named after an enormous linden tree on the grounds. Continental breakfast is included. ~ 26 King Street, Rockport; 978-546-2494, 800-865-2122, fax 978-546-3297; www.lindentreeinn.com, e-mail ltree@shore.net. MODERATE TO DELUXE.

Rockport's **Seaward Inn**, a rambling brown-shingle building, sits on a beautiful bluff overlooking the ocean. Surrounded by flower gardens, lawns and stone walls, it has a spring-fed swimming pond and bird sanctuary laced with nature paths. Cottages with kitchenettes and fireplaces, located behind the main inn, are ideal for families. Thirty-seven guest rooms, some with ocean views and fireplaces, are simply appointed with homey-looking Colonial-style furnishings. The Adirondack-style chairs on a grassy knoll overlooking the windswept shore are perfect for relaxing and reading. Rates include a full breakfast. Cottages unavailable during the off-season; closed November to mid-April. ~ 44 Marmion Way, Rockport; 978-546-3471, 877-473-2927, fax 978-546-7661; www.seawardinn.com, e-mail info@seaward inn.com. ULTRA-DELUXE.

A reasonably priced bed and breakfast in the heart of Rockport is hard to come by, but **Lantana House** fits the bill. The three-story cedar shake-shingled inn has five charming guest rooms, each with distinctive decor. There are two decks where guests can enjoy breakfast or a quiet afternoon. All rooms have private baths and air conditioning, and continental breakfast is included. ~ 22 Broadway, Rockport; 978-546-3535, 800-291-3535, fax 978-546-3231; www.shore.net/~lantana, e-mail lantana_house@yahoo.com. BUDGET TO MODERATE.

Guests at the **George Fuller House** will get the full Essex treatment. The house was built in 1830 by shipwrights who built many of the fishing schooners that plied Cape Ann's waters during the whaling era. Many of the original Federal-style details have been preserved, including the interior folding shutters, paneling and carved fireplace mantels. The seven rooms are furnished with antiques and reproductions; all have private baths, some have canopy beds and five have working fireplaces. The innkeeper serves a full breakfast every morning in the dining room, and tea is available on the porch or in the living room in the late afternoon. ~ 148 Main Street, Route 133, Essex; 978-768-7766, 800-477-0148, fax 978-768-6178; www.cape-ann.com/fuller-house, e-mail gfuller@ziplink.net. DELUXE TO ULTRA-DELUXE.

The **Clark Currier Inn** is a beautiful 1803 Federal home in the square style of the period. The woodwork and other details throughout the house are splendid, and the antiques and reproductions are, for the most part, true to the Federal period. The eight rooms are individually named for former owners or well-known visitors. Some rooms have canopy beds, and some have twin beds or are convertible to suites for parents who would rather have their children sleeping in an adjoining room. All rooms have private baths. The backyard boasts a lovely garden and a gazebo. ~ 45 Green Street, Newburyport; 978-465-8363; www.clarkcurrierinn.com. DELUXE TO ULTRA-DELUXE.

The **Morrill Place Inn**, a three-story, 1806 Federal-style mansion, stands on historic High Street, where wealthy shipbuilders lived in the 19th century. The inn's 12 spacious rooms are beautifully decorated. The Henry W. Kinsman room (named for a former owner) is a rich hunter green with an enormous white canopy bed, while the Daniel Webster room has a four-poster antique bed and sleigh dresser. Rooms on the third floor are less formal but charming in their own way, with Colonial-style antiques. Some rooms share baths; pets are allowed. Breakfast and afternoon tea are included. ~ 209 High Street, Newburyport; 978-462-2808, 888-594-4667, fax 978-462-9966. MODERATE TO DELUXE.

◄ HIDDEN

DINING

Rockport has the majority of restaurants on the North Shore, but few are outstanding. Restaurants with a steady local clientele in nearby towns are generally better.

The **Driftwood Restaurant** is something of an institution. Homey, friendly and colorful, it attracts fishermen in the wee hours (it opens at 5:30 a.m.) and young professionals late on weekend mornings. The fare is traditional and plentiful: ham and eggs, pancakes, fried dough, clam chowder, burgers, fried seafood. The interior of this modest little establishment is plain and simple with red-and-white checked tablecloths. Tables are jammed close together, and there's a counter. No dinner. ~ 63 Front Street, Marblehead; 781-631-1145. BUDGET TO MODERATE.

Portions of *The Perfect Storm* were shot in Gloucester. The movie, starring George Clooney, focused on a swordfishing crew that set sail in 1991, never to return.

The **Landing** features entrées like lobster basilico and baked scrod, plus non-seafood options like tenderloin medallions or pasta primavera, in a nautical-themed setting. The waterfront deck juts out over Marblehead Harbor. Sunday brunch is also offered. ~ 81 Front Street, Marblehead; 781-639-1266; www.thelandingrestaurant.com. DELUXE TO ULTRA-DELUXE.

The **Sail Loft Restaurant** offers hearty portions of award-winning clam chowder, sandwiches, fish and chips and a seafood platter. Be careful, though—the bar is known for its very potent drinks. ~ 15 State Street, Marblehead; 781-631-9824. MODERATE.

Pellino's owner and chef Francesco Pellino was born in Naples and occasionally returns to Italy to bring back more authentic recipes. Sample pan-roasted littleneck clams or porcini mushroom strudel for appetizers. Entrées include the signature veal Pellino, with port wine, shiitake mushrooms and sun-dried tomatoes, as well as roasted chicken with butternut risotto and veal saltimbocca. Dinner only. ~ 261 Washington Street, Marblehead; 781-631-3344, fax 978-777-5920; www.pellinos.com. MODERATE TO DELUXE.

If the diner urge strikes, head for **Red's Sandwich**. Its booths and two horseshoe-shaped bars are always crowded with regulars who all seem to know one another. The menu includes all the diner favorites, from pancakes at breakfast to hamburgers for lunch. No dinner. ~ 15 Central Street, Salem; 978-745-3527, fax 978-745-5262. BUDGET.

Lyceum Bar and Grill blends international flavors into unique appetizers like Szechwan seared ahi tuna with baby sprout salad and sake sauce. For an entrée, you can choose from artichoke-crusted salmon Napoleon with braised Swiss chard and black Mediterranean olives, or a barbecued half-chicken with peach bourbon sauce. No lunch on Saturday and Sunday; Sunday brunch. ~ 43 Church Street; Salem; 978-745-7665, fax 978-744-7699; www.lyceumsalem.com, e-mail ebrewin@hotmail.com. DELUXE.

Located in the Hawthorne Hotel, **Nathaniel's** is an elegant choice for American and European classics, including seared duckling breast, lamb porterhouse and veal fricassee. The appetizers (wild mushroom Napolean, pan-seared *fois gras*) are rich enough for a meal. ~ 18 Washington Square West, Salem; 978-744-4080, 800-729-7829, fax 978-745-9842; www.hawthorne hotel.com, e-mail info@hawthornehotel.com. DELUXE TO ULTRA-DELUXE.

HIDDEN ►

The North Shore has two first-rate gourmet delis perfect for unforgettable picnics. **Grange Gourmet** and **Bruni's** offer items such as breakfast pastries, leek soup, cucumber soup, homemade salsa and chips, tortellini primavera salad, chicken salad with green grapes and almonds, healthy sandwiches, gourmet desserts and baked goods. You can also pick up different types of coffee and tea, natural sodas and more. The Grange has no dinner on Sunday. ~ Grange Gourmet: 457 Washington Street, Gloucester; 978-283-2639, 800-236-2639; www.grangegourmet.com, e-mail info@grangegourmet.com. Bruni's: 36 Essex Road, Route 133, Ipswich; 978-356-4877, fax 978-356-8921. BUDGET.

Passports is the perfect place to bring picky kids. Their international menu features just about every kind of cuisine imaginable, from Adriatic stew to Southwestern pasta to steak *au poivre*. Daily lunch and dinner specials include pasta, seafood and sandwiches. No lunch on Sunday. ~ 110 Main Street, Gloucester; 978-281-3680. MODERATE.

The Rudder is a quaint waterfront restaurant with low-beam ceilings and a natural wood decor that creates an atmosphere of casual dining. On any given night you'll find an array of seafood, along with steak dishes. Dinner only. Lunch on weekends during summer. Closed mid-October to mid-May. ~ 73 Rocky Neck Avenue, Gloucester; 978-283-7967, fax 978-281-7004. MODERATE TO DELUXE.

The Greenery, located near the entrance to Bearskin Neck, has sandwiches, a salad bar, bakery goods and desserts to go. The back dining room facing the harbor serves all these dishes plus entrées such as pesto pizza, lobster, filet mignon and roast chicken. The restaurant is appointed with blond wood, brass light fixtures and touches of green throughout. Closed November through February. ~ 15 Dock Square, Rockport; 978-546-9593; www.thegreenery restaurant.com, e-mail general2@thegreeneryrestaurant.com. MODERATE.

Portside Chowder House & Grill is a good place for a cup of chowder on a cold, blustery day. The cozy dark wood restaurant has low-beamed ceilings, a fireplace, Windsor chairs and ocean views. Specialties include New England and corn chowders, grilled sausage, crab and chicken. Lunch is served year-round; dinner is served during the summer only. ~ 2 Doyle's Cove Road, Rockport; 978-546-7045; www.portsidechowderhouse.com, e-mail info@portsidechowderhouse.com. BUDGET TO MODERATE.

Follow Bearskin Neck as far as it goes (resisting the urge to stop for a lobster roll or bowl of chowder along the way) and you reach **My Place By-the-Sea**. Here the view of the ocean competes with the food for your attention. If the weather's nice, grab a table outside: this is Cape Ann's prettiest dining spot. For both lunch and dinner you'll find lots of seafood specialties, including lobster prepared several different ways. The lunch menu also includes an array of salads and sandwiches. Closed winter and early spring; no dinner on Monday and Wednesday in spring. ~ 68 South Road, Bearskin Neck, Rockport; 978-546-9667, fax 978-546-2033. DELUXE TO ULTRA-DELUXE.

Downhome and lively, **Woodman's** hasn't changed anything except the prices since it opened in 1914. The menu includes steamers, lobster, clam cakes, scallops and corn on the cob. Sit inside at old wooden booths or outside at picnic tables in back. There's a raw bar upstairs and a full liquor bar downstairs. Locals like to come here after a day at nearby Crane's Beach. ~ 121 Main Street, Route 133, Essex; 978-768-6057, 800-649-1773; www.wood mans.com, e-mail yankeetradition@woodmans.com. BUDGET TO DELUXE.

> If you've come to Massachusetts in search of history and tradition, don't miss Woodman's: this roadside institution claims to have created the fried clam.

Tom Shea's is a fine quality seafood restaurant with large picture windows overlooking Essex River—a perfect spot for watching the sunset. The wooden interior gives the restaurant an understated, nautical look. The fare is traditional—baked stuffed lobster, fried clams, stuffed sole, grilled teriyaki shrimp, pasta, Cajun dishes plus some beef and chicken dishes. ~ 122 Main Street, Route 133, Essex; 978-768-6931, fax 707-768-7907. DELUXE TO ULTRA-DELUXE.

Grog is a large, dark, woody college bar–type place in a noncollege town. The burgers and caesar salads are particularly good, and the cheerful staff may entice you into hanging out for longer than you'd planned. There's live music Wednesday through Sunday. ~ 13 Middle Street, Newburyport; 978-465-8008; www.the grog.com, e-mail thegrog@aol.com. BUDGET TO MODERATE.

SHOPPING

HIDDEN ►

Located in a former tavern, **Antique Wear** offers beautiful earrings, stick pins, broaches, pendants and tie pins made out of antique buttons, some dating back to the 19th century. ~ 82–84 Front Street, Marblehead; 781-639-0070.

One of Salem's biggest attractions is a witch shop once owned by Jody Cabot, the city's most illustrious witch. **Crows Haven Corner** is filled with gargoyles, unicorns, crystal balls, magic wands and the full assortment of herbs, powders and seeds necessary for attracting good spirits or warding off bad ones. ~ 125 Essex Street, Salem; 978-745-8763.

In Salem, the **Peabody Essex Museum Gift Shop** offers a wonderful assortment of reproductions from around the world, as well as posters and regional history books. You'll also find children's books, Indian jewelry and ceramic plates from China. ~ 161 Essex Street, Salem; 978-745-1876.

Across from the House of Seven Gables is **Ye Old Pepper Candy Companie**. Established in 1806, it claims to be the oldest candy company in America. Specialties include gibralters, black jacks and other old-fashioned candies made on the premises. ~ 122 Derby Street, Salem; 978-745-2744.

HIDDEN ►

Nearby is the **Pickering Wharf Antique Gallery**, which at first glance looks like your garden-variety antique shop. Upon closer examination you'll find an astounding arena for dozens of antique dealers. ~ 69 Wharf Street, on Pickering Wharf, Salem; 978-741-3113.

Hanna Wingate House sells American pine antiques, French country furniture and accessories. Open weekends January through March. ~ 11 Main Street, Rockport; 978-546-1008.

New England Goods specializes in wooden toys, salt-glazed pottery, Maine wind bells and other quality crafts made in New

AUTHOR FAVORITE

If your sweet tooth is as ravenous as mine, don't leave Salem without stopping off at **Harbor Sweets**, which carries sweet sloop chocolates (a combination of white and dark chocolate with almond butter crunch) that are frighteningly delicious. You can take a tour of the factory if you call ahead for an appointment (groups only). Fortunately, Harbor Sweets does mail-order, so before leaving fill out an address card to receive mailings. At Valentine's Day you can order a dozen tiny red boxes of sloops for all the loves in your life. ~ 85 Leavitt Street, Salem; 978-745-7648.

England. Occasionally closed from January through March. ~ 57 Main Street, Rockport; 978-546-9677.

Rockport has almost as many galleries as bed and breakfasts. The majority sell seascapes—some good, many bad. For an excellent selection of Cape Ann art, visit the **Rockport Art Association**. All the work on view is for sale. Closed January; closed Monday from October through May. ~ 12 Main Street, Rockport; 978-546-6604.

Walker Creek, a real find, offers reasonably priced, finely crafted wood tables, hutches, four-poster beds, one-of-a-kind pieces and custom work loosely based on Shaker or Colonial designs. Closed Monday. ~ 57 Eastern Avenue, Route 133, Essex; 978-768-7622; www.walkercreekfurniture.com.

◄ HIDDEN

Essex's 50 antique dealers run the price-range gamut. Always ask an antique dealer if you can do better on a price—you're expected to bargain. Don't hope for major savings, however. The **White Elephant** is bargain-basement heaven. ~ 32 Main Street, Essex; 978-768-6901. At the high end of the spectrum is A. P. H. **Waller & Sons,** which carries quality European antiques from the 18th and 19th centuries. Closed Monday and Tuesday. ~ 140 Main Street, Essex; 978-768-6269. **The Scrapbook** specializes in historical and decorative prints, and maps from the 16th to 19th centuries. Call ahead for winter hours. ~ 34 Main Street, Essex; 978-768-7922. **Main Street Antiques** carries antique wicker, accessories, jewelry and textiles from the late-18th- to the mid-19th-century. ~ 44 Main Street, Essex; 978-768-7039. **North Hill Antiques** has 18th- and 19th-century furniture. ~ 155 Main Street, Essex; 978-768-7365.

If you've ever spent a lengthy period of time in the British Isles and you miss such examples of British cuisine as Bovril, Irn-br or Smarties, you'll have a ball at **Best of British**, which imports a variety of English, Scottish, Irish and Welsh goods for Anglophiles who just can't do without 'em. ~ 22 State Street, Newburyport; 978-465-6976.

Every Sunday afternoon, Le Grand David and his Spectacular Magic Company perform a highly skilled magic show at the **Cabot Street Cinema Theatre**, featuring levitations, vanishing acts, comedy skits and energetic song-and-dance routines, complete with outrageous costumes and sets. (The magic show is closed August to late September). The rest of the week the theater shows first-rate foreign and domestic films. ~ 286 Cabot Street, Beverly; 978-927-3677.

NIGHTLIFE

◄ HIDDEN

The **Larlcom Theatre**, built in 1912, features classic stage magic and a variety of entertainment also performed by Le Grande David Magic Company. Call for scheduling. ~ 13 Wallace Street, Beverly; 978-927-3677.

Symphony by the Sea concerts take place in the Peabody Museum's spectacular East Indian Marine Hall and Abbot Hall in Marblehead. Pre-concert talks are given by the conductor. ~ 181 Essex Street, Salem; 978-745-4955; www.symphonybythesea.org.

Nathaniel's in the Hawthorne Hotel features live piano music Thursday through Saturday nights. ~ 18 Washington Square West, Salem; 978-744-4080, 800-729-7829.

The **Gloucester Stage Company**, under the direction of playwright Israel Horovitz, stages first-rate plays in an old fish warehouse from May through September. With a focus on contemporary plays the company stages six productions each season. ~ 267 East Main Street, Gloucester; 978-281-4433.

The **Rockport Chamber Music Festival** performs in the Hibbard Gallery of the Rockport Art Association and offers evening concerts in June. Music ranges from Baroque to contemporary. ~ 12 Main Street, Rockport; 978-546-7391; www.rcmf.org, e-mail rcmf@shore.net.

From mid-July to mid-August, **The Crane Estate at Castle Hill** presents local musicians for its thursday-night concerts held on the manicured grounds of Castle Hill Mansion. ~ 290 Argilla Road, Ipswich; 978-356-4351; www.thetrustees.org.

The Grog is an attractive restaurant and cabaret with live entertainment ranging from reggae, rock and rhythm-and-blues to oldies and dance bands. Cover. ~ 13 Middle Street, Newburyport; 978-465-8008; www.thegrog.com.

BEACHES & PARKS

DEVEREUX BEACH 🏊 🐟 ⛵ On the causeway leading to scenic Marblehead Neck, Devereux is a small, clean beach. There's a lot to see here. The affluent town lies immediately behind the beach on a hill, while across the street lies a windsurfing cove and busy Marblehead harbor. Devereux is popular with families and teens, yet, unlike most North Shore beaches, it isn't always packed on summer weekends. Swimming and fishing are good here. You'll find picnic areas, restrooms, a playground, a bike rack and a lifeguard from mid-June to Labor Day. Parking fee, $5. ~ Located on Ocean Avenue, to the south of Marblehead harbor; 781-631-3350, fax 781-639-3420.

HIDDEN ►

SALEM WILLOWS 🏊 ⛵ ⛵ Don't be thrown off by the tawdry-looking Chinese take-out joints and arcade you see when you enter the parking lot. Salem Willows holds some pleasant surprises, including a nostalgic old amusement park overlooking Salem Sound that is shaded with graceful willow trees planted in 1801 to provide a protected area for smallpox victims. Next to the park is a small beach. People come here to stroll in the park, admire the view, rent rowboats and fish from the shore or a short pier. The waters are a little rough, and may not be ideal for swimming. Locals swear by the popcorn and chop suey sandwiches sold in the parking lot. Facilities include picnic areas, restrooms, lifeguards, a snack bar and rowboat rentals from mid-April to mid-October. ~ Located at the end of Derby Street, Salem; 978-744-0180, fax 978-740-9299.

SINGING BEACH 🏊 This jewel of a beach, only a quarter mile long, has pristine sand that literally squeaks underfoot. Hidden away in a lovely affluent neighborhood, the beach is surrounded by steep cliffs and spectacular mansions. The crowd matches the conservative neighborhood—blond and preppy. The parking lot is for residents only, and parking in the immediate area is impossible. But that doesn't keep out-of-towners away. Bostonians like this beach so much, they take the commuter train to Manchester, then walk one long, sweaty half mile to the shore. There are restrooms, a lifeguard and a snack bar Memorial Day through Labor Day. Day-use fee, $1 on Friday and weekends. ~ At the end of Beach Street, Manchester; 978-526-1242, fax 978-526-2001.

Families with young children frequent Wingaersheek Beach because it has good climbing rocks that aren't too slippery.

GOOD HARBOR BEACH 🏊 🐚 Located in a spectacular natural setting outside of Gloucester proper, this sweeping, half-mile beach is all ocean, sand dunes, marsh grass and big sky. A small shrub-covered island, positioned between two rocky headlands and accessible at low tide, is fun to explore. The beach is raked clean every day in the summer. There are restrooms, showers, a lifeguard and a snack bar. Closed early September to Memorial Day; open weekends only the rest of the year. Parking fee, $15 to $20. ~ On Thatcher Road, East Gloucester; 978-281-9790, fax 978-281-3896.

WINGAERSHEEK BEACH 🏊 This gentle, sloping, fine sand beach on Ipswich Bay is surrounded by rocks, tall marsh grass and homey summer cottages hidden in the woods. There are also tidepools to explore. The beach is quite close to downtown Gloucester and Rockport, but it feels as though it's far out in the country. There are restrooms, showers, lifeguards and a snack bar. Closed September through March; open weekends only the rest of the year. Parking fee, $15 to $20. ~ On Atlantic Street, West Gloucester; 978-281-9790, fax 978-281-3896.

◄ HIDDEN

ROCKPORT BEACHES 🏊 🐚 Rockport has two small beaches right in the heart of town. **Front Beach**, a favorite with small children, has a parallel sidewalk that gives everyone in town a perfect view of the beach. **Back Beach** is on the other side of a small bluff and is much more private. Restrooms, lifeguards (Front Beach only) and snack bar can be found here. ~ Both beaches are on Beach Street, Rockport; 978-546-3525, fax 978-546-3562.

HIDDEN ▶ **HALIBUT POINT STATE PARK** 🧍 🏊 🦆 🛶 This wild and rugged 62-acre oceanfront park, formerly the site of a granite quarry, has one of the most spectacular views on the North Shore. A walking path goes past the old quarry down a gentle incline to a vast, treeless plain of scrub thicket and wildflowers overlooking the ocean. The stark, rugged shoreline has tidepools and smooth granite rocks large enough for a group of people to picnic on. Swimming is permitted, but not recommended since the shore is covered with big, slippery rocks. There is also a World War II observatory tower. Amenities include restrooms, walking trails and guided tours. Parking fee, $2. ~ Three miles north of Rockport off Route 127; 978-546-2997, fax 978-546-9107; e-mail halibut.point@state.ma.us.

HIDDEN ▶ **THE COX RESERVATION** 🧍 🐾 Formerly the home of famed muralist Allyn Cox, this 31-acre salt marsh farmland is now headquarters for the Essex County Greenbelt Association. Peaceful and pastoral, it has winding paths, a salt marsh, woods, orchards and open farmland down to winding Essex River. Artists come here in the late afternoon when the river and graceful marsh grass are bathed in a soft golden light, creating a dreamlike environment. It's easy to see why a muralist lived in this romantic and private place. ~ Off Route 133, Essex; 978-768-7241, fax 978-768-3286; www.ecga.org, e-mail ecga@ecga.org.

CRANE BEACH 🧍 🏊 🛶 This massive, four-mile, dune-backed beach is surrounded by over 1000 acres of salt marsh, shrub thicket and woods. In the off-season, the wide beach seems to go on forever. In the summer it's wall-to-wall people. Nature and beachgoers coexist peacefully, however. At certain times of the year, sections of the beach are fenced off to protect nesting birds. Boardwalks leading to the beach protect the sand dunes. There are restrooms, showers, lifeguards, picnic areas and a snack bar. Parking fee, $10 to $20. ~ Located on Argilla Road, Ipswich; 978-356-4351, fax 978-356-2143; www.thetrustees.org.

PARKER RIVER NATIONAL WILDLIFE REFUGE 🧍 🚴 🏊 🎣 🛶 This magnificent oceanfront wildlife refuge on Plum Island is only about ten minutes from downtown Newburyport, but it feels very far away from civilization. One third of Plum Island is covered with ramshackle summer beach houses; the rest is the refuge—4662 acres of bogs, tidal marshes, sand dunes and beach. It's a good beach for surf fishing, although a strong undertow discourages swimming. Several boardwalks lead to the beach, and a few trails meander throughout the refuge. The abundant wildlife includes seals, geese, ducks, deer, coyote and over 300 species of birds. Parker River is dearly loved by Newburyport residents. From April through August, most of the beach is closed to accommodate nesting piper plovers. The only facilities here are restrooms. Parking fee, $5. ~ On Plum Island, Newburyport; 978-465-5753, fax 978-465-2807; parkerriver.fws.gov.

Plymouth Area

This area is a mix of cranberries and Pilgrims, small scenic villages, pastoral farmland, clean beaches and one main town, Plymouth, about 50 minutes south of Boston. Plymouth, of course, is where the Pilgrims landed, and it draws over one million tourists annually. It has enough historic sights to occupy an entire weekend, although most people can't take more than a day of Pilgrim lore.

To reach Plymouth from Boston, drive south on Route 3 or take scenic Route 3A. It winds along the coastline past beautiful, affluent commuter villages with lovely coves and harbors, historic lighthouses, stately mansions and winding streets.

SIGHTS

A few miles south of Quincy lies one of the region's most attractive coastal communities, **Hingham**, settled in 1635. Sailing yachts bob in its picturesque harbor, and the downtown retains the characteristics of a small village, with mom-and-pop shops, restaurants and a vintage movie theater surrounding **Hingham Square**. A drive along the long and wide **Main Street** rewards you with views of stately 18th- and 19th-century homes sporting neat black shutters. A number of them are on the National Register of Historic Places. These houses are private, but many are open to the public during the **Hingham Historical Society's** annual house tour in June, reputed to be the oldest historical house tour in the country, held since 1924. ~ Old Derby Academy, Hingham; 781-749-7721, fax 781-740-2084.

> The Old Ordinary counted Daniel Webster among its many patrons.

There are two private houses worth driving by. One is the **Hersey House**, a handsome gray mansion in Italianate style, with a flat-roofed, pillared porch, which dates to about 1857, and was once home to John Andrew, the Civil War governor of Massachusetts. ~ 104 South Street, Hingham. The other is the **Joshua Wilder House**, a beautifully restored house that probably dates to 1760. ~ 605 Main Street, Hingham.

The Old Ordinary, dating to 1680, numbered among its many owners tavern keepers who provided an "ordinary" meal of the day at fixed prices. Halfway on the day-long stagecoach ride from Plymouth to Boston, the Old Ordinary did a brisk business. Additions were made to the house in the mid-18th century. Now a museum of Hingham history, the house has an 18th-century taproom, complete with wooden grill, pewter plates and rum kegs. There's also an 18th-century kitchen outfitted with large hearth and butter churn, and a den, dining room and front parlor. Upstairs are four bedrooms furnished in period style. There are a number of rare objects among the collection, including "mourning" samplers, embroidered to honor the dead; a 17th-century Bible box; an 18th-century Queen Anne mirror; a chinoiserie; and paintings of Hingham ships that sailed to China. The Old Ordinary is open for public tours mid-June to mid-September. Closed Sunday and Monday, and early September to mid-June. Admission. ~ 21 Lincoln Street, Hingham; 781-749-0013, phone/fax 781-749-1851; www.hinghamhistorical.org, e-mail info@hinghamhistorical.org.

The Puritan congregation of the **Old Ship Church** gathered in 1635. Built in 1681, it is the oldest building in continuous ecclesiastical service in the United States, and the nation's only surviving Puritan meetinghouse. Unlike later New England churches with white spires and sides, Old Ship is built of mustard-colored wooden clapboards in Elizabethan Gothic style, as its Puritan worshippers saw fit. Crafted by ships' carpenters, the building has curved oak roof frames like the knees of a ship, and the unusual roof structure resembles an inverted ship's hull. ~ 90 Main Street, Hingham; 781-749-1679.

Not far from Hingham, on a peninsula jutting out into Boston Harbor, is **Hull**, site of **Boston Light,** the oldest lighthouse in America. Immediately south, on Jerusalem Road, is **Cohasset,** known for magnificent homes with sweeping ocean views.

Scituate, a village directly south of Cohasset, is famous for an event that took place during the War of 1812 involving Abigail and Rebecca Bates, the young daughters of the town's lighthouse keeper. When the girls noticed two barges from the British frigate *La Hogue* approaching the shore, they hid behind some trees and made so much noise with a fife and drum that the soldiers mistook them for an entire regiment and hightailed it back to safety. Scituate has quite a few historic homes plus many elegant shops along Front Street.

Continuing south, you'll arrive in **Marshfield**, where Daniel Webster lived for 20 years. His law office is located in the **Winslow House,** a historic home built in 1699 by the grandson of Mayflower passenger Edward Winslow. Visitors can tour the house and premises June through September, Wednesday to Sunday. Admission. ~ 644 Careswell Street, Marshfield; 781-837-5753.

HIDDEN ►   A few miles south of Marshfield is **Duxbury,** an aristocratic residential area of elegant homes. Stop by **The King Caesar House,** one of the state's most beautiful historic homes, located off Route 3A on a winding coastal road. A fresh yellow and white Federal-era mansion with green shutters, a sweeping lawn and climbing roses, the house stands across from a massive stone wharf where ships were once rigged. The house has finely crafted wood cornices, moldings, fanlights and balustrades, plus original handpainted

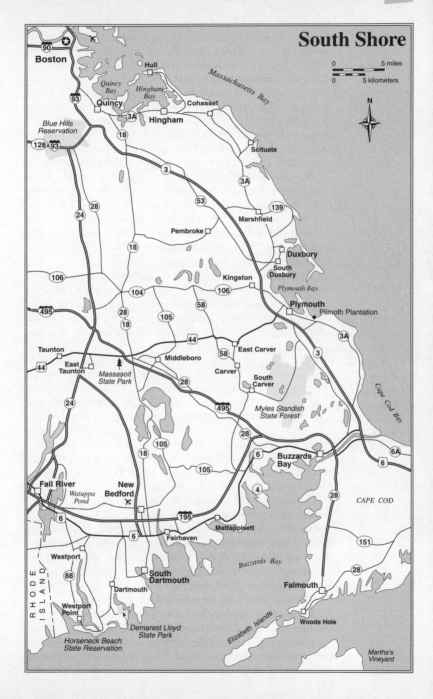

South Shore

0 ———— 5 miles
0 ———— 5 kilometers

N

Boston

Hull

Quincy Bay

Hingham Bay

Cohasset

Quincy

3A

Hingham

Massachusetts Bay

Blue Hills Reservation

18

Scituate

128 93

3

3A

24

28

53

139

Marshfield

Pembroke

18

Duxbury

106

South Duxbury

Kingston

Plymouth Bay

495

104

106

Plymouth

Plimoth Plantation

28

18

58

105

44

East Carver

3A

Taunton

East Taunton

Massasoit State Park

Middleboro

58

Carver

3

44

28

South Carver

24

495

Myles Standish State Forest

105

28

Buzzards Bay

6A

18

6

Fall River

Watuppa Pond

New Bedford

105

4

6

28

CAPE COD

195

Mattapoisett

6

Fairhaven

151

Westport

Buzzards Bay

88

South Dartmouth

Dartmouth

Falmouth

RHODE ISLAND

Westport Point

Demarest Lloyd State Park

Elizabeth Islands

Woods Hole

Cape Cod Bay

Horseneck Beach State Reservation

Martha's Vineyard

French wallpaper and fine antiques. Open Wednesday through Sunday from June through August, and weekends only in September. Admission. ~ King Caesar Road, Duxbury; 781-934-2378, 781-934-6106, fax 781-934-5730; www.duxburyhistory.org, e-mail pbrowne@duxburyhistory.org.

From Duxbury head south for **Plymouth**. "America's Home Town" can't seem to make up its mind whether to be a tourist trap or a scenic, historic village. The town is a jarring mix of historic homes, cobblestone streets, '50s-style motels, souvenir shops, a tacky waterfront and tour buses everywhere you look. It's not particularly scenic in parts, yet the town is rich with history.

Plymouth is small, and without trying you bump into everything there is to see. The **Plymouth Area Chamber of Commerce** is thrilled to dispense tourist information. ~ Water Street, Plymouth; 508-830-1620, fax 508-830-1621; www.plymouthchamber. com, e-mail info@plymouthchamber.com. So is **Destination Plymouth**. ~ 170 Water Street, Plymouth; 800-872-1620, fax 508-757-7535; www.visit-plymouth.com.

The first thing everyone heads for is **Plymouth Rock** on Water Street on the harbor. Believed to be the landing place of the Pilgrims, it is housed inside a Greek canopy with stately columns. Don't expect to see a big impressive rock; it's only large enough to hold two very small Pilgrims.

At the Plimoth Plantation, there's not one contemporary detail in sight—just the village, the ocean and settlers going about the daily tasks of the time, tending the vegetable garden or building a house with 17th-century tools.

Right next to the rock is the **Mayflower II**, a brightly painted reproduction of the real *Mayflower* that looks like the pirate ship at Disneyland. The self-guided tour is worthwhile, even though there's occasionally a line to get in. The *Mayflower* is shockingly small. It's hard to imagine how 102 people ever survived 66 days at sea in such cramped quarters. Closed December through March. Admission. ~ State Pier, Plymouth; 508-830-6021, fax 508-746-7037; www.plimoth.org.

For more Pilgrim lore, head for **Pilgrim Hall Museum**, on the main drag. Continuously operating since 1824, the museum houses the nation's largest collection of Pilgrim possessions, including richly styled Jacobean furniture and the relic of a ship that brought colonists to America. Its hull is made out of naturally curved tree trunks and branches, a crude but effective design. Closed in January. Admission. ~ 75 Court Street, Plymouth; 508-746-1620, fax 508-747-4228; www.pilgrimhall.org.

Three miles south of Plymouth is **Plimoth Plantation**, a "living museum" where men and women in period costumes portray the residents of a 1627 Pilgrim village. This sounds contrived, but it's authentic and well-done. The re-created village, situated on a dusty, straw-strewn road overlooking the ocean, is comprised of many wooden dwellings with deeply thatched roofs. The villagers speak in period dialect, and you can ask them questions about anything—including the politics of the 17th century. There's also a Wampanoag Indian site that re-creates a typical native homesite with woven and bark dome-shaped dwellings. Call ahead for reservations. Closed December through March. Admission. ~ Route 3 Exit 4, Plymouth; 508-746-1622, fax 508-830-6022; www.plimoth.org.

From Plymouth go west on Route 44, then south on Route 58 to rural **Carver**, cranberry capital of the world. In the fall the harvesting process, a breathtaking sight, can be witnessed from the road. (See "Exploring Cranberry Country" in this chapter.)

◄ HIDDEN

The Plymouth area has an abundance of very ordinary motels that attract families and tour groups, but there is also a sprinkling of hidden bed and breakfasts that is quite special.

LODGING

For a romantic getaway try the **Winsor House Inn**, 15 minutes north of Plymouth. This graceful 1812 inn stands on a street lined with houses listed on the National Register of Historic Places, and it's next to a classic white-steepled church. Down the street are a few elegant little shops, a French bakery and a small wharf. Winsor House has two tastefully decorated guest rooms and two beautiful suites. All guest rooms are furnished with Shaker- and Colonial-style antiques. A dark, cozy restaurant on the ground floor looks like an ancient seafaring tavern. A full breakfast is included. ~ 390 Washington Street, Duxbury; 781-934-0991, 800-934-0993, fax 781-934-5955. MODERATE TO ULTRA-DELUXE.

◄ HIDDEN

Route 3A in Plymouth is lined with indistinguishable motels, but the **Best Western Cold Spring** is one of the most attractive. The motel is in pristine condition and beautifully landscaped. In the summer, thick yellow marigolds border brick paths leading to the 58 units. These are spacious and simply appointed with standard-issue motel furnishings. There's a heated outdoor pool. Closed January through March. ~ 188 Court Street, Plymouth; 508-746-2222, 800-780-7234, fax 508-746-2744; www.cold springmotel.com. MODERATE TO DELUXE.

The **John Carver Inn**, a large, imposing, Colonial-style hotel, gets very crowded in the summer. But it's in the most scenic part of Plymouth, across the street from a row of 17th-century historic homes and a beautiful grist mill. Eighty rooms and five suites are pleasantly decorated in soft shades of beige and Colonial-style reproduction antiques. A full-service hotel, it has a restaurant, a lounge, a gift shop and an indoor pool with a waterslide and whirlpool. ~ 25 Summer Street, Plymouth; 508-746-7100, 800-

Text continued on page 246.

Exploring Cranberry Country

Hidden away in Carver, a scenic rural area ten minutes east of Plymouth, you'll find one of Massachusetts' most spectacular and least-known autumn attractions—**cranberry harvesting**. If you think fall foliage is a beautiful sight, wait until you see this dazzling display of color.

Cranberries are the state's number-one agricultural product, valued at about $100 million annually. Around 500 growers, with several hundred employees, work more than 14,400 acres of cranberry bogs. Little Carver alone produces one third the nation's crop, while Cape Cod and Nantucket also have cranberry farms.

One of the few fruits native to North America, cranberries were known to Indians as sassamenesh. They ate the tart red berries raw and mixed them with venison and fat to make small cakes called pemmicans. The cranberry's slender, cone-shaped flower reminded early European settlers of the beak of a crane—hence the present name. Nineteenth-century sea captains sailing from New England ports supplied cranberries to their crews because it was the most readily available source of vitamin C to prevent scurvy.

The popularity of cranberries was limited to a harvest time until 1930, when a Massachusetts lawyer-turned-cranberry-grower joined with two other growers to form a marketing cooperative promoting demand for cranberry juice cocktails. The cooperative, which became Ocean Spray Cranberries, now has 904 members—more than 90 percent of all independent cranberry growers—and continues to explore ways to boost demand by touting the berries' health benefits and trying to popularize them in other countries. The co-op held a near-monopoly until the 1990s, when the Wisconsin-based Northland Corporation went public, raising investor capital to buy up bogs around Cape Cod, and quickly became the world's largest cranberry producer. Today, a "cranberry war" rages between the two companies, while cranberry surpluses have reached unprecedented levels.

Harvest time starts September 15 and continues until the first week of November. During this time, restaurants and bakeries in southern Massachusetts use the berry in a number of creative dishes, ranging from cranberry horseradish and salsa to cranberry soup, bread, muffins, sorbet and tarts. Other innovative recipes involve mixing cranberries with applesauce, wild rice and cole slaw. To experience the full range of creative cranberry cookery, head for the **Massachusetts Cranberry Festival**, held in South Carver on Columbus Day weekend.

To explore the cranberry bogs, from Plymouth take Route 44 east to Route 58 south. Bogs line both routes, and the harvest process is very easy to see from the road. Many farmers don't mind if you observe from the elevated dirt paths bordering the bogs, as long as you stay well out of their way.

The short, scruffy, dark green cranberry vines are grown in shallow bogs surrounded by deep woods. When the cranberries are ripe, they are picked by either dry or wet harvesting. Dry-picked berries are often sold fresh, while wet-picked fruit usually becomes juice or canned cranberry sauce.

Dry-harvested berries are combed off the vine with a machine. But it's wet harvesting that's the real treat to watch. First the bogs are flooded with about 18 inches of water. Then farmers in bright yellow slickers beat the fruit off the vine with large water reels that look like giant eggbeaters stirring up a waterfall of crimson berries. The buoyant berries float to the water's surface, creating a scarlet sea surrounded by a fiery ring of woods ablaze with fall colors.

The wind blows the floating berries to one end of the pond, where they are corralled with wooden brooms. Giant vacuum cleaners then suck the berries into dechaffing machines. Helicopters and trucks transport the berries to packing houses, where they are graded according to size, color and quality.

For a cranberry-themed family amusement park, try **Edaville USA**, featuring rides, children's events and a cranberry park. Admission. ~ 7 Eda Avenue, Carver; 877-332-8455, fax 508-866-7921; www.edaville.org.

Plymouth Colony Winery, off Route 44, is in a former berry-screening house in the middle of a ten-acre cranberry bog. It offers free tastings. Closed January through March. ~ 56 Pinewood Road, Plymouth; 508-747-3334; www.plymouthcolonywinery.com, e-mail pcwinery@ plymouthcolonywinery.com.

274-1620, fax 508-746-8299; www.johncarverinn.com, e-mail info@johncarverinn.com. DELUXE TO ULTRA-DELUXE.

DINING

You may have to wait to get a table at the crowded **Run of the Mill Tavern**, but it's worth the wait for golden battered onion rings and their famous burgers. ~ 6 Spring Lane, Plymouth; 508-830-1262. BUDGET TO MODERATE.

For traditional New England–style fare, swing by **Isaac's**. They bake, they fry—you'll even find steak, lamb and seafood on the menu. ~ 114 Water Street, Plymouth Harbor; 508-830-0001, fax 508-830-0758; www.isaacsonline.com. MODERATE.

Though a magnet for tourists, **The Lobster Hut** should not be avoided. Here you can feast on clam chowder, fried clams and lobster at outdoor picnic tables overlooking the harbor, or you can eat inside, though the atmosphere may be a bit too fast-food for your liking. Closed in January. ~ On the Town Wharf, Plymouth Harbor; 508-746-2270, fax 508-746-5655. BUDGET TO MODERATE.

HIDDEN ►

A ramshackle red-shingle restaurant a few miles north of Plymouth, **Persy's Place** claims to have "New England's largest breakfast menu," and that's no joke. The menu takes about an hour to read; some of its offerings include fish cakes, buttermilk pancakes, chipped beef on toast, catfish and eggs, hickory-smoked bacon, raisin, corn, wheat and pumpernickel bread, finnan haddie, no-cholesterol eggs and much more. Persy's looks like a cross between a coffee shop and a country general store. No dinner. ~ 119 Main Street, Route 3A, Kingston; phone/fax 781-585-5464. BUDGET.

HIDDEN ►

The lovely **Crane Brook Restaurant and Tea Room** is a must if you're touring cranberry country. Located in a former iron foundry, the cozy, antiques-filled restaurant overlooks a pretty pond and is surrounded by gardens and cranberry bogs. The restaurant started out serving only tea and pastries, but now it also offers lunch. A perfect place for a long, leisurely meal, the Crane Brook has a changing menu of dishes such as grilled duck breast sandwich, rack of lamb and spicy pork loin roast and imaginative salads. Closed Sunday and Monday. ~ 229 Tremont Street, South Carver; 508-866-3235, fax 508-866-3289. MODERATE.

NIGHTLIFE

Occasional free summer concerts at the **Village Landing Gazebo** range from swing bands to Irish balladeers and children's performances. ~ Water Street, Plymouth.

Live bands can be heard free on Friday and Saturday at the **Sheraton Plymouth Pub**. ~ Village Landing, 180 Water Street, Plymouth; 508-747-4900; www.sheratonplymouth.com.

BEACHES & PARKS

DUXBURY BEACH 🏊 This five-mile stretch of clean white sand is one of the finest barrier beaches on the Massachusetts coast. The beach juts out into Cape Cod Bay and is bordered by a little harbor on one side and the Atlantic on the other. Stretches are dotted with salt marsh, and parts are accessible only by four-wheel-drive vehicles. Located in an affluent residential neighborhood, it attracts a well-heeled crowd. There are restrooms, showers, a changing room, lifeguards, a snack bar and a restaurant. No dogs allowed. Parking fee, $5 to $8. ~ Located off Route 3 on Route 139 in Duxbury, north of Plymouth; 781-837-3112.

MYLES STANDISH STATE FOREST 🚶 🚲 🐎 🏕 🏊 🎣 🚣

Locals joke that once you're in this 16,000-acre park, you'll never find your way out again. The park is enormous, and the roads winding through the forest and meadows seem to go on forever. Because of its size, it feels remote and peaceful even in the summer. Beautiful and clean, the park has 15 ponds with two beaches. You can fish most of the ponds and swim at College and Fearings beaches. Motorized vehicles are not allowed off-road. Bicycle, bridle and hiking paths wind through the forest. Non-motorized boats are allowed. Among the amenities are picnic areas, restrooms and interpretive programs. Day-use fee, $5. ~ Located off Route 3 on Long Pond Road, Plymouth; 508-866-2526, fax 508-866-5043.

It takes more than 4000 cranberries to produce a gallon of juice—good thing nearly 640 million pounds are harvested in the U.S. annually.

▲ There are 475 tent/RV sites (no hookups) with restrooms, hot showers, fireplaces and picnic tables; $10 per night for state residents, $12 per night for visitors. ~ 508-422-6762.

PLYMOUTH BEACH 🏊 🚣 🎣 🏖 Located in a half-rural, half-residential area, this straight, three-mile beach dotted with beach grass and clear stretches of sand serves as a nesting ground for migratory shore birds such as terns and plovers. The nesting area is fenced off for protection, but the birds are easily observed. In summer this busy beach attracts families and local kids. Facilities included are restrooms, lifeguards and a snack bar. Parking fee, $8 on weekdays, $10 on weekends. ~ Located off Route 3A, three miles south of Plymouth; 508-830-4095, fax 508-830-4062; www.townofplymouth.org.

New Bedford Area

About a half-hour's drive southeast of Carver lies the former whaling town of New Bedford, which gained immortality in Herman Melville's *Moby Dick*. It still looks and feels a lot like a 19th-century whaling city, with a bustling waterfront and large Portuguese population.

Until the early 1980s the waterfront area was in disarray. Then, to attract tourists, the town restored more than 100 buildings. Fortunately New Bedford didn't go overboard with cute, contrived tourist attractions. Today it has a number of fine museums, restaurants, antique shops and galleries alongside the harbor. There's something genuine and tasteful about this miniature city.

SIGHTS   The **New Bedford National Park Visitor Center** offers brochures, maps and tours. ~ 33 William Street, New Bedford; 508-979-1745.

The **Rotch-Jones-Duff House and Garden Museum** is a 19th-century Greek Revival with a picturesque rose garden that becomes a Christmas showplace during the holidays and is the site of summer concerts, lecture series and educational programs. Named for three families who owned the property, it features many of their fine antiques and chronicles the history of New Bedford. This 28-room mansion is one of the region's best. Guided and audio tours are available. Admission. ~ 396 County Street, New Bedford; 508-997-1401, fax 508-997-6846; www.rjdmuseum.org, e-mail info@rjdmuseum.org.

For three sights that shouldn't be missed, begin with the Whaling Museum. Continue on to Seaman's Bethel, a church across from the whaling museum, and County Street, where wealthy sea captains built homes in the 19th century.

Wealthy mill owners built their mansions on Columbia Street in the 1830s, but by the 1850s, immigrants began to settle here to be closer to the mills and the owners moved up the hill to Fall River.

Start with the **New Bedford Whaling Museum**, then enter Seamen's Bethel, and New Bedford won't look the same again. The museum depicts whaling's profound impact on this town, telling the story beautifully with large, dramatic paintings of life aboard whaling ships and an enormous mural created in 1848. You can climb aboard a half-scale model of a fully rigged whaling ship housed in a large room with harpoons and figureheads. There's also a 66-foot complete skeleton of a blue whale. The museum is spacious, airy and absorbing. Admission. ~ 18 Johnny Cake Hill, New Bedford; 508-997-0046, fax 508-997-0018; www.whalingmuseum.org.

Across the street is **Seamen's Bethel**, where whalers prayed before setting out to sea. The pulpit of this plain, sturdy church is shaped like a ship's bluff bows. Its walls are covered with memorial tablets to men who died at sea. A visit to this church is a sobering experience. ~ Located at 15 Johnny Cake Hill, New Bedford.

HIDDEN ►   "Nowhere in America will you find more patrician-like houses," wrote Herman Melville of **County Street**, located a few of blocks up a slight hill from the whaling museum. The impeccably restored Federal-style mansions and elaborate Victorians along this picturesque street illustrate how grand life was in 19th-century New Bedford.

HIDDEN ►   For a unique change of pace, consider visiting **Cuttyhunk**, an island 14 miles offshore from New Bedford accessible by ferry (see the "Transportation" section at the end of this chapter). It's part of the Elizabeth Islands, a chain of 16 tiny islands, 14 of them owned by the Boston Brahmin Forbes family. The island is practically all sand and scrub bushes with a rocky beach but it does have a general store, two restaurants and about 100 homes. Cuttyhunk is the opposite of busy, crowded Cape Cod—there's nothing to do but walk and fish—and therein lies its charm.

Immediately southwest of New Bedford off Route 6 are the affluent rural communities of **Dartmouth** and **Westport**, where you'll find some of the most exquisite coastal farmland in all of Massachusetts. Like Kentucky bluegrass country, this area has miles of ancient stone walls, lovely old houses, shingled dairy barns, rolling pastures and elegant horse farms.

Off Slocums Road in South Dartmouth sits **Padanaram**, a fashionable yachting resort on Apponagansett Bay. It's home to the famous boatyard Concordia, where beautiful old wooden yachts are restored. The village is only two blocks long, but it has a number of fine restaurants and shops.

Not far from Padanaram is the **Lloyd Center for Environmental Studies**, a nonprofit organization that studies coastal and estuarine environments. Open to the public are an aquarium with an Interactive Touch Tank, six walking trails and changing exhibits featuring such work as naturalist photography. The best thing here is the dazzling view from the observation deck, which overlooks winding Slocums River and miles of wetlands. The center offers weekly walks, canoe and kayaking trips and educational programs. Closed Saturday from October through March. ~ 430 Potomska Road, South Dartmouth; 508-990-0505, fax 508-993-7868; www.thelloydcenter.org, e-mail admin@thelloydcenter.org.   ◄ *HIDDEN*

Heading back to New Bedford, you can take Route 195 west to Fall River 15 minutes away. Factory outlets (see the "Shopping" section below) and Battleship Cove are this town's claims to fame.

At the turn of the 20th century **Fall River** had more than 100 textile mills, but in 1927 the industry sagged and the town went through serious hard times. Today its large granite mills are occupied by electronics and metals firms and factory outlets, but the effects of the depression still linger.

Fall River's downtown has been spruced up, but there are so many "for lease" signs tacked to its grand 19th-century buildings that the town looks a little lost.

Columbia Street, the Portuguese section of downtown, is a colorful place to stroll, sample treats from the many good bakeries and discover the beautiful mosaic sidewalks. Television chef Emeril Lagasse grew up here, and can occasionally be spotted in the midst of this vibrant ethnic community. For travel information, call the **Bristol County Convention and Visitors Bureau**. ~ 70 North 2nd Street, New Bedford; 508-997-1250, 800-288-6263, fax 508-997-9090; www.bristol-county.org, e-mail visitorinfo@bristol-county.org.   ◄ *HIDDEN*

There's also an information center at **Battleship Cove,** a harbor and park area right in town off Route 195 at Exit 5. Docked in the water at Battleship Cove are a World War II battleship, destroyer, attack submarine and PT boat that you can tour. Not surprisingly, these vessels, which are in excellent condition, are filled with children playing war. Hundreds of scout troops make pilgrimages to this John Wayne playground. Admission for boat tours. ~ Fall River; 508-678-1100, fax 508-674-5597; www.battleshipcove.com, e-mail battleshipcove@battleshipcove.com.

Next to the boats is the **Fall River Heritage State Park Visitors Center.** It has an attractive waterfront park and a building with a number of exhibits about the town's former textile industry. ~ 200 Davol Street, Fall River; 508-675-5759, fax 508-675-5758.

LODGING

In the heart of cranberry country, **On Cranberry Pond** is a great place to stay if you want to get away from the crowds in Plymouth (which is just 25 minutes away). The house is surrounded by ponds, horse pastures and cranberry bogs. The six bedrooms are furnished with country decor. The enormous back porch is a great place to while away a morning or an afternoon. A gourmet breakfast is included in the rates. ~ 43 Fuller Street, Middleboro; 508-946-0768, fax 508-947-8221; www.oncranberrypond.com, e-mail oncranberrypond@aol.com. MODERATE TO ULTRA-DELUXE.

HIDDEN ▶

Off-the-beaten-path **Mattapoisett Inn** is in a scenic little seaside village of doll-sized clapboard houses with white picket fences and window boxes. The inn stands right across the street from the harbor. The village, which is only four blocks long, consists of a small dock, a picnic area, a museum and the inn. The white-clapboard inn with black shutters has a restaurant and pub on the ground floor. Three spacious guest rooms upstairs all have balconies overlooking the ocean. The rooms aren't "decorated," but they're neat, clean, bright and comfortable. ~ 13 Water Street, Mattapoisett; 508-758-4922, fax 508-758-6353; www. mattapoisettinn.com, e-mail mattapoisettinn@aol.com. MODERATE.

A 1760 brown-shingle bed and breakfast, **The Edgewater** is so close to the water you'd swear you were on a boat when you look out the window. The inn seems miles away from civilization, yet it's only a five-minute drive from New Bedford's historic wharf district. A perfect spot for romance, the handsome house has soft taupe walls and crisp white arched moldings. The blue-and-white Captain's Suite, the best room in the house, has a sitting room, fireplace and spectacular views. The remaining two suites and three guest rooms are attractive and comfortable. All are appointed with contemporary and antique furnishings. ~ 2 Oxford Street, Fairhaven; 508-997-5512, fax 508-997-5784; www.rixsan.com/edgewater, e-mail kprof@aol.com. BUDGET TO MODERATE.

DINING

The **Candleworks** is housed in an 1810 granite candle factory half a block from New Bedford's major sights. An atriumlike room in front is appointed with wooden tables and Windsor chairs. The main dining room has a low-beamed ceiling and rich wood. The menu features Italian cuisine and a wide variety of American food including veal medallions sautéed with lobster and asparagus; breast of chicken stuffed with prosciutto, provolone and roasted peppers and served with a pesto cream sauce; and grilled swordfish with lemon butter. ~ 72 North Water Street, New Bedford; 508-997-1294; www.thecandleworks.com, e-mail info@thecandleworks.com. MODERATE TO DELUXE.

New Bedford has many Portuguese restaurants, but **Antonio's** is one of the most popular. Try the seafood paella and the *carne a ribatejana*, a casserole of pork, clams, shrimp and potatoes. Be prepared to wait for a seat, especially on the weekends. ~ 267 Coggeshall Street, New Bedford; 508-990-3636. MODERATE.

It may look like a coffee shop, but **Bayside** serves classic clam-bar fare as well as such specials as chicken burritos and eggplant parmigiana. More "in" than it seems, the restaurant has a clientele ranging from construction workers, senior citizens and families to yuppies and arty types dressed entirely in black. Bayside overlooks salt marsh, stone walls and the ocean. Breakfast on weekends only. Call ahead for winter hours. ~ 1253 Horseneck Road, Westport; 508-636-5882, fax 508-636-6496; www.thebaysiderestaurant.com. BUDGET TO MODERATE.

◄ HIDDEN

SHOPPING

This is outlet country. Fall River has over 100 outlets, and New Bedford has quite a few, too. Until the 1980s these were novel, but today there are so many discount shopping places across the country that they don't seem unique. Choices are somewhat limited because the same brands are sold everywhere: Bass, Farberware, American Tourister, Jonathan Logan, Van Heusen and Vanity Fair to name a few.

AUTHOR FAVORITE

There are many Portuguese restaurants in New Bedford, but my favorite is **Café Portugal**. A large, festive restaurant popular with Portuguese families, it features house specialties such as an enormous platter of succulent shrimp and marinated steak served with eggs on top. With its acoustical tile ceiling and plastic flower arrangements, Café Portugal looks a little bit like a banquet hall. ~ 1280 Acushnet Avenue, New Bedford; 508-992-8216. MODERATE.

Driving the expressway in Fall River, you can't help but notice the mammoth, six-story granite textile mills transformed into factory outlets—**Fall River Outlets**. All the outlets are close together, and each building has between 50 and 100 retailers selling clothes, dishes, sheets, towels, jewelry, handbags and more. Prices are rock bottom, and the merchandise is pretty low-end. Natural fiber clothing is difficult to find. ~ To visit them from Route 195, which runs through town, take Route 24 south to the Brayton exit and follow the signs.

Salt Marsh Pottery specializes in handpainted pottery and tiles designed with wildflower motifs. ~ 1167 Russells Mills Road, South Dartmouth; 508-636-4813, fax 508-636-3622; www.salt marsh.com, e-mail mail@saltmarsh.com.

NIGHTLIFE   **Zeiterion Theatre** presents a wide range of year-round musical and dramatic performances—everything from *Guys and Dolls* to *The Nutcracker*. Located in historic downtown New Bedford, the 1200-seat Zeiterion is a masterfully restored 1923 vaudeville theater with gilded Grecian friezes, elaborate crystal light fixtures and a glamorous atmosphere. Box office is closed Sunday and Monday. ~ 684 Purchase Street, New Bedford; 508-994-2900; www.zeiterion.org, e-mail zeiterion@usa.net.

BEACHES & PARKS

HIDDEN ►

HORSENECK BEACH STATE RESERVATION 🏃 🚲 🏊 This vast, breezy beach is one of the state's most spectacular and least known. Bordered by fragile dunes that create a barrier between the huge parking lot and the beach, it has crunchy white sand and fine waves. **Gooseberry Island** is a narrow, mile-long stretch of land jutting out into the ocean and laced with paths. There's an abandoned World War II lookout tower at the end. Right before Gooseberry Island is a small parking lot and a tiny beach popular with windsurfers. There are also restrooms, showers, a seasonal concession stand and seasonal lifeguards. Day-use fee, $7. ~ At the end of Route 88, Westport; 508-636-8816, fax 508-636-3968.

▲ Permitted in 100 RV sites (no hookups); $12 to $15 per night. ~ 508-636-8817.

HIDDEN ►

DEMAREST LLOYD STATE PARK 🏃 🏊 🏊 🛶 This little-known state park has everything: natural grassy areas for picnics, rambling hills of beach grass, winding rivers, abundant wildlife—deer, hawks, egrets—and a fairly isolated beach. At low tide a long sand bar juts out into the calm, warm waters. Located in the bucolic Dartmouth area, Demarest is a real find. Closed from Labor Day through Memorial Day. Facilities include picnic areas, portable restrooms and lifeguards. Day-use fee, $7. ~ Located at the end of Route 88, east of Horseneck Beach, South Dartmouth; 508-636-3298, fax 508-636-3968; www.state.ma.us/dem/forparks. htm, e-mail mass.parks@state.ma.us.

Bluefish, striped bass, tuna, cod and flounder are abundant on the Massachusetts coast. No license is required to fish, and tackle shops are everywhere. For detailed information on what to catch when, where and how, call the **Massachusetts Division of Marine Fisheries.** ~ 251 Causeway Street, Suite 400, Boston, MA 02114; 617-626-1520; www.state.ma.us/dfwele.

NORTH SHORE Captain Bill's Deep Sea Fishing provides half-day trips on Saturday and Sunday for deep-sea fishing on double-decker boats July to Labor Day. ~ 30 Harbor Loop, Gloucester; 978-283-6995. **Hilton's Fishing Dock** is a fishing, bait and tackle shop. Contact **Newburyport Whalewatch** for daily whale-watching tours May to mid-October. ~ 54-R Merrimac Street; 978-465-9885; www.newburyportwhalewatch.com.

PLYMOUTH AREA Half- and full-day cod fishing trips are available daily through **Captain John Boats** April through October. ~ 10 Town Wharf, Plymouth; 508-746-2643; www.captjohn.com.

NEW BEDFORD AREA Captain Leroy Inc. charters cabin boats for fishing and full-day party boat excursions May to late September. ~ Route 6, on the Fairhaven Bridge, New Bedford; 508-992-8907.

Marblehead, on the North Shore, is sailboat country. **Coastal Sailing School** has boats for excursion rides. Lessons are available from May through September. ~ P.O. Box 1001, Marblehead; 781-639-0553; www.coastalsailingschool.com.

The Massachusetts coast offers an enormous number of whale-watching excursions, some conducted by naturalists. The season starts in May and runs through October.

NORTH SHORE Gloucester is the North Shore's gateway to whale watching. **Cape Ann Whale Watch** offers two daily ventures from June to mid-September. ~ 415 Main Street; 978-283-5110; www.caww.com. The **Newburyport Whale Watch** runs half-day

Outdoor Adventures

FISHING

SAILING

WHALE WATCHING

AUTHOR FAVORITE

The more chances I have to encounter whales up close, the happier I am that we humans are learning to interact with them instead of killing them. In fact, these days whale watching seems to be Gloucester's main industry. **Yankee Fleet** is the oldest and largest whale-watching outfit, with trips to Stellwagon Bank and Jefferey's Ledge. Charter and fishing party excursions are also available. ~ 75 Essex Avenue; 978-283-0313; www.yankeefleet.com.

trips twice daily May to mid-October. They also organize dinner cruises. ~ Hilton's Fishing Dock, 54 Merrimac Street; 978-465-7165.

PLYMOUTH AREA Captain John Boats goes to Stellwagen Bank to spot whales. ~ Town Wharf, Plymouth; 508-746-2643; www.captjohn.com.

CANOEING & SEA KAYAKING

NORTH SHORE One of the most beautiful canoe trips in New England is along the North Shore's Ipswich River, through the 3000-acre **Ipswich River Wildlife Sanctuary**. Here you can spot deer, beaver and fox, among other animals, on a naturalist-guided half-day trip. ~ Perkins Row, Topsfield; 978-887-9264; www.massaudubon.org. For canoe rentals, contact **Foote Brothers Canoes**. You can enter the Ipswich River on Route 97. Closed November through March. ~ 230 Topsfield Road, Ipswich; 978-356-9771; www.footebrotherscanoes.com. **Essex River Basin Adventures** explores the surrounding estuaries in kayaks. ~ Essex; 978-768-3722, 800-519-1504; www.erba.com. **North Shore Kayak Outdoor Center** provides guided kayak tours of Rockport Harbor. ~ 9 Tuna Wharf, Rockport; 978-546-5050; www.northshorekayak.com.

NEW BEDFORD AREA South of New Bedford, near Dartmouth, are many rivers ideal for canoeing. The **Lloyd Center for Environmental Studies** organizes guided canoe and kayaking trips that focus on the natural history of local rivers. ~ 430 Potomska Road, South Dartmouth; 508-990-0505. **Palmer River Canoe** rents kayaks and canoes and provides half-day narrated trips. Shuttles are available. ~ At the rear of Deans Plaza, Route 44, Raynham; 508-336-2274, 800-689-7884.

GOLF

NORTH SHORE Public golf courses are rare on the North Shore, but there is one beautiful semiprivate, 18-hole course surrounded by deep woods, the **Beverly Golf and Tennis Club**. The signature par-3 15th hole is called the Wedding Cake. ~ 134 McKay Street, Beverly; 978-927-5200. **Harwich Port Golf** is a nine-hole public course of par 3s and par 4s that offers pull carts. ~ Forest and South streets, Harwich Port; 508-432-0250.

ICE SAILING

Ice sailing is a tradition on **Watuppa Pond** in Fall River. This graceful sport takes tremendous skill and specially designed sailcrafts. Rentals aren't available, but it's a delight to watch these lighter-than-air boats glide along the icy pond.

PLYMOUTH AREA Golfing opportunities on the South Shore are limited. There aren't any public golf courses close to Plymouth, but about 30 minutes out of town is the par-71 **Pembroke Country Club**, a semiprivate 18-hole course. ~ West Elm Street, Pembroke; 781-826-3983; www.pembrokecc.com.

NEW BEDFORD AREA **Bay Pointe Country Club** is nearby and offers a full course with an island hole—completely surrounded by water. ~ Bay Pointe Drive, off Onset Avenue, Onset; 508-759-8802, 800-248-8463; www.baypointecc.com.

TENNIS

NORTH SHORE A few municipal courts are available throughout the North Shore towns. The best spot here is the **Beverly Golf and Tennis Club**. It has ten clay courts open to the public; a tennis pro is available for lessons. Fee. ~ 134 McKay Street, Beverly; 978-927-5200.

NEW BEDFORD AREA Six clay municipal courts can be found in New Bedford's woodsy **Buttonwood Park**. ~ Rockdale and Hawthorne avenues. **Hazelwood Park** is a city park with five lighted courts. ~ Brock Avenue, New Bedford; 508-991-6175.

RIDING STABLES

Chipaway Stables has hay rides. Call for reservations. ~ 152 Quaker Lane, Acushnet; 508-763-5158.

BIKING

The North Shore and South Shore have limited bicycling areas, but a few choice spots are described below.

NORTH SHORE Cyclists in the area recommend scenic **Route 127** between Beverly, Manchester and Magnolia. The tree-lined road dips and turns past seaside mansions and historic homes. It's cool and peaceful in the summer.

PLYMOUTH AREA Some of the best and least crowded biking in the area is at **Wompatuck State Park**, where there are 15 miles of trails through old forest groves. ~ Union Street, Hingham; 781-749-7160; www.reserveamerica.com.

NEW BEDFORD AREA The **Westport** and **Dartmouth** area on the South Shore doesn't have many cars, and the flat country roads wind past elegant horse farms, pastures and ocean. From Route 195, take Exit 12 and head south to Chase or Tucker Road. At this point it doesn't matter which road you take; they're all lovely, and as long as you head south you'll wind up at the beach. **Bike Rentals** **North Shore Kayak Outdoor Center** rents bikes. ~ 9 Tuna Wharf, Rockport; 978-546-5050; www.northshore kayak.com. You can rent a hybrid at **Cesar's Cyclery**. ~ 739 Ashley Boulevard, New Bedford; 508-998-8777.

HIKING

The Massachusetts coast offers excellent opportunities to hike through salt marsh, forest, sand dunes and moors bordering freshwater ponds and the ocean. Many of these hikes are short and easy. The rest of the Massachusetts coast has a limited number of marked trails. All distances listed for hiking trails are one way unless otherwise noted.

For more information on hikes throughout the state, contact the **Massachusetts Department of Environmental Management Trails Program.** ~ 251 Causeway Street, Boston; 617-626-1250.

NORTH SHORE   Art's Trail (1 mile), in Dogtown Common, a 3000-acre park in Gloucester, winds through red oak forest past a highland of scrub oak, grey birch, blueberries and huckleberries. Several low areas flood in late winter and spring, forming frog-breeding ponds. Of moderate difficulty, the trail is rocky in parts and requires careful walking.

Also in Dogtown Common, **Whale's Jaw Trail** (4.5 miles) is a rugged, rocky, hilly hike starting at Blackburn Industrial Park off Route 128. The trail meanders through former grazing land and past Babson Reservoir, birch groves and cattail marsh. It ends at the top of a hill, where you'll see an enormous split granite boulder that looks like a whale's jaw.

PLYMOUTH AREA   East Head Reservoir Trail (3 miles round-trip) starts behind the Myles Standish State Forest headquarters building in South Carver. The best thing about this hike is that it covers the full spectrum of habitats in the 14,635-acre park. The relatively flat trail winds past deep forest, marsh, hardwood and soft wood groves and a pristine pond. A pamphlet available at headquarters explains the flora and fauna of each environment. A couple of benches are located along the way.

The **Peter Adams Trail** (3 miles) in Massasoit State Park in East Taunton meanders through white-pine forest and hardwoods and past swamps and brooks. Skirting Lake Rico, it ends at a large, secluded sandy beach. Along the way, you might spot deer, fox, turkey and owls. To get a map, call 508-824-0687 (summer only) or 508-822-7405.

▼▼▼▼▼▼▼▼▼▼
Transportation

CAR

On the North Shore, **Route 128** is the main artery connecting Salem, Manchester, Magnolia, Gloucester and Rockport. **Route 95** is the major north–south artery to Essex, Ipswich and Newburyport.

Route 3 links Boston to Plymouth and ends at the Sagamore Bridge to Cape Cod. **Route 195** is the main east–west artery connecting Fall River and New Bedford.

AIR

Many people visiting this area come into **Logan International Airport** in Boston (see Chapter Two). Also serving the southern coastal area is the **New Bedford Regional Airport**. Cape Air flies into New Bedford Regional Airport.

Ferries and boats between Boston, Plymouth, New Bedford, Cape
Cod, Martha's Vineyard and Nantucket require reservations during the summer.

The following ferries and boats operate seasonally and do not
transport cars:

Captain John Boats goes between Plymouth and Province-
town. ~ State Pier, Plymouth; 508-747-2400, 800-242-2469.
Martha's Vineyard Ferry operates between New Bedford and
Oak Bluffs on Martha's Vineyard. ~ 1494 East Rodney French
Boulevard, Billy Woods Wharf, New Bedford; 508-997-1688;
www.islandferry.com. The **Cuttyhunk Boat Line** connects New
Bedford and Cuttyhunk Island. ~ Fisherman's Wharf, Pier 3,
New Bedford; 508-992-1432; www.cuttyhunk.com.

Greyhound Bus Lines offers frequent service to Newburyport
and Boston. ~ 617-526-1801, 800-231-2222; www.greyhound.
com. **Bonanza** runs buses to and from Logan Airport, Hyannis,
Woods Hole, Falmouth, Bourne, New Bedford, Fall River, Connecticut, Rhode Island and New York. ~ 700 Atlantic Avenue,
South Station, Boston, 617-720-4110; 59 Depot Road, Falmouth, 508-548-7588.

Many Boston commuters live on the North Shore; hence **Massa-
chusetts Bay Transportation Authority** runs numerous buses from
Boston's Haymarket Square and trains from North Station to
Salem, Beverly, Gloucester and Rockport. ~ 617-222-5000. **Cape
Ann Transit Authority** provides bus service from Gloucester and
Rockport. ~ 978-283-7916.

Plymouth does not have public transportation. **South Eastern
Regional Transit Authority** provides bus service throughout Fall
River and New Bedford. ~ 508-997-6767.

The New Bedford Regional Airport is serviced by **Checker Standard Taxi** (508-997-9404) and **Yellow Cab** (508-999-5213).

Index

Lodging Index

Dining Index

HIDDEN GUIDES

Adventure travel or a relaxing vacation?—"Hidden" guidebooks are the only travel books in the business to provide detailed information on both. Aimed at environmentally aware travelers, our motto is "Where Vacations Meet Adventures." These books combine details on unique hotels, restaurants and sightseeing with information on camping, sports and hiking for the outdoor enthusiast.

THE NEW KEY GUIDES

Based on the concept of ecotourism, The New Key Guides are dedicated to the preservation of Central America's rare and endangered species, architecture and archaeology. Filled with helpful tips, they give travelers everything they need to know about these exotic destinations.

Ulysses Press books are available at bookstores everywhere. If any of the following titles are unavailable at your local bookstore, ask the bookseller to order them.

You can also order books directly from Ulysses Press
P.O. Box 3440, Berkeley, CA 94703
800-377-2542 or 510-601-8301
fax: 510-601-8307
www.ulyssespress.com
e-mail: ulysses@ulyssespress.com

Order Form

HIDDEN GUIDEBOOKS

____ Hidden Arizona, $16.95

____ Hidden Bahamas, $14.95

____ Hidden Baja, $14.95

____ Hidden Belize, $15.95

____ Hidden Boston & Cape Cod, $14.95

____ Hidden British Columbia, $17.95

____ Hidden Cancún & the Yucatán, $16.95

____ Hidden Carolinas, $17.95

____ Hidden Coast of California, $18.95

____ Hidden Colorado, $15.95

____ Hidden Disneyland, $13.95

____ Hidden Florida, $18.95

____ Hidden Florida Keys & Everglades, $12.95

____ Hidden Georgia, $16.95

____ Hidden Guatemala, $16.95

____ Hidden Hawaii, $18.95

____ Hidden Idaho, $14.95

____ Hidden Kauai, $13.95

____ Hidden Maui, $13.95

____ Hidden Montana, $15.95

____ Hidden New England, $18.95

____ Hidden New Mexico, $15.95

____ Hidden Oahu, $13.95

____ Hidden Oregon, $15.95

____ Hidden Pacific Northwest, $18.95

____ Hidden Salt Lake City, $14.95

____ Hidden San Francisco & Northern California, $18.95

____ Hidden Southern California, $18.95

____ Hidden Southwest, $19.95

____ Hidden Tahiti, $17.95

____ Hidden Tennessee, $16.95

____ Hidden Utah, $16.95

____ Hidden Walt Disney World, $13.95

____ Hidden Washington, $15.95

____ Hidden Wine Country, $13.95

____ Hidden Wyoming, $15.95

THE NEW KEY GUIDEBOOKS

____ The New Key to Costa Rica, $18.95

____ The New Key to Ecuador and the Galápagos, $17.95

Mark the book(s) you're ordering and enter the total cost here ⇨ [   ]

California residents add 8.25% sales tax here ⇨ [   ]

Shipping, check box for your preferred method and enter cost here ⇨ [   ]

❑ BOOK RATE   **FREE! FREE! FREE!**

❑ PRIORITY MAIL/UPS GROUND   cost of postage

❑ UPS OVERNIGHT OR 2-DAY AIR   cost of postage   [   ]

Billing, enter total amount due here and check method of payment ⇨

❑ CHECK   ❑ MONEY ORDER

❑ VISA/MASTERCARD _____ EXP. DATE_____

NAME _____PHONE_____

ADDRESS _____

_____

CITY_____ STATE _____ ZIP_____

MONEY-BACK GUARANTEE ON DIRECT ORDERS PLACED THROUGH ULYSSES PRESS.

ABOUT THE AUTHORS

PATRICIA MANDELL is co-author of *Hidden New England* and author of *Massachusetts: Off the Beaten Path* (Globe Pequot Press). Her travel articles have appeared in numerous publications including *Yankee*, the *Washington Post*, the *New York Times*, the *Miami Herald*, *New England Monthly*, the *Boston Globe*, the *Houston Post* and the *Baltimore Sun*. She is a member of the Travel Journalists' Guild and the American Society of Journalists and Authors.

RYAN VOLLMER is the author of *Affordable Spas and Fitness Resorts* (Ventana Press) and co-author of *Hidden New England*. She has written for the *New York Times*, *Rolling Stone*, the *New York Daily News*, the *San Francisco Chronicle*, *Psychology Today*, *Ladies Home Journal* and *Woman's Day*.

ABOUT THE ILLUSTRATOR

NORMAN NICHOLSON, a graduate of the Art Center College of Design in Los Angeles, has successfully combined a career in illustration and painting. His artwork has appeared in national ads, book and magazine illustrations, and posters. His paintings are included in a couple of important government collections as well as private and corporate collections throughout the United States. He has taught at the California College of Arts and Crafts in Oakland and at Art Academy College in San Francisco.